THE POWER OF TWO

CARL BREWER'S BATTLE WITH HOCKEY'S POWER BROKERS

With best wishes!
Susan Foster

THE POWER OF TWO

CARL BREWER'S BATTLE WITH HOCKEY'S POWER BROKERS

Susan Foster

with Carl Brewer
Foreword by Stevie Cameron

Fenn Publishing Company Ltd.

Fenn Publishing Company Ltd.

THE POWER OF TWO
A Fenn Publishing Book / First Published in 2006

We acknowledge the financial support of the Government of Canada through the Book
Publishing Industry Development Program (BPIDP) for our publishing activities.

Fenn Publishing Company Ltd.
Bolton, Ontario, Canada

Distributed in Canada by H. B. Fenn and Company Ltd.
Bolton, Ontario, Canada, L7E 1W2
www.hbfenn.com

Library and Archives Canada Cataloguing in Publication

Foster, Susan, 1944-
    The Power of Two : the Carl Brewer story / Susan Foster and Carl Brewer ;
foreword by Stevie Cameron.

ISBN-13: 978-1-55168-289-1
ISBN-10: 1-55168-289-3

    1. Brewer, Carl. 2. Toronto Maple Leafs (Hockey team)--Biography. 3. Hockey
players--Canada--Biography. 4. Hockey players--Pensions--History. I. Brewer, Carl
II. Title.

GV848.5.B74F68 2006   796.962092   C2006-903768-X

In loving memory of Carl Thomas Brewer, my anam cara, forever—beyond time and space, and Dr. Thomas J. Pashby, my "other father," with deep gratitude

CONTENTS

FOREWORD

In 1993, Dennis Mills, the former Liberal MP for Toronto Danforth, asked me to meet one of his constituents about a potential story. The man, he told me, had built a strong fraud case against a powerful lawyer, but couldn't interest anyone in the media. Would I be willing to meet his constituent and listen to his story?

Then he told me the constituent was Carl Brewer. The name meant nothing to me. Dennis told me he was a famous hockey player. Still nothing. In fact, I wasn't interested. Hockey? I didn't know anything about hockey. Get a sports reporter. Dennis convinced me to meet Brewer anyway, and I finally agreed, but only with great skepticism and only because of the fraud angle. Fraud always interests me. Dennis had also mentioned that the powerful lawyer, Alan Eagleson, was politically connected to both major parties and considered untouchable. Politics also interests me.

I called Carl, and we arranged to meet at the McDonald's at Eglinton Avenue and Bayview in Leaside; he told me he would have a friend with him… and that I would recognize him by his hair. When I arrived, I looked around and saw a large man — completely bald — sitting at a table with a short, smiling woman.

This is how I met Carl Brewer and his partner, Susan Foster, and started work on one of the best stories of my life. The hockey aspect never did interest me, and the names of the great athletes paraded before me meant very little. What grabbed my attention was the corruption they described, especially the way the crimes — if they were indeed crimes — had been papered over and brushed aside by Liberal and Conservative politicians, the police, the Law Society of Upper Canada, the National Hockey League, and sports reporters who had all been told, more than once, of the evidence Brewer and Foster had gathered.

Up to that time, only two journalists had shown any interest in the story. One was Russ Conway, the sports editor and hockey writer for the Lawrence *Eagle-Tribune*, a small paper in a small town in Massachusetts. Russ was a friend of Bobby Orr — a name I *did* recognize — and Orr had tipped him to Eagleson's activities. In Canada, CBC sports reporter Bruce Dowbiggin called Carl and Sue; he said he'd heard about the story and was interested. He dug into it, in the face of skepticism and outright hostility from his colleagues.

When I took Carl and Sue's documentation to *The Globe and Mail* in 1993, they were interested, but only because the storm Conway had stirred up was embarrassing and had made powerful Canadians, including journalists, look complicit in Eagleson's crimes. The newspaper put together a team of reporters and we produced a short series that essentially restated material Conway had already published. Later, I worked on the story for *Maclean's* magazine.

As we all know now, on the basis of evidence collected almost entirely by Susan Foster and Carl Brewer, courts in Toronto and Boston finally convicted Alan Eagleson of fraud. He was sentenced to serve time in a Canadian jail.

Seems like a wonderful story that has been told many times, right? Not at all. Even though I was at the heart of the story for several years, I didn't know it all. I didn't know the most important part of it — the story of Carl Brewer and Susan Foster themselves.

I didn't know about the torment of Carl's early life, about the poverty and unhappiness. I didn't know about his intellectual ambitions, or how much he despised the world of professional hockey, where the owners treated their players like serfs. (One thing I did know, having flown to Boston with him and Sue, was that he was terrified of flying.) Carl was a brilliant athlete, one of the best in the game, but he couldn't stomach the business he was in. Indeed, I didn't know what a legend he was until he took me to a game at Maple Leaf Gardens, and I watched grown men bring their children and grandchildren to get his autograph and shake his hand, or until I walked down streets with him and saw the awe in the faces of men and women who never failed to stop and wish him well.

I didn't know about their first meeting, in 1963, when they immediately felt connected to one another. That six months later, they met again by accident in Montreal, when Susan — a student at McGill — walked into the lobby of the Mount Royal Hotel, which just happened to be the Leafs' hotel when they were in town to play the Canadiens. I didn't know that they fell in love right away and soon began a long and secret affair, or that she was the only one Carl could talk to about how frustrated he was with his life in hockey.

I did know about Carl's long friendship with Alan Eagleson, and his trust in him. Eagleson was his agent, as well as a friend and a father figure. I knew they'd been so close that Carl was the godfather to Eagleson's daughter, Jill. I also knew about Carl's suspicions, and the fury when he discovered the extent of Eagleson's greed and dishonesty. Eventually, Carl and Sue saw the hockey players win their battle to get the pension monies that National Hockey League owners, with Eagleson's acquiescence, had stolen or withheld. They saw justice done in many ways.

That story has been told and it was my great privilege to work on it. The untold story is the personal one. Carl and Sue's story is a love story, one so deep and profound that you will never forget it. They were a great team, never losing faith, full of courage. Carl always told me he was just the front man and Susan was the brains; he always wanted to make sure Susan got the credit for the brilliant forensic research she did on Eagleson's many frauds that made it possible to put him behind bars. Make no mistake about this: as Carl told us all, Susan can run rings around most investigative reporters when it comes to finding paper trails, and he was so proud of her. But Susan also made a comfortable, welcoming home for Carl. She is a great cook, a collector of antiques and a gardener; their house was always a haven for him.

Susan's story is one of great passion and courage. It is also a gripping detective story with a strong cast of characters — heroes and villains alike.

The Power of Two is a book you will love. It tells a story that will make you proud, and one that will break your heart.

Stevie Cameron
Toronto, 2006

ACKNOWLEDGMENTS

This book has been in the works for many years. Carl treasured a letter that John Robertson, a columnist with the *Toronto Telegram*, sent to him in 1968, suggesting that he think of writing a book. John's letter inspired Carl to write short vignettes and a few stories about his hockey life. On Carl's behalf, thank you, John. We began to give serious thought to a book back in 1982 and worked at it sporadically over the years. Shortly before he died, Carl asked me to finish the story. This book could never have come to fruition without the generous help and support of many exceptional friends.

First of all, I am grateful for the opportunity of working with Jordan Fenn of Fenn Publishing. Jordan's enthusiasm, commitment and dedication to this story have been unrelenting. I truly appreciate his patience as I worked my way through grief and the process of writing this story. Jordan had the excellent foresight to bring Lloyd Davis in as my editor. Lloyd has been fabulous, and it was a very empowering experience working with such a caring, sensitive, knowledgeable and skilled editor. Thank you to my agent, Suzanne Depoe of CTI Artists Management, for her guidance.

Dr. Tom Pashby didn't live to see this book completed, but he gave me tremendous encouragement, telling me pointedly, soon after Carl's death, that I must complete this work because I had the ability to do so and because there was no end to the people who would be glad of the opportunity to help me. Dr. Pashby, a world-renowned ophthalmologist, dedicated his life to championing the cause of safety in hockey and the prevention of catastrophic injuries. He was responsible for introducing almost every piece of protective equipment that is now considered regulation in hockey at all levels and has saved countless eyes and lives.

A group of men from some of the greatest hockey teams of all time gave me incredible help and encouragement. Carl's old Leaf teammates and friends Johnny Bower, Kent Douglas, Dick Duff, Ed Litzenberger, the

Honourable Frank Mahovlich, Bob Nevin and David Keon — I owe each of you a huge debt of gratitude. Thanks for taking my seemingly endless phone calls and always being so patient, gracious and helpful! David Hutchison, who played with the Leafs during Carl's comeback of 1979–80, was a delight, sharing his memories of that turbulent era. My sincere thanks to "Mr. Hockey," Gordie Howe, Carl's old Detroit teammate and loyal friend, and Del Reddy of Howe Enterprises; and former Boston Bruin Rick Smith. Jim Roberts, an old friend and Carl's teammate in St. Louis, stepped right up to assist and contribute his insights and memories. And finally, Ralph Backstrom of Montreal Canadiens fame, Carl's archrival in hockey and a cherished friend to both of us, was always ready and willing to help in every way. From my heart, thank you, gentlemen, for honouring Carl and me with your participation — I love you dearly.

This book has a "godmother," and her name is Stevie Cameron. No one could have been more devoted and protective, more defensive and involved, more caring and supportive than my friend Stevie. Thank you seems so inadequate!

I am fortunate to have several friends who are terrific authors and who offered me advice, encouragement and support. In addition to Stevie, my heartfelt thanks to my dear friend, author/journalist/broadcaster Bruce Dowbiggin, for his constant support and for telling me that I could write this myself long before I understood that. Jack Batten, one of Carl's and my most admired writers, was incredibly generous in reading my original manuscript and giving me his candid advice and direction—and especially his wise counsel, which helped me stay focused during the moments of despair. Jack's wife, author Marjorie Harris, always shared her thoughts in her matter-of-fact way—thanks indeed, Jack and Marjorie! Russ Conway, thank you for your excitement and enthusiasm on learning of this project and for your friendship and help. You are our hero, pal! Brian Nolan, thank you for your interest, encouragement and journalistic advice, even during your own dark night of the soul.

Carl's childhood pals and lifelong friends, Bob McAleese, Lloyd Quance and Bill Agnew, were always eager to help, and I thank you for all your effort in getting all the old childhood friends together with me and digging up pictures and sharing the memories. It has been a pleasure to get to know Carl's German teacher, Mrs. Anne Ellis Taylor. You have all added significantly to this story.

Acknowledgments

My heartfelt thanks to Allan Dick. Allan, our legal adviser but first and foremost a cherished friend always to Carl and me, has been a source of constant and extraordinary support throughout, monitoring everything for me and believing in me from the beginning. Allan contributed the title for the book.

Many thanks to hockey historian Paul Patskou, who was his usual generous self, confirming hockey facts and details for me and cheering me on. I am grateful for the help and support of Mary Ormsby of the *Toronto Star*, Francine Bellefeuille of *The Globe and Mail* photo archives, numerous people at the Hockey Hall of Fame — Craig Campbell, Phil Pritchard, Ron Ellis — Mark Askin of Leafs TV, Carl's big sister, Shirley Thomas, who always shared her memories with Carl and me, and my Aunt Vivian Foster. Kevin Shea and Amy Cameron, thank you for helping give direction to this book at the early stages. Many thanks to Ben Daube. Without his frequent help with my computer challenges, this book would still be a work in progress. Special thanks to Ritch Winter — a courageous and loyal friend who helped make it all happen — Lorraine Mahoney and Tom Lockwood.

There are literally hundreds of wonderful people within the hockey community who have constantly rallied around me with their love, encouragement and interest: I cherish your presence in my life. Special mention to Al Shaw, Jim Anderson and their wives for all the love and the contribution you make to the NHL Oldtimers.

I am blessed by the friendship of my former husband, David Horton, and his wife, Beverley. Stephanie Ashton Smith is a joy and has honoured me as her "surrogate mother" since she was about 10. Finally, my children, Melanie and Dan: thank you for always being there for me with all your love, admiration, protection and wisdom. I love you with all my heart — you make being your mother my proudest role in life.

CHAPTER 1

FOREVER

"Sue, our ship transcends time and space."

Over the years, when people asked me how long I'd known Carl Brewer, I'd frequently reply "forever." It may sound melodramatic, but it was never intended to be. Indeed, it has always seemed to me to be the only true answer. Upon hearing this, some would look at me, perplexed, while others would smile knowingly and nod in understanding.

The course of our lives was altered the moment we met in March 1963. I was 18, a shy, retiring teenager studying for my Grade 13 exams at West Hill Collegiate in Scarborough, Ontario. That fall, I hoped to be accepted at McGill University, majoring in French. My goal was to be a high school French teacher.

Carl, meanwhile, was well established as a defenseman with the Toronto Maple Leafs — a Stanley Cup winner, an NHL All-Star, and an eccentric who cut the palms out of his gloves and gripped his hockey stick barehanded. He was also recently married.

My father, Newton Foster, was employed as an industrial engineer at Johns Manville, an asbestos insulation factory at Port Union Road and Lawrence Avenue in Scarborough. The man who ran food services at Johns Manville also operated the coffee shop at Maple Leaf Gardens. He'd arranged for the Leaf team to tour the factory and have dinner. I'd heard my dad mention the event, but never expected to be part of it. When he came home one evening and told my sister and me that we'd be meeting the Leafs, I was delighted. It was a welcome and exciting break from my studies. I grabbed a notepad for autographs and off we went.

We arrived just as the dinner was winding up. I'd no sooner entered the dining area that evening than Cam Granger, a colleague of my father's and a close family friend who was hosting the event, approached me and said, "Come with me; there's someone I want you to meet."

Cam had always been special to me. A French-Canadian from St. Boniface, Manitoba, he had taught me French songs as a youngster and encouraged my efforts to learn the language. He enthusiastically supported my plans to study at McGill and teach French.

Cam ushered me past the long tables where the players sat, laughing and chatting with my father's peers, to where Carl Brewer was sitting, alone, finishing his meal. Cam introduced us, Carl immediately stood up and we were standing face to face. At that instant, before a word was spoken, we both felt an extraordinarily powerful connection and attraction for one another — "soul recognition" is the only way I can describe it. We both had a deep sense of knowing one another and felt comfortable and relaxed in each other's presence. We stood smiling and gazing at each other for several moments. I sensed at once his gentle nature and was charmed by his warm and welcoming expression. He was soft-spoken and inquired with genuine interest about my studies and plans for university. That peaceful, strong sense of ageless connection never left us. We both just knew, even then, that our lives were somehow inextricably intertwined.

When I was introduced to Carl that March day, I knew nothing more about him than that he played defense for the Toronto Maple Leafs. As in so many homes of the day, our family followed hockey, the national pastime, with keen interest. On Saturday nights we gathered in front of the black-and-white television set in the living room. With a fire crackling in the fireplace and the wonderful aromas of a delicious dinner prepared by my mother still permeating the air, we sat transfixed to the grainy screen, listening to the catchy theme song and the voices of *Hockey Night in Canada*, Foster and Bill Hewitt, as the game got underway. Later on, a high school classmate, Gary Milroy, played for the Junior A Toronto Marlboros, and we often went to the Sunday-afternoon doubleheaders at the Gardens to cheer for the Marlies, many of whom were the Leafs of the future, until our voices were hoarse. So, to meet the Leafs was a tremendous thrill for my sister and me — not to mention our father!

Although we didn't realize it at the time, Carl and I shared many similar traits. We were both shy, almost to the point of being outsiders. I was uncomfortable with people my own age, and Carl was often on a different wavelength from his teammates. Carl and I would come to see hockey as his temporary calling, and not the thing that defined his life. I always felt this was the reason our relationship grew and endured. It wouldn't have mattered what he did; our strong connection came from a dimension beyond the sport.

The Toronto Maple Leafs won the Stanley Cup that spring; in the final minutes of the final game, Carl broke his arm, badly. That summer, I got a note from Carl, and he signed a copy of the photograph that had been taken of us the moment we met. However, we never needed that picture to remember the moment.

In the autumn of 1963, I enrolled at McGill University in Montreal. One evening early in the academic year, I walked over to the Sheraton Mount Royal Hotel to purchase a Toronto newspaper. To my surprise, I noticed several of the Leafs wandering about the lobby. I hadn't known that the Mount Royal was the Leafs' home when they were in Montreal. To my bigger surprise, Eddie Shack came up to speak to me. In conversation, I mentioned having met Carl back in March. He told me that Carl would really like to see me and suggested that I return to the hotel around six o'clock, when the guys would be leaving for the Forum.

I did return to the Mount Royal that evening and met up with Carl. He actually spotted me first — recognizing the McGill logo on a notepad I was carrying — and approached me. I hadn't noticed him because he was wearing his black-rimmed "camouflage" glasses! We chatted amicably and arranged to meet after the game.

During the years that I was at McGill and Carl was with the Leafs, we had an understanding — we'd meet in the hotel lobby at six (sometimes he'd have a ticket for me for the game), or, if we missed one another, meet at Ben's Deli after the game. Carl loved the smoked meat sandwiches at Ben's. We used to sit at the back of the restaurant, Carl hoping not to be recognized by any hockey fans, eating our smoked meat. Carl would down about a half a dozen glasses of Coke. In the 1960s, a glass of Coke was the size of a small juice glass and cost a dime; the smoked meat sandwiches cost 35 cents. Afterwards, we'd walk; sometimes Carl would walk me back to the university residence, Royal Victoria College on Sherbrooke Street, or, if time was tight, I'd walk with him to Central Station, where the Leafs would catch the midnight train back to Toronto. One night when we were saying goodbye at the station, Frank Mahovlich walked by and called over, "Hello, Susan." Carl was befuddled, and he asked me, "How does Frank know your name?" I had no idea; we had never been introduced.

Our frequent visits to Ben's didn't go unnoticed by the waiters. Whenever I went there with friends from McGill for a coffee or a latenight snack, it wasn't unusual for one of the waiters to crack to me, "Where's your boyfriend?" or "How's your boyfriend?"

Our visits were important for Carl. Most importantly, he had someone to talk to, someone with whom he felt incredibly close, to unburden his soul and release a little of his incessant intensity. He'd talk to me about the dynamics of the dressing room that night, tell me who had played well and who hadn't. He talked a great deal about Leafs coach Punch Imlach and his demeaning attitude towards the players. It angered and upset him terribly. He would talk to me about a lot of things that he contemplated constantly — his life's work, his frustrations with hockey, and his desire to teach. He spoke a great deal about his religion — Catholicism. I realized early on how important his religion and his faith were to him and how much they dominated his life. I learned that, as a child, Carl had attended Mass every morning before going to school and that he had been an altar boy. In a letter home to my parents, I wrote: "Carl asked me to meet him after the game for something to eat. But when he showed up late (because Punch had called a team meeting), he said he was too uptight to eat and preferred to go for a walk. He looked like a prizefighter — one bloodshot eye, one black eye, a big, stitched gash on his face and a finger absolutely green and yellow from stopping a shot. I think he is trying to convert me to Catholicism — it was all he talked about."

Carl was always keenly interested in my studies at McGill, my experiences living in Montreal and my plans to teach high school French. He thought that was a most admirable career decision. He observed with noticeable envy how quickly I was getting my university credits and how much longer it was taking him as he studied in the off-season. It was apparent to me that Carl was somewhat of an outsider among his teammates. He didn't drink in those days, and that made it more difficult for him to socialize with the other players. Many a time, he said: "The guys are either out drinking or looking for someone to get laid, and me, I'm better off than any of them because I have you."

One of the first friends I made at McGill was a physiotherapy student from Port Hope, Ontario: Lynne Roberts. Her brother was Jim Roberts, a role player with the Montreal Canadiens. Lynne and I became close friends and we frequently attended the Habs' games together with tickets provided by Jimmy. I can remember the first time I watched Gordie Howe, known as "Mr. Hockey", on the ice — live, instead of on television. I could see so much more from my seat in the Forum than on TV: how much space he got on the ice *and* how much of his dirty play and elbowing the refs ignored. The kid-glove treatment Gordie seemed to get drove Lynne right up the wall! Of course, it was always amazing to watch the Canadiens as well: Henri Richard (The Pocket Rocket), Jean Beliveau, Dickie Moore, Claude Provost, Terry Harper, Jim Roberts, Ralph Backstrom and Charlie Hodge or Gump Worsley in goal.

However, because I was a Leafs fan, Jim Roberts refused to give me any of his tickets for the Toronto games. So I went only if Carl was able to secure one for me. Because I was acquainted with several of the Marlboros, I also went to many of the Junior Canadiens' games at the Forum. The Marlies won the Memorial Cup in the spring of 1964, with such future Leaf stars on their roster as Peter Stemkowski, Ron Ellis, Brit Selby and Jim McKenny. I always cheered for the Toronto teams and would invariably find myself covered in popcorn tossed at me by the rabid Montreal fans. It was a special privilege to be an "insider" and to meet such former NHL legends as Harry Watson, who accompanied the team with his son Barry, a left-winger with the Marlies.

During the summers, when I was home in Toronto, it was not unusual for Carl to phone and have long chats, or simply to show up at my door and ask me to go with him for a coffee and talk. My involvement with Carl during my university days, I learned much later, was troublesome to some of my friends. Mary Ella Magill, a close friend from our days at McGill, was prompted to comment: "What did Susan do at McGill? She studied and went out with Carl. We all thought she was throwing her life away, but what did we know?"

In the late winter of 1963, Carl Thomas Brewer was on top of the hockey world. He and his defense partner, Bobby Baun, along with Tim Horton and Allan Stanley, comprised what was arguably the most effective defense corps in the National Hockey League. By the end of the 1962–63 hockey season, the Leafs had won their second consecutive Stanley Cup and Carl Brewer was chosen a first-team All-Star.

Despite all the attention, the accolades and the awards, however, Carl remained somewhat separate from hockey. The game consumed his life but he didn't fit in. He never would truly fit in.

CHAPTER 2

THE BEGINNING

"Hockey players in general were from the lower economic grouping and were humble and self-effacing. I had no idea of my potential."

Carl seemed destined for a life in athletics from the moment he was born in Toronto on October 21, 1938. The third son of Carl Sr. and Elizabeth (McAvoy), Carl grew up in a family where athletic prowess reigned. Carl's older brother, Frank, was an excellent athlete; his younger brother, Jack, also played hockey. (A third brother, Roy, was older than Carl, but he died around age four of suspected meningitis.)

Their father, an intense-looking man with deep-set eyes that Carl inherited, was a sandlot softball legend in the east end of Toronto. In fact, both Carl Sr. and his twin brother, Willie, nicknamed "Wee," were local sports heroes in their day. Carl loved to tell the story about the Brewer twins. His Uncle Willie was playing in a game; Carl Sr. was not on the roster and was watching from the sidelines. During the game, Willie was injured, so Carl's dad raced into the dressing room, shaved off his moustache, threw on his brother's uniform and played the remainder of the game. No one knew the difference!

Riverdale, the east-end neighbourhood where Carl was born and raised, was a blue-collar part of the city. Danforth Avenue, the main shopping street, was lined with Italian greengrocers — Cirra's at the corner of Carlaw, and Simio's — as well as Tip Top Tailors, Woolworth's, pastry shops, numerous car dealerships, and five movie theatres between Broadview and Greenwood avenues.

The area was a hotbed for hockey and other sports. Several wonderful parks provided places for skating on the outdoor rinks in winter and softball in the summer. Many top athletes came from this part of town: Ron Stewart of the Canadian Football League's Ottawa Rough Riders grew up here; Billy Harris and Ray Timgren became Maple Leafs, and Tom McCarthy became a Detroit Red Wing. Many other promising Riverdale athletes had to abandon their dreams of playing pro sports because they had to go to work.

While it is true that Carl's father excelled in sports, he was not, however, very successful at providing a stable living for his family. During the late 1930s and early '40s, Carl Sr. and his brothers operated a photography business. Using a pony as a prop and calling the enterprise "Kidnapping," they worked the residential streets of Riverdale, taking pictures of the children of the immigrant families. These families were thrilled to have nice photographs to send home to relatives in the "old country." Carl used to curse when he recalled the many times the pony got away from his uncles and he was summoned to chase after it and bring it back.

This little enterprise was not as unusual as it might appear today. I remember, from times spent with my grandparents who lived in this same neighbourhood, when bread and milk were delivered door to door by horse-drawn carts. The ice man delivered blocks of ice, which was the only means of refrigeration in many homes. Children followed after the ice cart, picking up the pieces of ice that fell as the blocks were chipped into smaller pieces.

Business was brisk, and customers paid in cash. Carl remembered there being literally bushel baskets of money around the house. It was, however, either feast or famine, because the Brewer men loved to don their top hats and tails and hit the Toronto nightclub scene. Money was quickly squandered, and Carl Sr. would occasionally sneak his family out of their rented accommodation in a midnight move because they couldn't afford the rent. Carl often said, sympathetically, "Life couldn't have been too bad because we always had toast and tea before we went to bed — although sometimes there was no milk for the tea and no bread for toast!"

It appears that there was little by way of security, either financially or emotionally, when Carl was growing up. When he was born, the family lived in rented space on Pape Avenue. Carl's older sister Shirley tells of the day her parents brought her new baby brother home from the hospital. She walked into the kitchen, and "the very first thing I saw was Carl's tiny feet kicking out of the bassinet." Then she noticed her parents, sitting at the kitchen table, counting out the money in her piggy bank. "I wasn't upset," she recalled, "just sad that they had to do that."

While the Brewer brothers squandered their money on good times and drink, Carl's mother, Elizabeth — nicknamed "Tote" because she was so petite — was at church or doing her best to take care of her children. The youngest of five children in her family, she had immigrated to Toronto from Prestwick, Scotland, as a young woman. She was typical of the people living in this part of Toronto — working-class, Anglo-Saxons of British stock who arrived in the early 1900s. She was a devout Roman Catholic. Even as a very young boy, Carl could sense the stress and lack of support his mother endured, and he always tried to appease her, to behave, and not cause her any further angst. He also followed her example and attended church regularly. Elizabeth once told Carl's school chums, Bob McAleese and Lloyd Quance, that she remembered how, as children back home in Scotland, she and her siblings were picked on by the Protestant kids in the neighbourhood. Similarly, Carl and his brothers were confronted, almost daily, by Protestant kids looking to pick fights with them as they made their way to school because they were Catholic.

Carl used to spend a good deal of his time as a young boy wandering on the Danforth. He showed me where, in front of Mrs. Chambers' fish store, "I used to walk along the Danforth and look at the cars — alone," he'd emphasize. "I was always alone. I'd cry and tell a passerby that I'd lost my car fare. They'd give me a dime and I would go to the movies," he confessed. All his life, Carl loved the old black-and-white or silent movies.

As close as Carl was to his mother, he longed for some sort of relationship with or even acknowledgement from his father, who was absent a great deal of the time. The church therefore came to represent security and safety in his otherwise unstable world.

In 1947, there was an abrupt change in Carl's life. The Brewer brothers had managed to bankrupt their photography business in Toronto, and so everyone, uncles and all, packed up and moved to Vancouver. There, they started up the family photography business again. "Dad worked with Uncle Fred, and I believe did reasonably well," Carl recalled. However, the wild partying and drinking started anew, causing Carl's mother deep anxiety and concern for her children. While certain of the Brewer brothers fared quite well — Fred and his wife, Elsie, lived in a nice home in Port Coquitlam — Carl Sr. moved his family into an unheated, converted garage near the foot of Burnaby Mountain. Elizabeth used sawdust for heating and cooking, and Carl recalled long walks to school and warnings not to go too far up the mountain because of bears. During this year in British Columbia — a year of boozing, partying and suspected philandering by the Brewer men — the highlight for nine-year-old Carl was Friday night, when his Uncle Fred would pick him up in his big Studebaker and take him downtown for fish and chips and a movie.

After a year, Carl's mother had had enough. Carl Sr.'s lifestyle was out of control — as was that of her in-laws — and Elizabeth worried about the effect it might have on her children. Also, it was lonely for her — the only person she had to talk to was her daughter, Shirley. She finally packed up the kids and caught a train back east to Toronto. It was traumatic for the kids — especially the sensitive Carl, who cried and begged his father to come with them. "I was terrified and worried that Dad would never return to Toronto," Carl told me. He also remembered the deep sense of relief he felt when his father looked at him and said, "Don't worry, Carl; I'll come back." Several months later, he did return.

Back in Toronto, the family moved in with relatives — Elizabeth's sister Nan and her husband, Bobby — at 44 Tennis Crescent, near Broadview and Danforth. "All six of us shared their house; it was crowded," Carl remembered. This household was representative of many Toronto families in post–World War II Toronto. "Their eldest son, Jack, was a paratrooper and he had been away at war. There was a memorable picture of him in his uniform on the living-room coffee table." The hilly terrain around Tennis Crescent and in Withrow Park made this an ideal place for Carl to develop those good skating legs, the ones that Carl's Leaf teammate Allan Stanley called "million-dollar legs."

Carl and Frank settled into school — they had both wanted to return to Pape Avenue Public School, but Carl was assigned to Withrow Avenue Public School. "It turned out to be fortuitous," Carl said. "Mrs. Featherstone's class at Withrow Avenue was a combined Grade 3 and 4, with the result that I skipped a grade [the next year] and went right into Grade 5. This made up for my earlier having to spend two years in kindergarten (probably because I was an October baby?)." As a teacher, I can only imagine that attending many different schools as a youngster, combined with skipping a grade, must have been very stressful and challenging for Carl, not only academically but socially.

Carl's mother was an excellent seamstress — she taught Carl how to mend and shorten his trousers. She also found part-time work as a cleaner at the Art Gallery of Toronto (now the Art Gallery of Ontario). She brought books home for Carl to read and introduced him to art. Carl would speak gratefully about his mother and how she helped him with his studies. No doubt her influence did a great deal to cultivate his love of learning, of books and of the arts. She had another occasional job as an assistant to a caterer, and Carl spoke fondly of the petits fours and eclairs that she brought home from those affairs. He always did have a sweet tooth!

Although Carl never spoke about it at length, it must have been a tough existence. The family never had enough money, and holidays and birthdays were rarely celebrated, but Carl remembered fondly that his mother somehow always had a quarter for him to buy a piece of pie at school.

At age 10, Carl experienced a child's worst nightmare: his father had the first of several heart attacks. "There was a quiet pall around the house as Dad's recuperation dominated our lives," he recalled. "I'm not sure I understood the difficulties. I was confused and upset and worried. Death was a word we talked about. I just hoped he would be around." But the relationship between father and son was never a warm one. Gary Corbie, a boyhood chum, has a vivid memory of Carl Sr. driving a bunch of kids home after a ball game. Carl had played well, making some incredible plays. In the car, Carl Sr. chastised his son for something he felt he hadn't done to perfection. Gary said he was stunned; Carl's dad didn't make one positive or complimentary remark about Carl's extraordinary game. The other kids in the car, including Gary, felt terribly sad for their friend. Carl mentioned that his father once told him he considered Frank a much better athlete. Carl knew, as did everyone else, that he was the much better, and more disciplined, athlete of the two, but the remark did anger and trouble him. Carl would try to justify his father's jibe, suggesting he'd only been trying to motivate him. But it was also clear that Carl was always highly motivated and dedicated about whatever he was doing, even as a child.

I have often thought that Carl's lifelong feelings of not being good enough and not being able to do anything right had their origins in the words and attitudes that came from his father at such an early age and critical stage in his development.

The Beginning

***

After his heart attacks, Carl Sr. was able to collect on two insurance policies, and the proceeds allowed the family to buy their first home of their own. It was a small semi-detached house at 25 Dingwall Avenue, off Pape Avenue. It was here that Carl spent the rest of his youth. Initially, the family lived on the first floor, while the upstairs was rented out. At the back of the house was an unheated sun porch that Carl shared with his brother Frank. In winter, their mother would open the back door and the boys would scramble across the icy floor and leap into bed. "It was like sleeping outdoors," said Carl. Though the Brewers had settled into a home, life was still anything but peaceful. Carl remembered that his Uncle Willie lived upstairs with his girlfriend, Irene. One night, Willie came tearing downstairs and crawled through the dining room window, into the sun porch and then out of the house. Irene, clutching a knife in her hand, was in hot pursuit.

At the time of the move, Carl and Frank were finally allowed to attend a Catholic school, Holy Name on Carlaw Avenue. "It was good for me, but not so great for Frank," Carl said. "I had good teachers and I flourished. 'Goodism' was my trademark — I was a very devout Catholic. Frank hung around with his buddies and he was always in trouble — he had brains but he didn't use them." Carl was industrious; he always had part-time jobs. On Friday nights, he'd take out his bike and deliver fish and chips to the Catholic families in the neighbourhood. He said he was paid a quarter for each delivery.

Meanwhile, Carl Sr. finally got a steady job — as a messenger for Burns Brothers, a Bay Street brokerage house. For the first time in young Carl's life, his father was bringing home a regular paycheque. The head of the brokerage, Charlie Burns, took a genuine liking to Carl Sr., and would invite him into his office every Monday to discuss the weekend's hockey games.

Carl felt that the last 10 years of his father's life were the best for the entire family. Both Carl and his sister, Shirley, had fond memories of their dad's singing in the kitchen in the mornings as he made the coffee in an old percolator.

However, it seemed that, all his life, Carl mourned the lack of paternal approval, communication and affection of a solid, reliable male role model. Carl told me that when he was 18, he didn't speak to his dad for about six months because he didn't like the way Carl Sr. treated his mother.

Carl was a very serious, and sensitive, child. He applied himself at school, became a voracious reader and was interested in the bigger issues of life from a very early age. His choice of subjects demonstrated that, even then, he followed his own interests, and not those of the herd. He studied German, French, Greek and Latin. His Grade 10 German teacher at Riverdale Collegiate, Anne Ellis Taylor, has said that having Carl as a student was her claim to fame. She remembers him well. "It was a joy for me to have Carl in my class. He was an intelligent, excellent student and his homework was mostly completed. He seemed to learn the language easily, and I could always count on him for a correct answer." In addition, "he was always volunteering his help to the students who had more difficulty learning German. One morning in class, I taught the German folk song 'Die Lorelei,' and he paused at my desk after the class and said, 'Good class, Mrs. Ellis — that was a great song.'" But it wasn't only his devotion to academics that stood out for Mrs. Ellis. "Carl's athletic abilities and skill in hockey, along with his cheerful personality, made him popular with his classmates."

When Carl was in Grade 10, he read a book called *The Search for Bridey Murphy*, by Morey Bernstein. It had a lifelong effect on him, introducing him to such concepts as reincarnation, thought transference, ESP, hypnosis and meditation — topics that intrigued him and studied and worked to integrate into his life. When we got together, we would share these interests.

Socially, he was very shy — painfully so around girls. He used to say that he never spoke to girls, and he blushingly recounted one very funny situation from Grade 11. "I was at my locker when Mary Jo Payne came up to me and asked if I'd like to go to the Sadie Hawkins Dance. I was very surprised and I answered, 'Sure... who with?'" Startled, she answered, "With *me*." Carl recalled that he was shocked because she was a grade ahead of him. "I never imagined that an older girl would be interested in going out with me." He spoke of going to the dance and walking his date home. "When we reached her door, I gave her a real quick peck on the cheek, then turned and ran home as fast as I could!" His buddy Lloyd Quance remembers how, for days in advance, Carl stressed about the date. "He was asking me all sorts of questions about what he should say and how he should conduct himself," Lloyd recalled with a smile.

The summer that Carl was 18, he worked as a counsellor at Camp Lakewood, an Easter Seals Camp for handicapped children at Port

Colborne, Ontario. Carl's lifelong friend Bob McAleese also worked there that summer and was impressed by the compassion Carl showed for the children. "The serious disabilities of these children in wheelchairs, many of whom couldn't move, was something neither Carl nor I had ever seen before," Bob said. "Carl was amazed at the young campers' determination and their desire to please, and he gently encouraged them to be as successful as their disabilities allowed when they were competing in sports or participating in musical programs."

Roz Bailey was dating Bob at the time; she remembers Carl as an impressive young man. "Carl was always very polite to the girls; a lot of guys weren't, but Carl never swore in front of girls." That summer, at the camp, Carl met Marilyn Rea, a Toronto girl, whom he would one day marry. Marilyn, a quiet, attractive, warm and proper woman, came from a very different socioeconomic background than Carl. Carl often talked about how uncomfortable he felt the first time he visited her home, which was in an upscale Toronto neighbourhood. "When I went into the living room, they had *two* chesterfields. I was really self-conscious, because I had no idea where I was supposed to sit."

***

Though his home life was unsettled, Carl quickly began proving himself in sports. He played football and softball in high school, and earned a tryout with the Cleveland Indians of Major League Baseball at age 18. According to his friends at the time, he was simply an exceptional all-around athlete and could have played football or baseball professionally. But, from the time that he first played for Holy Name at the age of 10, he was hooked on hockey.

Cliff Cooper was the coach of the Toronto Marlboros' bantam and midget teams, as well as a peewee team in the Toronto Hockey League (now the Greater Toronto Hockey League). Carl began playing with Cooper's peewee team, sponsored by Riverdale Garage and known as the Riverdale Meteors. Billy Harris, who would become a teammate of Carl's on the Leafs, started out the same way, playing for the Riverdale Mercurys. "I liked [the Mercurys'] sweaters and sleek emblem much better than ours," Carl commented. "Cliff was as good a coach as I ever had," he stated. "The teams I played on for Cliff won league titles at every level." As a 13-year-old, Carl moved up to Cooper's Marlboro minor bantam team, as a centre. The Marlie bantams won the THL championship, the King Clancy tournament and the Ontario Minor Hockey Association title. Carl remembered that his first championship banquet was held at Shopsy's because, as he explained, "Sam Shopsowitz and Harold Ballard were friends. Staff Smythe addressed us that night and told us, 'Champions beget champions.' This was the basis for the Toronto Maple Leafs' 'glory years.' The foundation had been laid many years before."

The following year, as Carl put it, "I left the Marlies, the Leafs, the mainstream, to pursue my own interests at De La Salle." De La Salle College was a Catholic high school on Avenue Road near St. Clair Avenue, and Carl was admitted as a scholarship student with a 90 percent average. His tenure at "Del" was to last only one year, however. He maintained his excellent grades, but this time 12 students were ranked ahead of him and he no longer qualified for a scholarship. "I couldn't afford the $85 tuition," Carl said. He did, however, want to return to the Marlboros bantam team, where he again played centre and won a league championship. "Winning championships was not new to the Marlboros," he observed. "It seemed this organization won a lot. It was clearly imparted on my mind that winning was the goal or 'modus operandi' of [Marlboros managers] Stafford Smythe and Harold Ballard."

Carl moved up to the Marlboro minor midget team as a centre, and won another championship. Then, in 1954–55, he graduated to the Marlboro's major midget team. "I came into my own as a defenseman with the midget Marlies," he recalled. "Our team was powerful and became league champions and Ontario Midget champions." During the season, several of Carl's teammates were called up to play Junior B with the Weston Dukes. "This confused me," Carl admitted, "as I guess hockey always did. Although I was our team's best defenseman, I never got the call. Of course, I never said anything, either. I was still considered small — I had not yet had my growth spurt. Being Roman Catholic, I was humble and would not celebrate myself but would rather denigrate myself." Carl confided. His teammate Lloyd Quance says that Carl began to come into his own, in terms of ability and size, during this season. "Prior to this year, Carl was small and an average hockey player, except for his excellent fine motor skills, but he had his growth spurt, and this gave him size and greater strength and speed and he really excelled."

The Beginning

That April, the Marlboro Midgets travelled to Noranda, Quebec, for the Ontario Hockey Association finals. Future Leaf great David Keon was playing for the home team. "I remember him," David told me. "You can talk to people in Noranda to this day who saw that hockey game, and they'll tell you that when they saw Carl play that night, they said, 'That guy's going to play in the NHL.'" Although Carl often spoke about what a thrill it had been for him to be part of this victory, his teachers at Riverdale were not amused that he missed school for hockey. Before he went to Noranda, he had been exempted from all his exams. When he returned, to his chagrin, his teachers had revoked the exemptions and he had to write all his exams. "Those were the decades of a whole lot of stupidity," David Keon remarked.

In 1955–56, Carl did get the call from the Junior B Weston Dukes, with whom he quickly established himself on defense. Lloyd Quance was impressed by Carl's dedication and determination. "Carl really wanted to make Junior A, and he went to bed at nine while the rest of us were out partying till all hours and hockey came second."

Late in the season, that diligence would pay off. "I got the call while sitting in Miss Tolchard's English class at Riverdale Collegiate. I was told to report to the St. Charles restaurant for the [Junior A] Marlies' 2:30 pre-game meal." Housed in a former fire hall on Yonge Street just above Carlton, the St. Charles's tall tower made it a local landmark. For Carl, there was only one problem. "You had to wear a jacket, shirt and tie and I didn't have them! I borrowed my brother Frank's. This was a thrill for me, although I still didn't understand why I had been called up.

"The dinner went well. I knew most of the guys and was in awe of their presence. Harry Neale, Al MacNeil, Gary Collins and others were cutting up with Walter 'Turk' Broda, the coach, who was acting as the willing dupe to most of the shenanigans. Turk Broda, the 'fabulous fatman,' had been one of the all-time great goaltenders. I came to love the man deeply, and I genuinely feel that he was the best coach I ever encountered. Turk put the fun back into high-stress competition." Before Carl's first Junior A game, played at the Hamilton Forum, Broda came into the dressing room to address the team. "I had to put my head between my legs because I was laughing so hard," remembered Carl. "Broda spoke as if he had a mouth full of marbles; I couldn't understand a word he said. But it was at this point that I learned I was going to be playing right wing. Yeah, that's right — right wing!"

Carl never returned to Weston, as he quickly established himself as an integral part of the Marlboros' Junior A team. Dr. Tom Pashby, the Leafs' eye consultant for many years as well as a friend, remembered Carl playing for the Marlies. "He was an outstanding player for the Toronto Marlboros. He was a terrific skater — one of those fellows who could get out there and skate and skate — forward and backwards." Harry Neale, who played alongside Carl, has stated emphatically, "Carl Brewer was the best athlete I ever saw." Finishing fourth in the seven-team Ontario Hockey Association Junior A league, Toronto upset the St. Catharines Tee Pees and Barrie Flyers in the playoffs to reclaim the Ontario crown. They went on to defeat the Montreal Junior Canadiens for the eastern Canadian championship, earning them the right to host the Memorial Cup series against the Regina Pats. The teams tied the first game, but Toronto won the next four in a row to win the Cup for the second year in a row. Only one team — the Oshawa Generals of 1939 and '40 — had done this before.

That autumn, Carl began his second year of Junior A. At the same time, he played football for Riverdale Collegiate and proved he could excel on the gridiron as well as on the ice. John Macdonald of the *Toronto Star* described him as a "hard-running halfback." In late October, he was named to the city's first All-Star team. The *Telegram* called him "the pony boy, who carried much of the valuable yardage Riverdale gained this season." Lloyd Quance, also a halfback, made the second team, as did another friend and teammate, quarterback Bob McAleese. Like Carl, Bob also played hockey for the Marlies that season. He recalls that Carl was unable to play in Riverdale's final game because of an injury, but he is certain that, had Carl been able to play, the "Dales" would unquestionably have won the championship that fall.

Where the Marlboros were concerned, Bob described Carl as "someone who got along with all his teammates. Players like Harry Neale and Ron Casey seemed to have an attitude of superiority about them, but that didn't seem to bother Carl." However, Bob also said: "Carl was the type of guy who didn't really want to get too close to anyone. You'd see that inquisitive look in his eye and know to keep away from him." Bob's wife, Roz, thought that Carl remained distant because his father was away so much and wasn't very dependable. Roz felt Carl was afraid to get too close to people for fear of being abandoned or hurt by them in the same manner.

Although Carl was a standout in junior hockey, the allure of sports did not distract him from his focus on his education. "Prior to my last year with the Marlies [1957–58], I decided to quit because my scholastic work was a disaster. My preference was to get a good education," he wrote. It troubled Carl that he had gone from being an honours student to a dropout. "Hockey consumed all my energies. The solution was simple: change the focus." This, one of his first retirements, was short-lived, however. Percy Topping of the Marlboros organization met with Carl, convinced him to return to hockey and agreed to provide tutors for him. After his return, Carl was tremendously successful on the ice, but the tutors did little to help his grades. "I was disappointed about my school failure, and my ego and confidence suffered," Carl wrote. McMaster summer school was his salvation. He took a six-week program studying German and English, earning Grade 13 credits. "I studied like hell and achieved 90 percent in both courses. My damaged psyche was healed and my confidence restored."

That season, the parent club took notice of Carl's capable and creative performance on the Marlboros' blue line. "I had a three-game tryout with the Toronto Maple Leafs. My first NHL game, against the Detroit Red Wings at the Olympia [on February 16, 1958], was a good performance for me. I partnered on defense with Ron Stewart, who was having an All-Star year," he explained. "Oddly enough, I saw little ice time in my next two games, against Chicago Blackhawks and New York Rangers. Because the Leafs were out of the playoffs, it seemed like an unnecessary waste of time not to play me more, but who the hell am I to judge? I guess the brain trust saw what they wanted." In his debut, Carl took the place of Jim Morrison alongside Stewart. Red Burnett of the *Star* called him "a decided improvement. He handled himself with more assurance than anyone Leafs have had on left defense this season." Another Leaf defenseman, Marc Reaume, was benched for the game in Detroit. Coach Billy Reay explained, "I wanted him to see what Carl Brewer, the Marlboro junior, was accomplishing by playing defense instead of trying to dash all over the ice. Carl looked more like a big leaguer than either Reaume or Morrison did in the past several games."

In 1957–58, Carl was the highest-scoring defenseman in the OHA, with 10 goals and 47 points in 50 games. He was an important reason why the Marlboros won the league championship, defeating St. Catharines and the Hamilton Tiger Cubs in the playoffs. In the eastern Canadian final against the Hull-Ottawa Canadiens, the Marlboros quickly fell behind two games to none. Gordon Campbell wrote in the *Star* that Carl "certainly hasn't looked anything like the take-charge guy he was during the OHA playoffs." After a Marlboros win, the powerful Canadiens, captained by future Montreal great Ralph Backstrom, took the next two to win the series. Hull-Ottawa went on to win the Memorial Cup. Carl was named an OHA Junior A All-Star, and was awarded the Banfield-Slater Memorial Trophy as the most valuable Marlboro. And at the age of 19, he still had a year of junior eligibility left.

"I expected to play the next season with the Marlboros," he said. "The 1957–58 season was an All-Star year for me, but the NHL still seemed like a distant dream. I was unaware that the NHL was [soon to become] my destiny."

CHAPTER 3

THE LEAFS

"As a Toronto native, when I secured a position with the Toronto Maple Leafs in 1958, it was absolutely awesome for me."

In August of 1958, a letter addressed to Carl arrived at the Brewer residence on Dingwall Avenue. It was his invitation to the Toronto Maple Leafs' training camp. The tone of the letter, dated the 14th, was indicative of the condescending manner in which team brass treated the players. "Kindly get this bit of information correct ... all players will proceed directly to Peterboro ... Golf will be a *must* in the training camp schedule ... I can only warn you..." The letter and enclosed training camp schedule read like something drafted by the drill sergeant at an army boot camp.

Carl was still eligible for another year of junior hockey with the Marlboros, and Leaf management invited him to camp primarily to give him some experience and seasoning and to have a look at him. But what no one could foresee was how quickly Carl would grab the attention of Leaf brass and the media alike. "Brewer is so Good, Leafs are Puzzled" read the headline above a story by Stan Houston of the *Toronto Telegram*. Carl was outshining many of the team's veterans, a group that included Tim Horton, Ron Stewart, Marc Reaume, George Armstrong and Allan Stanley. "None of the veteran players have shown all the facets of the amazing Brewer," Houston wrote. "Nothing of rubber or flesh passes him; he can hit hard, clear the pass accurately and skate and manoeuvre exceptionally well. And, on top of that, he plays the notoriously weak left side." At the time, Leaf management had no intention of promoting Carl to the pro ranks too early and running the risk of damaging the poise and confidence he exuded, but, their resolve quickly began to dissolve. Leafs' coach Billy Reay called Carl "the brightest prospect to come up for that position [defense] in years."

Without a doubt, the Leafs were a team in transition. The year before, they had finished dead last in the six-team NHL, missing the playoffs for the second year in a row. Howie Meeker had been fired as coach for finishing fifth in 1956–57, then was rehired as the general manager, only to be let go again. His coaching replacement, Reay, hadn't fared much better. But changes were in the offing, and Carl soon figured in the Leafs' plans. At the end of camp, he was offered a five-game tryout. He played the first of these games in the American Hockey League with the Leafs' farm team, the Rochester Americans. After that, he was called up for good.

Although Carl had played at Maple Leaf Gardens as a Marlboro, doing so in a Leafs uniform was another matter. "I had been fortunate enough to see a few games at Maple Leaf Gardens — not many — but I particularly remember going down to watch one Leaf game when I was in junior. Bobby Pulford, who had been a teammate of mine, had moved up and was playing his first year with the Leafs. I saw him wearing that beautiful Maple Leaf sweater and it was really exciting to see. When my turn came, it was unbelievably exciting for me."

In the last game of Carl's tryout, against the Boston Bruins, he scored his first NHL goal. Carl's skill, poise and tenacity impressed Leaf brass enough that they offered him a pro contract, which he signed on October 21, 1958, his 20th birthday — but not without dickering about the salary. Carl spoke disdainfully about the signing bonus the Leafs offered him. "I knew that my buddy and junior teammate, Bob Nevin, got $4,500 as a signing bonus. They offered me $1,600 — and Bob had not yet made the team (he was playing in Rochester). So I refused to sign. I held out." It was challenging for him to do so because his father kept pressuring him, saying, "Carl, just sign!" He wanted his son to be a Maple Leaf. After this, his first of what would be many standoffs with Leaf coach and General Manager Punch Imlach, Carl ended up with a signing bonus of $4,000 (still less than Nevin, he often lamented) and a two-year contract for $16,000.

On the ice, Carl made an instant name for himself. His outstanding skating ability, his smarts, his sharp passing skills and notorious head fakes, which always succeeded in putting opposing players off their game, were a thrill for the fans to watch. It was all rather confusing for Carl at first, especially all the attention focused upon him. He said, perplexed, that all of a sudden everyone wanted to know everything about him — even what he ate for breakfast. But he adapted well to his new environment and enjoyed playing for Reay. "I really liked what he had to say. He was always incredibly supportive of me and inspiring — especially because he told me that I could play the game like Doug Harvey played. Doug Harvey was my hero," Carl said at the time. Harvey, who was then playing for the Montreal Canadiens, was the foremost defenseman of his era — he won the Norris Trophy, awarded to the NHL's top defenseman, seven times in an eight-year span. He could skate, pass the puck effectively and lead the rush. Above all, he had an amazing ability to control the pace and tempo of the game. Reay saw the same attributes in Carl.

However, Reay's tenure as coach was short-lived. In 1958, George "Punch" Imlach was hired as assistant general manager — the irony was that the Leafs didn't actually have a general manager. In November, Imlach was named GM, and shortly thereafter, in one of his first moves, he fired Reay and assumed the coaching duties himself. The change would prove to be disastrous for Carl and would change the course of his career.

Johnny Bower, who joined the Leafs the same year as Carl, was another player who was sad to see the coaching change. "I got along really good with Billy. I remember him coming to me once and he said, 'John, this is a really important game for me; they're putting the pressure on me because we're losing, and if we lose this game, I've got a feeling I might go.' I was very sorry to hear that they did let him go and they brought up Punch Imlach."

Carl was also disappointed, as the coaching change meant a return to business as usual at Maple Leaf Gardens. Under Hap Day's management in the 1950s, the Leafs had played a very stifling style of hockey. After the woeful 1956–57 season, when Day was dismissed, Stafford Smythe said, "As far as I'm concerned, you can develop a system and stay with it until it goes sour … It's time we put a little enjoyment back in the game for the players." With that in mind, Reay was hired away from the Montreal Canadiens organization. The Habs were known as the Flying Frenchmen, the masters of "fire-wagon hockey." But Imlach's style, like Day's, emphasized defense.

Carl knew it well. "We played this system all the way up to pro. Centres forechecked, wingers peeled off with wingers, and the defensemen stood up at the blue line and crunched whomever. The system won championships and Stanley Cups. Much later, this system became lionized as the 'trap,' the system of Scotty Bowman, Roger Neilson and Lou Lamoriello. The trap became king, but it was godawful — boring, then as now."

Every player stayed in his groove, like the plastic players on a table-hockey game. Kent Douglas described the game plan for me: "The defensemen backed up and took the play off to the side when they could, and that took about half the ice out of play because there were no openings." This meant the puck carrier had no option but to shoot the puck in. Ralph Backstrom, who broke in with the Habs the same year that Carl became a Leaf, told me that he remembers going out with his teammates for a few beers after a game at the Gardens and commenting, "They've shrunk the rink in Toronto."

The Leafs' defensive style drove Carl crazy. "I clearly remember sitting in the Leafs' dressing room after another Imlachian 2–1 victory and thinking how embarrassing it was to play such boring hockey. However, 16,000 diehard fans only savour a victory, not style." He eventually came to revere the European game, with its panache and beauty.

In some respects, it's remarkable that Carl, whose style and talents ran counter to such a system, would have lasted any amount of time with the Leafs. It must have been because he was an exceptional player, as Dr. Tom Pashby recognized. "You need three things to be a good hockey player: brains, brawn and heart. He had all kinds of brains and he wasn't lacking in the other two, either."

Johnny Bower agrees. "I had the best seat in the house to watch Carl! He was good at stickhandling — moving the puck. He really helped me a great deal moving some of those guys [out of the way]." Johnny was really taken by Carl's determination. "Carl played rough hockey; he was a great competitor, too. He wanted to win; he didn't know what the words 'to lose' meant. I could say to Carl, 'Carl, there's a guy behind you' — because a lot of times he couldn't see him — and he'd turn around. He was so good at turning side to side. Carl wasn't afraid to block shots for me, either. Carl always gave me a good angle to look, and sometimes when he gave me a good angle, the player, instead of shooting the puck because he couldn't score, he'd try to hit Carl right on the pants — and boy, does that hurt! But Carl never pulled his leg up or anything. He'd say to me, 'If it hits me, it hits me, but if it gets past me, it might hit the net.' He was really focused."

In spite of his many talents, Carl felt he had a weak shot. "I spent countless hours practising my shot. I could shoot left or right with equal ineptitude. No matter how I practised, I never did have a good shot. I shot pucks off the boards at Withrow Park endlessly. I hammered nails into the puck to make it harder … nothing! Lesson learned: a player is born with a shot, or the lack of same. Practice is irrelevant. Look around the NHL and figure out how many guys can actually shoot the puck!"

It didn't take long for him to make a name for himself around the league. On November 22, he was named one of the three stars of the Leafs' game against the New York Rangers. In February, Red Burnett wrote that "Carl has a chance to develop into an all-star defenseman, something Leafs have lacked [for] several seasons."

Carl wasn't only an immediate sensation as a player. He also gained a measure of notoriety when it was discovered that he cut the palms out of his gloves — just one of his many eccentricities. He'd actually begun to modify his gloves since he was a 16-year-old playing with the Weston Dukes. "We were given hand-me-down gloves," he explained, "and they had been repaired more than once. The pair I got had been reinforced with a thick piece of leather sewn in. When I started using them, I felt clumsy. I couldn't get a feel for the stick. So I removed the leather pad and found that I got a better grip and a better feel with my palms bare. I've liked it that way ever since." There was another advantage, one that Johnny Bower thought was ingenious: "When he got in a scrap, he could get a better grip on the guy's sweater. Everyone had their tricks, but I think Carl's was the best."

Carl's memories of his early days as a pro remained vivid and poignant throughout his life. He had particular respect for the Montreal Canadiens, who were in the midst of a five-year run as Stanley Cup champions. "The Canadiens were awesome," he enthused. "For me, Dickie Moore was the toughest, smartest left winger I ever saw play, and I include everyone in that category — Ted Lindsay and everybody else. Moore could do it all, and he was magnificent to watch — the tricks he could do were unbelievable. I didn't play against him because he came down the opposite side of the ice. The line of Henri Richard — as good a player as his brother, in my mind — Rocket Richard and Dickie Moore was the most exciting line in hockey at the time. Moore did things that were simply amazing, and he contributed a great deal to Montreal because he had leadership qualities." Goaltender Jacques Plante, "he of toque and mask, the game's most creative thinker," also ranked highly in Carl's estimation.

Carl characterized his very first game against the Habs, a 5–0 loss, as unforgettable. "I was totally and completely in awe," he remembered, "playing against the powerful Montreal Canadiens, perhaps the most talented and glorious club ever assembled. At this point, I knew I could play in the NHL, but having just turned 20, and with a year of Junior A still left, I was not sure I was ready to take on the Canadiens — Doug Harvey, Tom Johnson, Dickie Moore, Henri Richard, Boom Boom Geoffrion, and the man of legend, Maurice, as he was endearingly denoted by the longtime voice of the Habs, Rene Lecavalier." Playing left defense meant he could see a lot of the legendary right winger, and an early encounter left a lifelong impression on him. "I was wearing number 18, and I don't know who my defense partner was, as Baun and I had not yet become a tandem. The only other recollection I have of the game is of Maurice breaking down the right side with the puck at our blue line. They say that, when you are near death, your whole life flashes through your consciousness. Well, at this precious moment, I was amazed at the number of things that flashed through my mind! I thought, 'What the hell do I do now?' I was backing up, stick in front of me, the left side covered by me alone and all sorts of negative thoughts running through my mind … fear, of course, was there. I always looked into a player's eyes; it had a hypnotic effect.

"Maurice crossed the blue line and made a move inside. I stripped him of the puck, and made a quick transition pass to my centreman. I was embarrassed; who the hell did I think I was? The Rocket taught me two lessons that night, all in the blink of an eye: firstly, that I was a pretty good hockey talent, and secondly, that even the greats of the game are human and make occasional mistakes — but they still make the great plays more often."

Carl was less than awestruck by Bert Olmstead, whom the Leafs had picked up from Montreal in the June 1958 intra-league draft. "He was an interesting phenomenon," Carl observed. "They expected Bert to be a leader with the Leafs, but I really didn't get along with him and I couldn't stand his act. I'm not suggesting that he could stand my act, either. It amazed me how the other players worshipped him. This, in my mind, was insane, because he really was a rather miserable person. We had lots of verbal battles, Bert and I; we really didn't get along at all." Later in life, Carl came to appreciate Bert, who became a staunch ally and supporter.

It was during Carl's rookie season that the indomitable Toronto Maple Leaf defense took shape — whether by luck or by design, it's hard to tell. In his memoir, *Lowering the Boom*, Bob Baun wrote, "[Imlach would] make a decision and never really be able to tell you why. He'd just live and die by his hunches." Either way, this decision was the best thing that could have happened to Carl. The foursome — the legendary Tim Horton paired with Allan Stanley, while Carl teamed up with Bob Baun — became the most formidable defense corps in the NHL in the late 1950s and early 1960s. It wasn't just the cornerstone of the Leafs' success; it was also a source of strength for Carl personally.

"We were indeed fortunate with the defense pairings," Carl recalled. "Horton and Stanley were inseparable; they played together and drank together. Baun and I played together and roomed together throughout the seven years I was with the Leafs. I didn't drink in those days — what a tragedy that was (I made up for it later). On the ice, we complemented each other." Carl was a very different player from Baun. They were both effective behind the blue line, but Carl was much more of an offensive player — a superior skater and much more of a playmaker. Baun used his brute force to crush opposing players as they approached the blue line. They covered for one another and, as Carl said, their relationship extended beyond the rink. He felt that their relationship at the time was strong. Johnny Bower, who was trying to establish himself in the big league, was grateful for the defense that played in front of him. "As a goalie, you're only as good as your defensemen. I really needed their help and they gave it to me and I appreciated it. I believe to this day that the reason I'm in the Hall of Fame is because of that defense foursome."

Carl valued the stability of the defense unit. Of course, injuries would occasionally create situations where someone had to fill in; the players who got the call were, in Carl's estimation, consistently impressive. "Larry Hillman, who was an outstanding defenseman and perhaps the greatest team player I ever saw because he fought a lot of battles, filled in on defense. Kent Douglas was another player who was an effective replacement on defense. Kent was, in my mind, the best athlete I ever encountered — he was a unique hockey player and a smart hockey player."

Carl had a terrific rookie season, appearing in 69 games, scoring three goals and assisting on 21 others. "I have to rate [him] as the find of the NHL season," Imlach said. "I'd hate to think of our defense without that waspish character." He clocked 125 minutes in penalties, third in the NHL, although many of them were misconducts for mouthing off to the referees.

The Leafs improved under Imlach's tutelage, but their slow start under Billy Reay had left them in a bind. With two weeks to go in the regular season, they were in fifth place, their playoff hopes dim. Improbably, however, the Leafs won five of their last six games, while the Rangers lost six out of seven. When the dust settled, the Leafs were in the playoffs. They met Boston in the semifinals, and the series went the full seven games. In the finale, Leafs eked out a 3–2 victory, with Carl assisting on Gerry Ehman's game-winning goal. "It was really very exciting for us because Boston at the time was a really impressive team," Carl recalled. For the first time since 1951, the Leafs were in the Stanley Cup finals. However, while they made a respectable showing against their archrival Montreal Canadiens, they lost four games to one. The Habs set a record by winning the Cup for the fourth year in a row.

While Carl was starring in his rookie season with the Leafs, a young man from Kirkland Lake, Ontario, Ralph Backstrom, was dazzling Montreal Canadiens fans in his debut. If Carl was the fastest-skating defenseman in the league, the 21-year-old Backstrom could easily claim that distinction among the league's forwards. Ralph was a clever playmaker who soon earned the moniker "Montreal's whiz kid." He was the third-line centre, behind Jean Beliveau and Henri Richard, but if he had played for any other team in the NHL that year, he would easily have been on the first line.

Apart from hockey talent, Ralph and Carl had many traits in common — both were intelligent, articulate, gentle and creative men — and they became good friends after their playing days. On the ice, they respected and admired one another — although, Ralph told me jokingly, "We had a pretty good rivalry going on the ice, too." Ralph remembered Carl fondly: "I had the opportunity to play against Carl, not only in the junior ranks, but at the NHL level, and I always considered him a world-class player. There's no question in my mind that he was one of the best defensemen I ever had the pleasure of playing against. I had the opportunity to play against Bobby Orr and I played with guys like Doug Harvey, and some of the very best — Serge Savard and some of these guys — and certainly Carl was right up there with those guys."

Carl's unique skills impressed Ralph. "He did a lot of little things," Ralph explained to me, "If he had the puck, he'd look you off like he was passing it right to another player, and you'd take that area away from him, either with your body or stick, and he'd just pass it the other way without even looking. It would drive the forecheckers, and everybody, nuts — including me." Carl had the greatest praise for Ralph, calling him "incredibly clever, fast-footed and smart."

At the season's end, Carl and Ralph were the top two contenders for the Calder Memorial Trophy, awarded to the rookie of the year. Ralph won soundly, with 141 points to Carl's 67. Years later, Ralph would kid Carl, calling him "Runner-up." He also sipped champagne from the Stanley Cup to cap off a sensational first year. Carl, on the other hand, earned the praises of coach Imlach, who said, "All I know is that I wouldn't trade Brewer even-up for Backstrom."

After the playoffs, Carl, Frank Mahovlich and Dick Duff got to chatting in the dressing room about their off-season plans. Since they were all more or less free and at loose ends, they decided to take a little vacation together. They went to Nassau in the Bahamas for a few days and stayed at the Nassau Beach Hotel. Dick Duff remembers, "We saw sand beaches, the ocean, we heard calypso music — we'd never seen anything like it!" Carl often laughed about the scenario. "Here we were, three good-looking guys, all of us Catholic. We didn't drink and we were too shy to speak to girls. We must have been quite a sight!" This trip just might have been the source of Carl's lifelong love of travel. Carl and I went to the Bahamas several times together over the years, and without fail, he'd take me to the Nassau Beach Hotel and show me around and tell me what they'd done. He always made a point of taking me downstairs to the piano bar, where he'd rave about the piano player who'd performed for them. We'd have a drink on the beach, and I could tell that Carl was lost in a wonderful memory.

Carl continued to shine and flourish with the Leafs in 1959–60, his second year as a pro. Midway through the season, the Leafs' assistant general manager, King Clancy, spoke to *Star Weekly* magazine in glowing terms about Carl: "Brewer is a fine young hockey player, believe me. He's up there with the top defensemen right now and he's only 21. He blocks well. He throws as stiff a bodycheck as anybody. If he didn't play defense, he'd make a fine centre. Sure the kid gets penalties. He's bound to because he plays all out."

Carl led the league in penalty minutes with 150, eclipsing his eye-popping total of the year before. Still, he insisted that he was no loose cannon when he was on the ice. "In professional hockey, it's important to be in position," he told the Star's Milt Dunnell. "You can't do that if you're running all over the ice attempting to knock everybody else off his feet. I play hard, but I feel some of my penalties were incurred because I was new to the league."

In February of 1960, the Leafs scored a coup, acquiring Leonard "Red" Kelly from Detroit in exchange for spare defenseman Marc Reaume. Kelly had refused a trade to the New York Rangers, but the Leaf brass was able to talk him out of retirement. Red had been a star defenseman with the Red Wings, but Punch Imlach moved him to centre, eventually on a line with Frank Mahovlich and Bob Nevin. "All great players make the players around them better," Carl observed. "Red Kelly had that effect — the 'Big M,' Mahovlich, matured, and Bob Nevin reached his potential." The Leafs finished the season in second place, and they defeated Red's old team in the semifinals, four games to two, but they were fated to lose once again to the Montreal Canadiens in the finals. This time the Habs swept them in four straight games.

***

By the autumn of 1960, on the eve of his third NHL season, Carl was already beginning to feel deep discontent with the hockey establishment. The Leafs owed Carl $100 because he'd been hospitalized with an ankle injury the previous year. But when he tried to collect, he was told to get lost. As Carl often told the story, as he was backing his car out of the laneway behind his parents' house, he had no idea whether he'd turn left and go to training camp in Peterborough or turn right and enroll at McMaster University in Hamilton. By the time he reached the highway, he'd decided to turn right. He knew his way around the McMaster campus, having taken high school equivalency and university summer courses there. Until a picture of him, clad in the uniform of the McMaster Marauders football team, appeared in *The Globe and Mail* on September 10, no one knew his whereabouts. In Peterborough, Punch Imlach had told the *Globe*'s Rex MacLeod: "I have no idea where Brewer is. He never told me he wouldn't be here for training camp. I thought a player of Brewer's intelligence would at least show up for training camp."

As soon as Carl's presence at McMaster came to light, the Leafs dispatched King Clancy, their designated diplomat, to meet with Carl. When King asked Carl what was wrong, he brought up the hundred dollars the team owed him. As Carl told the story, Clancy reached into his pocket, handed him $200 and asked, "Now will you come to camp?" Carl declined, telling Clancy that he thought they'd better get a contract signed first. As Carl told Red Burnett of the *Star*, "It isn't the amount of money involved, it's the principle of the thing. If I let them kick me around this early in my hockey career, it will be that way all through my career." Carl did, of course, sign a new contract and return to play the 1960–61 season. However, he made it very clear to me time and time again that his decision to return was prompted by his realization that he needed one more year of service to be vested in the NHL pension plan. Many years later, his awareness of — and concern about — pension issues would play a defining role in his life, and improve the lives of his colleagues.

There was a new face on the Leaf roster in 1960 — that of David Keon. Whenever Carl was asked about his teammates over the years, he always answered, "David Keon was the most complete hockey player I ever saw play the game." Keon had a stellar 15-year career with Toronto and was named captain in 1969. He spoke with me about turning pro. "When I came to the Leafs, Carl helped me a great deal because I had played against him in junior — I was with St. Mike's and he was with the Marlies. He was my closest contact, and I remember talking to him about the difference between playing junior and playing pro. He told me that basically [the game] was the same — it just happened quicker." David found that difference to be more dramatic, particularly where Punch's approach to practice was concerned. "It was totally different. At St. Mike's, the emphasis was on improving your skills and learning to play. And then, playing with the Leafs, I remember my first practice I had with Punch Imlach — I was just thinking, 'Holy cow, is this all there is to it?' It was just mind-numbing. It was just a total physical beat-down all the time."

On the ice, Carl exuded all the confidence and poise of a superbly skilled superstar. He considered himself a team player in every sense of the word, and no one could dispute that assessment. But away from the rink, he was the outsider, the guy who just didn't seem to fit in. Carl was deeply religious, incredibly sensitive, studious, an intellectual, and unrelentingly intense. He didn't drink in those days, which made it difficult for him to socialize with his teammates. They seemed uncomfortable with him, and certainly were at a loss to understand the complexity or intensity of his personality — they nicknamed him "Skitz," short for schizophrenic. Fellow defenseman Allan Stanley assessed the situation: "The defense corps was pretty close; we went everywhere together. Except Carl. He didn't really hang with the group; he was the odd guy out — not like the rest of us." Childhood friend and teammate Billy Harris once remarked: "We'd go to a party after a game and Carl didn't sit and discuss how the game went. He could communicate with the lawyers and the doctors. He felt comfortable discussing the ballet and opera. He was very philosophical."

Adding to Carl's troubles, he simply could not relax or learn to unwind. He couldn't sleep, especially after a game, and was known to pace the corridors of the train if they were travelling, or of the hotel room he shared with Bobby Baun. He worried about everything. There was no such thing as peace of mind for Carl Brewer. "It was hell playing the game," he said. However, like Keon, it was the practices that he found particularly demoralizing and exhausting — physically as well as emotionally.

Many of the Leafs, who found themselves needing to rest up to prepare for games, shared this viewpoint. Bob Nevin, another teammate and long-time friend, looks back on the practices and calls them stupid — "stupid because they were so tough." Bob felt the practices were physically draining, and he remembers that it hindered his play in games. "There were a lot of times when, during the games, I had openings to make a bigger play, but I had to move back because I knew I didn't have the stamina to carry it out." Nevin believes that he, too, would have been a much better hockey player had it not been for the gruelling workouts — especially the ones held on game days. On one occasion, Bob remembers Imlach ordering him to stay behind after a practice and skate 200 laps around the ice. "To this day, I have no idea what I did to incur such wrath from Punch," he told me, "nor have I any idea why or how this exercise was supposed to make me a better hockey player!"

David Keon remarked, "He tried to exhaust you physically — he did it because he was the boss, and if you wanted to play, that's what you went through." Carl and Bob both found it galling that Imlach routinely excused certain players from these practices, usually Allan Stanley, sometimes Red Kelly, and often, "Imlach's favourite player, David Keon." Carl could never understand that. "If it were a good idea to excuse these guys, why wasn't it a good idea to excuse all the players?" he'd ask.

"There was a great deal of friction between Carl and Punch Imlach," Johnny Bower told me. "A lot of times, if he made a mistake — and Carl was only human — Imlach would tell him about it. Carl kept a lot [of the anger] to himself, but every once in a while, he'd explode. He'd say his piece, and that's what I liked about him. Carl never criticized the other players, either, like some of the others did." Dr. Tom Pashby could also see the problems between Carl and Punch. "Sometimes I thought Carl was a little too smart. He could see through the coach. [Imlach would] say stupid things that Carl knew were stupid, and he didn't mind telling him."

Carl took particular offence at Punch's dictatorial approach. "We're just puppets," he once charged. "You expect us to dance when you holler." On another occasion, after Carl had played what Punch considered an outstanding game, Punch approached Carl to offer his congratulations. Carl dismissed the compliment, retorting that in his mind, all of his games were of the same calibre. Imlach reportedly stormed away in disbelief. I asked Keon if he was aware of the trouble Carl was having playing under Imlach. "I think so," he replied. "It was like that for a lot of the players. I think of what we could have become, and what we did become in spite of what we were put through. Carl was a great player, a great teammate, and he had great skills. Along with other players — like Frank, for instance — I just don't think we were ever used to the best of our ability with the talent we had on the team."

It also ate away at Carl whenever he thought about the way hockey players were treated by management — like serfs, chattels. The complete lack of dignity and respect shown the players deeply offended him, and as time went on, he fought against it in unusual ways. These feelings were put to productive use when Carl later assumed the role of a players' rights advocate.

Historically, the balance of power in hockey was tilted completely in the owners' favour. The vast majority of the players of this era came from families at the low end of the economic scale, so the personal sacrifices expected of them didn't seem so bad to most. Ralph Backstrom, for example, often spoke to us about growing up in the northern Ontario mining town of Kirkland Lake. From an early age, he saw that the choice for him was hockey or the mines. As he often said, "This was a tremendous incentive for me to succeed in hockey." Ralph recalled that, when he was 17, the Montreal Canadiens dispatched Kenny Reardon, the former All-Star defenseman, to meet with the Backstroms. Reardon placed five $100 bills on the kitchen table, alongside a Montreal Canadiens contract. "My parents and I had never seen a hundred-dollar bill, let alone five," Ralph said. He signed the contract and gathered his belongings to leave for Montreal. As he left the house, Reardon reached into his vest pocket and pulled out another five $100 bills, flashed them in Ralph's face and told him in a flippant manner that he had actually been authorized to pay twice as much for Backstrom's signature. Then he stuffed the bills back into his pocket.

Ralph doesn't harbour any lingering bitterness over the incident, but when he told me about it over lunch one day, I instantly got a visceral sense of the pain and indignity Ralph and his parents must have felt. His parents, Esther and John Albin, were salt-of-the-earth immigrants from Finland, though both were from Swedish backgrounds. They met in Kirkland Lake. Ralph's dad went to work in the mines every day of his working life for $1.40 an hour. It was clear that Ralph's family could have used the extra $500 that Reardon waved at them so cavalierly.

Though money was scarce, there was always someone in Kirkland Lake whose needs were even greater. Dick Duff's family — in which there were 13 children — were neighbours of the Backstroms. When Dick went to Toronto, Mrs. Backstrom pointed out to Ralph that Dick didn't have a jacket. She insisted that Ralph give him one of his own — even though Ralph only owned two. Ralph spent a sleepless night agonizing over which jacket to give up!

Carl and I had accompanied Ralph on several of his visits with his mom, and I found her to be a wonderful, strong, warm lady. "She was a great old lady," Ralph recently agreed. The story of his signing was so profoundly moving that I was able to understand, for the first time, exactly what it was that drove Carl so hard in later years to right some of the wrongs the NHL had done to its players.

***

The unabated stress Carl was under began to take its toll on him, both physically and psychologically. Early in his pro career, his hair began to fall out in patches. He explained that at first, the patches were the size of a dime; then they grew to the size of a quarter. Team doctors routinely injected cortisone into the patches, but while the hair grew back, it fell out in similar fashion elsewhere.

Needless to say, Carl kept all his inner conflict and agitation well hidden from those he saw on a regular basis, his teammates and his family. Pretty much from the moment we met in 1963, I was the one person to whom he did open up, and with whom he did discuss his innermost, deepest feelings and conflicts. I was his confidante, his soft place to fall. He came to depend on me to be there for him, to listen to him, to accept him, to encourage him and sympathize with him — to be a stabilizing presence in his life. He felt totally safe with me, and I saw and appreciated his kind, gentle spirit, his warmth, his brilliance and his delightful sense of humour. I respected his ideals and his feelings. Over many years, Carl frequently told me that I was the only person in his life who ever really knew him — that I knew him better than anyone ever had. He'd say, "I have one friend, and that is you."

The Leafs and Canadiens were the class of the league in 1960–61, locked in a battle for first place that went down to the wire: Montreal ended up with 92 points, Toronto with 90. The Habs' Boom Boom Geoffrion scored 50 goals, becoming only the second NHLer to reach that plateau, while Frank Mahovlich was right on his heels, setting a Leaf team record with 48. Aided by the defensive play of Carl and his mates, Johnny Bower won the Vezina Trophy, while Keon and Bob Nevin were one-two in the Calder voting. Mahovlich and Bower were named to the first All-Star team. Both Montreal and Toronto were upset in the playoffs, by Chicago and Detroit, respectively. The Blackhawks went on to win the Cup.

In September 1961, just prior to training camp, Carl suffered a severe personal blow — his father, Carl Sr., died of a heart attack at the age of 52. Every detail of the night was indelibly imprinted on Carl's mind. He recalled returning home from a team practice and finding that all the lights were on in the house and the front door was open, but there was no one home. Immediately, he sensed that something was wrong; his first thought was that something had happened to his mother, because she had been unwell. According to Carl, he was no sooner in the house than the phone rang; it was his uncle, Johnny McAvoy, who told him, "Carl, I'm not going to mince words: your father died tonight."

Carl recounted this story many times over the years, and every time he did, I noticed the colour drain from his face and his body tense up, indicating that the memory of the shock he had felt at the moment he got the news was still fresh. Carl was proud to say that his father's funeral was the biggest, and the funeral procession the longest, that he had ever experienced.

Carl spoke about how difficult it was for him to look up in the stands that season and not see his dad sitting in his usual seat, wearing the tweed overcoat he'd bought at the Salvation Army because it was all he could afford. Carl regretted all his life that he did not buy his dad a new car when he turned pro. Carl said later, "I could have done it financially, but I didn't understand that I could, because our family had never had money." He would often say that his dad had said very little to him over the years, but one thing he did remember his dad telling him was about his play with the Leafs: "Carl, you're awfully good and they're out to get you; you have to get back in position faster."

The Leafs completed the 1961–62 season firmly ensconced in second place, and a trio of Maple Leafs earned berths on the second All-Star team: Mahovlich, whose 33 goals tied him for second behind Bobby Hull; Dave Keon, who also won the Lady Byng Trophy for gentlemanly play; and on defense, Carl Brewer. Carl did something that could also be described as gentlemanly. Canadiens executive Frank Selke Sr. made it a habit to send congratulatory telegrams to players voted to the All-Star teams. He was amazed that spring to receive his first-ever thank-you note — from Carl!

The Maple Leafs met the New York Rangers in the semifinals and took the series, four games to two, then met the Chicago Blackhawks, who had upset the Habs powerhouse, in the finals. "Chicago was always a tough customer," Carl remembered. "They had a great hockey team with all those All-Stars — Stan Mikita, Bobby Hull, Glenn Hall. Hall was a great goaltender; he was known as Mr. Goalie in Chicago." Carl absolutely hated playing in Chicago Stadium — he talked with great disdain about the filthy, rat-infested building that was located in the worst part of the city. The dressing room was in the basement, and the players had to climb about 30 steps to reach ice level. "And the fans — the fans were terrible; they'd indiscriminately throw things on the ice and were a menace to the players as they departed the rink — often, with a police escort!"

The Leafs won the first two at home, while the Hawks followed suit at Chicago Stadium. The fourth game was particularly intense — Mahovlich and Stan Mikita were ejected after they got into a stick-swinging battle. Back at home, the Leafs steamrolled their way to an 8–4 victory, as Don Simmons stepped into the net in place of an injured Johnny Bower. When Bower was unable to play game six in Chicago, the team helped Simmons out by buckling down — allowing the Hawks only 21 shots on goal. Dick

Duff scored the game-winning goal late in the third period to give Toronto its first championship since 1951, the year that Bill Barilko scored his dramatic overtime goal mere months before his plane disappeared in the wilderness of northern Ontario. In an eerie coincidence, the wreckage of Barilko's plane was found in June 1962.

The Cup win was a thrill for Carl. "The night we won the Cup was a really significant time for me," Carl said. However, his feelings towards Imlach were not mellowing at all. Reports of the victory mentioned that Carl was so excited that he was rolling around on the dressing room floor. He, Duff and Ron Stewart started singing. That's when Imlach entered the room and threw a damper on their exhilaration; instead of sharing their joy and enthusiasm, he snarled, "Oh, for fuck's sake — get on the plane."

Carl thought Imlach's attitude was uncalled for. But in retrospect, he also found fault with *himself* — he always wondered why the hell he'd obeyed Imlach's order instead of staying in Chicago for a couple of days to savour the victory. After all, the season was over! When the players did return to Toronto, they were greeted by ecstatic fans, who turned out by the thousands to salute their hockey heroes as they paraded in open cars up Bay Street to City Hall for a civic reception.

***

It was in the early 1960s that Carl first became acquainted with a lawyer by the name of R. Alan Eagleson. Eagleson, the son of working-class Irish immigrant parents, was a buddy of Carl's teammate Bob Pulford. The Eagleson and Pulford families had known each other since Pulford was a teenager. Bob and Al played lacrosse together in the 1950s, and before long Eagleson began hanging around with "Pully" socially. In this way, he was introduced to Carl, Billy Harris, Bob Baun, Bob Nevin, and others. Carl admitted that he was impressed to be rubbing shoulders with a lawyer, having grown up poor in the east end. Carl soon began to view Eagleson as a possible ally in his conflicts with Leafs management. In those days, players didn't have agents, or anyone else, to help hammer out contracts, but at age 25, Carl engaged Eagleson to negotiate his deal with Imlach. It was an unprecedented move, and one that met with resistance from Punch, who advised Carl that if Eagleson could play hockey, he'd talk to him. Carl replied: "He's my lawyer." Imlach stuck to his guns; he wasn't about to get involved with a third party. Ultimately, he would have no choice.

Alan Eagleson would dominate Carl's life from this time forward, and Carl soon realized that getting involved with him had been a terrible error in judgment. Perhaps Imlach was right in refusing to deal with Eagleson — although not for the same reasons that the players would eventually have!

***

For years, NHL teams had travelled primarily by train, but by the early '60s they were increasingly flying between cities for games. It was during the 1962–63 season that Carl's fear of flying reached its zenith. It happened in New York, at Idlewild (now John F. Kennedy) Airport, after a game at Madison Square Garden against the Rangers. As Carl told the story, he was the last in line to board the Vickers Vanguard turboprop that morning. "As George Armstrong put his foot on the stairway ramp, I grabbed his arm and told him, 'That's it; see you around.'" Carl turned on his heel and walked back to the terminal.

The problem he now faced was how to get back to Toronto. He first grabbed a taxi to Grand Central Station where, almost immediately, he was able to catch a train to Buffalo. "The train was dirty, uncomfortable and cold. I had yet to discover the marvels of European train travel — the TGV of France, the Transalpine Express from Zurich to Innsbruck, the German high-speed ICE," Carl mused. It took eight hours to reach Buffalo, but as Carl said, "At least I was on the ground." In a veritable irony of ironies, the book Carl read on the train had been a Christmas present from Punch Imlach — Norman Vincent Peale's *The Power of Positive Thinking*. "It was a great book," Carl said, "but I wasn't ready for it at the time." Carl then climbed into another cab and arrived at home at two o'clock in the morning. He missed practice that morning, but the next day he approached Imlach and told him, "That's it; I can't fly anymore." Carl was stunned at Imlach's response. Without hesitation, he replied, "Get to the games the best way you can," and walked away. For the remainder of the season, Carl drove to the games, usually alone. Reflecting back on this time, Carl remarked on what he called "the many complexities of Punch Imlach; the strange complexity of our relationship." Sometime after this, Carl sought psychological counselling to deal with his fear of flying. However, he found it of little value; first of all, the therapist confirmed to him that a fear of flying is "real"; then he proceeded to tell Carl that he, himself, was petrified of flying!

At the end of the 1962-63 season, for the first time since 1947–48, the Toronto Maple Leafs finished first overall in the NHL, in one of the tightest regular-season races in history. Only five points separated the Leafs from the fourth-place Detroit Red Wings. Despite the parity, the Leafs had a relatively easy time of it in the playoffs, needing only five games each to dispense with Montreal and then Detroit. Johnny Bower was especially effective, allowing only 16 goals in the 10 games and chalking up a pair of shutouts in the semi-finals against the Habs. This time, the Leafs won the Cup on home ice, on April 18. Regrettably, in the closing minutes of that fifth game, Carl broke his arm when he crashed awkwardly into the boards while trying to check Andre Pronovost. In great pain, he remained in the Leaf dressing room until he heard the roar of the crowd after Eddie Shack's winning goal and David Keon's insurance goal before consenting to be taken to hospital. He missed the Stanley Cup presentation on the ice at Maple Leaf Gardens and the subsequent celebration in the dressing room afterwards. X-rays showed a fracture of the radius of his left forearm, and he underwent surgery the next morning to put the broken arm back in place with a plate. Ironically, Carl had managed to remain injury-free to that point, playing in all 70 regular-season games and all 10 playoff games.

This final game was the 13th consecutive playoff game the Toronto Maple Leafs had won at home. Apparently, everyone was reluctant to mention this detail to the very superstitious Imlach — who, Hal Walker of the *Telegram* suggested, "might not have shown up, even with his rabbit's paw, chewed-up coins and assorted bric-a-brac he believes are his good luck charms."

The season was satisfying for Carl on a personal note, as he was named to the first All-Star team. Frank Mahovlich was also on the first team, at left wing, while Tim Horton made the second squad. The Calder Trophy went to Kent Douglas, a defenseman who made his NHL debut at the "advanced" age of 26.

What a marvellous time for Carl Brewer, the hometown boy, to be playing hockey! "Throughout the 1960s, I'd been lucky," Carl concluded. "It was a fantastic experience to be part of a championship team and to be selected an All-Star. I did understand that I could play the game, and I was grateful to be able to attain this." Carl understood, too, that in his day, hockey careers were fairly short-lived. "Back in those days, a player was doing well to last 10 years. If you lasted 10 years, they shot you. Remember the movie *They Shoot Horses, Don't They?* Well, they used to 'shoot' hockey players, too," he often said.

"The rivalries in those days were very intense — especially with Montreal," Carl remembered. "We played games, usually back to back — on Saturday night in Toronto against the Bruins, for example, and then on the following night back in Boston. That was hell!"

Ralph Backstrom concurs. "There's no question the rivalry was intense. The grudges from one game carried over to the next because they were fresh in your mind." Players on opposing teams didn't talk or associate with one another, and many have admitted that, if they were walking down the street and an opponent approached, they'd immediately cross the street. In May 1965, television cameras captured the extent to which opposing players avoided each other. The Habs had just defeated Chicago to win the Stanley Cup. The Leafs had been eliminated in the semifinals, so Carl, who had gained a reputation early on as an insightful and articulate commentator, was working with the *Hockey Night in Canada* crew. He was in the Montreal dressing room with *HNIC* host Ward Cornell to interview the victorious Canadiens. As the players filed in, they turned abruptly the moment they spotted Carl, and walked away from him! Two players did come forward to talk to Carl on camera that night: Ralph Backstrom, always a class act, and Dick Duff, Carl's former Leaf teammate and friend, who spoke with him at length about the Canadiens' Stanley Cup victory.

Carl played against some of the all-time greats. He admired Bobby Hull, describing him as "flamboyant, with great flair — a player who was absolutely magnificent." He also believed Hull was the most exciting hockey player who ever played the game. "Bobby Hull wouldn't hurt anyone. He was a clean guy to play against — always a gentleman on the ice. He'd hit you, but it was always clean." Carl never forgot the continuing feud, if you will, between Hull and Bobby Baun: "It was nothing short of amazing, because Hull came down the left wing and Baun was the right defenseman, and they'd hammer one another. Bobby Hull didn't try to hurt Baun — they just wanted to run at each other. But it was intense, nonetheless. They were two powerful guys."

Of course, Carl also played against the one and only Gordie Howe. He referred to Gordie as "a great hockey player," but qualified his remark by explaining, "He got a lot of room because he'd sooner carve your eye out as look at you."

Of all the cities the Leafs visited throughout the season, Carl's favourite was Montreal, and he never ceased to be charmed by it. "Everybody's favourite city — every hockey player's favourite city — was Montreal for its flair, panache and *joie de vivre*," Carl explained. "The city of Montreal was free and open — you could get a drink there, and the restaurants were superior and abundant. They served steaks that were always blue — blood rare to you." By contrast, Toronto was well known as "Toronto the Good" because of its insufferable blue laws — there were no sports on Sundays, and no drinks served in restaurants on Sundays, either. The restaurants in Montreal really did put Toronto's to shame, as I soon learned when I went to study at McGill in the fall of 1963. Toronto had no restaurants to rival Ben's Deli, Mother Martin's, Joe's Steak House, or the Kon Tiki at the Mount Royal Hotel.

Carl could enjoy the Montreal experience all the more because they travelled there by train, which he considered "an absolute treat." He remembered the team ritual: "Board the train at Toronto's still-magnificent Union Station — there were alternatives for the departure time, depending on the particular whim of the superstitious Punch Imlach." Sometimes they departed at 11:00 a.m., arriving in Montreal in time for dinner; other times they travelled overnight, arriving in time for breakfast. Carl loved the sonorous tone of the porter shouting "All aboard" as the train was about to pull away from the station. "As was the custom of the time, team members were required to wear jackets and ties — models of sartorial elegance." However, the highlight of the train trip for Carl was the dining car experience. "The best was yet to come! The dining car — this was a memorable experience, with the white linen tablecloths, silver cutlery and waiters decked out in white jackets. Formal dining at its best." The players' five-dollar-a-day meal money went a long way because a sumptuous repast cost about $2.95. Carl's usual meal was roast beef, medium. Carl, who had been so dedicated to learning and was very well read, could never forget the first time Eddie Shack sat down to eat with him in the dining car. At the time, patrons had to choose from the menu and then write their meal choices on a chit provided at the table. Eddie asked Carl what he was ordering, then asked him to make it two of everything. It was the first time that Carl really understood that Eddie was illiterate — unable to read the menu or fill out his own meal request.

Once they arrived in Montreal, the players made their way to the Mount Royal Hotel, a Montreal landmark on Peel Street, a few blocks from the Montreal Forum. Carl enjoyed relaxing in the wonderful Turkish baths on the hotel's mezzanine level. The operator, a huge Hungarian man, was able to adjust and manipulate his back and release some of the perpetual tightness caused by Carl's ever-present tension and stress. Across the street from the hotel were two of Carl's favourite restaurants — Ben's Deli and Joe's Steak House.

As the Toronto Maple Leafs prepared for the 1963–64 hockey season, they seemed unstoppable, with two consecutive Stanley Cup victories behind them and a roster that went largely unchanged from the year before. Carl's debut with the team was delayed several weeks while he waited for the arm he broke in the last game of the Stanley Cup finals to mend itself. When he eventually did return to play in early December, his arm still was not properly healed and his mobility was limited.

Although Carl seemed at first glance to be thriving and tremendously successful professionally, he was no less troubled. In one of Carl's first games back with the Leafs, and with his broken arm still not completely rehabilitated, he got involved in an incident that would affect him psychologically for the rest of his life. It happened on December 7, 1963, in a game at Maple Leaf Gardens against the Chicago Blackhawks. It was a very chippy game right from the opening face-off, and by the third period, with the Leafs leading 3–0, a real donnybrook broke out. It started when Chicago's Reggie Fleming speared Eddie Shack. Fleming was assessed a major penalty, and while he was in the penalty box, Bob Baun took after him and they began fighting. From there, it quickly erupted into a bench-clearing brawl, with nine separate fights taking place on the ice. At the edge of the fray, Carl began mixing it up with Murray Balfour. Balfour started the confrontation by whacking Carl on the back of the head while Carl was holding on to Hawk Ab McDonald, then proceeding to strip Carl of his sweater. The two danced around until Balfour began pushing Carl towards the boards by the players' bench. In an interview with Brian McFarlane for Leafs TV years later, Carl related his version of what transpired: "Murray Balfour put his head down and was running me into the boards. I didn't realize the [gate to the] bench was open, and as it turned out, I fell back through the bench — under the bench — and that was the end of the fight.

"Fortunately, a friend of mine came down from the stands, by the name of Shatto — Dick Shatto, who proceeded to punch out Balfour." Why did the Argonauts' star halfback get involved? "Dick's son, Randy, was a goalie, and I was his favourite hockey player, so Dick Shatto and I had a relationship of sorts," Carl explained. Bob Nevin was on the ice at the time, and he told me that he recalls noticing what was going on between Carl and Balfour, but he was tangled up in a fight of his own. He thought it very odd and unusual that Balfour, one of Chicago's tough guys, went for Brewer; the unwritten code would have called for Balfour to go after an opposing tough guy, someone like Tim Horton or Larry Hillman.

For Carl, the experience was one he was unable to surmount emotionally. "This fight left an indelible imprint on my mind," he told Brian McFarlane, "although nothing really happened. I was coming back from a broken arm and couldn't use my left arm. I was stupid to be playing." Towards the end of the interview, he described, for the very first time, how the incident had affected him. "I never recovered; I was never the same player after that. Psychologically, it destroyed me. I really wanted to get past this, but I was unable to do so, to make the quantum leap." Before he took his seat in the television studio that day, the producer, Mark Askin, asked whether there was anything Carl didn't want to talk about. Mark promised he would never put Carl in a position where he might be embarrassed. Carl replied that he trusted Mark and was comfortable talking about whatever came up. After the taping was over, Mark remembers that Carl approached him and told him, "That's the first time I've ever spoken about it. I'm so glad I did that." Carl respected Mark, and the feeling was mutual. Mark recently told me, "He trusted me and he thought I was a good guy, and for Carl Brewer to think that I was a good guy, means the world to me."

Perhaps the most revealing insight into how Carl felt about the Balfour incident comes from Carl's own random notes: "Murray Balfour — he ruined my life because our fight shamed me. I forgive myself for being afraid. I was afraid because Murray caused it. Yet I was brave, I played the games, but lived with the destructiveness of fear. I could have confronted my fear; I did not. My fear was unnecessary."

Carl's unrelenting irritation with the way Punch Imlach treated the players also simmered beneath the surface, eating away at his psyche. Carl was not the only Leaf who couldn't tolerate Imlach's temperament. Carl's teammate and close friend Frank Mahovlich also had tremendous difficulty dealing with Imlach. During 1964, both Frank and Carl suffered from severe nervous tension. Both were sent to the same psychiatrist. The doctor assessed Carl, told him that he'd be okay and instructed him to go back and play hockey. Frank, on the other hand, was hospitalized for severe depression and tension in November. For the rest of his life, Carl complained that he was as emotionally distressed as Frank had been, but they "wouldn't let me have my nervous breakdown." Somehow Carl managed to keep going, and his play on the ice continued to be impressive, offering no hint of the angst he felt.

It struck me as remarkable that several of the Leafs of this era were bright, sensitive young men who happened to suffer emotionally under Imlach — in addition to Carl and Frank, there was also Mike Walton. Could environment have played a role? I asked Dick Duff, who played for the Leafs as well as the Canadiens, who dominated the second half of the 1960s, to compare his experiences with both teams. "First of all, Frank Selke [the Habs' general manager from 1946 until 1964] was a superb human being," Dick said. He also said that, while both teams were coached by tough, demanding men, "Toe Blake had come through the NHL ranks; he knew what it was like. Imlach had not played in the NHL. In Toronto, they beat the guys down. If you were having a bad spell, they never offered to help you — they didn't talk to you. Then they got rid of you. In Montreal, Toe Blake was fair — he played everyone. But if something was bothering a player, if he wasn't playing up to his best, they'd come to you and, first off, reassure you that you'd be back in form very soon. And they'd also ask if there was anything going on, any problem they could help you with." Perhaps Lloyd Percival, the physical fitness expert whose writings were viewed as gospel by the Soviet hockey hierarchy, put it best in a February 1964 interview with the *Toronto Star*: "The Leafs, especially, stress that hockey is a man's game — players shouldn't be bothered by a little thing called nerves. NHL owners will have to realize someday that hockey players have minds as well as bodies."

Events during the 1963–64 season support what Dick said about players being cast aside. In January and February of 1964, the Maple Leafs fell into a terrible slump, during which they couldn't seem to score goals. To remedy the situation, on February 22 Imlach pulled the trigger on a blockbuster deal with the New York Rangers, who happened to be in town for a game that night. Duff and Nevin, along with Arnie Brown, Bill Collins and Rod Seiling, were sent to New York in exchange for Andy Bathgate and Don McKenney. It was a textbook Imlach trade: youth for experience. At the time, Dick told the *Star*: "It won't look like such a good trade three years from now. These other guys and I will be playing and the fellows Toronto got will be ready to pack it in." When he spoke to me about it decades later, the hurt and bitterness were still evident in the expression on his face.

"There was no purpose in the trade, other than for Imlach to show everybody who was running the show," Nevin told me recently. And Carl felt the trade was absolutely absurd. "We gave up Dick Duff, who was probably one of the greatest playoff performers of all time, and Bob Nevin, who went on to play for the Rangers for seven years as their captain." A year later, Duff was traded to Montreal, where he helped the Habs win four Stanley Cups. Brown and Seiling went on to become solid NHL defensemen. And Dick's comments in the press proved to be prophetic: Bathgate was traded to Detroit after the 1964–65 season, while McKenney was claimed on waivers by the Detroit Red Wings in June of '65 — the Leafs got nothing in return except for the waiver fee.

Leaf defenseman Kent Douglas was no fan of Bathgate's; he didn't consider him a team player. Kent told me a story about how Tim Horton took the ex-Ranger to task in the dressing room. "Tim Horton never said a word — he'd say hello, but other than that he never said anything. One day, Bathgate made some comment in rebuttal to criticism about the team's play, to the effect that he wasn't the player at fault. Tim Horton got up, stared him down and yelled, 'Bathtub — sit down and shut up! You might have been a big star in New York, but here you're just one of the guys.'" When I asked Ed Litzenberger what Andy Bathgate brought to the team, he answered, "He was a 'me, me, me' guy."

Despite the animosity around the deal, it did prove effective in the short run. Both new Leafs helped boost the club's offence, and the team turned on the jets late in the season. They carried that renewed momentum through the playoffs, eliminating the Canadiens in a semifinal series that went the full seven games, then defeating Detroit in a final series that also lasted seven games. This was the series in which Bobby Baun scored his famous goal, reportedly on a broken leg, to win game six in overtime and tie the series at three games each. The Leafs had an easier time of it in game seven, shutting out the Wings 4–0 and winning the Cup yet again.

The third championship in as many years was sweet, but it did not completely eliminate the aftertaste left by the Bathgate trade. At the end of the year, reflecting on the deal, Carl said: "We gave up an awful lot. Did we need to do this? Not in my humble opinion. Was there a lack on the team? I think not. Could it have been a lack behind the bench? I think that, more than likely, it could have been. In my opinion, our Leaf team as it was originally constituted was good enough to become a dynasty."

In 1964–65, there were bright spots — Bower and Terry Sawchuk combined to win the Vezina Trophy, while Carl was named to the second All-Star team. His career-high 177 penalty minutes, which led the league, suggested he'd regained his edge. In his syndicated newspaper column, Gordie Howe paid tribute to Carl. "One of the reasons Carl Brewer is such an outstanding defenseman is because of his ability to move quickly either to his right or left. He's got the moves and he gets your dander up once in a while with his antics. You get a little mad and take a run at him. You find he's a very difficult man to hit, too." As if forecasting the future, Howe added, "He's still a man I'd like to see back on our blue line, too, as much as he gets you mad when you're playing against him."

In the playoffs, however, the Canadiens were too much for the Leafs, who had clearly lost their drive. At the time, no hockey fan could have imagined that it would be more than 14 years before they would see Carl play again in a Toronto uniform.

***

It didn't come as a surprise to me when Carl left the Leafs in the fall of 1965. In Montreal, after the playoff series with the Habs came to an end, Carl hinted at his plans a couple of times in conversation. "If I'm with the Leafs next year," he would say. At the time, I was struck by his emphasis on the word "if." I felt certain that the Leafs weren't about to get rid of him; knowing of his deep torment as I did, it seemed entirely possible to me that he might walk away. On the other hand, it seemed unfathomable — given Carl's tremendous talent, his skills and his apparent confidence and power. These latter qualities, which others saw, were not, however, qualities that Carl perceived in himself. Carl was playing hockey in the NHL, something every young man in the country would love to be doing. However, it didn't satisfy Carl.

He couldn't find the meaning he was searching for. He was questioning all of the bigger issues of life, what it was all about, at the same time as he struggled with emotional turmoil and a psyche that was being destroyed by playing under Punch Imlach. Years later, he explained, "It was an ongoing battle with Punch Imlach. I didn't agree with his methods; I didn't agree with his approach to hockey, and I didn't agree with his unnecessary disciplinary measures. If he required discipline of us, he should have demanded the same discipline of himself." He realized that there were players on the team who thought the same way, but they were able to keep it from getting to them. "He got to me and he got to Frank Mahovlich and Mike Walton. He destroyed our psyches," Carl said. He was never able to learn to let go of hurts, annoyances, grievances about anything. He let these things gnaw away at him, adding to his ever-present stress and anxiety.

In the summer of 1965, during one of our phone conversations, he inquired about my second-year results at McGill. He suddenly interjected, asking me if I realized that what I had accomplished in only two years had taken him more than five by taking summer courses at McMaster. I remember the anxiety and tension in his voice, conveying the sense that he was frightened, that he felt that he was losing ground and not getting where he wanted to go quickly enough.

The critical moment came in Peterborough during an exhibition game on the night of October 14, 1965. Carl had arrived at training camp confused and uncertain about playing hockey at all. His defense partner, Bobby Baun, was holding out, and Carl was anxious and unsettled. That night, Carl seemed to have neither his head nor his heart in the game, and he made a couple of plays that left goaltender Johnny Bower vulnerable.

In his book *Hockey Is a Battle*, Punch Imlach described the scene: "We were playing an exhibition game in Peterborough this particular night when the puck went into the corner and Johnny Bower yelled at Carl to get in there and get it out. All I could see from the behind the bench was that Brewer went into the corner and shot it right out in front. Someone on the opposite team took a swipe at it and almost hit Bower in the face. Then the puck went back in the corner and damned if Brewer didn't go in for it and shoot it out in front again and once more Bower almost got creamed."

Kent Douglas remembers that, in the final moments of the first period, Imlach hollered something at Carl. "I heard Carl shout angrily back at Punch, 'The hell with it!' and he stormed off the ice as the bell rang to signal the conclusion of the period."

In the dressing room, the tension escalated, as Carl and Bower exchanged angry words. Then Carl hurled an orange in Johnny's direction, almost hitting him. Johnny, who holds no grudge about what happened that night, talked to me about it for this book. "Carl was very stubborn. He wanted to do things his way. I had a little tiff with Carl — but I had one with Tim Horton, too — actually, I had a tiff with just about everybody because they were backing in on me too much or cutting in front of me, and I'd get mad at them. Then I'd ask myself, 'What are you doing?' I depended so much on these guys. After I'd said something, I was sorry I'd said anything to them." Nonetheless, Johnny and Carl remained lifelong friends. Carl always spoke affectionately about Johnny, and the feeling was mutual. "It's part of the game," he told me. "We were still friends on the ice and off the ice."

Douglas was in the dressing room and remembers that Carl was absolutely furious; he'd never seen him so upset. However, it never occurred to Kent that this just might be it for Carl. As Kent explained, "You just didn't do that, quit." As the players were about to head back onto the ice for the second period, Imlach told them, "If any of you don't want to play, stay in the room." That was all Carl needed to hear; when the players returned to the ice, Carl remained behind, and was soon in his street clothes.

Bob Tindall, who subsequently had a long career as a scout for the Boston Bruins, was in Peterborough at the time. Bob has told me that he had been at the golf course the afternoon of this game, and something about Carl's demeanour told him that he was going to quit. That night, Bob was watching the game in the arena and, when Carl did not reappear at the beginning of the second period, he knew immediately that something was up. Next, he saw King Clancy come out and look anxiously around the stands. By then, Bob was certain that his premonition was unfolding. It was Bob Tindall who drove Carl back to Toronto that night. Just as they were about to pull away from the Empress Hotel, Carl hopped out of the car. He had spotted sports reporter Paul Rimstead in the hotel lobby, and told Bob that he had to speak to Paul, because if Rimstead didn't have the story for the next day's paper, when a number of the other journalists did, he would look stupid. Even under times of great personal stress, Carl was concerned about someone else's needs.

The following day, naturally, Carl's defection was headline news. George Gross's column in the *Telegram* was headed, "Brewer: His Last

Game?" "I want you to know that this has nothing to do with my contract," Carl told Gross. "I didn't want to talk contract with Punch until I reached a conclusion about my future. And Johnny is a keen competitor, a great guy. You're bound to exchange words in a game." Gross went on to say: "Brewer looked tired and worried last night. He gave the impression of a man who has a big decision to make and is not certain which road to choose. On the ice, Brewer is an emotional individual, deeply engrossed in the game. He can't sleep for hours after a hockey game and he can't relax before a game. Even yesterday while the team was resting in the afternoon, Brewer was restlessly walking around the hotel — thinking. Off the ice, he's an intelligent, amiable fellow with whom it is a pleasure to discuss any topic of interest. In the past, he talked of a career in teaching. He has also shown interest in a job as a sportscaster. He studies French and German." Carl was further quoted as saying, "It takes a lot of sacrifice to be a hockey player. I don't know if I can handle it."

Carl did not make this decision lightly. He felt retirement was the only option available, given the trouble he was having with Imlach. "My damaged psyche — destroyed by Imlach — would no longer allow me to accommodate playing hockey and being a hockey player," he said. Back in Toronto a few days later, he went to Maple Leaf Gardens to talk to Punch. "At first, Imlach wouldn't see me," Carl recalled. "I sat outside his office in Maple Leaf Gardens and waited. [Imlach loved to keep people waiting.]" Training camp was just winding down, and Tim Horton, Bob Pulford and Bobby Baun had not yet signed their contracts for 1965–66. "Baun was Imlach's biggest problem," Carl continued. "He was to pay the ultimate price for upstaging Imlach — that is, not kissing Imlach's ass. What was the ultimate price, you ask? Baun, he with the Maple Leaf tattooed on his ass, was ignominiously dealt off to the fledgling Oakland Seals in the summer of 1967." Baun, who was relegated to the fifth defenseman's role in Carl's absence, was left exposed — and was selected by Oakland — in the June 1967 draft held to stock the six expansion teams.

Carl continued to wait.

Still Imlach wouldn't see me. King Clancy, everybody's favourite gofer, kept coming out of Imlach's office to inform me that I would have to wait a little longer. Finally, I told King that I would see Punch right away and I walked into his office.

"That's it," I informed him.

"Can I trade you?" he asked.

"You can do whatever you want, but I'm not playing hockey," I replied.

With that, I left his office. Any meeting I ever had with Imlach was brief.

Out on the street, the full, harsh impact of what had just transpired finally struck Carl. He described how he felt at that moment.

I started walking. It was a big decision, and one that I hadn't really wanted to make. I didn't feel good. I didn't feel relieved. I felt barren and empty. What the hell had I done? I was 27 years of age. For my entire life, I wanted to be a hockey player. My ultimate choice was to be a Toronto Maple Leaf, and I had done it — with élan, with style, with alacrity, with noise and ability. Suddenly, I was no longer a Maple Leaf ... a dream quashed.

Feeling tormented and distraught, he looked to the only source of comfort and support he knew. Being deeply religious, a devout Roman Catholic, he headed to church.

My solitary walk took me to St. Pat's, a Roman Catholic church at Dundas and McCaul streets. My mother made frequent novenas and retreats there. I was still, at this stage of my life, devoutly religious. I always found peace and comfort in a Catholic church. Knowing this was a special place for my mother was in itself solace and comfort for me. I meditated for a while. I knelt and prayed — hard. (I always did things with intensity — with teeth grinding and jaws clenched.) And then I went to confession. Confession is good for the soul, but not in this case. I wanted to talk about my dilemma. My confessor knew nothing about hockey — strange for a priest — and my queries were to go unresolved. The priest was able to offer little in the way of

*comfort and support. I left the confessional feeling even
more empty and alone. I was in the twilight zone.*

*I was no longer a Maple Leaf. It had been my only goal
in life.*

CHAPTER 4

"WE WANT BREWER!"

"It seems strange to me to hear others say that I was a smart, tough negotiator. I hear this in reference to my many retirements, as if they were obviously just a ploy. In fact, at no time were money or contract benefits part of my game plan. Where I somehow got the strength to stand up for what I considered to be my rights, I do not know. And why most of my colleagues lived in fear, I do not know. I was reacting to the dictates of my conscience, and it seemed to be the natural order of events."

In the weeks and months following Carl's departure from the Leafs, the rumour mill worked overtime. Commentators speculated about his imminent return, suggested that he'd see the folly of his decision and return to the pro ranks. "It was flattering," he said. "I was constantly being besieged to return to the Leafs. Many thought that this was a contract ploy — it had nothing to do with money. I was a vegetable and I was out. I was amused by the comments of the cognoscenti — Ballard, Smythe, Campbell and others — who harangued that I would be back by Christmas. For me, these comments were an incentive and a challenge to stick with my original premise."

Having committed to leaving the Leafs, Carl intended to take some time to heal his damaged psyche, find some work involving physical labour, perhaps in construction, after which he planned to complete his university education. Alan Eagleson, however, convinced Carl to apply, albeit late in the academic year, to the University of Toronto. This he did in the late autumn of 1965. Although most of Carl's credits had been earned at McMaster University in Hamilton, and in spite of his late application, he was accepted and assigned five courses for a makeup year to complete his bachelor's degree in Political Science and French. He found it difficult to catch up, and felt he never really adjusted, but it all worked out very nicely for him and he was delighted to graduate with his B.A. in November 1966. In his absence, the Leafs' defense suffered greatly, and fans urged him to reconsider his retirement. A Mrs. McLean in Scarborough wrote: "There has been an aura of gloom in our home since we heard the unbelievable news that you have retired.... The Toronto Maple Leaf organization will have a hard time filling [the] #2 sweater as capably as you have." Another, from a Mrs. Friessen in Saskatoon: "I cannot explain my feelings; my first reaction was anger, then there followed a sincere regret. I simply cannot believe that I will no longer see Carl Brewer in his dominant role in Maple Leaf Gardens."

By the summer of 1966, Carl momentarily relented and agreed to meet with Punch Imlach to discuss the possibility of rejoining the Maple Leafs. During the meeting, the two men even got to the point of discussing specific terms — Carl recalled asking for $25,000 plus bonuses over two years. Carl asked that the meeting be kept in the strictest confidence while he pondered the implications of their discussion, and Imlach agreed. However, Carl had no sooner left Imlach's office and driven away from the Gardens, than he heard all the details of the meeting, including the figures discussed, being revealed on radio station CKEY by sportscaster Joe Morgan. Morgan made comments, which Carl knew were coming directly from Imlach, suggesting that Brewer's demands were excessive. Carl was furious that Imlach had leaked word of their meeting to the press, and that put an immediate end to any possibility of his returning to the Leafs.

On September 30, 1966, the Toronto Maple Leafs tendered a contract, with a base salary of $25,000, to Carl for the 1966–67 season. They made this overture in spite of the fact that Carl had already formally asked the Leafs for his release. Two weeks later, Carl's lawyer, Alan Eagleson, returned the contract, reminding Punch Imlach that "Mr. Brewer has previously indicated to you that he wishes to retire from professional hockey."

***

Imlach's refusal to grant Carl his release threw a monkey wrench into his plans for his next move: to be reinstated as an amateur and join Canada's National team, managed by Father David Bauer. Carl wanted to play for Canada at the World Championships in Vienna in March 1967. There were many facets to Carl's desire to join the Nats, aside from playing hockey. Carl was an intellectual, and education had always been of paramount importance to him. He was fascinated by the concept of combining education with hockey, as the National team program did. From experience, he knew all too well that it was not easy to excel at both. Also, Carl felt confused about, and somewhat estranged from, his devout Catholic background; in his younger years, he had aspired to become a priest, and he sincerely hoped that working with Father Bauer would help him regain his faith and find his purpose in life.

In early September, Carl made his intentions known at a press conference. Immediately, a strong wall of resistance went up all through the hockey community, while the Canadian public at large was supportive and enthusiastic. Hockey fans from coast to coast sympathized with Carl's situation and wanted to see him free to play for Canada. It was an exciting prospect for all hockey fans, but particularly those who remembered the bygone days when the Trail Smoke Eaters and Whitby Dunlops triumphed at the Worlds.

In *The Globe and Mail*, Scott Young wrote an insightful article entitled "Hockey's Dilemma." The piece was particularly sympathetic to Brewer — which was quite a tribute insomuch as Young was often considered to be a conduit for Punch Imlach's viewpoints.

> *Punch Imlach, the general manager and coach of the Leafs, has refused to grant Brewer's release. Only a hopeless romantic would expect him to do otherwise. Brewer is one of the best hockey players in the world.*
>
> *You will read in the sports pages that Brewer's chances of playing with Canada's National team face impossible obstacles.... [U]nder hockey law, to become an amateur, Brewer must be waived by every team in professional hockey. Some hockey officials have been quoted as saying they would certainly claim him at the $30,000 waiver price. However, that obstacle would be final only if the courts had tested the validity of professional hockey contracts and found them binding forever. No such test has been made. If Brewer's association with lawyer Alan Eagleson means what it seems to mean, this could be the*

time — unless professional hockey gulps hard a few times and then passes the order from on high that Brewer is to be waived....

The facts of life in hockey are that when Brewer, in his early teens, signed with a Toronto farm club, he signed, in effect, for life. Each autumn since then, he had two choices: either go where he was told, or quit his profession. The iniquitous arrangement by which any hockey suspension is recognized reciprocally by amateurs and professionals alike the world over had him hog-tied, handcuffed, arm-locked, trussed like a prize beef.

Most players don't mind going along with this. But can you imagine an oil geologist being told he must work for Imperial Oil, or no one? Can you imagine an artist being told that he painted for the Toronto Gallery, or he wouldn't be allowed to paint at all? How would you like to be told that if your present employer blacklisted you, there wouldn't be a job open for you in your profession anywhere?...

As any adult citizen of a free country, he should be able to live his life exactly as he chooses. This brings us to the main event, which is not Brewer vs. Imlach at all, but Brewer vs. the National Hockey League's player's contract — a matter long overdue in the courts....

A court decision to upset professional hockey's standard contract would make hockey either change the contract or face chaos. Traditionally, this threat has caused professional hockey to back away, give ground, settle out of court, every time a contract has been challenged or the legality of a suspension has been challenged. To me, Brewer holds all the high cards if he and his lawyer decide that this is the time to look across the table in a courtroom and call hockey's bluff.

On September 15, Imlach told Red Burnett of the *Toronto Star*, "I don't want to hear [Carl's] name again and will refuse to answer any questions regarding his status. I've had all I can take of the Brewer business." Eight days later, headlines in *The Globe and Mail* announced, "Maple Leafs Give

Carl Brewer Release." Stafford Smythe stated his position in a letter to Clarence Campbell, president of the NHL:

> *[M]ay I make it quite clear that if Carl is to abandon professional hockey in favour of playing for our country's National team, then we have no objection. I realize that the final disposition of this matter rests with the National Hockey League and other professional leagues, but ... we would be delighted to have a former Leaf player wearing the national uniform in competition with other countries of the world.*

Reached at training camp in Peterborough, Imlach was furious: "It's stupid. They can't do it," he told *Globe* reporter Louis Cauz.

In spite of the Leafs' concession, other general managers, particularly Tommy Ivan of Chicago, made it clear that if Carl were put on waivers, they'd claim him. The impasse continued.

Sports fans across the country followed Carl's predicament with keen interest. A Montrealer, Bill Shields, wrote in a letter to Carl: "I used to play ball with your dad and your Uncle 'Wee.' I thought you might be interested in my rather brusque note to Clarence Campbell."

> *Come off it, Mr. Campbell. When you decide arbitrarily that Carl Brewer cannot play for Canada's National team unless he has been waived by every professional hockey team in the world, you have done a disservice to Canada, the NHL and to professional hockey in general. And you don't come out of it very well yourself. Which brings me to the point at issue. Here we have a good Canadian, certainly one of the finest defensemen in the NHL, who, at his own expense, and certainly at the cost of retaining any semblance of friendly relations with the Toronto Maple Leaf professional hockey club, elects to throw his lot with Canada's National team — surely you, the NHL decision maker, can be big enough to permit a good Canadian to make a worthwhile athletic contribution to the country.*

Negotiations dragged on for months and, needless to say, given Carl's makeup, the delay was very difficult for him to endure. By the end of October, it appeared that almost every professional team in the National, American, Western and Central leagues had agreed not to obstruct Carl's amateur reinstatement. The one holdout was Eddie Shore, the maverick owner of the Springfield Indians of the AHL.

On October 20, the NHL's board of governors met in New York, and Carl's case was on the agenda. At the end of the day, although there were agreements in principle, there was still no final resolution. After this meeting, a very upset and frustrated Carl spoke to the media: "Tell me, what has changed from yesterday? I'm still waiting, and my patience has grown thin. I can't play today, tomorrow or next week. How long can a Canadian citizen be deprived of his right to represent Canada? Why should American teams be allowed to hold me back? Last year, I was allowed to play in exhibition games; now, I can't even practise with the National team. I'm fed up with it all. Why can't they act in my case as fast as they did in Sid Smith's? [Smith, the former Leaf, was granted amateur status in a matter of hours to play for the Whitby Dunlops in 1957.] What are they worried about? That the National team will be stronger than some NHL teams? Well, they already are stronger. They are so good they could make the playoffs if they were playing in the NHL."

In November, Carl attended his convocation from University of Toronto, while he waited for the final decision concerning his hockey future. The International Ice Hockey Federation, which oversees the World Championships, was prepared to declare him eligible, but had to wait until the Canadian Amateur Hockey Association reinstated Carl as an amateur. And the CAHA would not do that until the NHL cleared him.

Finally, on December 1, 1966, Carl learned from Clarence Campbell that the waiting was over. In a letter to Carl, Campbell wrote: "This is to formally advise you that the National Hockey League has amended its by-laws in such a way as to make it possible to bring about an amateur reinstatement for a person in your position. You are now in a position to formally apply for amateur reinstatement in accordance with the revised procedure, and when the necessary documents are delivered to Central Registry at this office, I assure you that every effort will be made to expedite the official granting of your reinstatement by the CAHA."

Shortly afterward, Carl received a handwritten letter from Alan

Eagleson: "You have gained a great deal in this effort in the eyes of the public, so don't risk your reputation on a minor matter." Carl had understood from the outset that Eagleson would not bill him for his involvement. So, when an invoice surfaced, Carl was annoyed and very upset about it. Eagleson wrote: "As I told you, if you had to pay one cent of my fee, there would not be one. We have become close friends and I am scarcely going to bill you. George Graham of Ostranders [Jewellers] and Jim Kerr of Shaw Laboratories told me that they would cover your costs. This still goes. So don't worry about such things." Eagleson went on to suggest that Max Bell, who supported Carl's decision to join the National team, might also contribute to paying his fees, but added:

> If [Bell] takes no such steps, I shall speak to Kerr and Graham about the fee. After all, I think I did hear my name mentioned in connection with yours a few times (or, was it yours mentioned in connection with mine?).
>
> If all goes well, maybe I shall see part of the Centennial Tournament. Tell Father Bauer I would like to make the Austrian trip if he can fit me into his suitcase free of charge.
>
> Keep your head up — I am very proud of the way you handled yourself throughout the tough times in this situation. Everyone I know is proud of you. Show the Nationals how hockey should be played. Take care of yourself, pal.

Even at this early point in Eagleson's involvement in hockey, his letters display his convoluted thinking, his ego, and his interest in getting perks at no cost to himself.

Carl remained adamant that the final resolution of this saga had little to do with Eagleson and much more to do with public opinion, legal concerns by the NHL, and intervention on his behalf by his father-in-law, Toronto businessman, W. Harold Rea. The Leafs and the NHL were also well aware of the legal implications should Carl bring a restraint-of-trade lawsuit before the courts.

With the months of struggle behind him, Carl was free to devote his attention and energy to playing hockey. While he was in Winnipeg working out with the team, he even gained experience as a writer, authoring a weekly column for the Winnipeg *Tribune*. Living in Winnipeg was a challenge — especially the severe winter weather. He recalled having to leave his car running while at practice at the arena, otherwise it wouldn't start. He also spoke of nearly freezing to death one night while walking a babysitter home. He always had a great deal of respect for Winnipeggers, admiring them as hard-working, highly motivated and honest individuals.

***

From late 1965, when Carl quit the Leafs — which meant he was no longer visiting Montreal every few weeks — through 1966, we continued to keep in touch, but even more sporadically than before. He'd drop me notes from time to time. When I was at home in Toronto during the summers, he'd phone and we'd have long, engaging conversations. Sometimes, he'd drop by and pick me up to go for a drive, or a coffee and a chat — whatever time permitted. Mostly, I followed the saga of his professional life through the newspapers.

From the very beginning, Carl had consistently given me a message that was very heartfelt and powerful. Because our time together was somewhat erratic and he himself admitted that he hated goodbyes, he often said to me, "Sue, remember this: our ship transcends time and space." He believed that, and so did I. It never mattered how long we were apart, because from the moment we were together again, it was as if no time had passed, nothing had changed and we immediately felt that strong feeling of connection, of comfort and closeness.

I received a brief note from Carl, dated September 11, 1966, congratulating me on my graduation from McGill and telling me that his convocation would be in November because he had failed one course but passed the supplemental. He told me that when he was next in Montreal, he'd be in touch. I had stayed on in Montreal after graduation from McGill because I wanted to spend some time in an environment where I could speak French in a professional as well as a social setting before returning to Ontario to teach high school French. So I worked as a bilingual customer service representative for Bell Canada that year.

A date that will be forever engraved in my memory is January 8, 1967. That afternoon, Canada's National team, of which Carl was now a member, played the Soviet Mational team at the Montreal Forum. Canada's centennial year was just getting underway, and the whole country was wrapped up in the excitement. That summer, Montreal was staging the World's Fair,

Expo 67, and pride and optimism for the country's future were at an un-precedented high from coast to coast. It therefore followed that there was a great deal of excitement and hype surrounding this particular hockey game. It's essential to remember that, although this game was certainly about hockey supremacy, it was also about a good deal more. It was seen as a battle between the "bad guys" — the Russians and the Communist system — and the "good guys": us! The rivalry went far beyond that of the Montreal Canadiens and Toronto Maple Leafs. This was about ideology and idealism — fuelled, no doubt, by propaganda on both sides. The issues were certainly painted as black and white in those days.

As I took my seat in the Forum that afternoon, it wasn't long before I noticed that the arena was filled to capacity. The atmosphere was electric, the energy level from the crowd extraordinary. There was an unbelievable sense of anticipation as the national anthems were played and the puck was dropped to start the game.

What was even more extraordinary was the reception Carl received from the Forum crowd that afternoon. In years past, when he was one of the Leafs' defensive stalwarts, he was naturally the subject of scorn and abuse from the Montreal fans. Not this afternoon, however; in fact, quite the contrary: Carl was every fan's hero. They screamed wildly and unrelent-ingly every time he stepped on the ice; they chanted his name — and "*Nous voulons Brewer*" — in unison and went wild over every move he made. The excitement was infectious, and it began to well up inside of me. The game was no less thrilling from a technical point of view, and the two sides bat-tled to a 3–3 tie.

The following day, the Montreal papers were full of praise for Carl. A headline in *The Gazette* read, "Forum Fans Turn It On for Brewer." In his column, *The Gazette*'s Ted Blackmore wrote:

> "*We want Brewer, we want Brewer,*" *was the unbelievable chant that rattled the building's rafters late in the third pe-riod of the Canada–Russia game, and that left the former Toronto Maple Leaf defenseman visibly rattled in the dressing room minutes later.*
>
> "*No, it wasn't a surprise, nothing in hockey surprises me anymore,*" *he said, trying again to open a soft drink bottle with trembling hands. Now his voice was trembling,*

too. "But it was quite a thrill. People are waiting for me to fall down, and then this. It's quite a thrill.

"Actually," he said, "people here have always yelled, 'We want Brewer' — but they would always finish it off: 'We want Brewer — dead.'"

He carried the puck in Doug Harvey fashion, stick-handling and setting up plays. Back in his zone, he took charge and reacted calmly to each Russian charge. He made subtle contributions, such as needling the Soviets and dis-arming the referee. And he hit a few people such as Alexander Ragulin. "Well," he explained, "I make like I'm going for the puck and then I hit him. Now he knows all about it."

After the game, I made my way down to the Canadian team's dressing room. I knew my way very well, having attended countless games since coming to Montreal in 1963. I waited and waited for Carl. There were a lot of media personnel milling about, and I knew they were primarily interested in talking to Carl. I continued to wait until most of the players had left and the arena staff was attempting to clear people out of the building. At this juncture, Barry MacKenzie emerged from the dressing room. I asked him if he would please tell Carl that Susan Foster was waiting for him. Barry soon re-emerged and said emphatically, "Carl says for you to *wait!*" I did. About 10 minutes later, Carl finally appeared. Flashbulbs popped in unison as he came directly up to me and we embraced. Carl put his arm around me and began heading towards the front exit of the Forum. As we walked, Carl said, "I hope you don't have any plans, because I want to make a night of it."

A French-language reporter followed us and asked, "*Carl, est-ce que vous pensez que les Russes sont plus rudes que vous autres?*" "What did he say?" Carl whispered. I replied on his behalf, "*Ce n'est pas évident?*" and we continued towards the exit. Out on the street, Carl suggested we grab a bite to eat and go to a movie, but added that he wanted to go someplace where he wouldn't be recognized. We hopped into a taxi and headed to the east end — Sherbrooke Street near Park Avenue. My friend Lynne Roberts lived in the apartment building there, and I knew of a movie theatre close by as well as several simple restaurant choices.

In all of the years I had known Carl, his domestic situation was something he had never discussed with me. I knew that he was married, and I always accepted that that was how it was, especially because he was such a devout Catholic. But I did have a general impression that his situation was less than ideal. I'd heard bits and pieces of gossip from time to time, and occasionally Carl would cast a disparaging glance as he passed quickly over some casual comment about having to get home.

This night in Montreal, the complexion, the intensity of our relationship deepened and expanded powerfully. For the first time, we acknowledged what we had always known and really felt for each other — just how totally we were attracted to one another, not only intellectually, emotionally and psychically, but physically. We had known it, but we had not allowed it to come to anything. Tonight, that changed.

We went into the restaurant on the ground floor of Lynne's building — a familiar place to me. We sat opposite one another — we were both wonderfully content, and delighted just to be together again, alone. It had been about six months since we'd seen each other, and that comfortable, secure feeling of togetherness that we knew with one another was very welcome. After we took stock of our cash to make sure we had enough between us for supper and a movie, Carl ordered a cheeseburger, fries and a Coke, while I ordered a grilled cheese sandwich and a coffee. Carl was embarrassed and explained to me that he had not yet been paid any of the money he was owed by the National team. He was visibly concerned about this fact (eventually, he did get his full salary, but only after appealing to Max Bell, the Canadian entrepreneur, businessman and philanthropist who was the first chairman of Hockey Canada and who helped Carl in his efforts to join Father Bauer's team). As we sat having our meal, Carl talked about the reaction of the fans. He was incredulous but thrilled by the reception. He also told me about the struggles he'd gone through to regain his amateur status. He mentioned that Eagleson had made a lot of noise, but that in the final analysis, Eagleson had had nothing to do with the result. I got up to make a phone call, and was aware that as I did so, Carl never once took his eyes off me.

We paid the bill, donned our coats and headed out into the streets of Montreal. It was still early, but by now darkness had fallen. It had been an overcast day, and very mild for Montreal in January. Now it was still mild, but snowing ever so gently. We began walking — strolling, actually. Carl immediately put his arm around me, snuggling me close to him. We stopped frequently for long, lingering kisses. We were both completely in the moment. Space on the sidewalk for two had only one in it. As we meandered I watched the huge, soft, fluffy snowflakes drift past the lights in the old, globe-shaped wrought-iron street lamps that lined the street. The air was completely silent — nothing but the sound of our footsteps. Carl was wearing only toe rubbers on his feet and they were getting wet, but he didn't seem to notice or care. That night, our souls merged permanently in a way that went beyond time and space.

Eventually, we entered the small east-end cinema where French films were the norm. *Un Homme et Une Femme*, the movie by Claude Lelouch, was playing. In the lobby of the theatre, about a dozen people were waiting to buy their tickets or take their seats. We weren't there many minutes before we heard the whispers — "...Brewer..." — and all eyes were on us. I was standing back a few paces while Carl stood in line to buy our tickets. He leaned over and whispered in my ear, "I thought you said no one would recognize me here!" I smiled warmly and suggested that there was probably nowhere in the entire city where he wouldn't be recognized that night, and that here, at least, there were only a few gawking people.

We took our seats at the rear of the theatre and, after we removed our coats, Carl pulled me close to him again. We thoroughly enjoyed the movie and the opportunity it provided us to be together. This, like all French movies that we saw and loved over the years, was very special, with a simple theme but poignant and beautifully played out. It was a pleasant couple of hours.

We left the theatre and hailed a taxi to go back to my apartment on Ridgewood Avenue. During the taxi ride, Carl told me he had been deeply moved by the film, all the more so because I was with him. Foreign movies remained our favourites over all the years to come.

For hours that night, we sat together, listening to the music of Al Martino and Jim Reeves, while Carl talked and talked. He was terribly burdened emotionally. It was frightening and alarming to see him in such despair — such a wonderful man, so gifted and talented, with so much to contribute in life, and yet so deeply tormented. He shared his fears, his hurts, his disillusions and confusion with me. Carl talked about his career as a hockey player and questioned what sense it made to chase a puck around the ice when so many people out there were doing things that made a real difference in the world. He talked about the way that playing for Punch Imlach had destroyed his psyche.

He related to me that he had fought long and hard to regain his amateur status, with the express purpose of playing for the National team, but Father Bauer seemed not to have taken him seriously or given him the time and attention he needed. This left him feeling let down and discouraged. It seemed that Father Bauer was the third significant male figure in Carl's life to whom he had looked for understanding, support and validation, only to be let down. The first had been his father, Carl Sr., who'd had trouble understanding his son and found fault even where Carl excelled, followed by Punch Imlach. Also, having finally succeeded in making the National team, Carl felt he wasn't really being accepted. He said that Jackie MacLeod, the coach, appeared to be threatened by his presence, as if Jackie feared that Carl had designs on his job. Carl vehemently denied this and told me the idea was nonsense. Also, it was weighing heavily on his mind that he had not yet received any of his salary from the Nats.

For the first time, Carl spoke to me of his marital situation that night. He confided to me that his marriage was in serious trouble and that he knew it had been a mistake from the very beginning. Carl told me that both his father and Bob Baun had told him very bluntly to think carefully about what he was doing because the marriage wouldn't work. He admitted he had not listened. There was deep sadness in his voice as he acknowledged what a terrible situation it was for his 18-month-old son, Christopher. His face lit up when he talked of Christopher, and it was obvious that he was the great joy in his life.

He talked about a possible future career as a teacher and asked me if I thought he'd be able to handle it. He was enthusiastic about my plans to teach, telling me what a worthwhile, ideal career path I had chosen.

It was not easy to take all this in, and I felt tremendously heavy-hearted for Carl. I listened and let him talk, trying to console him and encourage him and let him know that I was there for him. However, seeing him so profoundly tormented and troubled at the core of his being left me feeling overwhelmed. He was terribly conflicted. As close as we had been over the years since we first met, we had never been so close, in every way, as we were this night.

The evening passed all too quickly. At close to midnight, Carl got up and said that he had to leave, but was doing so reluctantly. He had to meet the team curfew, and he said that he thought that it was really stupid for grown men to have curfews. On the other hand, he added that he couldn't mess with the rules when he was just getting established with the team. As he was leaving, he kissed me and said, "This will continue." He asked me to write to him. When he got into the taxi that night, I felt that part of my soul was leaving with him.

Throughout that evening, I began to see just how much Carl took things to heart, and how he was torn apart by his thoughts. All his life, he would replay things over and over in his mind, unable to let go of anything he experienced or saw. He often talked about his guilt and shame — none of which made any sense to me at the time. This wasn't the only time I witnessed this wounded part of Carl; his deep-seated troubles and torment were never far from the surface. Over the rest of his lifetime, in long, searching conversations, we would explore the source of these feelings, and his need to hold onto such negative thoughts — without ever reaching any real understanding or resolution.

On January 10, the National team played the Soviets in Toronto. It was hyped as a homecoming of sorts for Carl Brewer. George Gross spoke to Carl before the game, having found him fretting in his hotel room, nursing injuries — a pulled groin and an elbow inflamed by bursitis. Gross reported that Carl was anguished over how he would be received at Maple Leaf Gardens. Gross marvelled at the greeting Carl had been afforded two nights earlier in Montreal. "The once-hostile Montreal Forum crowd gave Brewer a thunderous standing ovation on Sunday.… It was in appreciation of Brewer's play and his intimidating tactics towards the Russians. The crowd loved it. They stomped their feet, clapped their hands and chanted, 'We want Brewer!'" Carl told Gross, "It was the greatest thrill of my life." In Toronto, in a packed Gardens, the fans' response was modest. There was little fanfare — aside from a banner in the stands that read, "Good Luck Carl — Punch" — and even a smattering of boos. The lack of enthusiasm was attributed to resentment at his walking out on the Leafs in 1965. Afterward, Carl said that the reception was about what he had expected, and he added, "Let's just say my biggest thrill was in Montreal on Sunday night. That was something I'll always remember." Carl did not figure as prominently as expected on the Gardens ice, but the Canadians prevailed, 4–3, giving them two wins and a tie in the three-game series.

The following week, the Maple Leafs played in Montreal. I knew several of the players — Peter Stemkowski was a good friend and he regularly gave me a ticket to the games, both in Montreal and Toronto, after Carl's departure from Leafs. Carl had a lot of respect for Peter. He appreciated the fact that, in Peter's first TV interview after being called up to the Leafs from the Marlies, he publicly expressed his gratitude to Carl for taking him under his wing and helping him make the adjustment. The first thing Peter asked me on this night in Montreal was whether I'd seen Carl, and he asked how he was. I told Peter that I'd spent the evening with Carl and that I was terribly worried about him. I filled Peter in briefly. Wisely, he said to me: "Sue, don't worry about him — write to him; it would mean a lot to him to hear from you."

The next time I saw Carl was in early March, when the team passed through Montreal en route to Europe for the World Championships. I had been allowed into the departure lounge at Dorval Airport, and I waited there for Carl. He didn't show up untill the last minute. He walked into the lounge, and the moment he saw me he let out a big sigh, telling me: "There you are! I've been out there phoning you for the last two hours." I, however, had come directly to the airport from work. We had only a very brief visit before he had to board the Air Canada flight. I watched the plane pull away from the gate, take off, and disappear into the night sky, bound for Europe. Little did I know just how many times Carl and I would depart for Europe together in the years to come.

In the first exhibition game in Prague, Carl suffered a serious thigh injury; Jackie MacLeod, his coach, didn't believe he had a bad bruise, but Carl summoned George Gross to his hotel room and showed him the leg. George described it as black and blue from hip to ankle. Carl missed the team's next exhibition game in Prague, and as well as one in Stockholm, but he refused to follow doctor's orders to stay on the sidelines any longer. He played the second exhibition game in Stockholm. He took the Canadians' 2–1 loss that night very hard.

During the tournament, word filtered out that Carl was playing his last hockey games. Gross reported, "Carl Brewer will end his career as a hockey player after the World Championships in Vienna." He quoted Carl as saying: "I don't want to play hockey again. It takes too much out of me. I joined the National team for one year, hoping that I could help. After the World Championships, I want to concentrate on something else, probably teaching school." However, by the time the team reached Vienna, Carl angrily tried to backpedal, asking, "Who said I said that?" Pressed further about his intentions, he answered brusquely, "No comment." Canada won the bronze medal at the Worlds, and Carl was chosen the tournament's outstanding defenseman. Carl would not be eligible to accompany the Nats to Grenoble, France, for the Winter Olympics the following year, however; unlike the IIHF, in those days the International Olympic Committee prohibited former pros from taking part in the Winter Games.

Back home, 1967 was a year of change for the National Hockey League, which expanded from six teams to 12. Carl wasn't eligible to return to the NHL, as a league rule stipulated that a player had to sit out for two years after regaining his amateur status. And under the reserve clause, his rights belonged to the NHL team he'd last played for — in Carl's case, of course, the Toronto Maple Leafs. Nevertheless, the California Seals — who drafted his former defense partner, Bobby Baun — were interested in Carl, as were the Minnesota North Stars. Alan Eagleson actually negotiated a contract for Carl with California; former Leaf great Charlie Conacher and Bing Crosby were involved in the Seals' ownership and hoped to have Carl challenge the reserve clause. The idea fascinated Carl, who had long deplored the way players were bound indefinitely to their teams, and he was keen to pursue this challenge. According to Carl, however, the matter dragged on, and in time he felt he was being pushed around, so he backed away from this opportunity. Carl remembered that at one point he said to Conacher, "I guess I'm rather naïve." Conacher replied, "Brewer, you're not naïve; you're just fucking stupid." I don't think Carl ever got over the shock of hearing that statement.

Carl was still searching for answers, trying to deal with the ever-burning question of what to do with his life. While he did, he relented and accepted another hockey offer. This time, he joined the Muskegon Mohawks of the International Hockey League as the playing coach. The decision accomplished a number of things. First, Carl had the chance to coach at a relatively young age (he turned 29 in October 1967). And, he was able to take his younger brother Jack — who he always felt had the potential to play pro hockey — with him. And although the IHL was officially an amateur league, Carl earned more money that year than he ever had before — indeed, he was thought to be among the highest-paid hockey players in the world. (However, since NHL salaries were such closely guarded secrets, this could never be confirmed.) Furthermore, he enjoyed the chance to work as a radio commentator in Muskegon.

It was a successful year for Carl, who was well accepted by the team. Attendance at the games steadily rose with Brewer in the lineup and the team advanced in the standings. The year before Carl's arrival, the Mohawks had been sixth in a seven-team league; in 1967–68, they were first overall and won the league championship. Carl was awarded the Governors' Trophy as the IHL's top defenseman. Jerry DeLise, the team owner, was thrilled with Carl's contribution in Muskegon. He stated: "He had our kids doing things with the puck none of them had ever done before. He meant a lot to all of them." DeLise hoped that Carl might return for a second year, but Carl decided against it.

Several years later, I was teaching high school with a young man who had played in Muskegon the season after Carl had been there. Joe Modeste still laughed about the comment one of the players made about Carl. Amazed, the player told Joe, "Carl Brewer used to bring books on the bus — and *read them!*"

It was at this time that Carl's first doubts about Alan Eagleson surfaced. Carl had negotiated his own contract with Muskegon and was proud of the deal he carved out for himself — $30,000 plus incentives. He was surprised, therefore, to receive an invoice from Eagleson, in the amount of $5,000, for contract negotiations with Muskegon. Carl considered it both absurd and unwarranted, so, according to Carl, he "gassed" Eagleson.

After his year in Muskegon and having disengaged himself from Eagleson, Carl received a phone call from Al asking if they could get together for dinner. As Carl explained, he took Al to the Granite Club — Carl was not a member, but his wife was at the time. Over dinner, Al told Carl that he was just getting started in hockey, and he asked Carl not to say anything bad about him. Carl frequently recalled how odd and strange the request seemed to him at the time. He was taken aback and asked: "Why would I say anything bad about you, Al?"

***

Later in 1968, Carl broadened his hockey horizons in a very significant way, both professionally and personally. He accepted an offer to become the playing coach of the Finnish team HIFK, based in Helsinki. Through this association, Carl Brewer's love affair with international hockey would continue and grow.

"We Want Brewer!"

Shortly after his arrival in Finland, Carl took time to record his impressions and his thoughts about hockey in Europe in general at the time:

In 1966–67, I had my first taste of international rules competition playing for Canada's Nats in the World Championships in Vienna. Prior to the tournament, the team had an extended tour of Europe, with games in Prague, Czechoslovakia; Stockholm, Sweden; Zweibrucken, Germany; and Feldkirch, Austria. This exposure whetted my appetite to spend a period of time abroad, and hockey would provide the ticket, as it has for so many Canadian hockey players.

The first thing that strikes a Canadian hockey player is the ice surface. It is considerably wider than those we are accustomed to in North America. This, more than any other feature, changes the complexion of European hockey. I was first confronted by this in Prague when, as I approached the ice from an alcove, I was hard put to figure out which was the length and which was the width. The larger ice surface lends itself more to artistic players, but any team not inclined to mix it up or get involved can effect a very dull performance for the fans. The smaller ice surfaces of North America — more by design than by accident — confine the area of play, thus giving the illusion of intensified action. From my experience, I would say that this works to the benefit of the fans, who would prefer to stand cheering as opposed to sitting on their hands.

Of course, body contact is the subject most widely discussed when contrasting the two brands of hockey. European hockey permits bodychecking in the defensive end only, and even then, only gentle exchanges are allowed. For European players, hockey is a great game, but only a game. When it comes to the moment of truth, they are inclined to say, "The heck with this. I'm only playing for fun." But this attitude is gradually changing — and so too, is their willingness to mix it up — as players in Europe are being better paid.

Carl loved living in Europe, and he took advantage of his situation to take some Phys. Ed. courses at the University of Helsinki. Technically, he was a huge success. He taught the Finns a great deal about hockey and impressed upon them just how talented they were. He raised their understanding of their abilities considerably. And guiding HIFK to the league championship was one of the highlights of his life. He later commented that this was as much of a thrill for him as the three Stanley Cup victories. He was embraced by the entire country, and was to be forever known and revered as Finland's "Father of Hockey" — and a national hero in this small, fascinating country. In a 2004 *Toronto Sun* column, George Gross quoted a former Canadian ambassador as saying, "Carl Brewer did more in one year for Canada in Finland than any ambassador could in 10 years."

Carl's year in Finland, away from the stress and scrutiny his public persona attracted in Canada, provided him with the necessary space and time for reflection, introspection and some deep soul-searching. Although being in Finland was an excellent experience for him in a number of ways, this aspect of his being did not change. His quest for purpose and peace of mind, and his self-doubts, continued to weigh heavily on his psyche. He was very open and candid about his feelings in Helsinki in February 1969:

> *The players here really feel a sense of accomplishment. And to be part of it is just as significant and joyous as winning the Stanley Cup.*
>
> *I think for the past four years I have just been kidding myself. I have made a conscious effort to relax and learn to live with the game, but unsuccessfully. I am more upset and wound up for these games than I was for the NHL. Perhaps my ego tells me that the outcome of the game depends on me alone. Since Xmas, I have just taken the attitude "the heck with it," and have tried not to care about the game at all. But this has been unsuccessful. The only result is that my conditioning has suffered and that my play has been inefficient.*
>
> *Of the billions of people in the world, I ask myself, "Why do I have this type of mentality? Why me?" The same with flying! Why is it me who is afraid? All through my youth, as is the case for so many Canadians, all I wanted to*

be was a hockey player. How many of those boys have the opportunity that I had — and still have? I don't love the game any less now than I did when I was 12, but I am just not able to live with it. The day of a game is just so bloody long and I am just in a trance, unable to do anything worthwhile with my time. And it's terrifying just walking around with your thoughts, especially when you magnify the negatives the way I do.

Fear plays such a strong role — fear of injury, fear of fighting. I was fearless in my youth, and this is the only way to minimize the injury factor. When you worry about being injured, that's when you get hurt.

I am inclined to feel that if I had had some direction when I entered the NHL, I would be in a different position today. I was so young and naïve and completely unaware of what I was undertaking. No one told me a thing. I suppose I could have asked, but in those days, a rookie was not accepted as a member of the team. I thought you were supposed to sleep all day, rest your body constantly, have a "mad on" all the time and think of nothing but hockey. The likes of Bert Olmstead and Punch Imlach didn't help. On the day of a game, if you even thought of anything but hockey, Olmstead went into a fit of rage.

Now that I look back, I can see how senseless this attitude was. I always envied Baun, who was out and active on the day of a game. Yet, this attitude is prevalent, and the only attitude to have. I think I was the exception. Lloyd Percival in his Hockey Handbook *— which, by the way, is the Bible of both Anatoli Tarasov and Harry Sinden — talks of the "Happy Warrior" as being the one who contributes the most to his team. I only read, and am re-reading, this book of late, but last year in Muskegon this is the type of attitude I wanted our players to have. Often before a game I would just keep them smiling and laughing and then tell them to go out and make sure they had a lot of fun. Here in Helsinki, the attitude is different — more fun-loving to start with — but when I feel them getting* *quiet and serious, I just start joking around and tell them to do their best, but only if they are having fun and enjoying themselves doing it.*

Probably, as a reaction to the Imlachian system and the general hockey attitude, I do not require any overt discipline, curfews, etc. I feel that the players are intelligent enough to know what is best, and, if it is a good team with a good team spirit, they stick together and they themselves castigate the delinquents. In view of what the Nats stand for, I could never understand why it had so many petty curfews and disciplines. These just pressure good men to be liars and cheats.

At any rate, the agony I go through to play the game no longer seems justifiable. Here, I have not trained since December 1. I have felt fine for about three weeks now, but I will not train. For over four years, I have detested practices, and I would be sick and overwrought just going to practice. Now I no longer delude myself; I just go out there and stand around for an hour and a half. I'm not accomplishing anything, but I don't worry about it, either.

About the future, I am certainly apprehensive. It's hard to face up to a new career after the security, leisure and recognition of a well-paid hockey player. I think I feel more apprehensive because I just don't know what I want to do — after four years of looking. I guess I just don't want to start at the bottom. Now the question arises, in terminal work such as that of a hockey player, what have I prepared for?

I am really impressed with the ability of the players on our team. Our average age is 20–21 years of age and our "sure-fire superstar" prospects are 19 and 20. Under the proper training conditions, I feel that in a year's time, this team could develop into one of the top teams in the world. But I am not saying that I am the right person to do the job. Last year in Muskegon, the coaching was easy. This year, I have learned how little I do know about the game. I envy the job that Tarasov and Arkady Chernyshev have done with their Russian team.

"We Want Brewer!"

I have been invited back here for another year. They are very anxious for me to return. The success — artistically and financially — that the team has achieved has been considerable. Hockey enthusiasm is at an unprecedented peak.

Yet, right now, I am inclined to think I will not come back.

CHAPTER 5

FEELING GOOD

"The best way I can describe my career in hockey is that it truly has been a love-hate relationship. I love the game; it hates me."

In March 1968, the hockey world was stunned when the Toronto Maple Leafs traded Frank Mahovlich, Peter Stemkowski and Garry Unger to Detroit, along with the NHL playing rights to Carl Brewer (who was then with Muskegon of the International league), for Floyd Smith, Norm Ullman and Paul Henderson. On several occasions after that, Carl's friend Mahovlich approached him on behalf of the Red Wings, hoping to convince him to come to Detroit. While in Finland, Carl even received a telegram from Detroit that read, "You can play the home games and any of the road games you want to go to." Carl's reaction: "I was flattered and amused. What the hell would that type of concession do to team ethics and team play?"

Back in Toronto, Carl was typically indecisive about his plans for the future. On March 27, 1969, I was pleased to get a phone call from him, telling me he was on his way out to visit me at my apartment in Oshawa, where I was living while I taught high school in nearby Whitby. He spent the evening and seemed exceptionally happy and in good spirits. As always, we had a lot of catching up to do, and just spending time together once again was delightful. He told me that he didn't want to talk about hockey, but he did indicate that his time in Finland had been gratifying. One thing, however, had not changed: he was still struggling with the emotional difficulties that had always come with playing professional hockey.

When he left late that night, he made no mention — and gave me not the slightest indication — that he was entertaining even the remotest thought of playing for Detroit, or any other NHL team for that matter. To be fair, he didn't know he was going to make this decision, either. Carl was notoriously indecisive, and there were always dozens of conflicting thoughts and ideas flashing about his mind at the same time.

Nonetheless, within a matter of days, Carl did agree to play for Detroit for the 1969–70 season. Carl recalled the bizarre set of circumstances that led to this turn of events:

> Bobby Baun dragged me down to a team party with the Detroit Red Wings. That night, I signed a blank contract just before midnight — after which time, my rights would have reverted back to Toronto — with John Ziegler. Ziegler was not then the president of the NHL — that came about in 1977 — but the legal functionary for the Red Wings. That's when I made my decision to come back to the NHL. I didn't know I was going to do it!
>
> As the night of partying unfolded, I had a discussion with a very drunk Bruce Norris about my contract. He told me to name my deal, and I wrote an amount on the back of a table napkin — $120,000. And he accepted without hesitation.

Carl also stipulated that the Red Wings buy up the pension benefits he had missed in the four years he had been out of the NHL. At every juncture of his pro hockey career, Carl was considering the impact of his decisions on his pension.

Carl's move to the Red Wings was well received by the team's management. It was imperative that coach Bill Gadsby and general manager Sid Abel convince Carl to join the Wings because they had been weak on defense for quite some time. Indeed, Detroit had been trying to acquire Carl's services since the summer of 1966, when they first opened trade talks with the Leafs. His new teammates also considered him a welcome addition to the dressing room. Gordie Howe, told me fondly: "In the early days when we faced him, faced his team, he had a way of getting on your nerves — he'd antagonize guys. But once he joined our team, the Red Wings, he became an excellent teammate. He was no longer the opponent I used to love to run over when playing against him!"

As the season began, there were many skeptics among the press corps. About Carl's absence, Dan Proudfoot of *The Globe and Mail* wrote: "It was a bewildering four years, admittedly, if only because of the lack of direction. But Brewer has been bewildering people for years." An enthusiastic endorsement of Carl's performance came from coach Bill Gadsby: "You saw how good Brewer is with the puck in our own end. That's what we've needed all along. Carl takes charge. He settles things down." Carl got along well with Bill and enjoyed playing for him, and he had trouble understanding why Gadsby was fired as coach only two games into the season — both of which the Wings had won — to be replaced by Sid Abel.

Carl flourished in the much more relaxed atmosphere that prevailed in the Detroit dressing room. Even on game days, the Red Wings were able to go to the racetrack and relax — quite a change from the rigorous workouts of Punch Imlach's Maple Leafs. "The Leaf system wasn't necessary. It's more relaxed now and you can see the difference," Carl remarked to Milt Dunnell of the *Toronto Star*. "You were always supposed to frown when you played for the Leafs," Carl added. "I don't do that anymore." Another change for Carl was that he started to take the occasional drink — particularly before getting on an airplane.

Reunited with his old friends from the Leafs — Bob Baun, Stemkowski and Mahovlich — Carl once again proved himself, showing that his tremendous talents had not diminished in the slightest. In fact, Carl played what was arguably the best hockey of his career that season. The Red Wings played in Toronto on February 21, 1970, and Carl had an outstanding game, skating effortlessly, gliding about the ice gracefully and fluidly. His passes were right on the mark time after time, connecting crisply but easily on his teammates' sticks. He had two assists that night, en route to a career high of 39 points, far more than he'd had during any season with the Leafs. At the end of the game, Bob Goldham, a wonderful gentleman and elder statesman who'd played defense for both Detroit and Toronto, selected the three stars. He gave Carl the third star and said, "Brewer, every time he had the puck, he slowed the game down to suit himself and I think he was the dominant figure on the back of the blue line for Detroit."

Carl enjoyed telling the story about one of the memorable goals he scored that year, in Montreal. "Canadiens were leading 5–4 late in the game. I picked up a loose puck at the point and launched an ice-level clearing shot in the direction of the Montreal goal. The weak shot found its way through a maze of legs and somehow ended up in the net. An important tie game! The goal I scored was at 19:59 of the third period. The name of the stick I used was, appropriately, 'Montreal Surprise,' one of the brands of stick I imported from Italy."

Carl's year with Detroit turned out to be significant for the great Gordie Howe. Gordie learned from Bob Baun just how badly Detroit had treated him financially over the years. Howe had been led to believe that he was the highest-paid player on the team, and every year, he simply signed the contract they put in front of him. It was Baun who broke the news that he was making twice as much as Gordie's $45,000 — but the real kicker was that Brewer was earning three times as much! An embarrassed and angry Howe finally realized how badly his team had duped him; fortified with this information, he was finally in a position to speak up and demand appropriate compensation from the team to which he had contributed so much. Colleen Howe talked to me years later about this being the first time in his life that she had known Gordie to stand up for himself. "I was very proud of him," she said.

In 1969–70, Carl played 70 regular-season games and 4 playoff games. He scored 2 goals and added 37 assists, and spent only 51 minutes in the penalty box — the fewest, by a large margin, of any of the full seasons he played in the NHL. As further evidence of his exceptional ability, Carl was selected to the second All-Star team, the fourth time in his career that he was named to an All-Star squad.

Carl enjoyed the camaraderie with his teammates and spoke fondly of going to the Howes' with Gordie after the games. "Gordie's sons would order pizza, and Gordie and I would sit around having pizza and a couple of beers, discussing the game with the boys." He remembered these as happy times. Gordie shared with me recently that these times were also cherished memories for him: "Carl and Bobby would visit our house in Lathrup Village, Michigan, after the games. Colleen would prepare some pizza for us. Carl and Bobby would have a few beers, and along with Mark and Marty we would discuss the hockey games. It was our pleasure to have Carl in our home." He added, "I remember driving to our place with Carl a few times, and he shared his unique views with me about so many things.

"I was happy to have the chance to play hockey with Carl," Gordie concluded. "Without a doubt, he was a star."

Things were not all sweetness and light on the ice, however. "The 1969–70 Detroit Red Wings were perhaps the best team in the NHL — in my mind, a dynasty — but unfortunately we exited the playoffs in the first round, losing four straight," Carl explained. "There is no doubt in my mind that our team had the right mixture of youth and veterans, with the incomparable Gordie Howe mixed in.

"We were convinced that the Red Wings could win the Stanley Cup," he said. "We had good young players and we had Howe. We'd all watch Howe, and when he slowed the game down to his tempo, we thought we could win. Then the Detroit management began trading players in and out. It destroyed the team's dignity."

Although Carl had agreed to a three-year contract, his sojourn in the Motor City lasted only one season. His departure was a huge disappointment for team personnel. "We'll certainly miss Carl because he figured prominently in our plans," Sid Abel commented at the time.

Carl's initial reason for deciding not to return to Detroit involved a health matter that caused him considerable distress at the end of the year — a frozen shoulder. When he raised his arm above his shoulder, he was unable to lower it without help. He was sent to the best orthopedic doctors in North America, but to no avail. Carl described the condition as "nervous arthritis." To add fuel to fire, a dispute developed over his contract. "I declined to return to the team as they shorted my contract by $500." They also refused to continue the arrangement they had made with Carl to have his brother Jack in their farm system. These various problems were enough for Carl to walk away once again. In so doing, he managed to avoid a new era for the Red Wings, one that Carl aptly described as "Darkness with Harkness."

In May, Sid Abel hired Ned Harkness, who'd been successful at Cornell University, to coach the Wings. Hiring a college coach was an unorthodox move in the early 1970s, and in this particular case it was a recipe for disaster. Carl summed up the situation this way: "And then Ned Harkness, he of the 'sophisticated' college background, proceeded to decimate the ranks of the entire team. This saw Gordie Howe's premature retirement, and Baun did not escape his purview." Harkness was a fierce disciplinarian; this quality made him especially ill-suited to get the best out of the Red Wings, many of whom were veterans expecting to be treated as professionals and adults. Before long, his verbal tirades were being greeted with laughter and ridicule, and the team limped to a record of 12 wins, 22 losses and 4 ties before Harkness was, rightly, relieved of the coaching reins. But in a bizarre twist, he was then promoted to general manager, replacing Abel! This only emboldened Harkness to trade away the players who hadn't bought into his authoritarian program. By season's end, Baun, Mahovlich, Stemkowski and Unger were all playing elsewhere — having already escaped Punch Imlach's clutches, they were probably relieved. Carl later found it amusing when Frank Mahovlich, who was traded to the Canadiens, asked him somewhat naïvely, "Carl, how did you know?" The Red Wings didn't start to recover from the changes implemented by Harkness until Steve Yzerman joined the team more than a decade later.

Baun was traded to St. Louis, but he didn't stay there long. Apparently, as Carl understood from Bob, he told the Blues to "get lost" and returned to his Detroit home. Subsequently, Carl would gain new and troubling insights into Bobby Baun, his old teammate, roommate, best man and friend.

It happened that I was passing through Detroit en route to a trade show in Chicago and, aware of the trade, stopped at Baun's house to say hello. We spent the night together as old friends and partners. At the time, we had a history of seven years together as partners and roommates. There were no idiosyncrasies that passed us by — or so I thought.

I got zapped unexpectedly twice that night, however. As Bob, the gourmet, cooked omelettes and we talked, I attempted to build his confidence in such distressing times by suggesting that I had always thought a lot of him. Bob's response: he had always been aware that I thought a lot more of him than he did of me! Zap number one. To continue, Bobby told me that he knew now how I must have felt over the years, now that he had just told the St. Louis Blues and Scotty Bowman to go to hell. He was implying that I was the one who had always been telling people to go to hell.

Ah, but in Bob's case there was a big difference! Don Giffin, a mutual friend, had already engineered a trade and made it possible for Baun to return to the Toronto Maple Leafs. Go to hell, indeed! Baun had been aware of what St. Louis had not! Baun was able to distinguish himself again as a Leaf but, on the other hand, I never had a birdie in the bush as he did!

Don Giffin owned Giffin Sheet Metal, and he had arranged financing for Harold Ballard twice — the first time to buy out John Bassett and the second to buy out the Smythe interests at the Gardens. Giffin was to become Ballard's minority partner, but this never took place. "Does it surprise you that Ballard had a short memory?" Carl asked rhetorically.

***

When he returned to Canada from Finland in 1969, Carl brought back Finnish-made hockey sticks with him. He had obtained the North American distribution rights to the Koho brand, and he began importing the company's products for sale throughout North America. It was a bold move, since names like Northland, Sher-Wood, Victoriaville, CCM and Hespeler dominated the market on this side of the Atlantic. Having parted ways with the Red Wings, Carl was able to devote his full attentions to introducing North America to the Koho brand. He also had an interest in a North Toronto travel agency — called, logically enough, Koho Travel.

Still, as Carl said so often, "Hockey never left my mind." On his way to a large sporting goods fair at Chicago's massive McCormack Place convention centre, he stopped off in Detroit to visit his former roommate, Garry Unger. It was here that he learned that Unger and Wayne Connelly were to be dealt to St. Louis in exchange for Red Berenson and Tim Ecclestone. And for the second time, Carl Brewer figured in a trade, even though he wasn't on active service. "Although I still maintain that *I* was never traded during my career, the St. Louis Blues did acquire the *rights* to Carl Brewer as an appendage to the deal," Carl later explained. "I was contacted in Chicago by Scotty Bowman, then the coach and general manager of the Blues, and asked if I'd consider playing in St. Louis. Scotty, an old acquaintance, seemed less than thrilled and was obviously acting on instructions from his boss, Sid Salomon III."

Apparently, Salomon was enamoured with Carl Brewer. Carl knew this because, while he was in Finland, Blues' assistant GM Cliff Fletcher had gone there. His mission was to scout several Finnish players... *and* Carl Brewer. Later, Salomon sent Carl a letter expressing his interest in having him join his team. Carl discouraged him, insisting he had no intention of returning to the NHL.

Feeling Good

***

"The owners sit in their offices and play chess with players'
lives, so I play my own game of chess with the owners."

Sid Salomon remained dogged in his efforts to sign Carl, and after lengthy
back-and-forth discussions, Carl finally came to terms on a two-year deal
with St. Louis. He signed for $60,000 the first season and $100,000 the next,
plus bonuses, a house and a car. His contract negotiations were unique in
and of themselves. It was clear that Salomon wanted Carl to make a long-
term commitment, as he offered a five-year, no-cut, no-trade deal at
$100,000 per annum. The real kicker was that Salomon also offered to have
the team purchase its own airplane to assuage Carl's intense fear of flying. "I
told Sid that I didn't want a long-term contract because he had been fair and
it seemed like I had trouble staying in any one place for any length of time,"
Carl remarked. "How prophetic," he added. He joined the Blues for the last
six weeks of the 1970–71 season, playing in 19 games and scoring 11 points.
"My stay in St. Louis was brief and not noteworthy, despite early optimism,"
Carl commented. About his own contribution, he was candid in his assessment. "My play was undistinguished and the team was in turmoil."

Jim Roberts, who joined the Blues from the Montreal Canadiens in
1967, disagreed. "Carl fit right into the mould [in St. Louis], along with
Doug Harvey, Dickie Moore and Phil Goyette, all guys who had played in
the 'Original Six' and had played in St. Louis before Carl arrived there," Jim
told me. "Carl came in here and he was a very good player still, and very talented. He made a big difference to our team." Jim remembers that Carl
seemed to be enjoying hockey in St. Louis. "He was away from the Toronto
pressure cooker and down here he was a *relaxed* player, and playing here, he
was as good as I think he ever was as a player. He brought a lot to the team."

Carl was in great physical condition when he reported to the Blues.
I fondly remember Jim Roberts's dad, Wilf, telling me that he had never
seen any athlete who could punch the speed bag as deftly as Carl did in the
St. Louis training room during this time.

Carl's fear of flying was something all his teammates were aware of.
Of course, flying was still fairly new for players in general, and in recent
years the itinerary had grown to include such outposts as Los Angeles,
Oakland and Vancouver. Carl wasn't the only one on the Blues with an in-

tense fear — Barclay Plager was also terrified to fly. Jim laughingly told me, "Carl always had a little flask with him and had a couple of shots before getting on that plane!" He remembers that Carl spent a lot of time in the cockpit, which was the only place where he could relax because the pilots would reassure him during the flight. Jim also has some fond and funny memories of Carl's efforts to stay loose and create some fun on road trips. "On one occasion, as the team was preparing to depart from San Francisco after a game on the west coast, Carl had already started to get himself prepared for the flight," Jim recalls. "And then he disappeared. As the players walked down the long corridor to board the plane, we came across this guy, sitting on the floor, a cap pulled down over his head and a cup held out, and he was rattling it asking for spare change." It was, of course, their teammate! On another occasion, again in San Francisco, the guys were relaxing in a tavern across from the hotel after practice. "There was a balcony in the bar. Next thing I hear, Carl, having had a couple of beers, jumps down from the balcony, landing plunk in the middle of a table below, where about 10 guys were seated having a drink. He was always up to something, getting enjoyment and having some fun, and it was really good for the team," Roberts told me.

In 1968, '69 and '70, the expansion Blues had made it all the way to the Stanley Cup finals. In the spring of 1971, however, they were eliminated in the first round by Minnesota. The night before the last playoff game, Carl was placed in an excruciatingly uncomfortable position. "Our team assembled at a St. Louis country club for a team meal prior to flying out to Minnesota. I was seated at a table with Sid Salomon III and five others. During the meal, out of the blue, Salomon confided quietly to me that things were not working out as he had planned. He wanted to lose the game in Minnesota so that he could fire Bowman! I was flabbergasted and speechless."

As it turned out, the Blues did indeed lose that next game. Not long afterward, at the Salomons' Florida retreat, where the team and their families had assembled for a postseason holiday, Bowman, Fletcher and trainer Tom Woodcock were all given the boot. Once again, Carl found himself not only flabbergasted but also right in the midst of all the controversy. Milt Dunnell, the dean of Canadian sports journalists, wrote that Scotty Bowman, although he hadn't come right out and said so, thought Brewer was bad for the St. Louis Blues. Apparently, he was unhappy that the Red Berenson trade had been forced upon him by his superiors. Dunnell pointed out that

Bowman's contract with St. Louis did not give him the right to make any major deal without consulting the owners. Dunnell further suggested that it was the Salomons, Sidney Jr. and Sid III, who thought "Brewer was the greatest thing to hit town since Anheuser-Busch." He further suggested that Carl was the "wild card" in a poker game in which Bowman's $100,000 contract was at stake. Hence the turmoil Carl had immediately sensed. Incidentally, Bowman's contract had been negotiated by Alan Eagleson, whose practice of representing players and management always raised a red flag in Carl's mind.

Jim Roberts says that he never heard any of the players mention Carl's name in connection with these moves. In fact, Jim remembers that there had been growing friction between Bowman and the Salomons for some time. "Scotty had dug his own hole," Jim told me. "He wanted more control, and the Salomons thought they knew more than some others who had been in hockey all their lives. Sid III started to think he had a lot of answers, and there's where the problem was. It's beyond me to think that anyone could blame Carl for that."

The 1971–72 season started out well enough, Carl felt, but it was soon obvious to him that the St. Louis fans objected to his low-key style of play and they started getting on his case. "The fans preferred the fighting style of the Plagers — brothers Bob, Barclay and Bill." Nonetheless, Carl felt that he played good hockey. Then, at Christmastime, he injured his left knee when he fell heavily into the boards with Paul Henderson in a game in Toronto. "No one on the St. Louis team saw me get injured and I hobbled off the ice to the Gardens hospital, unbeknownst to anyone on my team," Carl explained. "I was examined by Leafs specialist Dr. Dave Hastings, the well-regarded orthopedic surgeon." Dr. Hastings's diagnosis indicated damage to Carl's left kneecap that resulted in pain when he moved the joint. He was advised that the injury would take six months to a year to heal. Time proved the doctor right.

For six weeks, Carl tried various types of rehab and was examined by several other doctors. He still was unable to skate without pain. At the same time, the team was again undergoing a front-office upheaval. "Al Arbour, an old friend, teammate from Toronto Maple Leaf days, and now the assistant general manager, was asked to take over as coach — just before Christmas and just before my injury. Before taking the job, he called me to ask for my thoughts. I told him that he probably would take the job and certainly he had my support 100 percent," Carl recalled. "But, he and his wife being old friends, I suggested to him that assistant general managers never get fired, and that he and his wife had a home and stability in St. Louis, something that they hadn't had for a long time, and it was a shame to put that in jeopardy." As Carl expected, Arbour did accept the coaching job, and was fired in November 1972. He worked briefly in Atlanta, with Cliff Fletcher, before finally establishing himself as the hugely successful coach of the New York Islanders, guiding that team to four Stanley Cups.

Carl described the continuing problems surrounding his injury. "The knee did not respond to treatment and I could not skate without pain, although I did train on the stationary bike and with weights. I was in great shape and wanted to be prepared for the abusive St. Louis fans when I did return." After about six weeks, Arbour asked Carl to give the knee a try again. After skating gingerly that night for about half an hour on new, soft ice at the St. Louis Arena, Carl agreed to give it a try the following night at home against the Montreal Canadiens. Carl expected Arbour to spot him in the lineup that night, but to Carl's surprise, he was sent out to take a regular shift. He felt he played pretty well, but "unfortunately, in the third period, I gave up the game-winning goal on a St. Louis power play when Claude Larose stripped me of the puck at the blue line and went in all alone and scored. Not an auspicious debut for me!"

In Philadelphia the following night, Arbour did not play Carl. The next morning, Carl tried to skate but could not. Arbour sent him to the dressing room and told him he wanted to speak to him after practice. It was at this point, Carl learned much later, that Arbour called the players together and informed them that Carl Brewer would never play in a St. Louis uniform again. "It was some years before I was ever informed of this fact. My 'friends' on the team neglected to inform me. Some team! Some friends!" a bitter Carl complained.

"After practice, I sat briefly with Arbour in his office. He informed me that I had not wanted to play in Philadelphia. I suggested to him that he never put me on the ice. He then proceeded to tell me that I was playing at a tenth of my ability and that I was hurting the hockey club. He further told me to go back home to Toronto until my knee was better and that if I didn't like it, I could go upstairs to the bosses if I wanted," Carl explained as he recounted this troubling experience. Carl told Arbour that his home was in St. Louis, not Toronto, and that he never went over anyone's head. The meeting ended on that note. Carl remained in St. Louis and trained by himself, but he never got a call from the team, nor did he ever again play for the St. Louis Blues.

For years, Carl chided himself for not having accepted the Salomons' initial offer. "What a fool I was not to lock up the guaranteed no-cut, no-trade contract! So much for doing my own negotiations. I always was a soft touch!" he complained. He was annoyed with himself for having relinquished such an opportunity, for not respecting the value of his services even when it was put before him on a silver platter, and his annoyance became more and more disturbing to him as he considered the unfortunate way he was treated by the Blues in the end.

Carl's days in St. Louis had come to an abrupt end, but it was not the last time he would play hockey professionally. Years later, Carl often looked back at his extraordinary hockey career and concluded that he must have been awfully good for teams to take him back repeatedly, in spite of his reputation.

***

Carl was an enthusiastic supporter of the World Hockey Association, the rival hockey league that began play in 1972. He felt that a competitor to the long-standing NHL monopoly could only be a good thing for professional hockey players.

"The WHA was the brainchild of two Americans — Gary Davidson and Dennis Murphy. The traditional hockey establishment — management, the media and the supposedly knowledgeable fans — maligned the concept. But I believe it was good entertainment and a calibre not much different than the NHL," Carl maintained. Carl understood that the NHL's monopoly had kept player salaries artificially low, and that the launch of a competitor would result in paycheques several times as large as those the players had known before. WHA player contracts also lacked the notorious reserve clause that bound players to their teams forever.

To erase doubts about its viability, the new league needed a star player to take the plunge and sign with one of its teams. And it landed one of the biggest in Bobby Hull, the owner of hockey's most devastating shot. The Winnipeg Jets made an unprecedented million-dollar offer that Hull couldn't refuse, and that Chicago owner Bill Wirtz wouldn't match. A number of prominent NHLers — including Gerry Cheevers, Jim Dorey,

Derek Sanderson, Frank Mahovlich and Ralph Backstrom — joined Hull in jumping to the new league.

"The Paul Newman movie *Slap Shot* had nothing on the history and folklore of the WHA!" Carl later said. "This league produced some memorable stories and some really good hockey — who could ever forget the Winnipeg Jets' line of Bobby Hull, Anders Hedberg and Ulf Nilsson? Goons also abounded in the WHA — strange, because its chief proponents were 'sophisticated' college men like Terry Slater, the psych major, in L.A., and Harry Neale and Glen Sonmor in Minnesota. These guys were incapable of coaching [beyond] simply [opening] the door for their goons." Neale, a childhood friend of Carl's, had plenty of talent to play in the NHL. "Harry was a better skater than Allan Stanley — just as smart, and mean to boot," Carl remarked. "However, Harry made his mark in hockey as the best wise-cracking television analyst."

At its outset the WHA had held a massive player draft in which the 12 charter franchises staked their claims to hundreds of pros, all the way from the NHL to the lowest minor leagues, as well as European talent from both sides of the Iron Curtain. The Los Angeles Sharks chose Carl Brewer, but a year or so later Johnny F. Bassett — son of former Leafs partner John W. Bassett — arranged to sign Carl for his new Toronto Toros franchise. At 35, Carl was one of the older players, not only on the team but in the league, and he was duly nicknamed "The General" by his Toro teammates. Of the countless legends and wild tales that emerged from the WHA during its lifetime, Carl was in the middle of some of the most outrageous. One of the longest-lived and most often recounted stories involved Carl and an airplane trip. Carl and I once discovered, first-hand, how this tale has taken on a life of its own over the years, the details aggrandized and embellished with the passage of time. As Carl recalled,

> *In the summer of 1995, Sue and I were spending a few nights in Niagara Falls at former NHLer Nick Ricci's hotel, and we went out to dinner at one of the town's better eateries, Casa di Oro. The restaurant was full, but we were directed to the last remaining table for two, which just happened to be right beside Steve Ludzik and his wife. We had never met, but knew one another by reputation. Steve had distinguished himself as a player with the Chicago Blackhawks and was*

coaching the Detroit Vipers of the International Hockey League at the time. Steve immediately began telling us about a phone call he had received the previous night from Darryl Sutter, who was then coaching the Blackhawks. During this call, Sutter related to Steve the "Carl Brewer airplane story" that took place back in 1974 — twenty years previous! There were some errors in the telling — it did not take place in Moncton and it was not a 747! — but the essence was very much intact.

We spent a most enjoyable evening with the Ludziks. Over dinner and the two bottles of Beaujolais that the Ludziks shared with us as a "thank you" for the recent pension victory, Sue and I heard more Carl Brewer stories from Steve than we ever knew existed!

This seems like the perfect time and place for Carl's personal — accurate — version to be told.

The Toronto Toros, for whom I played the 1973–74 season, were in Winnipeg, and on the previous night had defeated Bobby Hull's Winnipeg Jets. This was always a major accomplishment because the Jets were the glamour team of the WHA. There was good reason for celebration, but in the days of the WHA anything was reason for a party! We awoke early at our airport hotel, the Winnipeg Inn, to catch our flight home to Toronto. A team meeting was called for 8:00 a.m. in [general manager] Buck Houle's room, and we were informed that because of dreadful weather we wouldn't be getting out of Winnipeg for two days. Winnipeg was entirely covered in a layer of ice two inches thick.

So we made plans — shopping, movies or reading. The Winnipeg Inn had a wonderful glass-enclosed swimming pool in the lobby, and I chose to go for a swim and a sauna. While in the pool, I was good-naturedly razzed by my teammates, but suddenly I was being waved in for yet another meeting: plans had changed. We rushed to pack and get on the bus to the airport. I detested flying under the best of conditions, and these were the worst! So I went into my usual flight-preparation mode — under no circumstances do I ever get on a plane sober! My medicine of choice in those days was rye whiskey — in a pinch, anything alcoholic would do. I rushed to the coffee shop and got a plastic milkshake container half-filled with milk and the other half filled with good old Canadian Club.

Fortified, I climbed on the bus. At the Air Canada ticket counter I spoke to a ground hostess who was married to a former teammate of mine. She told me there would absolutely be no flights arriving or departing this day. We moved on to Canadian Pacific's counter, and sure enough, they had a plane that would be departing in short order. I gulped my drink, but to no avail. They de-iced the wings of the 727, and finally the flight was called and my "medicine" took effect. What the hell, I figured, and I paid another $90 and upgraded to first class. The team boarded and I grabbed Brit Selby, my buddy, and told him to sit down with me. The cabin steward asked him to pay for the upgrade — eight dollars!

Brit stayed and we continued to drink champagne while they de-iced the wings twice more. Eventually we were airborne, and within minutes our 727 was above the haze and cloud cover into a perfect sunny day.

It was at this point that I made a deal with the convivial cabin steward and went into the first-class toilet and changed into my Winnipeg Inn swimsuit. I poured water over my head, soaking my hair — yes, I had hair in those days. I came out from behind the first-class cabin and proceeded to walk the length of the plane while towelling myself dry with my oversized towel from the Winnipeg Inn. I asked the aghast passengers in economy, "Would anyone like to come up to first class for a swim?"

As I sauntered back, I overheard confused passengers asking each other, "Do they really have a swimming pool in first class?" Buck Houle and coach Billy Harris — although they'd had as much to drink as I had and could barely

stumble off the plane — were not impressed, and I was
fined for my "swimming pool" escapade.

In April 1974, Carl was involved in a different type of incident, this one serious and terribly upsetting for him. It happened in a playoff game against the Cleveland Crusaders. During the game, Gerry Pinder, a small, clever scorer, broke clean down the right wing with only the Toros' goalie, Gilles Gratton, to beat. Carl was in pursuit, and he made a move with his stick to harass Pinder and impede his momentum. As Carl explained, "Usually, this was a harmless yet effective play." However, in this instance, Pinder fell abruptly to the ice, writhing in pain and covering his face. "I couldn't fathom what had happened. Pinder had a history of being melodramatic, but in this case he was badly hurt. How? I have no idea, but it seems my slash had deflected off Pinder's stick and struck him in the eye, causing a serious injury."

The day after the incident, Carl went to visit Gerry in the hospital. As he said, "I would never purposely injure anyone," and he was dismayed by cool reception he got from Gerry, who had been a longtime friend. Carl had first met Gerry and his older brother Herb at the Canadian National team's training camp in Winnipeg in the summer of 1967. "The Pinder brothers, from Saskatoon, were scoring phenoms in the Western Hockey League — both were good players, but Herb's skating was deficient," Carl assessed. "I was considered to be the resident genius by the Nats, and I worked closely with these fellows and they developed as a result." In fact, just prior to the incident with Gerry, while on a Toros road trip in Boston, Carl received a phone call from Herb Pinder, then a law school graduate. He was calling to thank Carl for helping him make the National team in 1967. Apparently, at the beginning of the training camp that year, coach Jackie MacLeod and Father Bauer had both told Herb he wouldn't make the team because of his skating. "This phone call from Herb Pinder was one of the most gratifying incidents of my involvement in hockey," Carl said.

Carl had a history with Gerry as well. In 1968, while coaching in Finland, Carl accompanied the Nats to the Soviet Union. "The team was hopelessly outmatched in the Izvestia Tournament, and the Canadians resorted to goon hockey, which doesn't work against the Russians," Carl said. According to Carl, Gerry Pinder was one of the worst offenders — slashing, spearing and goading. Then he pushed the wrong guy, and the big, burly

Russian grabbed Gerry, lifted him over his head and threw him heavily to the ice. Carl remembered, "I assisted the crying and whimpering Pinder to the dressing room, trying to settle him down, but he refused to return to the ice."

The Crusaders' management, and the local press, used the incident between Carl and Gerry to incite the players against Carl, and the Toros' next game in Cleveland was terrifying. "In contrast to Canadian fans, American fans are fanatical — they scream for blood and guts," Carl recalled. "The Cleveland fans wanted Brewer — preferably dead! The Cleveland players were in a frenzy." Goalie Gerry Cheevers was the Crusaders' acknowledged leader, and although he agreed that the injury had been an accident, he did nothing to mitigate his mates' bloodlust. The game was played in the old Cleveland Arena, which had wire screening instead of Plexiglas atop the boards. Carl was caught at a bad angle and had the wind knocked out of him. He was not injured, but he recalled that all 7,000 fans were rabid and bent on retribution. "It was the most difficult and terrifying hockey experience I ever participated in," he admitted. Later in the game, Russ Walker — who, according to Carl, "lacked one hockey ingredient as a player: talent" — ran him into the corner and "cut me *good* — not well, good, with a high stick." Walker wasn't penalized.

Another lighthearted story from Carl's WHA days reduced him to hysterics every time he recounted it — and that was frequently! It was very early in the morning — the sun had not yet risen — and the team bus was parked in front of a Holiday Inn in an unknown city, waiting to take the players to Quebec City. Everyone was on the bus except for defenseman Billy Orr. Orr eventually stumbled out of the hotel, completely unable to find the bus, which was no farther than five feet away from him. He was bouncing off the walls as he tried to find his way. According to Carl, the players were in hysterics as they watched the performance, and finally a couple guys got off to assist Billy onto the bus. The coach was Billy Harris, an old Maple Leaf teammate of Carl's. Harris, a placid, soft-spoken man, got up and quietly announced: "Anybody who has a drink between here and Quebec City, it will cost you a thousand dollars." Tommy Martin, a right winger with an incredible shot, and a glib, funny man to boot, saw this as a golden opportunity. He asked Carl if he still had the thousand-dollar bill he was known to carry in his pocket. As everyone on the bus watched, Carl handed Tommy the bill, and Tommy went to the front of the bus and announced to the coach, "Billy, Carl would like a rye and Coke!" The entire bus erupted in laughter. Carl characterized it as "just a typical Toro road trip."

Carl spent only one season with the Toros — he pulled a hamstring during the off-season while training in Riverdale's Withrow Park, where he ran the hills to keep in shape, and the injury was slow to heal. Also, Carl said that his wife had put the gun to his head about hockey, telling him he had to get a regular job or else.

The WHA lasted seven seasons, and in 1979 a "merger" was agreed to, whereby the NHL would absorb its adversary's four strongest teams — Edmonton, Hartford, Quebec and Winnipeg. "God save the WHA, because Alan Eagleson sure as hell wouldn't," Carl used to say. The reasons for his condemnation of Eagleson were many. First of all, the real losers in this truce were the players. The restoration of the NHL's monopoly threatened to put the brakes on the salary gains the players had enjoyed throughout the 1970s. Eagleson represented many of them as their agent, while at the same time acting as executive director of the NHL Players' Association. Instead of working to protect the players, Eagleson co-operated with the NHL owners. For instance, he agreed to reopen, with no reciprocal concession to the players, the collective bargaining agreement that had been signed in 1975, to allow teams to buy out players they didn't want or need for only one-third of their contract amounts. Eagleson's conflicts of interest were visible in every aspect of the so-called merger. Although he talked tough about what rights the players would demand, as time went on, he gave in to one concession after another. The NHL put forth financial statements that failed to include revenues from such sources as arena rentals, parking receipts and concession stands; the statements therefore made the teams appear much weaker than they really were. Eagleson did not call the NHL owners to task on details like these. Carl remarked to our friend, journalist Bruce Dowbiggin, "Either he knew and did nothing about it, or he didn't know and is a fool — and I haven't heard anyone describe Alan Eagleson as stupid." It was understood at the time that the NHL was to contribute $7.5 million to the players' pension plan in consideration of this merger. Years later, it was impossible for us to locate a single copy of that merger agreement, and we learned that no such payment had ever been made to the pension plan.

Carl always felt that Toros owner Johnny Bassett treated his players fairly and with dignity, and he had tremendous respect for the man. May 14,

1986, was an overcast spring day in Toronto. Around three o'clock, Carl came in with a can of Coke in his hand, looking very upset. He said to me, "I want a drink — I need a drink ... Johnny Bassett died." Deep sadness and regret were written all over Carl's face. The funeral was held at noon on Friday, May 17, and Carl was ready early and dressed handsomely in a new suit and trench coat he'd bought specially for the funeral. Afterwards, we met for lunch at Ricky and Ricardo's, a neighbourhood restaurant we frequented, and he told me all about the funeral service. He described the service as truly "him," Johnny Bassett. The choir from Upper Canada College had sung two hymns — "Praise Him, Praise Him" and "The Battle Hymn of the Republic" — that Carl thought were wonderful. He had seen Harold Ballard there, and commented on how dreadful he looked.

Carl looked very weary, and when I suggested to him that it had been a very emotionally draining day for him, he answered, "It is sad, but sadness is allowed," as he smiled warmly at me and glanced at the book he had taken with him, his "bible" at the time: *Feeling Good* by Dr. David Burns.

CHAPTER 6

THE BROKEN ROAD BACK TO HOCKEY

"I've been tilting at windmills all my life."

Our evening together in Montreal back in 1967 had left absolutely no doubt, in Carl's mind or mine, about the deep feelings we had for one another. Our bond was deep and inexorably forged. After 1967, although we were in touch more sporadically, the feelings, the closeness never changed, and we were never far from each other's thoughts.

It had always been my intention to teach, and I accepted a position at Anderson Collegiate in Whitby, Ontario. I spent part of the summer of 1967 at Queen's University in Kingston, taking the requisite courses to begin my career as a high school French and English teacher. All the while, Carl, who had recently completed his degree, was trying to find a niche in life — someplace to fit in and make a difference, to exorcise his demons and find peace and fulfillment.

Although we acknowledged the feelings we had for each other, a future with him never crossed my mind. In the 1960s, divorce was not even a legal option in Canada and was frowned upon socially. I could never imagine Carl's domestic situation changing. He was a married man, and one with exceptionally strong religious convictions. I saw his situation as set in stone, regardless of his talk of discord.

I felt it was time to move on with my life, and I met and married a terrific man, David Horton, also a teacher, in 1969. When Carl learned of my plans, he was speechless and quite distraught. Although he wished me well and I knew he was sincere, he was upset, alarmed by this change. Years later, he admonished me, saying, "I'll never understand why you ever got married," as if he somehow perceived it as a betrayal.

For the next six years, from 1969 to 1975, Carl and I were not in touch with one another. I had a beautiful daughter, Melanie Amelia, and later a delightful son, Daniel John Foster, and I was busy teaching and taking care of my family. During this period, Carl was back playing hockey professionally in two leagues — the NHL and later the WHA. After Carl quit the Toros in 1974, he went to work at Global Television as a colour commentator on broadcasts of the Toros games. Over the years, Carl had demonstrated his outstanding capabilities as a media personality. He was articulate and insightful, and he did a terrific job for Global, commenting on games that were often pretty uninspiring. At the same time, he was busy importing and promoting Koho's sporting goods.

This venture dated back to 1969, when a Finnish acquaintance, Joukko Paavola, showed up at Carl's door in Toronto and announced that they were going into business together. The business was called Sisu Sports International. Initially, they kept their inventory in Carl's mother's garage before leasing space in an office/warehouse complex at 1111 Finch Avenue West in Downsview. Carl was excited about the prospects for this business, and he put all his energy into it, confident that it held the promise of a lucrative post-hockey career.

Like most hockey players of his time, he lacked business acumen. He had a terribly underdeveloped sense of whom he could trust. That was understandable considering that, as Carl was always quick to point out, playing pro hockey required total concentration and commitment, and players missed out on many of the usual lessons young men learn when they are growing up — like learning who their friends really were, or even how to change a tire or make minor repairs around the house. In later life, Carl lamented this state of affairs and was inclined to feel inept and frustrated when faced with such challenges, most of which were of a minor nature.

In the summer of 1975, Carl teamed up with Bob Thorndyke and moved his hockey stick importing business to Oshawa, where Thorndyke was based. This was a newsworthy event locally, and a widely publicized open house was held at the office/warehouse complex in the industrial area of the city. I was surprised when I heard about this move and saw Carl's picture in the *Oshawa Times*.

On August 7, 1975, at about six-thirty in the evening, my phone rang. When I answered, I heard a male voice say "Susan?" I recognized the soft-spoken voice instantly, even before, after a pause, he said "Carl." I was over-come with emotion and pleased to hear the warm, gentle tone of his voice. All the good feelings I had held in my heart for him came rushing back. We chatted amicably and enthusiastically for over an hour that night; we had a lot of catching up to do. Carl was excited about his new business partner-ship. He talked to me about the circumstances of his leaving the Toros and gave me an update on some of our mutual friends from hockey. He ad-mired Brit Selby, whom he told me "hated hockey" and was very happy in his new career teaching high school in Toronto. By now, Carl and Marilyn had three children — Christopher, Michael and Anna-Lisa — and he men-tioned the arrival of his daughter, but said nothing else about his domestic situation. As we settled into the conversation, Carl told me that he had missed me — had missed our visits, the talks, the easy, close communica-tion. He said, "I hope that doesn't have to end." He asked me if we could get together, and without hesitating for a second, I agreed. That phone call turned out to be a pivotal moment in our lives.

Early one morning about two weeks later, Carl called again and asked if I could get away and meet him — he'd be waiting for me in Oshawa Park, behind the hospital and next to the Oshawa Golf Course. I walked there, and as I reached the south end of the park, I caught my first glimpse of him — standing there, waiting for me. As I approached, he held his arms out to me and I fell into them. He drew me very close, holding me tightly — and kissed me with years of pent-up passion. My knees were trembling and felt like jelly; he steadied me and guided me to a nearby bench. After catching our breath, he walked me to his car, his brown Olds 98. The first thing I re-member Carl's telling me was: "I've never stopped dreaming about our night in Montreal. I've kicked myself ever since." When I asked why, he replied, "I should have stayed then." We remarked incredulously about how we hadn't seen each other in six years. "Six years!" Carl said. "It will never again be six years. I hope it's never more than six minutes." We drove that morning, and he held me close beside him — there were no seat belts or seat belt laws in 1975 — as we headed out to the country, near Windfield Farms. We made love in his car and vowed we'd never be out of touch again.

As Carl had plenty of reasons to be in the area, we saw one another more frequently, but it continued to be a clandestine affair for years to come. Now, he spoke often about leaving his marriage and was open about the continuing deterioration and the impossible differences in the relationship.

THE POWER OF TWO

On July 15, 1975, I met Carl at his office in Downsview. It was a glorious summer day and we went for a drive in the country, up to Maple. There, we went for a long walk in the woods. While he was driving that day, Carl was very emotional. He said, "Sue, I've never had feelings like this in my entire life and I don't know what to do about it." He went on to tell me: "Yesterday, I was driving and it was a beautiful sunny day, and I had the radio on and I started singing to the music. All of a sudden, I started to cry and I was saying to myself, 'Carl, you don't deserve to be this happy.'" It was a very moving moment. I didn't know how to respond. After a few moments of silence while I contemplated what he'd just told me, I told Carl that it wasn't a one-way street. I promised him that we'd work it out, whatever it was — together.

It was around this time that Carl's business world began to fall apart and embark on a rapid downhill slide. Carl became increasingly dependent on me for advice and emotional support.

His adjustment to life after hockey was really not any easier or more successful than that of many of his peers. Ron Ellis, a one-time teammate of Carl's, confronted this harsh reality and described it candidly in his memoir *Over the Boards*: "It all came to a head in 1986. I had retired in 1981 and it's always hard for pro athletes to make the transition to the working world." Ron tried different avenues, searching for a niche, and opened Ron Ellis Sports. A sporting goods store would have seemed a natural venture for a former pro athlete who was well respected and well liked in the community. But instead of setting out on the road to success, Ellis was headed down a path that led to the depths of depression.

Carl understood intellectually that a segment of the public was often fickle towards sports celebrities. They were anxious to rub shoulders with the players at the peak of their game, to use the contacts and the connections, mostly for self-serving purposes; but once the stars were out of the limelight, such hangers-on were quick to exit the scene and move on to the next star, and not return phone calls. Carl, unfortunately, had difficulty translating this knowledge into practice; time and time again he got involved with people in business ventures, only to be used. If Carl and I had one area over the years where we had disagreements, it was almost always about the people he was anxious to get involved with.

One evening in November 1975, Carl came out to Oshawa to play in an oldtimers' hockey game. The game was cancelled at the last minute, and we were going out for a few drinks and a visit. As we got into his car, Carl reached for my hand just as he always did, intertwining his fingers with mine and squeezing tightly. This night, however, I just knew something was wrong — something ominous was in the air. Alone at last, he broke the news to me that Koho had fallen apart, his hopes and aspirations dashed. The parent company had moved quickly and unexpectedly to sever the relationship with Carl. Of course, all the while, Carl never really knew what kind of deals his partners had made with home base, either. Years later, when we were visiting friends in Finland, we heard for the first time that Carl's partner had purportedly cut a side deal that paid him a dollar for every stick sold in North America. Upon hearing this, Carl and I just looked at one another in disbelief — and at the same time total belief! The night Carl told me about the collapse of Koho, he was noticeably shaken up and very angry. He spoke of having consulted Toronto lawyer Bill McMurtry, and he was determined to go after a substantial financial settlement. This never came to pass, and Carl and Koho went their separate ways. It never had been a lucrative business; Carl had taken out large lines of credit, he had excess inventory, and there was always a long list of receivables yet to be collected. From then on, whenever Carl heard of yet another former player going into the sporting goods business, he saw it as a disaster waiting to happen.

Shortly after the demise of Koho, Carl's business arrangements with Bob Thorndyke went sour as well. After two consecutive disappointments, Carl focused on the travel agency and other ventures. He soon found there was little money in the travel business, so he represented several sporting goods companies. As with everything Carl did, he invested a great deal of effort in these opportunities and was generous with his contacts and ideas. He attended trade fairs as a rep, especially the large international fair in Munich, Germany, where he was a definite asset because he spoke fluent German. However, once his contacts were known, his services became redundant. All of these ventures left a trail of unresolved problems, some of which required legal assistance to get Carl his due or to extricate him from the entanglements. I have to say that I never ceased to be amazed and impressed by Carl's resilience. Time and again, having put his heart and energy into ventures only to see them blow up in his face, he'd pull himself up, dust himself off and move on to something else — with the same optimism and energy.

One of Carl's last business experiences of the 1970s was as owner of a used car dealership — Koho Compact Cars. Need I say more? The business was located at the corner of Woodbine Avenue and Highway 7 in Markham, at an old garage on Steve Stavro's Knob Hill Farms property. If ever there were a business for which Carl wasn't suited, this was the one. His partners and employees were old pros in the business. Friends, or rather hangers-on, expected to use cars and not pay. One even happened to take a car to New York and leave it there; Carl had to go and fetch it. It was a disaster, not only from a financial standpoint, but also for Carl's well-being and confidence. As this debacle dragged on, I watched Carl lose ground. We'd meet for lunch, and there were days when he looked terrible — stressed out, drained, unkempt and sleep-deprived. He was in over his head, and we both knew it.

The stress manifested itself physically: Carl developed full-blown alopecia and all his hair fell out. The only body hair he had, for the most part, were — thankfully — his eyebrows. For quite some time he was uncomfortable being seen in public, although he eventually did come to terms with his bald head, which became his trademark feature. For years, he'd joke about it. Often, when he met someone and sensed they were staring at his bald head, he would say, "You'll remember me — my blue eyes!" This cracked most people up. Other times, when people asked him about it, he'd answer, "Grass doesn't grow on a busy street." It was surprising to me that reporters wrote over the years about Carl's "shaved head." He didn't shave his head — there was no hair there to shave!

In 1978, seeking a career change, I had taken the Ontario real estate course. My first listing in real estate was a lot with a small house on it with the potential for severance. Carl had always been interested in property development and had an acquaintance, a builder who built low-end homes and small strip plazas in small towns. Carl and his builder friend bought this piece of land and I helped them get the severance approval. Then this fell apart, too. There was an acrimonious split between Carl and the builder, who put a lien on the property as a stink bid, and I spent weeks negotiating a settlement on Carl's behalf because he was too angry and hostile towards his erstwhile partner to resolve the issues himself. I got the partner to sign a quit claim deed, effectively giving Carl clear title to the land — which was not unreasonable, given that Carl had put up all the money.

By the late spring of 1979, Carl's car business had deteriorated badly. He had taken a financial beating and was trying to liquidate his inventory.

Working in real estate left me with a more flexible schedule than teaching had, so I found myself devoting more and more of my time to helping Carl sort out his problems. The main avenue for getting rid of the cars was the weekly auto auction in Courtice, Ontario, just east of Oshawa. He took cars out there every week, hoping to sell off as many as possible. On auction day, I would meet him there, usually around noon. He expected me to be there to provide moral support and keep him company. Sometimes I'd make a lunch and we'd drive down to Lake Ontario and have a picnic for a brief respite from the negative environment of the auction. Again, these were times when Carl was very open about his innermost feelings, and he spoke with me about his self-doubts, frustrations, regrets, unhappiness, fears and despair.

On July 4, 1979, we were at the lake, sitting in his car together, talking. Carl had some vodka and had brought along a couple cans of Coke from the auction barn. Yes, Carl's medicine of choice was vodka and Coke, a drink he'd first tried in Finland. As we were having a drink, Carl turned to me and said: "Sue, do you see? I can't handle this. I just can't take any more of this shit." The tone of desolation and defeat in his voice was troubling. I realized he was referring not only to the car business but to the entire litany of business battles of the past several years. I assured Carl that I did understand, that I did see his discouragement. I tried telling him there was light at the end of the tunnel and that he had to take things one step at a time, persevere a little longer and not be so hard on himself. Carl's self-esteem, confidence and outlook seemed to me to be at an all-time low. I was worried about him. For months, I had been witness to this long, agonizing decline playing out in him.

At the same time, in Toronto, an interesting coincidence was playing out. A press conference was held at Maple Leaf Gardens to announce the return of Punch Imlach as general manager of the Leafs. Sports reporter Paul Rimstead wrote about the announcement in the next day's *Toronto Sun*. Specifically, he wrote about his conversation with Punch about Carl Brewer.

> *"What about bringing Carl Brewer back on defense?" I asked.*
>
> *Brewer, of course, has been out of competitive hockey for years but still is playing age. He is as bald as a billiard*

ball, tremendously eccentric, and while playing here under Punch had more than one tiff with him.

Punch just smiled. After the Oldtimers' game last winter in Montreal, I said, "I suspect Carl Brewer could make the team today."

"He'd have to be in shape," Punch said.

"What if he got in shape?" I asked. "Would you invite him to training camp?"

"He'd have to come to me and say he wanted to play," Imlach said.

Somehow I think the challenge would be interesting to a guy like Brewer.

The game Rimstead referred to had been played in March 1979, when the Toronto Maple Leaf Oldtimers played in Montreal against Les Anciens Canadiens. Carl reminisced about the game: "All the greats were there — Keon, Richard, Mahovlichs 1 and 2, Doug Harvey, Johnny Bower, Dollard St. Laurent, Jean Beliveau, and so on. It was a stirring game before a sold-out, enthusiastic crowd. The game was well-played. The unemployed Punch Imlach was our coach. At the postgame press conference, Imlach was asked if he thought any of the players could still play in the NHL. Imlach replied that he thought Henri Richard and Carl Brewer could still play. Thus the bug was placed in my ear."

Throughout that summer, Carl gave serious thought to a return to competitive hockey and had discussions about joining a team in Augsburg, Germany, for the purpose of training, conditioning and playing. It looked like the possibility, however remote, for a return to the NHL might just be available to him.

After reading Rimstead's column on July 5, Carl phoned him. "I called Rimstead and said I wanted the challenge, hoping it would come in February when I was in shape and after I'd come back from Germany."

Carl's reasons for wanting to play in Germany were many — to get away and clear his head, and to distance himself from the long list of residual matters still outstanding from his various business entanglements of the past few years. He was also intrigued by the possibility of obtaining a German passport — his paternal grandfather, Fritz Oldschwager, had immigrated to Canada from Flensburg in the north of Germany. (When he got to Canada he changed the family name to that of his wife, Ada Brewer, because in those days after World War I it wasn't popular to have a German surname.) Carl was always fascinated with the idea of living and working overseas, and he knew that a European passport would facilitate any such eventuality. The really important motivation for Carl, however, was to find out whether he could still play hockey of NHL calibre. Playing in Germany would give him a much-needed income as well. In his mind, if things worked out, he could play the short season in Germany (the seasons end in late February in the European leagues) and possibly return to Toronto and join the Leafs for the remainder of the 1979–80 season. This latter consideration was anything but a flight of fantasy for Carl.

The day he left for Germany, we spent the afternoon together at Fuller's Restaurant on Yonge Street just south of Sheppard Avenue. We had a long lunch and sat talking for hours. He thanked me profusely for standing by him and for being there for him through all the problems. He told me how special my friendship was to him and, in a very heartfelt tone, said: "Thank you for always accepting me as I am. It seems that everybody looks at me askance, but you, you accept me, you put up with me exactly as I am." When it came time to part, Carl handed me $40 and asked me to look after it for him. He also showed me a bank draft for $8,000 and told me it was what he'd salvaged from the cars — and that it was all the money he had. I put the two $20 bills in my wallet and they stayed there until I saw him again, many weeks later.

Years later, Carl told me it had been very difficult for him to leave me that afternoon because he honestly believed there was a possibility he might never return to Canada. From the airport, he phoned me at the real estate office. He expressed his relief at getting away from all the problems. I promised him that whatever problems needed to be dealt with, I would support him and that we would clear things up when he returned. I heard and felt the relief and gratitude in his voice.

The couple of months Carl spent in Augsburg were not free of hassles. He took his brother, Jack, with him, and when they arrived, Carl told me that the club management informed him that Jack couldn't stay. Carl made it clear that if his brother didn't stay, he wouldn't, either. But, according to Carl, Jack had been dissatisfied with the way things were being handled, and Carl felt that Jack was blaming *him*. When he returned, he told me, "Over in Germany, I kissed Jack's ass; I did everything to try to please him and he complained — nothing suited him." As an added frustration, Carl did not receive the pay he'd been promised in timely fashion (eventually, he was paid some of what he was owed). Conditions apparently declined from difficult to intolerable very quickly. He told me how, after a game, he put the money in his shoe, gathered his belongings and quietly left town. He took a train to Munich to get a flight back to Toronto. This was a very uncomfortable experience for him, and he told me numerous times about waiting for his flight in Munich's airport and hearing — or at least he thought he was hearing — his name being called on the public address system.

The one truly positive thing that came out of his brief time in Germany was that he was reassured, both by his brother Jack and his Austrian friend Alfred Fischnaller, that he definitely still had the skills and ability to play in the NHL. Carl told me that Jack had been awestruck by just how well he had played, and Jack's endorsement was very important to Carl.

The night Carl arrived back in Toronto, he phoned me and we arranged meet the following day for lunch. It was wonderful to see him again. We spent the entire afternoon together talking, and he told me all about his experiences in Augsburg — good, bad *and* ugly! One major disappointment was that he hadn't stayed long enough to get the club to help him get his German passport. That afternoon, Carl mentioned to me that he didn't have any money. I took the 40 dollars out of my wallet and handed it to him. He had forgotten all about it, and the look that came over his face spoke volumes.

Soon after his return to Toronto, Carl followed up on the possibility of playing with the Leafs. "In November, I returned from Germany and contacted Rimstead. He suggested that the door was still open," he explained. "I made a number of attempts to contact Imlach. Finally, we chatted on the phone, concurred as to the possibilities and probabilities, and agreed to meet in two weeks when the team returned from a road trip."

A brief meeting in Imlach's office followed, and the two men agreed that it was possible for him to return and play for the Leafs. Nothing was made definite, however, and they planned to meet again a week later.

On December 13, 1979, Carl phoned me and asked me to have lunch with him. We went to what was then the Howard Johnson's hotel at Highway 401 and Markham Road. I remember that it was an unseasonably mild, overcast day. We had a long, leisurely lunch and a very good visit. I was uncertain as to why Carl was so insistent on seeing me that day; it seemed to be just another one of those times when he needed my presence for support, or to give him the courage he needed at a particular moment, or to help him settle down given all the conflicting thoughts that were always running through his mind. This day, the possibility of his returning to the Leafs seemed remote and unlikely. He did make some comments that indicated he was thinking about the flying he'd have to do if he went back to play. There had recently been a couple of big air crashes involving DC-10s and he was concerned about that. At one point he said, "I wouldn't have to fly if it's a DC-10." Over lunch and a good heart-to-heart talk, he was otherwise very relaxed and not in the least bit hurried. As we were leaving, standing in the parking lot, he just stood there for many long minutes, saying nothing but reluctant to leave.

* * *

The next morning, the papers and newscasts were full of the story of Carl Brewer's comeback. It took me completely by surprise. He told me later, apologetically, that when he left me that day after lunch, he had definitely decided not to go back. "When we had lunch that Wednesday, I didn't know I was going. In fact, after I left you, I had decided to say no. I was just going to go in and say, 'Look, forget it; I don't want to do it.'" Yet that same day he visited Imlach and committed to a return to the Leafs — Carl's indecisiveness was a lifelong trait!

Later, he described what transpired when he went to see Imlach at the Gardens.

> *I showed up on Wednesday, December 13 at 5:00 p.m. The Leafs were playing that night, and Imlach had been looking for me. I hadn't even made up my mind, but Imlach had already made up a press release indicating that I would be starting back with Leafs the next day. A copy was in the hands of [broadcaster] Dave Hodge. With that, I decided to give it a try.*
>
> *Upon considering the Leafs' heavy schedule — six to eight games in the next 10 days — I suggested that I would prefer to go to [the New Brunswick Hawks, the Maple Leafs' farm team in] Moncton for a week or so in order to*

*avoid the pressures of the press, to play a few games in the
AHL and to work under coach Joe Crozier's rigid and demanding conditions. It was agreed that I would return to
the Leaf lineup on December 26 in a game against the
Washington Capitals.*

*Imlach reached across the table and shook my hand
and said that, starting the next day, I was on the payroll at
$125,000 prorated. He then rewrote and distributed the
press release about Moncton and arranged forthwith, in the
office, my ticket for my flight.*

For the most part, the press greeted the news with cynicism and derision. I heard sportscaster Pat Marsden say, "If this is what professional hockey has to resort to, then I've lost a lot of respect for the Leafs." They couldn't have known how serious Carl was about his return to competitive hockey. "Sue," he told me, "if I get the opportunity to play the way I know I'm capable of playing, I want to make this work for the next four or five years." By the time Carl arrived, the Leafs were in chaos. After assembling a successful young team as Buffalo's general manager during the 1970s, Imlach had returned to Toronto as GM to encounter a new generation of hockey players who would not submissively accept his dictatorial style. Darryl Sittler was the Leafs' captain — and vice-president of the NHL Players' Association — and his contract contained a no-trade clause. The battle lines were irrevocably drawn early in November 1979, when Sittler gave his grievances against Imlach a public airing, something that would have been unheard of during Imlach's heyday with the Leafs in the 1960s. In a full-page article in *The Globe and Mail*, written by James Christie and headed "Darryl Sittler Drops the Gloves," Sittler castigated Imlach for his public criticism of the play of both Sittler and goalie Mike Palmateer, as well as his controversial decision to put winger Lanny McDonald and defenseman Ian Turnbull on waivers.

Speaking for the players, Sittler expressed anger about the loss of certain perks they had attained under previous coaches and general managers, including Roger Neilson, Red Kelly and Jim Gregory — such as the serving of beer on the charter flights after games and the disappearance of the Ping Pong table from the Leafs' dressing room. Carl followed this saga with amusement and interest at the time. He found the Sittler–Imlach power play absurd. He also understood that it was really Sittler's agent, Alan Eagleson, who was inciting the conflict and trying to control the Leaf team.

David Hutchison was playing with the Leafs at the time of Carl's comeback. We had a great chat about the Leafs for this book. Dave says that, with players like Palmateer, Sittler, McDonald, Tiger Williams, Borje Salming and Turnbull, "We were a good, strong team but we couldn't beat the Habs, so after 1979, Harold [Ballard] fired Jim Gregory and our coach, Roger Neilson, and brought in Punch Imlach. Now, that's where the problems started. The problem was with Punch Imlach. He came in and was laying the law down to us, telling us what was going to happen. He traded Lanny. We had a nice ship running and all of a sudden, we hit a big wave with Imlach. This was a team that was in the top four or five in the league, that turned into a team that went straight into futility for 10 or 15 years after that year with Punch."

Carl went to Moncton and played three games with the Hawks. Initially, his play was tentative, but no one could say he didn't have the skills of old. Paul Rimstead went to watch Carl and was favourably impressed, as was Joe Crozier. Imlach, along with King Clancy and Johnny Bower, showed up for his first game, against the Nova Scotia Voyageurs, and Imlach was enthusiastic about Carl's play: "You can be sure he'll be playing for the Leafs on December 26. I thought he made good plays. He passes the puck as well as any defenseman I know, but he can't make up for the mistakes of others."

Crozier had fond memories of Carl Brewer from decades earlier. He told Rex MacLeod of the *Toronto Star* about being called up to the Leafs when Bob Baun was injured. "I had Brewer as a defense partner and it was a breeze. All I did was give him the puck and sic him on the enemy." When Baun returned and Imlach sent him back down, Crozier said, "I cried."

Given the atmosphere that prevailed within the organization at the time of his arrival, the players were immediately suspicious of the way in which Carl came to be part of the team. It struck them as just one more irritation and blatant insult from Punch Imlach. The team by this point was in such disarray that sportswriter Frank Orr characterized the Leafs as "not a team but rather a collection of bodies." The players began referring to Carl as "CIA" and "Sting," suspecting that the sole purpose of his presence was to be a spy, a pipeline, for Imlach. It isn't difficult to see how they could reach such a conclusion, but anyone who knew anything at all about

Carl's history with the Leafs would have realized that this was a most unlikely proposition!

Carl played his first game with the Leafs on December 26, 1979, at Maple Leaf Gardens against the Washington Capitals. Just before the game, Carl signed his contract with Imlach. "Previously, I had not signed a Leaf contract," Carl explained, "but I had signed some papers blindly with Joe Crozier in Moncton which I believed constituted an amateur tryout. Before the game, Imlach called me out of the Leaf dressing room, and told me in private he had received a complaint from the NHL saying I was not eligible to play but that he was going to play me anyway. The next day, I signed my contract — Imlach said he could tell everyone that it had been in his desk for 10 days [to fulfill NHL requirements that contracts had to be filed with league headquarters within 10 days after signing]."

The players were openly hostile to Carl. Borje Salming, his defense partner, refused to pass the puck to him. On one occasion in practice he was cut in a nasty collision with a goalpost after some of the players pushed him. The gash to his head required the work of a plastic surgeon. When players Joel Quenneville, Pat Boutette and Lanny McDonald were traded away, the whole city was in an uproar and Imlach was criticized for favouring Carl Brewer over them. Hutchison, who was benched to make room for Carl, told Rex MacLeod, "A lot of guys in this league would rather play 80 games against Brewer than one against me."

Carl felt that the disapproval of his presence went beyond the players. "As for Floyd Smith, he is totally noncommittal and noncommitted. If there was subterfuge, he was part of it. On several occasions he said he didn't want to play me 'now' because 'those guys won't even talk to you, let alone pass you the puck; they won't come back when you're on the ice, either.'"

Scott Young, who had covered Carl's early years with the Leafs, was more supportive and sympathetic. On January 5, 1980, he wrote in his column: "Even that first night, although he did not carry the puck much (or have it passed to him), it was obvious there were enough old Brewer watchers around to make themselves heard. There would be a murmur around the rink as he did a head fake or that little trick where he lifts his stick a few inches from the ice and makes a series of dazzling moves with it while the puck just keeps on going."

Friday, January 10 was the first opportunity Carl and I had to spend any quality time together, and we met for a late lunch at Fuller's. Carl came in directly from practice and said, "Right now, I'm exhausted. I'm just shaking, I'm so beat." He spoke at length about the discord: "It's just incredible. I was the first out of the dressing room. I don't want to be in there." He went on to tell me, "I'm between the devil and the deep blue sea… they don't know how I feel." We talked about the media's reaction to his return, and I asked him if he had expected anything like it. He hadn't. I told Carl that I'd had a lot of trouble coping with all the negativity, the mockery and the snide remarks, especially because I knew what a bad place he'd been in for such a long time. Carl advised me not to read the papers anymore. "Do what I do: don't read anything. That's why I feel so good."

Nonetheless, Carl was aware that the team was in the centre of a media circus. He saw the problem: "Ballard and Imlach don't give a shit if they win games — they have never had so much publicity, and there has never been a greater demand for tickets." Aware of the impact of all the trades made by Imlach, he took some comfort in that saying, "I think they'll bring David Farrish up soon; we'll soon have a whole new team and then I'll be okay. Hutchison [traded to the Blackhawks in January 1980] is supposed to be ready for me in Chicago, but that's all right. I'll handle him."

Carl really didn't get a chance to play much that season — certainly not regularly. This left Carl confused and disappointed. "I continued to practise, train and hope," he said at the time. "I was told to be patient. In early to mid-January I called Rimstead and told him I was prepared to quit. He prevailed on me to hang in, and I did. But I never did get the chance to play." Carl played in a total of 20 games and was chosen one of the three stars of a game he played in Buffalo. However, he got mixed messages from the media as well. "I felt unquestionably that I had the ability to help the Leafs. After the game when I was selected a star, Imlach seemed to be my most enthusiastic supporter. The quiet whispers, a campaign of silence at which Imlach excels — one is left with one's own mind to play tricks on oneself." He began to question Imlach's original motives, especially when Scott Young, Imlach's mouthpiece, wrote that Brewer's stay would be short-lived. On a CFRB radio phone-in show, Imlach talked about what a shame it was, the way the players were treating Carl Brewer, and that he wouldn't blame Carl for quitting but wouldn't cut him.

"During the playoffs they kept saying I was injured. I was not. I wasn't even allowed to attend the team meetings," Carl lamented. "The quiet assassination continued, but failed. I stayed."

David Hutchison told me a story that is not only comical but adds new insights into why Carl was having trouble being accepted by the team. "We were heading out — taking a charter flight out of Skyport at the back of Toronto Airport — to Montreal. We were going to play the Habs that night and fly right back to Toronto after the game, so we're all parking at the Skyport. Pat Boutette is the last guy on the plane. Boutette says to us, 'Check it out, boys,' so we're all looking out the back window and, sure enough, here comes Carl with Punch. Carl was riding with Punch Imlach — that was a no-no; players never travelled with the coach or general manager! Well, Punch had left his lights on in his car. It's a foggy, kind of rainy morning, around eight-thirty, nine o'clock. So, of course, we don't say anything.

"We go to Montreal and we lose 3–2 and we come back to Toronto. Punch and Carl go to the car — they're the first off the plane because they're sitting in the front. They go to the car and the battery is dead. So, Punch sends Carl out to see if any players have booster cables. I'm driving with Ian Turnbull at the time, and Ian has a set of cables in his trunk, so he grabs them and he sort of slams them into the back door of his Cadillac Seville. Anyway, he's got these cables dangling out the back door — maybe 15 feet of cables hanging out the right side back door — and he's driving around the parking lot with these at two o'clock in the morning. The cables, you can imagine, are sparking off the ground as he's driving around the parking lot. I'm in the front and I've got my window down and my arm out the window as we make a big swoop past Imlach. Punch sees me and he thinks it's all my trick. Traded to Chicago two days later. That's when I was gone!

"This wasn't about Carl," Hutchison insisted. "This is the way we guys did things back then; pranks were part of everything."

In retrospect, it seems very strange indeed that Carl would ride with Punch and sit with him on the plane, especially given the history they had! It would be difficult for anybody not to understand the players' suspicions toward Carl under these circumstances. On the other hand, it is indicative of Carl's gall. He always did do things his way!

Imlach was soon out of the picture, and for reasons Carl saw and understood. "Punch Imlach, the bastard who had his ass run out of Toronto, not once, but twice by… you guessed it, Alan Eagleson. The second time, Palmateer, Sittler, Williams and McDonald were the protagonists. Eagleson was the director. There was no love lost between Eagleson and Imlach.

Imlach sat in the reds of the Gardens after his demise, licking his wounds. Maple Leaf Gardens was his Taj Mahal — mine, too!"

Dave Hutchison was an Eagleson client. "That's the reason all this went down," he told me. "Anybody who had Eagleson as agent — and we had a lot of them, when we look back — it's pretty clear the feud was between Punch Imlach and Eagleson, but everybody that had Al as an agent was gone." Carl saw this as a power play, with Eagleson using Sittler as a pawn. Mike "Shakey" Walton remembers that, when he was with the Leafs back in the late 1960s, team practices saw Imlach line up the Eagleson clients against the rest of the guys for drills. Carl often took shots at Eagleson, saying that, had he really been interested in looking after Sittler's best interests, he would have backed off and made sure that Darryl got to finish his career with dignity with the Toronto Maple Leafs, the team he had done so proud.

After the season, Carl continued to hold onto a glimmer of hope that the Leafs would honour his contract and give him a real chance to be part of the team. He was also wrestling with a deficiency in his pay. Carl had no doubt that Imlach had told him on December 13 that, as of the following day, he was on the payroll at $125,000 prorated. When he received his first cheque in mid-January, he noticed that his pay had started only on December 26. He hadn't addressed this issue at the time because, as he explained, "I was avoiding any communication with Imlach because of the spying allegations." He quietly made this shortfall known to assistant coach Dick Duff, but got no response from the front office. Carl knew that Imlach wanted him to ask him directly for the money — some $8,200 — but Carl felt strongly against doing so. "I went to Imlach on bended knee for a purpose — to be a Maple Leaf. I do not intend to cower on bended knee again."

We engaged a young lawyer, Donald Fiske, to follow up on the matter of the shortfall in Carl's pay. The fallout would consume our time and lives for the next 20 years.

CHAPTER 7

THE BIG BEAR HUNT

"I had for years wanted to take on the sceptre of Alan Eagleson and his evil influence on hockey as perceived by me — as judge, jury and executioner."

Early in the morning on Boxing Day 1980, Carl phoned me. He didn't sound in a relaxed or festive mood; he sounded down — even despondent. He faked some pleasantries, thanked me for my Christmas gift, then implored me to help him. He told me bluntly that he was flat broke and discouraged by the way in which everything he had worked at in the recent past had failed. By now it was apparent to both of us that the Leafs had no intention of including him in their plans. He asked me to help him do something in business because he was convinced that together we could make something work and split any profits 50/50.

I was working in real estate and was frequently in demand as a substitute French teacher, especially for long-term maternity or illness leaves of absence. Carl had taken the real estate course, but he continued to flounder.

Carl's builder acquaintance — the one he'd had the falling-out with years earlier — was doing a rehab job on a mixed residential/commercial property on Danforth Avenue near Broadview in the east end of the city. This neighbourhood held a lot of fond memories for Carl because he had grown up there. Carl and the builder had reconciled their differences and they discussed purchasing the property that was being refitted. However, one day, the builder let it slip to me that he intended to obtain financing and purchase the property alone — without "the Brewer," as he called him. Naturally, I broke this news to Carl and he decided that we ought to approach the owners of the property, two restaurateurs in Mississauga. The renovations had dragged on for ages, and Carl's former friend was letting out the rooms and apartments and collecting rents. We became friends with the restaurateurs and, before long, they had kicked the contractor off the premises. Carl and I were put in charge of overseeing the completion of the work and clearing up the outstanding work orders the city had issued against the building. It was a piece of cake for Carl, who got a great deal of co-operation from every department, to navigate his way around City Hall, so things went quickly. As time went on, we decided that we should consider purchasing the building. We made a deal with the current owners, arranged financing and went ahead and bought the building. I had to cash in my RRSP and my teacher's pension to come up with the necessary down payment. We closed the transaction in 1981.

We worked very hard for over six years to make this property work — to keep repairs up to municipal standards, to screen tenants and collect the rents. Carl made weekly trips to Goodwill in his old pickup truck to get furniture, mattresses and kitchen items to furnish the rooms. We had some help from time to time, but for the most part it was just Carl and I — seven days a week, night and day. On Saturdays we cleaned all the bathrooms and the hallways and tried to collect the rents that were due — or, usually, overdue. After this weekly ritual, we would treat ourselves to lunch at one of our favourite Greek restaurants. Riverdale had changed dramatically since Carl's youth. Formerly dominated by Anglo-Saxons, the district was now known as Greektown. Immigrants, initially from Italy and then from Greece, had moved into the area, and souvlaki and baklava were the specialties where fish and chips had once been served. Gentrification was beginning to take place, too, as young professionals bought and renovated the old homes that lined the streets Carl had so often walked alone.

Still, the transformation was not yet complete: we had a lengthy, ever-changing succession of tenants, most of them on some form of social assistance. It was a bizarre and colourful cast of characters, indeed. We had Deb, a prostitute, living in one of the apartments. She was very pleasant and was one of the few who paid her rent and paid it on time. However, she got hooked on an evangelical television program and gave all her money "to God." She fell behind in her rent, and eventually we had to take her to court and have her evicted, after patiently waiting for her to come up with the money she owed. Then there was Ed from Newfoundland. He was one of the few who went to work each day, at a junk store downtown where they sold everything from food and kitchen supplies to furniture. When his rent was due, he'd invite Carl and me to come to the store and help ourselves to whatever we needed. This didn't help us meet our payments for the mortgage, taxes and utilities however. Young Derek, a cross-dresser, lived in one of our rooms; his middle-aged lover paid his rent.

We had another tenant, a Mr. Hart, who turned out to be a serious problem. He was consistently menacing and ended up taking me to court, alleging that we had charged him illegal rents. It turned out that he had been in jail for years and, while incarcerated, had learned how to be a professional litigator. The process took months and cost us hugely in legal fees. I couldn't contain myself sufficiently to sit beside our lawyer, Allan Dick, in court because the man's lies were so preposterous. In the end, we won — a pyrrhic victory — and the judge declared that she wished she could order the plaintiff to pay our costs, but the applicable act prevented this. We would never recoup the thousands of dollars it took to defend this nuisance case. Mr. Hart was ordered off our premises, and he may well have moved on to another unsuspecting landlord whose life he would turn into a living hell sooner or later.

Many of the tenants left in the middle of the night with rent owing. Others didn't pay their rent, but stayed. They knew how long, under the lengthy, tedious court process required under the Landlord and Tenant Act, they could prolong eviction. I initiated that process more times than I can remember. In any of these cases, the best we could hope for was an order to evict the tenant, because there was never any money available to pay the arrears. No matter how pleasant these people might have appeared at the outset when they wanted to rent a room or an apartment, by the time they left they often had the police on their trail. We were amused at how frequently a tenant would disappear and then, about two weeks later, the police would show up asking for information about them.

One day, a young punk who lived in one of our rooms pulled a knife on me. Fortunately, I kept my cool, walked past him and called the police. The police showed me the weapon so that I would recognize it in court and marched the kid away. I never heard another thing — about the kid, or any charges. We had another bizarre tenant, whom Carl felt sorry for him and befriended. His behaviour and conduct were erratic and unpredictable. One afternoon, out of the blue, and with Carl off the premises, he stormed into our quarters and threatened me. He told me that he hated me because Carl loved me — and *he* wanted Carl! The police were called and they removed him, then returned a few hours later to inform me that he had a lengthy string of convictions for some very unsavoury crimes, and that if I ever saw him around the building again I was to call them immediately! When Carl returned and heard about my ordeal, he wept and said, "Sue, I'm so sorry. If anything ever happened to you, I don't know what I'd do."

Early on, Carl let a sportswriter, Don Ramsay, rent our choice unit — a main-floor studio that we called our "garden suite" because it opened into a courtyard. Carl was intrigued with Don's insights into the corruption in hockey, and they had long, wide-ranging discussions about many topics. However, he was another person who never paid any rent. Routine promises to pay went unfulfilled. After many weeks, he made a specific agreement to meet Carl at two o'clock on a Saturday afternoon to pay up the rent owing. On the appointed day, we were busy doing chores when Don phoned and told Carl that he was in a very important meeting and just couldn't get away. Carl bought Ramsay's line and told me very sympathetically about Don's predicament. That's when I lost it. I told him sternly that Don was not in any meeting, that I believed he was in a bar somewhere and never had any intention of showing up to pay him. Carl in turn became furious with me and stormed off.

Having witnessed Carl's previous business fiascos at first hand, especially with the used-car business, I was not prepared to allow this to go on a minute longer, especially when it affected me directly. I proceeded to enter Don's suite — Landlord and Tenant Act be damned — and threw all his belongings in garbage bags and boxes. I moved every stick of furniture to the basement, where he would not be able to get at it. He returned later that night to an empty apartment; undaunted, he just bunked with another tenant in the building.

After he'd had time to think about this, Carl phoned a mutual friend and told him sheepishly, "Sue was right." The friend then called me to tell me how Carl felt, because Carl, never having seen me so furious with him — even more so than I was with Don — was afraid, not only to call me but that I wouldn't accompany him to a very important meeting concerning his grievance with the Leafs. On the following Monday, I met Carl for lunch at the Press Club before his meeting, and he was most apologetic about his reaction and wondered aloud how it was that I was so much more able than he was to see through people. We found out later from Rick Fraser and his wife, Gloria, that Ramsay owed money to many people around town at the time, and we were just another name on an already long list. And no, we never did get any rent money from him. He moved on — and never did come to reclaim his things.

It was incredibly difficult to soldier on with this property. By 1982 my husband and I had separated amicably and I moved with our children, Melanie and Daniel, into a small semi-detached house in North Toronto that I'd bought a couple years earlier as an investment/rental property. To make ends meet I took in two boarders from the nearby Canadian Memorial Chiropractic College and did some supply teaching, although Carl did not hide his displeasure when I accepted occasional teaching assignments. My daughter, Melanie, made an insightful comment to me recently: "Mum, when you consider what you and Carl accomplished, it is remarkable, given that the odds were so stacked against you. But more than that, every day you were looking failure in the face with all the tenants in that building." Fortunately, the real estate market was rising, and we were able to refinance every 18 months or so, which freed up a little money to get the past-due hydro and property tax bills paid, with a little left over to live on.

When we wanted to refinance, it was important that all of the space in the building be rented. But we had a small storefront that had been difficult to rent. A political candidate took it briefly as a campaign office, but stiffed us for the rent when he left. We had a tenant in one of our apartments, a pleasant woman who had previously run an escort service in Montreal and was now in Toronto; from our building she made phone-sex calls for a company that advertised in some local rags. She suggested that she'd like to run a lingerie/sex-toy store in this space. We both liked the woman and agreed to be her "silent partners," and she set up shop. The merchandise she ordered consisted of lingerie and all sorts of other unusual items — at least, unusual to Carl and me! A huge box of these items arrived one day. I opened it and was carrying a full armload of stock a few doors down the street to the building when I heard a voice behind me say, "Oh, hi, Susan." I turned around and it was Brit Selby, walking past on his way home from his day of teaching. I was mortified, although I'm sure Brit didn't realize what I was doing!

Having our personal quarters in this building over the six years enabled us to spend much of our time together and to research and pursue Carl's ever-mounting problems with his recent hockey experience and his concerns over the business of hockey in general. This was our home through our years of legal struggles to get Carl his salary for the first days of his comeback with the Leafs, to have Carl's contract upheld after the Leafs unceremoniously ignored him at the end of the 1979–80 season and to investigate a wide range of pension issues — and, particularly, the conduct of Alan Eagleson, the executive director of the NHL Players' Association. I spent hours every day assembling information, reading and studying. It was excruciatingly difficult to get my hands on many relevant documents, such as the collective bargaining agreements and bylaws of the NHL, the NHL Pension Society and the NHLPA. They were certainly not available directly from the source, and we had to go through hoops and numerous layers of people — player agents, sports reporters and others — before we eventually obtained copies of them. Years later, many of these very documents would prove indispensable to authorities investigating the same matters. I spent hours writing letters, preparing documents for court and assembling books of authorities that outlined Carl's positions, our evidence and reasoning. We had no money to speak of, so we had to learn to do everything ourselves. I relied heavily on my teaching skills for research and preparation of material, and we had some help from friends in the legal profession from time to time, but for the most part we were on our own. We were a team of two.

It seemed that we had nothing but struggle in our lives for most of the six years. First of all, just to keep our building functioning was exhausting. There were always repairs to be done and our tenants were, with few exceptions, transient types who routinely left without notice and without paying. On one of our walls, I had a large piece of bristol board upon which I had outlined all of the battles Carl was embroiled in — there were about a dozen to start with. Apart from the Leaf matters, many were residual problems left over from Carl's business debacles of the 1970s. Some were the subject of legal action and some required that we get legal direction to fend people off or get Carl his due.

It was extremely stressful for Carl, but equally so for me. I couldn't help but worry about him. There were many times when he couldn't handle the pressure and got so wound up that he would go up to his mum's home in nearby Leaside to sleep all afternoon, or just go off by himself and ski for an afternoon to try and relax a little. While I sympathized with Carl and understood his predicament, it meant that I had to look after everything at the building. There was a moment around this time that really struck a chord with me and made me laugh. My dear friend Lynne Roberts (by now Lynne Skeie) came to visit me and told me that, when she mentioned to her brother Jim — the former Canadien and Blue — that Carl and I were together, he said, "Well, Sue never was one to back down from a challenge." I had a whole new respect for Jim's insights!

I felt heartsick that Carl, such a genuinely decent, generous and selfless man, had so many people taking advantage of him or trying to use him. Obviously, some thought he had money — what an erroneous notion that was! It was I who wrote letters, consulted with friendly lawyers, prepared documents and negotiated settlements for most of these matters. However, it often seemed that I had no sooner got one problem cleared up than a couple of new ones would be added to the list.

Carl had a cute little story he used to recite to our friends about our relationship. He called it "The Big Bear Hunt." The story was about a husband and a wife living in a little cabin out in the wilderness. Every morning, the husband would go out hunting bears. Later in the day, he'd return — exhausted, out of breath, grappling with a big black bear, fighting to drag it home. The man would throw open the door, push the bear inside and say to his wife, "Here, you take care of him; I'm going out to look for another one." Carl thought this story was hilarious and described perfectly our life together. I couldn't disagree.

***

Carl's dispute with the Leafs over his unpaid salary came to a head when his lawyer's demand letter, dated April 14, 1980, for arrears of $8,287.32 went unanswered. We found ourselves involved in a lawsuit: Brewer v. Toronto Maple Leaf Hockey Club. On January 5, 1982, after months of preparation with lawyer Don Fiske, we headed to a Toronto courtroom for the trial.

Carl was exceptionally anxious, nervous and tense as we rode the escalator to the second-floor courtroom. He was uncomfortable because he knew the press would be present to observe the proceedings. I tried to encourage him, to calm him down and assure him he'd do just fine on the stand. I didn't succeed.

The courtroom was indeed filled with reporters from all the Toronto newspapers and television stations. The Leafs' current general manager,

Gerry McNamara, and other members of the Leaf brass were also in attendance. In the witness box, Carl was tense, but throughout his testimony he remained poised and, as always, articulate. He responded to all the questions clearly and confidently.

The proceedings were, if nothing else, entertaining, particularly when Punch Imlach was in the box. He conducted himself with a high-handed attitude and colourful language, and he ran afoul of Judge Keith Gibson on more than one occasion. When asked why he had not let Carl go during the 1979–80 season, he replied: "Maybe I'm too soft. Just the fact that he won three Stanley Cups. He should get the money. He has it coming to him." At another point in the cross-examination, Imlach took at shot at Don Fiske, saying, "Well, you don't know much about the hockey business so what the hell would you know about that?" The judge reprimanded Imlach, saying, "Mr. Imlach, Mr. Fiske is doing his job and if you are not able to answer…" Imlach apologized. Later on, when Fiske kept the pressure on Imlach for more information about what had been said in the meeting of December 13, 1979, Imlach retorted: "Well, it's [Brewer who's lying]. He doesn't know what the hell he's talking about. He is a little unstable as it is at times." Again the judge interjected: "Mr. Imlach, this is not the dressing room. This is a court of law." When Imlach apologized yet again, Judge Gibson persisted, "I appreciate that, but you have to exercise some restraint." When asked by Carl's lawyer if he had discussed bringing Brewer back to the Leafs with any of the players, Imlach replied: "I am the manager of the hockey club, correct? Players have bugger all to say about what I do and who I hire or who I don't hire, and that's one of the troubles with the Maple Leafs. Everybody seems to think that they run it, and maybe you got that impression, too, and that's why you asked the question. I don't know, but that is a stupid question." Later, when asked if he had discussed the Brewer comeback with owner Harold Ballard, Imlach replied, "I don't have to ask Mr. Ballard what the hell I do." Despite the judge's admonishments, Carl was struck by just how deferential the court was to Imlach.

At the end of the day, we left the court not really knowing what to expect. We had spent months preparing for this day. Carl was never willing to surrender exclusive control of one of the files to any lawyer, and that meant we were intimately involved in every situation. I'd had to conduct countless hours of research and, with Carl, attend many luncheon meetings with

Don Fiske to go over the details and prepare for court. The preparations involved as much work as a lengthy, complicated trial.

All along, I was uncertain as to whether Carl had any chance of winning. Clause 21 of the NHL's standard player's contract stipulated that the entire agreement was embodied in the contract and there could be no side agreements unless they, too, were written in the contract. Carl's contract clearly showed the effective date as December 26. The verbal agreement he understood that he had with Imlach was not documented anywhere.

Fortunately, we didn't have to wait long for a decision. On January 8, the judgment was handed down, and it was not favourable for Carl. Punch and Carl had given vastly opposing accounts of what had been said in the meeting in Imlach's office, so the judge based his decision on Clause 21. "In my view the Plaintiff is bound by the contract and Clause 21 does not permit the introduction of oral evidence as to any alleged agreement," he wrote. "The Plaintiff, if he felt at the time he executed the contract it did not reflect the true agreement, ought to have brought it up then and sought to have the contract amended."

He went on to say: "If I was of the view that there had been an alleged oral agreement, I would have seriously considered allowing the rectification of the contract as of that date. However, I am not satisfied on the evidence that the Plaintiff… has proved the alleged oral agreement so as to entitle him to rectification of the contract and damages." The action was dismissed with costs, meaning Carl was on the hook for the Leafs' legal bills.

Personally, I never doubted that Carl's understanding of what transpired in the meeting was correct. I'd never known Carl to be as resolute or definite about anything as he was with his recollection of the handshake and Imlach's words to him that day.

Although the conflicts between Carl and Punch had a very long history, I was with Carl on a grey, damp afternoon — December 1, 1987 — when we first learned that Imlach had died. We were relaxing together that afternoon in a bar when the news came over the television. Carl was immediately overcome with emotion and began to weep inconsolably. He went to the washroom to try to compose himself, but on returning to our table, immediately broke down again. A number of patrons in the bar, realizing that Carl was present, approached us, but Carl was unable to look at any of them or even to speak. He kept his head down and sobbed. I quietly and politely asked people to leave him alone. He took the news of Imlach's passing extremely hard indeed. I feel that Imlach's death was akin to the loss of his father for Carl — it left so many unresolved issues.

***

The costs of the legal action had been assessed against Carl, and it was a financial stretch for us to pay. Eventually, the Leafs sued Carl for the money. The plaintiff suing him was "The Toronto Maple Leaf Hockey Club." Richard Sankey was a lawyer with a brilliant mind — though he enjoyed his drink and hadn't paid his dues to the Law Society of Upper Canada. He'd been introduced to us by a mutual friend and had taken to hanging around our building with us. Richard had terrific insights and was very helpful, especially to me, giving me guidance about what forms needed to be filled out, how to file documents with courts, and so on. Well, Richard looked at the legal papers that had been served on Carl and immediately asked us, "What's this Toronto Maple Leaf Hockey Club?" He asked me if I'd checked it out. I hadn't, but I knew immediately where he was headed with the question. I searched the name at the Ontario Ministry of Consumer and Commercial Relations and found that no such business was registered. We asked the courts to dismiss the action because the Toronto Maple Leaf Hockey Club, not being a legal entity, could not bring an action. Immediately the Leafs' lawyers were scrambling to amend their documents; meanwhile, we had continued to investigate the matter and we filed papers to register the Toronto Maple Leaf Hockey Club name ourselves.

I obtained the required search showing that the name was not registered. Carl filed forms for a sole proprietorship under the name, and had no problem doing so. Next, I completed the forms to incorporate the company with Carl Brewer as president and sole shareholder. When Carl first took the papers to the ministry, they told him he couldn't register the name. Carl persisted, and they suggested that we return in two weeks because they would have to conduct a more in-depth search of the archives. We did return, and they relented, telling us we had been correct. The documents were registered. On July 25, 1983, Carl became the owner of the Toronto Maple Leaf Hockey Club Ltd., at least on paper.

We kept this quiet for several months. One afternoon we were at the Toronto Press Club having drinks with Rick Fraser, then a sports columnist for the *Toronto Star*. Carl and Rick went way back to Toronto Toros days and were good friends. For some reason, Carl decided that afternoon to let Rick in on our story. At first, Rick wouldn't believe that Carl was serious and, thinking Carl might have had one too many vodka and cokes, took me aside to check the story out. When I assured Rick that it was absolutely true, he got very excited and said he wanted to break the story. The *Star* did its own due diligence and decided to run with the story. As Carl remembered it: "Surprise! On Friday, November 11, 1983, headlines in the *Toronto Star* read, 'Guess Who Owns the Toronto Maple Hockey Club Ltd.?' The story also made the CBC National News! Briefly, I crawled into a hole, more embarrassed than pleased."

Maple Leaf Gardens, having already become aware of Carl's incorporation, had quietly filed an objection with the Ministry of Consumer and Commercial Relations on October 12, 1983. "Maple Leaf Gardens Limited was incorporated by Letters Patent on February 24, 1931, amalgamated with Hamilton Tiger-Cat Football Club Limited on May 31, 1980, and thereafter continued under the corporate name Maple Leaf Gardens Limited," they alleged. "'The Toronto Maple Leaf Hockey Club' is an unincorporated association of professional athletes which has carried on business as a division of Maple Leaf Gardens Limited since on or about February 24, 1931." Letters were exchanged for several months. We paid Richard's Law Society dues so that he could represent Carl in the dispute.

Richard helped me compose the first letter from Carl in response to MLG's objection. "There is no violation of Section 9 as alleged by Maple Leaf Gardens Limited," we stated. "There is no other corporation, trust, association, partnership, sole proprietorship, or individual with a name which is the same or similar to [Carl's corporation]." We stated that MLG's assertion that the Toronto Maple Leaf Hockey Club was an incorporated association of professional athletes was

a fiction. There is in fact no association or club to which the individual team members belong and which identifies itself as Toronto Maple Leaf Hockey Club.…

Moreover, to state that this association is a division of Maple Leaf Gardens is totally incorrect. It is simply impossible legally for an unincorporated association to act as a division of a limited company. Indeed, an inquiry made at the chartered accounting firm of Thorne Riddell, the

*accountants for Maple Leaf Gardens, Limited, revealed
that the Toronto Maple Leaf Hockey Club does not exist
as a separate entity apart from Maple Leaf Gardens for accounting purposes.*

In conclusion, we asked the ministry to conclude that there had been
no violation of Section 9 of the legislation. The letter was signed: Carl
Brewer and his solicitor, Richard V. Sankey.

Eventually, we received notice of a hearing scheduled for May 11, 1984,
at the offices of the ministry. With Richard now in good standing with the
Law Society, Carl felt he had good representation. On the afternoon of the
10th, we met with Richard and he laid out his intended defense of Carl's
position. He was citing case law and comparative situations eloquently and
convincingly. We were enthralled by his conviction and knowledge. He certainly seemed up to the task. The next morning, Carl went to his house to
pick him up early — at seven-thirty, so we could take him to breakfast and
make sure that he didn't start drinking. Well, surprise, when Carl picked
him up, he told us he had been up all night and it didn't take us long to
figure out what he'd been doing.

We were concerned as we assembled in a boardroom at the ministry.
"It was interesting," Carl said, "not because the functionary was capable of
doing anything interesting, but rather because of the case history of Maple
Leaf Gardens that their lawyers presented." It was all quite fascinating and
interesting. Our legal representative, regrettably, seemed more in awe of
what he was learning and was enthusiastically complimentary to the Leafs'
lawyers. He seemed to have forgotten everything he had known so well the
day before. In the end, the ministry ruled that Carl could not keep the corporate name of Toronto Maple Leaf Hockey Club Ltd. The reason had little
to do with the evidence at the hearing; in the relatively recent past, the
ministry had adopted a new regulation: if a name had ever previously been
in existence, even though it may have been deregistered or the registration
had lapsed, should someone else incorporate the same name and the original owner objected, the name would revert to the original owner. We
learned in the course of the hearing that, back in 1946, Conn Smythe had
deregistered the name Toronto Maple Leaf Hockey Club and replaced it
with Maple Leaf Gardens Ltd. Carl's incorporation therefore became
simply a numbered company.

Carl was disgusted by the attitude one of the Leaf lawyers had shown him. "Arthur Gans, the small-minded lawyer... was more intent on belittling me than he was in presenting the law. Lawyers have so little appreciation for the largesse that I have bestowed on their monthly billings. Gans would have been better served by offering his sincere thanks to me." Sometime later, in connection with another unrelated matter, lawyers for the Leafs inadvertently sent a copy of their legal bill to our lawyer, Allan Dick. The papers showed that the Leafs had incurred legal costs of approximately $250,000. Carl often shook his head and wondered why they simply hadn't bought him out. On a lighter note, Carl joked, "I bought the front page of the *Toronto Star* for $320!"

THE NHL'S KANGAROO COURT

*"The NHL's reserve system was used to restrict the move-
ment of players and tied them to indentured servitude for
all of their hockey-playing lives."*

At the same time that Carl was stressing about the salary shortfall with the
Toronto Maple Leafs, he was also keeping a keen eye on his contract, in particular the infamous Clause 18, formerly known as the reserve clause.
Ironically, this was the same passage Carl had run up against in 1966, when
he sought to be reinstated as an amateur, and which the California Seals
had hoped to test in their aborted attempt to sign Carl in 1967. The passage
had been modified somewhat to avoid U.S. restraint-of-trade laws, but the
essence was the same: a player was not free to sign with a new team after he
had fulfilled his contract. "True free agency has always been near and dear
to my heart," Carl wrote. "The NHL's reserve system was used to restrict the
movement of players and tied them to indentured servitude for all of their
hockey-playing lives."

Under Clause 18, a team had until August 10 of the final year of a
player's contract to offer him a termination contract, upon completion of
which the player would be a free agent. Or, if the player had 50 games of
pensionable service in his final year, the team had until September 10 to
offer him a new standard player's contract that included another Clause 18.
If the club did not offer either of these, the player could either elect to become a free agent or request an option contract before September 10 of the
final year. If the player requested an option contract, the team was obliged
to give him one by the 25th.

In Carl's case, neither party had taken any of these actions. As training camp began in the fall of 1980 and Carl was not invited, he became increasingly determined to do something about his status. In November, Carl and his lawyer, Don Fiske, met with Alan Eagleson to discuss the matter. According to Carl, Eagleson looked at the contract, tossed it on the table and said to Carl, "Yeah, you've got 'em," then advised him to wait until the end of the hockey season and collect his money. Carl didn't like that advice; he still wanted to play hockey, so he felt he needed to act more promptly and make his position known to the Leafs. It was our view that Carl's situation was covered by subsection (d) of Clause 18, which said that if the team didn't offer either of the two contracts, and the player didn't request an option contract, then the parties were deemed to have entered into a new standard player's contract — including another Clause 18 — for the following season, with the same terms and conditions as the previous deal with the exception of salary. Because of the reserve clause, Carl and the Leafs were bound together for a string of one-year contracts that would continue indefinitely until one side or the other made a move.

On November 27, Don Fiske wrote to Harold Ballard: "My client advises me that he has no record of receiving any applicable notice under Clause 18 (a) of the Standard Player's Contract, nor has he complied with conditions under 18 (c). Thus it is our position that 18 (d) becomes operative in this situation." He concluded, "My client advises me that he has been prepared to meet the obligations under the terms of the contract dated December 26, 1979, and has been prepared since the season commenced." The reply from Ross McGregor of the law firm Miller Thompson Sedgewick was dismissive: "Quite simply, our client takes the position that Section 18 (d) of the subject Standard Player's Contract is not operative under the circumstances and the Toronto Maple Leaf Hockey Club has no outstanding obligations to your client."

The collective bargaining agreement in effect at the time called for a grievance such as Carl's to be referred to the president of the NHL for arbitration. Carl was anxious to move forward, so on February 26, 1981, Fiske wrote to John Ziegler to request a hearing. A flurry of correspondence followed, as the submissions of both Carl and the Leafs were exchanged and various dates were proposed for a hearing. In the fall, the Leafs requested an indefinite delay because Punch Imlach had fallen ill. In the meantime, the 1980–81 season had come and gone, as had the deadlines under Clause 18. As far as we were concerned, it amounted to one more year that the Leafs had breached their contractual obligations to Carl, and the damages were mounting. On September 17, 1981, we learned from player agent Bill Watters that Carl's name was on the Leafs' reserve list. That meant the Toronto Maple Leafs still considered themselves the owners of Carl's NHL playing rights, and it supported our belief that the team was obligated to him.

In spite of his request for arbitration, Carl continued to make it known that he considered himself under contract and was ready, willing and able to play hockey. He scribbled letters to Harold Ballard that I typed for him. On March 8, 1982, he wrote:

Dear Harold:

It is so difficult for so many of us to watch the hapless inconsistencies of the "new" Leafs. Obviously their immaturity has been a detriment to the emblem.

As in my previously stated queries to you, my services are available to you for the purposes of stabilizing a young defense. And, in addition, as previously stated, it is unfortunate that you are so unwilling to avail yourself of this opportunity even though I am still under contract to you and wish to honour that contract.

While you are considering my aspirations, perhaps you would care to get your bookkeeping up to date by forwarding to me my delinquent paycheques.

On May 31, 1981, he again wrote to Ballard:

My Dear Harold:

With the draft meetings just completed, Leafs should be looking forward, as usual, to a successful season.

Don't delude yourself, Harold, with outworn concepts. The "youth movement" has failed.

My hope still prevails. A superbly conditioned athlete to stabilize a young team — just the right ingredient.

Each day, I wait in anxious anticipation for the mail-man in hopes that, this time around, more sensible heads will prevail and I will justly be invited to training camp.

Yours in hope,
Carl Brewer

Ballard did not reply to either of these.

Meanwhile, in an attempt to learn everything we could about Carl's contractual situation, I spent countless hours over a period of months reading the collective bargaining agreement (CBA), looking up case histories in libraries and finding out whatever I could about arbitration and contract law. I wrote letters for Carl and organized our mounting evidence and data. Carl set up frequent meetings for us with player agents, lawyers and anyone else he thought might be able to shed some light on the vagaries of our concerns. We seemed to spend most of our waking hours discussing these issues — among ourselves and others — trying to decide what steps to take.

We were absolutely astounded by what we learned from our research. Carl had always been aware of the injustices the players had suffered, but it was only now that we realized how extensive they were. For example, the CBA stipulated that grievances such as Carl's had to be referred to the president of the league as sole arbiter. If either side wished to appeal, their recourse was the NHL's board of governors. Imagine a worker at General Motors, a member of the Canadian Auto Workers union, having his disputes adjudicated by the president of GM! That Eagleson — who negotiated the CBA in his role as the NHLPA's executive director — had allowed players to be put in such an unfair and ridiculous situation particularly angered Carl. It was a clear-cut example of how Eagleson had sold the players out time and again, something Carl had suspected for years. Eagleson's coziness with the league establishment, particularly John Ziegler and Chicago owner Bill Wirtz, was a growing source of discomfort and agitation for Carl.

During the first part of 1982, dates for the hearing were set and cancelled for various reasons. Carl grew increasingly frustrated with the delays, but sometimes they were on account of our inability to find suitable counsel. We had parted company with Don Fiske and, to avoid incurring legal costs, continued to research and study the issues ourselves. Several lawyers had input into our case. Tim Danson was on the case briefly, until he changed a date without advising Carl, who fired him. Bill Sasso was helpful to us, but Carl felt that Ziegler was taking advantage of him by arbitrarily changing dates on more than one occasion, so, feeling that a change was in order, he dismissed Bill.

On July 7, 1982, Ziegler informed both sides that he intended to convene a hearing on the 21st. Carl advised Ziegler that he would not be available on that date, as we were in the process of engaging new counsel. Carl learned after the fact that Ziegler went ahead and arranged the hearing in his absence, for the purpose of taking evidence from Punch Imlach. We were alarmed and annoyed that Carl was not represented and had no one to cross-examine Imlach. We already had serious doubts about the impartiality of the process. Eagleson and Ziegler both said that Greg Britz, who was employed by the NHLPA, had been in attendance to represent Carl. However, Carl never agreed to have Britz represent him and had always made it known that he would have his own legal adviser. Years later, thanks to the U.S. criminal indictment of Alan Eagleson, we discovered just how meaningless Britz's representation had been that day: he had only four years of legal experience, and that had been more than a decade before. Furthermore, Britz "had little or no background or legal training or experience in arbitration matters."

By this time, Carl had hired a friend of his, Michael Gordon, a labour lawyer with the firm Beard Winter Gordon. Michael focused solely on the question of the jurisdiction of the arbitration process. Before we went any further with arbitration, Gordon wanted Ziegler to rule on the issue — was he a statutory arbitrator, in which case the process came under the Ontario Labour Relations Act, or a consensual arbitrator, in which case it came under the Arbitrations Act of Ontario? Michael found the lack of establishment of jurisdiction so inappropriate that he met to discuss the matter informally with a friend and colleague: George Adams, who, at the time, was chair of the Ontario Labour Relations Board. Michael reported to us that, at the end of their conversation, Adams told him he'd love to have the matter show up on his desk. This wasn't the only time Adams' name would be significant to us.

Meanwhile, the 1981–82 season had concluded. On September 7, 1982, three days before the deadline for filing, I hand-delivered a letter to Harold Ballard on Carl's behalf. In part, it read:

I wish to notify you of my wish to sign a Player's Option Contract.... It is my further understanding that the option contract shall be on the same terms and conditions as my original contract and that it shall be for one additional season only and that as of June 1, 1983, I shall be a free agent without any further obligation to provide services under this contract.

When I returned to the Toronto Maple Leaf Hockey Club in December of 1979, it was my ardent wish and intention to remain in the employ of the club for a period of four or five years. However, time passes on. I am not getting any younger and it is apparent now that you have no interest in my services.

Once again, there was no response from the Leafs.

John Ziegler set a new date of September 30, 1982, to "reconvene" the arbitration of Carl's contract dispute. Michael Gordon represented Carl and continued to pressure Ziegler to make a determination about jurisdiction. He made reference to the Dale McCourt case — one that Carl had followed intently in the newspapers when it played out back in 1978 — in which it was determined that there was a valid agreement negotiated between the NHL and the NHLPA and, therefore, the National Labour Relations Board in the United States had jurisdiction. Gordon argued that it followed that the process would, in Ontario, come under the auspices of the Ontario Labour Relations Act and the arbitrator's decision could be filed with the office of the registrar of the Supreme Court. He further argued that the Arbitrations Act of Ontario did not apply. Ziegler, however, continued to refuse to deal with this issue, nor would he agree to stand aside.

We continued to gather more evidence in support of Carl's position. One day, as I looked over a copy of one of Carl's pay slips from Maple Leaf Gardens, it occurred to me that the team had deducted unemployment insurance premiums from his salary. Therefore, if he had been terminated by his employer, as the Leafs tried to claim, he ought to be eligible to collect unemployment insurance. At no time, however, had Maple Leaf Gardens issued Carl a record of employment — a form that would confirm that his employment had been terminated, as the team now alleged, and which employers were required by law to issue within five days after the last day worked.

I prepared all the relevant documentation and we eventually appeared before a tribunal at the Toronto offices of the Unemployment Insurance Commission. At the end of the meeting, the members of the tribunal complimented me on my presentation and on the material put before them. They were keenly interested in Carl's situation and tremendously sympathetic. After deliberating for several weeks, they came back to us with their decision. They informed us that they felt that, if they granted the benefits to Carl, it would jeopardize his continuing entitlements under what appeared to them to be a legally binding contract between Carl and Maple Leaf Gardens.

But Carl and I were losing faith in the arbitration proceedings altogether. Carl began to describe the process, aptly, as a "kangaroo court." We had parted company with Michael Gordon because we couldn't afford his fees. Encouraged by Richard Sankey, who had become a rather permanent fixture in our lives, Carl agreed that we ought to abandon arbitration and ask the Ontario courts to assume jurisdiction of the complaint.

There were numerous grounds for taking this route. We believed, first of all, that it was a violation of the laws of natural justice and of the Canadian Charter of Rights and Freedoms for John Ziegler to be the arbitrator. Secondly, Sankey was adamant that this was really not a question of interpretation of a contract, as the Leafs never denied entering into the contract; he saw this as a matter of collecting monies owed under a contract that had been breached. Finally, he felt this was a matter for the courts because Ziegler, although asked several times to do so, had refused to make a determination about his jurisdiction under Ontario law.

Richard assured us that we could proceed ourselves without legal representation. He guided me through the preparation of all the relevant documents, and on July 29, 1983, I filed an action in the Supreme Court of Ontario for arrears of salary for 1980–81, 1981–82, 1982–83 and 1983–84 in the amount of $507,250. A court date was set for October 17.

Not long afterward, Carl received a letter from John Ziegler, scheduling another date for the continuation of the arbitration: October 18 — the day after our scheduled court appearance.

On September 16, Carl responded with a strongly worded letter that Richard Sankey helped me compose. It read in part:

One could accept this newly appointed hearing date of October 18, 1983, as a coincidence, but the sudden interest on your part to schedule a hearing one day after my motion does strain credulity in so much as:

> *(i) you have not actively pursued this matter for almost a year;*
>
> *(ii) you have been informed of my recent lawsuit... and you appear to be coordinating your plans to support the Leaf defense.*

All of the foregoing, I consider to be totally pertinent.

My position has been, and will continue to be, consistent. Until you establish to any relevant person's satisfaction (that is, other than your own), that:

> *(i) you have any legal authority to adjudicate the grievance between myself and the Toronto Maple Leaf Hockey Club; and*
>
> *(ii) even if it should be determined that the arbitration process as outlined in the NHL–NHLPA Collective Bargaining Agreement is properly constituted legally, and that you, Mr. Ziegler, have complete independence from the Toronto Maple Leaf Hockey Club — a member of a league of which you are president,*

for me to submit myself to any further proceedings under your aegis might appear to prejudice my legal rights under the Judicature Act and the Rules of Practice of the Province of Ontario and the courts constituted thereof.

I do not intend to be present at any of your future hearings until all matters have been settled by the courts of Ontario...

On October 17, we appeared before Mr. Justice Robert Reid. Carl represented himself; I sat beside him to prompt him. Carl requested that, because of his serious apprehension of bias on the part of John Ziegler, the courts assume jurisdiction over the matter. The proceedings were tense; Carl was nervous and the judge chastised him for being there without a lawyer, even though it is any citizen's right to do so. In the end, the judge took the path of least resistance and concluded that there was a valid collectively bargained agreement in existence and Carl would have to live with it. A court of law was apparently not the forum in which to deliberate over conflicts of interest and abuses of the laws of natural justice. Later, I would find it interesting to see Mr. Justice Reid's name listed in *The Globe and Mail* among the guests at one of Alan Eagleson's social functions.

In the spring of 1984, another player, Vaclav Nedomansky, was suing Alan Eagleson over his contract with the Detroit Red Wings. "Big Ned" had been a perennial scoring champion in his native Czechoslovakia before escaping to the West in 1974. He joined the Toros the year after Carl played there, and in 1977 became one of the few players ever to be traded between the WHA and the NHL. In 1979, Eagleson's partner at the time, Bill Watters, negotiated an attractive, guaranteed contract for him. Watters and Ted Lindsay, Detroit's GM, agreed to the terms in principle, then Watters handed the matter over to Eagleson, who was to get the deal signed by Detroit's front office.

For whatever reason, the Red Wings never signed the deal. The contract that both sides did eventually sign was not as lucrative. The case, which was being heard by Mr. Justice Marvin Catzman of the Supreme Court of Ontario, was of considerable interest to Carl and me, and I sat through most of the trial. I came to know Ned and his wife, Vera, and felt a lot of empathy for them.

This suit offered up the first indication that Eagleson had been lending out the monies he was supposed to be managing for his clients, like Nedomansky, to family and close friends. One such loan was made from Nedomansky's account to Nanjill, a company owned by Eagleson family members — "Nan" for his wife, Nancy, and "Jill" for his daughter. Also, Russ Conway reported that *Toronto Sun* columnist George Gross received an interest-free loan of $10,000 from Nedomansky's funds. These were early hints of a continuing pattern of conflicts and professional indiscretions in the use of other people's money over which Eagleson had control.

High-profile Toronto lawyer — and future Supreme Court of Canada justice — John Sopinka represented his friend Eagleson. I remember watching Eagleson in the witness box during this trial and thought his performance was incredible: he was cocky, arrogant, brash — and he spoke out of both sides of his mouth, contradicting himself. Years later, of course, I would get to see him in court again.

Regrettably, Nedomansky's suit was dismissed, and he was ordered to pay Eagleson's agent fees going back many years. He didn't have to pay Eagleson's legal costs, but his own bills had mounted, causing him financial hardship. Sadly, Ned and Vera's marriage didn't survive, either.

There were several problems with Big Ned's case. His lawyer, Mort Greenglass, was experiencing personal problems at the time. Also, Bill Watters, who had handled the actual negotiations, had parted company with Eagleson and was bound by a confidentiality agreement —a gag order. As a result, Watters' testimony was less than candid, probably because of concerns about the confidentiality agreement. Furthermore, Greenglass decided not to call Ted Lindsay as a witness. He was concerned that Lindsay might not stand up very well under cross-examination. Greenglass and his junior — our friend Allan Dick — disagreed on that point. Allan felt strongly that they needed Lindsay to testify that, had the contract been placed on his desk, he would have signed it. Allan said that he didn't feel confident in pressing the point, however, because he was just 48 hours out of law school at the time.

Nedomansky, using another law firm, appealed his case. The young lawyer who first worked on this file went on to become Dean of Law at Queen's University. Years later, she told Stevie Cameron that when she read the file, she found it full of errors in handling and procedure; she felt strongly that the case for appeal was very strong and that victory was almost assured. She was stunned when a senior lawyer with the firm told her the matter had been settled. When she expressed her shock and argued that there was no way the matter should be settled, she was told in no uncertain terms to leave it alone. She suspected improper interference in this case and was upset to the point that she left the law firm on principle. The lawyer who told her to drop the appeal was Peter Atkinson, indicted in the United States in 2005 in connection with fraud allegations against Conrad Black and Hollinger International.

For Carl and me, Nedomansky's case yielded a bright spot. We finally found a lawyer who was thoroughly versed in the hockey matters that we had been struggling with for years. Finding the right lawyer had long been a problem for us. The business practices of the NHL were so convoluted that lawyers had trouble unravelling the details or even getting information. As an example, as we were trying to prepare for Carl's arbitration, we asked for information about previously arbitrated cases involving other players with similar grievances. We were told there were no precedents to be had and that the results of arbitration hearings were confidential. There was also the challenge involved with paying an experienced lawyer's fees. Finally, we met our man in Allan Dick.

At first, Mort Greenglass had been representing us, as he had done for Vaclav, and some progress was being made, which encouraged us. Before long, however, the road ahead of us shaped up to be a long one, and we were uncertain as to how long we'd be able to go on paying Greenglass's fees. At this point, I went to lunch one day with Allan, who mentioned that he was leaving Greenglass and Associates and moving to the law firm of Macaulay, Chusid. I knew immediately that our file would go with Allan. We were both tremendously impressed with his brilliance, wisdom, diplomacy, and especially his ability to recommend the most efficient and least costly avenues for us to take. We worked closely with Allan, and preparations began for the final arbitration hearing before John Ziegler, which was now our only option, since we had exhausted the possibility that the courts would take the matter on.

***

I knew that Carl had something serious on his mind on May 25, 1985, when he took me by the arm and asked me to go with him for a drink. We went to the little restaurant adjacent to our building, Ricky and Ricardo's. After the half-litre of white wine was poured, Carl looked at me intently and said, "I'm leaving." At first I didn't know what he meant. Seeing the shocked look on my face, he immediately reached for my hand and exclaimed: "NO, no, no, no, God, no — I'm leaving my marriage. This is it!" He went on to say: "You've been so incredibly gracious; you've never pressured me; you've always said, 'Carl, do what you have to do.'" Because we had spent most of our time together for the past five years, I didn't feel that I'd been missing out on much, and I was taken aback by his sudden conviction and decisiveness. He told me he was going to deal with it and then get out of town for a few days, but that he'd be in touch shortly. Then he told me he'd left a note for me. After we finished our wine and he left, I went to find my note. It read:

Susan:

Your friendship is special,
Your loyalty unrelenting,
Your strength awesome,
Your brilliance incomparable.
Thank you.

   Love,
   Carl

In July of that year, we took a welcome break from the intensity of Carl's legal battles and travelled overseas together for the first time. It would be the first of many such journeys together. On this trip we travelled by train, the Transalpine Express, from Zurich, Switzerland, to Innsbruck, Austria, through some of the most magnificent scenery in the world. We visited with Carl's old friends, Walter and Erma Rothauer, from the days when he played summer hockey in Innsbruck to keep in playing shape.

In spite of this pleasant break, Carl's contract battles were never far from our minds. Allan Dick had done a superb job of getting things on track for us, and he arranged for the arbitration proceedings to continue in Toronto on July 17, 1986, an overcast, rainy day. It was, it seemed to Carl and me, to Allan's credit that the date had not been changed; it had been the norm for this to happen, and just the day before, when Allan interrupted our phone conversation to take a call from John Ziegler, I instantly feared there would be yet another postponement. Not this time, however.

Perhaps the most positive development in this six-year saga occurred early in the week when, for the very first time, the Leafs made an offer to settle. The sum was quickly increased, from $30,000 to $40,000. Allan assessed the offer from all angles and in his usual cool, reasoned manner. He felt we were dealing from a position of strength and advised us to refuse the offer. "I've spent the whole weekend on this case," he reminded us, "and I don't think any less of it now than I ever have."

Carl drove me down to the Westin Hotel at Richmond Street and University Avenue just before one o'clock to meet Allan Dick. Carl had decided not to attend the hearing; he was far too emotionally involved, too angry and frustrated, to be present. Art Gans had also, on many previous occasions, attacked Carl personally and unrelentingly, and Carl didn't want to listen to his abuse. I would act as Carl's eyes and ears. I knew that it would be no less difficult for Carl not to be present, to have to sit and wait throughout the afternoon and fret about what was transpiring.

When I entered the hotel, Allan was huddled in earnest discussion with Greg Britz, the NHL Players' Association's outside legal counsel. They both rose to acknowledge me, and I encouraged them to carry on and not allow me to interrupt. Gans arrived shortly afterward, and we waited by the elevators for Britz to find out which room Ziegler was in. As we waited, Gans queried Allan about Britz, saying, "Some nice free ride he's on," and asking, "Who *is* he — another Eagleson flunky?" Allan looked at me and we laughed. Gans was certainly on the right track, as we both knew. Back in October 1981, during a meeting at his office, Bill Watters had told Carl and me that Britz had been fired by American Airlines for giving too many free passes to Eagleson. In turn, Eagleson rewarded him by making him outside legal counsel for the NHLPA. In 1994, Britz's situation was confirmed when it was included among the charges laid by the U.S. Department of Justice against Alan Eagleson. As the indictment read:

> *From in or about 1975 through 1991, Eagleson did obtain money and property from the NHLPA and its members by means of fraud and by causing the payment of fees, benefits and expenses to Gregory Britz as a payback for years of friendship and free airline travel [on American Airlines] and while knowing that Britz was not performing the duties and responsibilities for which he was allegedly retained.*

Britz had been paid between $75 and $200 an hour, plus expenses, and he also received pension benefits and medical insurance, among other perks, paid for in full by the NHLPA in return for basically nothing.

We entered Ziegler's room, and he rose to greet us in a terse, businesslike manner. The court reporter was already set up. After we got enough seats organized and removed the lamps from the side tables so that Allan Dick and Arthur Gans had some work space, Ziegler commenced the hearing by explaining the order of the proceedings. First, Allan would present his facts and argument, followed by Britz, then Gans, and finally Allan would conclude.

There was a pause before Allan began to speak. I was nervous — my stomach in knots, my mind frantic with random thoughts. When Allan did speak, it was slowly and quietly — much lower than his norm — but he knew exactly what he was doing. Very quickly, his confidence put me at ease. He began by explaining that there were two issues he would address: jurisdiction, and the facts, which Allan said "are hard to dispute."

With respect to jurisdiction, Allan explained clearly that his client had instituted proceedings to have the arbitrator interpret Clause 18 of the NHL's standard player's contract, to apply that section to Carl and to order payment under the contract, plus interest. "I submit that, as arbitrator, your sole function is to interpret, apply and rule on Clause 18, and further, that you can do no more," Allan continued. He said that the law was very clear about Ziegler's function: to rule on the player's rights under the contract. Throughout his statement, Allan spoke deliberately and with awesome authority, pausing for effect after each point, while Ziegler feverishly took notes.

Next, Allan turned his attention to the facts. "I submit that you should find two things: one, that there was a violation of the standard player's contract… and two, that you should rule on the particular manner of remedying the violation."

Ziegler interrupted to ask, "So, are you saying that Mr. Brewer has three years due to him under the contract — '80–81, '81–82 and '82–83?"

"We submit that the relationship continued," Allan replied.

"So, if I understand you correctly," Ziegler pressed on, "you don't think that Carl Brewer's request for an option year is tantamount to his termination of the agreement?"

Allan replied that Brewer had taken a step that he was entitled to take, the Leafs had ignored him, and then they further breached their responsibilities by not tendering an option contract, as was clearly their obligation. Allan continued that the interpretation of Clause 18 (d) calls for a series of one–year contracts from 1980–81 onward, each one including another Clause 18. "I'm suggesting this is part of the breach and the damages which you will have to consider," Allan told Ziegler. He summarized this point by adding, "A breach has occurred and you are required to be the mechanism for repairing the said breach."

Throughout his presentation, I was awestruck by how Allan left no angle to any argument open for attack or an escape. He concluded his facts and argument most impressively.

Greg Britz, representing the NHLPA, followed and made a general, benign statement that did nothing to influence Carl's case one way or the other. He suggested that the terms of the contract should "dictate." He mentioned also that the NHLPA's position was that the Leafs had maintained a proprietary interest in Brewer by keeping him on their reserve list, indicating some action on the team's part to protect Carl's playing rights.

All the while, I was thinking about Carl, wishing there were some way of letting him know that things were going well. I was not looking forward to the arrogance or the dramatics of Arthur Gans. His disparaging remarks about Carl had the ability to stir up my emotions as well as Carl's.

When Gans began to speak, half of my mind was elsewhere. He tried to discredit Allan at one point, only to have Ziegler interject that Allan was correct in his premise. Ziegler said that the particular matter had been negotiated between the NHLPA and the league and, just as Allan had advised, he couldn't do anything to negate that agreement. Gans backed down quickly, blaming his junior, John Chapman, for not submitting the information correctly. I heard bits and pieces of Gans's assertions — "Brewer was laying in the woods… opportunist… found out about Clause 18 after the fact — almost fraud." (If Gans knew anything about Carl, he would have known that the reserve clause had been important to Carl for years.) But all through them my mind was drifting back, to July 15, 1976, when Carl and I sat in his car on a sideroad near Maple, Ontario. He was desperately upset and profoundly unhappy. Things had turned sour with his business dealings with Bob Thorndyke in Oshawa. "Grovel, that's what I do," he lamented. "I'm not treated with any dignity."

Then back to Gans yelling, "He doesn't deserve a nickel of interest.… He said he'd play for nothing." I flashed back to that July day in 1979, at the automobile auction, when Carl told me he was going to Germany — in part to prepare for the possibility of playing for the Leafs. I had always known so much about Carl intuitively over so many years, and when he told me this, I already knew. Carl was so discouraged at this time that he was barely holding himself together. But by the end of his stint in Germany, there was no doubt in his mind that he could still play in the NHL.

Gans ranted on about how the Leafs did Carl a favour by letting him play in 1979–80. My thoughts immediately went back to December 26, 1979 — Carl's first night back with the Leafs. I could not fathom the hostility and the ridicule from the members of the press. I knew how hard Carl had worked for this, how sincere he was, how much he needed it — financially *and* for his self-esteem. It was no joke to Carl. On January 10, 1980, over lunch, Carl said to me, "Sue, if I get a chance to play, the way I know I can play, then I want to make this work for five years."

As I listened to Gans pontificate, I was thinking about how Carl must be very weary of fighting all the time on so many fronts.

At the end of his argument, Gans asked Ziegler to rectify the contract. In a nutshell, he was saying, "If we have to live with this thing, at least allow us to turn back the clock so we can buy him out." When Ziegler asked Allan Dick if he would agree that the team should be allowed to buy out any contract awarded, Allan replied that he did not agree they should be allowed to go back and retroactively do anything.

During the course of his argument, Gans made several belittling remarks about hockey players in general. At one point, when trying to justify a "mistake" in the preparation of the contract, he said that it was important to remember that Imlach, just like the hockey players, was not a lawyer, not a businessman, not an educated person accustomed to crossing *t*'s and dotting *i*'s. Hockey players were entertainers — just interested in putting on a show, not doing paperwork, Gans said. Allan countered this remark by saying that, as a general manager, preparing contracts was Imlach's job, his responsibility, and something he was accustomed to doing and experienced at doing.

I reflected on how Gans's comments seemed to mirror Eagleson's attitude, and that of so many others who exploited the naïveté of the players for their own benefits.

After an emotionally and intellectually draining afternoon, it was time for Allan's final summation. I wondered how we would look at the end of the day. My mind flashed back to a little note about this case that Carl had passed to me in February 1981, in which he said, "Gawd, it's important!"

Allan countered each and every silly point raised by Gans. Allan told Ziegler that for the Leafs to try to suggest that Carl entered into a contract for any predetermined period of time was patently absurd — he was good enough to play indefinitely as long as he was of value. He reiterated that the Leafs did not cut Carl, and that Carl fulfilled a role for the balance of the 1979–80 season. With respect to Gans's suggestion that a newspaper article had stated that Carl had retired, Allan said that if the Leafs believed everything they read in the newspapers they'd have left town a long time ago. This drew a hearty laugh from everyone in the room.

Allan pointed out that a subsequent article by John Iaboni of the *Toronto Sun* refuted the earlier story, and he reminded Ziegler that he had a copy of it in the brief. Next, Allan asked why, if Leafs were so aware of this "retirement" article, nobody from the Gardens had picked up the phone and called his client to confirm or deny the story. He suggested it would have been reasonable for the Leafs to call Carl and, if he really wanted to retire, arrange to meet to execute the appropriate paperwork.

At the end of the hearing, John Ziegler looked at Allan and, with obvious sincerity, complimented him on his excellent submissions and argument. Ziegler explained that, with so much material before him, it would be impossible to hand down a decision the next day, but he promised to turn his attention to it immediately.

As we made our way down to the hotel lobby, Allan was optimistic that the Leafs could be pressured into offering a decent settlement, and he felt Ziegler was leaning towards some action that would reward Carl monetarily. He felt that Ziegler would have a hell of a time finding entirely in favour of the Toronto Maple Leafs. For my part, I couldn't think; my head was spinning. But it was obvious to me that Ziegler was impressed, and that Carl could not have had better or more supportive representation.

All the way back to the Danforth on the subway, I was in a trance, numb. I was overawed by Allan's efforts and emotionally exhausted. When I emerged from the subway at Chester station, Carl was standing there in the late-afternoon sun, thumbs hooked in his jeans pockets (he stood that way so often!), looking extremely pensive and worried, waiting for me. Carl was always aware of just how much pressure he put on my shoulders, and he was never insensitive to that. He knew this would have been a terribly exhausting day, mentally and emotionally, for me. I felt tremendously happy and relieved to see him. We went to dinner at Omonia, a nearby Greek restaurant that we frequented. Over a few drinks — which I appreciated as much as Carl, especially as my mind and body both began to relax — and a delicious dinner of roast lamb with Carl's favourite roasted potatoes, it was for once a real joy to be able to tell Carl just how well Allan had represented him. It was a joy for both of us to see this six-year battle finally in capable hands, and coming to some resolution — whatever that outcome might be. I was neither optimistic nor pessimistic, but I did know that, where this situation was concerned, Carl never looked better than he did this afternoon.

On October 31, 1986, John Ziegler released his decision. While he never did rule on the issue of jurisdiction, we were pleasantly surprised that he upheld the validity of the contract (which we believed was the only conclusion he could reach). Ironically, the case meant that Carl had been able to turn the restrictive reserve clause to his own advantage. Nonetheless, having become thoroughly cynical about the system, we were half expecting Ziegler to come up with some creative manoeuvre to deny Carl's claim. And although the decision was positive, there were still many disappointments.

First of all, Ziegler ruled that Carl would not receive the contracted amount of $125,000 and instead awarded him the league minimum — approximately $22,000 per season. Ziegler also decided arbitrarily that the Leafs would have terminated the contract for the second year by buying Carl out at one-third of the contract's value. So much for justice NHL style! We felt that this was cutting Carl's entitlement way too short. Allan Dick explained to me that Ziegler's finding, which was made without any evidence, essentially said that Toronto Maple Leaf management didn't understand how the standard player's contract worked; otherwise, they would have taken action to terminate it and reduce Carl's entitlement. In a sense, Ziegler was excusing the club for not knowing its rights and obligations in contract matters, and giving them a mulligan — a "do-over." What was worse was that the only recourse was to appeal Ziegler's decision to the Board of Governors of the NHL. We doubted that any other union leader would have allowed such unfairness for its members as Eagleson had negotiated for NHL players.

In computing the amount with interest to be awarded to Carl, errors of arithmetic were made, and the total reflected these. Allan Dick wrote to request a correction. However, with typical arrogance, Ziegler refused to correct the math — tough luck for us! The final award, in the amount of $42,363.86, was paid on August 27, 1987. This sum barely covered our legal expenses, let alone our other costs. It was a Pyrrhic victory at best. After taxes were deducted and approximately $6,000 transferred directly to Carl's RRSP, Carl was left with a cheque for $27,418 in back pay. We had had every reason to believe that, if his contract were upheld properly, his award ought to have been in the hundreds of thousands of dollars.

Then there was the most troubling aspect of the entire arbitration process. Incredibly, the final award — with the errors in arithmetic that Ziegler and Eagleson both refused to correct — matched exactly the amount that Allan had been offered prior to the hearing on July 17, 1986. At that time, when Allan had asked the Leafs' lawyer why he felt this was a reasonable settlement, he had replied, "Just trust me." It was as if Ziegler and the Leafs had decided the outcome of the case before we even went into the July hearing.

Of the ongoing battles between Brewer and Ballard, Carl remarked, "I guess I'm one for three," taking into account his unsuccessful suit to collect the salary he had been promised and the matter of the corporate name Toronto Maple Leaf Hockey Club Ltd. Asked by Rick Fraser why he spent all this time and money on these battles, Carl replied: "I have the same sense of humour Harold Ballard does. Harold's not the only one with a sense of humour." Then, when asked if his run-ins with the Leafs were through, Carl replied: "I'm not so sure. There are a couple of other things I want to check out. You'd better stay tuned for a while yet."

Now that the contract issue had been dealt with, there was another matter to address: that of the pension benefits owed to Carl because his contract with the Leafs had been upheld and extended. It seemed to us to be a "no-brainer" — Carl would get the requisite pension benefits, because he was clearly entitled to them under the NHL Pension Society's bylaws. However, Carl's dealings with the NHL and the Toronto Maple Leafs had never been straightforward, and this situation would prove to be no different.

What would be different was that this next battle ended up having a resounding impact on all of the players of Carl's era.

CHAPTER 9

THE PURSUIT OF
R. ALAN EAGLESON

For Alan Eagleson, there are only two types of people in this world: those who are with him and those who are against him. The latter are not on thin ice; they're swimming with their skates on like cement boots!

Carl knew he had upset Alan Eagleson when he received the following personal note, dated August 3, 1983.

After a great deal of thought, Nancy and I have decided to change the godparents of our daughter Jill. We consider godparents to be important and our daughter Jill in her seventeen years has not heard from you and your wife. For that reason, Nancy and I do not wish to impose on you further as godparents. We will ask another couple to replace you. Thank you for your co-operation.

Yours truly, Alan

Carl referred to it affectionately as his "Godfather letter." He thought it was hilarious, and I think it pleased him more than a little bit to know he had succeeded in getting under Al's skin ever so slightly! Carl enjoyed discussing the subject of whether one can actually "fire" a godparent with a number of acquaintances in the clergy. They were unanimous in replying that it is simply not possible.

"Obviously, Al was neither a friend nor a fan of mine," Carl said publicly at the time. "His personal bias came out in a letter."

The Pursuit of R. Alan Eagleson

Carl had first become acquainted with Alan Eagleson back in the early 1960s, while playing for the Toronto Maple Leafs. Carl had taken the unprecedented step of hiring Eagleson to negotiate a contract for him. The Leafs' general manager and coach, Punch Imlach, refused at first to negotiate with him. The two grew so close that Alan asked Carl to be godfather to the Eaglesons' daughter, Jill. When Eagleson ran for Parliament, as a Progressive Conservative, in the 1963 general election, Carl, along with Bob Baun and Bob Pulford, campaigned for him — even though their teammate, Red Kelly, was the Liberal incumbent in that riding. Kelly defeated Eagleson by 17,000 votes. A few months later, Eagleson ran in the provincial election and did win.

During the early days of his involvement with several of the Leaf players, Eagleson set up an investment group known as the Blue and White Group, after the Leafs' colours. Members included Baun, Pulford, Billy Harris and Carl, as well as several of Eagleson's business colleagues, including George Graham of Ostranders Jewellers and Herb Kearney of the Hearn Pontiac car dealership. Eagleson was quick to notice how much the businessmen enjoyed rubbing shoulders with the players, and he learned to use that to his own advantage for years to come. The Blue and White Group gave Eagleson his entrée into the world of professional hockey; his influence would quickly spread, and before long he would come to dominate all aspects of the sport.

Eagleson was always hard-nosed, brash, loud and confrontational. Canadian author Jack Batten was a classmate of Al's at the University of Toronto Law School. "I never knew anyone who swore as much and as innovatively as Al did!" Jack told me. What was worse, Carl used to say, was that Nancy Eagleson, Al's wife, used even saltier language — he said she could swear Al under the table!

Carl soon came to realize that enabling Alan Eagleson to ascend to his powerful position in the hockey world had been a terrible error in judgment. During his contract disputes with the Maple Leafs in the 1980s, the NHL Players' Association — Eagleson's creation — proved to be no help at all. Carl said, cynically, "I've always maintained that the Players' Association doesn't exist, and I feel sorry for the young players who think they have a union."

During the contract battles, Carl consulted several times with Alan Eagleson in his capacity as executive director of the NHLPA. Eagleson offered token support, but seemed unable to conceal his displeasure that Carl was challenging the system so doggedly. Early on, Carl understood Alan to say that the players' association would pay his legal fees in the arbitration case. Later, when Carl attempted to get this confirmed in writing, Eagleson replied: "Your interpretation of our meeting is quite incorrect. Any legal expenses incurred in this matter are your obligation." Eagleson offered to provide the services of the NHLPA's lawyer, Greg Britz, an American with dubious connections to Eagleson. In July 1982, when NHL President John Ziegler convened an arbitration hearing in spite of the fact that Carl and his lawyer couldn't attend, Carl complained about the injustice to Eagleson. In a letter dated August 3, 1982, Eagleson replied: "It is difficult for the NHLPA to continue to help you because of your attitude. The NHLPA did object to the commencement of the arbitration but Mr. Ziegler chose to proceed with Mr. Imlach's testimony. Mr. Britz examined Mr. Imlach in your absence and we attempted to protect your interests." Britz, however, was not Carl's lawyer, and he had little to offer in terms of experience or expertise. This really frustrated Carl, who always asked me to sit beside him whenever he called Eagleson so that I would be witness to the conversations.

***

By early 1982, the extent to which Carl's mind was preoccupied with concerns about Alan Eagleson had become apparent to me. Eagleson's activities, behaviour, and the multitudinous conflicts of interest, as Carl perceived them, were a topic of daily conversation; he routinely filled me in on the latest news or explained to me the ploys or misdeeds that Al was perpetrating. I could see the anger and agitation mounting within him as he contemplated these issues and became more and more consumed by them. Carl was keenly astute and tended to look at things from different angles than most people; it frustrated him when others couldn't — or wouldn't — see what was obvious to him. This was true in many areas, but especially where Eagleson was concerned. Players, journalists and the public at large seemed oblivious to what Carl was perceiving — things that, in his mind, were egregious conflicts of interest and indications of abuse and neglect of the players' rights.

Above all, I could see that Carl was haunted by a deep sense of responsibility for having helped create this "monster," Alan Eagleson. Eagleson had been front and centre in 1966, when he represented Carl in his high-profile effort to regain his amateur status so that he could play for Canada's National team. Eagleson became a household name as a result, giving him even more exposure to, and credibility among, hockey players and the public at large.

By the time Carl returned to the NHL in 1969, Eagleson was firmly ensconced as head of the NHLPA. He had systematically endeared himself to the players of the six established teams — he credited Ralph Backstrom with introducing him to the Montreal players and helping him get them on side. Ralph explained to me that he was the Habs player rep at the time and added: "I was somewhat helpful to him, but not entirely." He told me about management's reluctance to have anything to do with him. "I was at the Forum, where we were practising, and Eagleson was sitting in the stands — he was there all by himself in this huge building, so he was pretty obvious to everybody, sitting there. Toe Blake looked over at him and said, 'What the hell is he doing in here?' He knew [Eagleson] was trying to start the Players' Association, and coaches and management were really against it at the time. So Blake called a couple of security guys, and they grabbed Eagleson by each arm and escorted him out of the building. As he was leaving the building, he yelled at us, 'I'll meet you across the street at the bar.' So, after practice, we all high-tailed it over there and had a meeting with Al."

One might well wonder how Eagleson had managed to launch the NHLPA when the resistance by NHL owners had been so fierce in the past — for example, when Ted Lindsay tried to form an association in 1957. David Cruise and Allison Griffiths, in their book *Net Worth*, proffered the notion that Eagleson had been in the hip pocket of the owners from the start; otherwise he would not have succeeded. Considering that, in 1969, the owners agreed to take over the "full funding of the pension" in exchange for the players' giving up their representation on the pension board — and the owners ended up paying even less than they were previously supposed to contribute, while the players were left with no access to information about the business of the pension plan — this speculation gains traction. Bruce Dowbiggin suggested that the unspoken deal boiled down to this: Eagleson was to allow the owners to do whatever they wanted with the pension plan, while Eagleson would have unfettered control over international hockey revenues. In 1972, of course, Eagleson was involved in the first of many international hockey tournaments; we later learned just how lucrative these events turned out to be. "In 1967, when the NHL owners agreed to Alan Eagleson as 'union leader,' there must have been conditions attached," Carl said. "The NHLPA was a 'company union' from the beginning. Eagleson's accession to his throne was hailed by all hockeydom, especially the owners. Boy, did things run smoothly under his aegis — no labour unrest, no freedoms (i.e., free agency, no openness, no player insurrections) — only quiet submission, acquiescence. A dictatorship of one."

Eagleson progressively built a position of unbridled power and influence over every aspect of Canadian hockey — the NHLPA, international hockey, Hockey Canada (a quasi-governmental organization), while at the same time operating his personal law practice and his agency business, which represented not only players but management personnel as well. Carl soon began to think that Eagleson was much more about self-promotion and self-interest, while players' rights seemed to take a very low — or non-existent — priority for him.

In March of 1983, Carl asked me a very searching question: "Sue, am I crazy — is it really as bad as I'm suggesting? Or am I just way off base?" He asked it with such intensity and concern that I was taken aback. I didn't answer him immediately, other than to assure him he wasn't crazy. Later, Carl remembered, "I'm not exactly lacking in brain power, but I had to ask, 'Am I crazy — can he *really* be this bad?'" Meanwhile, I took some time to reflect on all of the things that Carl had spoken to me about over what was, by now, a period of many years. I knew this was very important to Carl and that my insights would mean a great deal to him. Over the next few days, I turned my attention to his question and made extensive notes that I entitled "Why Eagleson?" My notes became the first step toward developing a basis to investigate Carl's concerns.

My notes included references to the multitude of "hats" Eagleson wore. I noted the concerns about the NHL pension plan — the absence of accounting, the unavailability of records, the walls of secrecy surrounding the pension. NHLPA insurance was a source of interest and concern: we had, for a long time, heard stories that players were being short-changed and ripped off. Favourable results seemed to be obtained more readily for Eagleson's personal clients, while players who had not hired him as their agent were left high and dry. Al's clients were also the ones who found jobs with NHL clubs after their playing days ended. Where player-management relations were concerned, the NHL–NHLPA Collective Bargaining Agreement appeared to cede all the power to the owners. The arbitration process specified by the CBA was what Carl labelled a "kangaroo court." The president of the NHL was the appointed arbitrator for various grievances, and there was no independent appeal process. Other arbitrators were appointed by the NHL and were not neutral because they had ties to the owners.

There was no legal status for the NHLPA — it was accountable to no government or legislative jurisdiction. It was impossible to find any real benefits the association had won for the players, and Eagleson obviously had a fiduciary duty to the players to act in their best interests. Bill Watters, a former associate of Eagleson's who went on to open his own firm, Branada Sports, subsequently informed us that Eagleson cronies and family members often had lucrative deals to perform functions of questionable merit at international hockey events; invariably a large contingent of his buddies went along for the ride, paid for by the unsuspecting players — or the taxpayers of Canada, through Hockey Canada. (As for why Watters had split with Eagleson, Watters explained that when Eagleson asked him to be general manager of Team Canada, he found out his salary would be paid by Hockey Canada, and not Eagleson's sports management company, and there was no benefit to Watters for the extra duties.)

I further noted the allegations about ways in which Eagleson was benefiting from deals with the NHL. Years later, we heard rumours that his condo in Florida had been his reward for supporting the NHL–WHA merger. This was never proven in the investigations. There were suspicions circulating that he was getting kickbacks from the sale of advertising on the rink boards in the Canada Cup and other international hockey tournaments. We had been told about secret bank accounts in Zug — a particularly tax-friendly canton in Switzerland — and about his associates carrying bags of cash to Switzerland for Al after the Canada Cup tournaments. Eagleson's overhead was paid by the NHLPA, but information surfaced that it was being subsidized by Hockey Canada and others.

Eagleson's suspected ties to the NHL's inner circle had a human element. If Eagleson had been a bona fide union boss, looking after the interests of players, it is impossible to explain his invisibility when players like Larry Mickey were in trouble. Mickey had not been able to adjust to life after his hockey career came to an end; his marriage fell apart around the same time, and it was reported that he killed himself the day after he was served with divorce papers. The NHLPA had no programs to help retired players make the transition. There ought to have been career counselling, as well as counselling for drug and alcohol abuse.

Severely injured players were similarly hung out to dry. Jim Harrison, the former Boston Bruin and Toronto Maple Leaf, was playing for the Chicago Blackhawks in 1977–78 when he began to experience excruciating back pain. He quickly found himself ensnared in the web that the NHL and Eagleson's NHLPA had spun. At first, team doctors treated Harrison as if the injury was all in his head, and cleared him to play. His coach and general manager, Bob Pulford, accused him of being a malingerer, put him on waivers and sent him to the minors. Harrison refused to go, and was suspended. Harrison's agent was Alan Eagleson — who also happened to be Pulford's agent, as well as his old friend and one of those who paved the way for Eagleson to enter the hockey world. Many point out that guys like Pulford managed, more often than not, to get plum positions in management after their playing careers were over.

The Chicago owner was Bill Wirtz, a close friend of Eagleson's, and of league president John Ziegler. It gradually became obvious to one and all that the triumvirate of Eagleson, Wirtz and Ziegler ran the league.

Harrison's grievance was adjudicated by none other than Ziegler. At the hearing, Ziegler didn't rule on Harrison's case because Pulford hadn't followed proper procedure in giving Jim notice that he was being demoted. Ziegler told them to work it out. Harrison had been sent out of the room before Ziegler chastised Pulford and the others about the notice. Eagleson came out of the meeting and lied to Jim, telling him that Ziegler had ruled that he had to report to Moncton and play. In reality, Eagleson had just made a deal that suited his other client, Pulford, with absolutely no regard for Harrison's welfare. In the end, Jim got $10,000 from his disability insurance — a small fraction of the $175,000 he was expecting. He was also told, again erroneously, that he wasn't entitled to worker's compensation in Illinois.

David Keon told me a story that gave me an interesting insight into Jim's predicament. When Jim Harrison signed with Cleveland of the WHA in 1974, he asked Keon, who had been his captain in Toronto, for the name of his lawyer. David told Jim, and Jim got the lawyer to negotiate his contract with Cleveland. "So [the lawyer] represented Jim and got him a good contract, and he sent him a bill. And Jim said to me, 'He sent me a bill!' I said, 'Jim, he doesn't work for nothing.'" David had paid attention to Harrison's struggles with Eagleson. Recently, he said to me, "I'm thinking to myself, if Jim Stevens was representing him against Pulford and John

Ziegler, he'd have been represented and not had someone representing him who was really in business with the other two guys!" David's story speaks directly to the lack of sophistication of young hockey players. Eagleson preyed upon that naïveté.

Nonetheless, how could most of the players really have had any idea that they couldn't trust Eagleson, given the unanimous support and acceptance he had from everyone? How could they really have been expected to know not to trust Eagleson under the circumstances? Carl, who seemed forever to be out of step with his colleagues, was one of the very first to recognize these conflicts of interest.

A few days after Carl had put his question to me about Eagleson, wondering whether he could be as bad as he thought, I talked to Carl about my deliberations and my notes. I told him that I was convinced, first of all, that he was absolutely right about everything. Carl was very bright, and his observations were always insightful and astute. There was not a shadow of a doubt in my mind about the validity of his concerns. I suggested that the problem was likely far worse and more extensive than he realized, or could even imagine. At that very moment, Carl asked me, "Sue, will you help me do something about it?"

The request did not seem at all unusual to me. For years, to the exclusion of almost everything else, I had been helping Carl — with the fallout from his many failed business ventures, to his battles with the Leafs and managing our real estate. However, for Carl, it was a pivotal moment when I answered, "Of course, I'll help." For the rest of his life, he often told people how significant this moment was for him, because he knew he could never have won the pension battle and brought down Eagleson on his own, but by working together we would have a good shot at it. In an article he wrote for the *Toronto Star* after Eagleson pled guilty, he explained: "Sue is not very smart. It was in the early 1980s when I asked her to help me. Silly girl, she said she would. It was a task too daunting for me alone. I had the courage — read that *cojones* — but not the emotional stability — read that 'bad nerves.'"

Carl was encouraged in February 1981, when Don Ramsay wrote a column in the *Toronto Sun* that put the spotlight on some of Eagleson's dubious activities. He explained how Eagleson's company, Sports Management Ltd., effectively loaned out its employees to Hockey Canada, a not-for-profit agency, who paid them — relieving Eagleson of the burden of paying them himself. Meanwhile, they continued to do their work for

Eagleson's firm. For example, Bill Watters was reportedly paid $65,000 by Hockey Canada between April 1977 and April 1978 for services rendered. At the same time, he generated approximately $675,000 worth of new business by bringing 13 first-round NHL draft picks into Eagleson's agency. Eagleson also pocketed the $45,000 he ordinarily would have paid Watters. Sports Management's full-time bookkeeper and comptroller, Marvin Goldblatt, was paid more than $75,000 by Hockey Canada for bookkeeping services, and that replaced at least some of the salary Eagleson owed him, Ramsay reported.

Both Carl and I were also moved and angered after reading Jack Batten's 1982 book, *In Court*. The last chapter told the story of former NHLer Mike Robitaille. Robitaille's background was typical of many NHL players — he'd been born in a small town, Midland, Ontario, into an impoverished and difficult family life. At age 14 he became the property of the New York Rangers, playing for their junior team in Kitchener and their farm team in Omaha before being traded to the Detroit Red Wings and later to the Buffalo Sabres. In 1974, at the age of 25, he was traded to the Vancouver Canucks. By this time, Mike was suffering from acute anxiety and was taking Valium, which was apparently readily available to players through team doctors. Mike eventually developed a drug dependency, for which he received medical attention and made a rapid recovery. However, team personnel were less than convinced of this recovery, or of the state of his mental health.

In a game against St., Louis, Robitaille suffered a shoulder injury. An orthopedic surgeon, Dr. Piper, advised Mike that X-rays showed bone chips that would eventually require surgery. He was advised simply to rest, but he had an uneasy feeling about this injury. Previously, he had experienced numbness in his right arm, and now he noticed it again. Canucks coach Phil Maloney scoffed at him and told him to play or face suspension. What choice did Mike have? Although the team doctor was correct about the bone chips, he reportedly made no effort to intervene on behalf of his patient. Meanwhile, Mike's teammates began making fun of his use of meditation tapes to help him cope with his anxiety. He found himself ostracized by his peers. This struck a very sensitive nerve with Carl, who had also had issues with extreme anxiety and had practised meditation and hypnosis in an effort to combat them. Carl, too, had been considered "strange" and treated as an outsider by his teammates.

Robitaille's troubles escalated. In a game against the New York Rangers, he was checked violently by Nick Fotiu, after which his right leg felt to him like rubber. A team doctor suggested it was just a pulled muscle. With pain overtaking his entire body, Mike knew something far more serious was going on. Canucks management showed little concern and benched him. He tried to see the team doctor, Dr. Piper, who put him off and didn't show up to see him. The following night in a game against the Minnesota North Stars, Mike was again pummelled. He felt nauseated and pain-ridden. Dr. Piper left the rink that night having completely ignored Mike. In another game against Pittsburgh, Robitaille was checked brutally by Dennis Owchar. Writhing in pain on the ice and unable to co-ordinate his body movements, he begged for help. Once again, the team doctor told him he'd be fine. At home, however, when he was unable to hold a spoon, his wife prevailed and convinced him they needed to take charge of the situation, and he went to hospital. (Carl always said that the players' wives knew what Eagleson was about, but that the guys didn't have a clue.)

The team doctor continued to insist the problems were psychosomatic. Outside doctors finally diagnosed a severe spinal-cord injury, which pre-dated the Owchar check. Nonetheless, Canucks officials would not bend from their position that Robitaille's injuries were in his mind. In the end, with the aid of lawyer James Laxton, Robitaille successfully sued the Canucks and was awarded more than $350,000 in damages.

Carl had an enormous capacity for compassion, and stories like Mike's really upset and angered him. He wrote a letter of support to Mike and Isobel Robitaille after we read this account. The questions forefront in our minds: Where was Eagleson? Where was the NHLPA? Robitaille had been abused, bullied, manipulated, threatened, goaded by his peers and management, and mishandled medically in every imaginable way.

Like the Jim Harrison case, Mike Robitaille's story went directly to the heart of the very important matter of just how little Eagleson did to protect the NHLPA's members in collective bargaining. Clause 5 of the NHL standard player's contract stipulated that only a team doctor could assess and diagnose a player's injuries and determine his readiness to play. This had been terribly detrimental to many players over the years; time after time, doctors didn't seem to consider the player as a "real" patient, and all too often they made decisions in line with management's wishes.

After "gassing" Eagleson in 1968, Carl became increasingly concerned about his conduct and his selling out of the players. From early in the 1970s, Carl began making an informal record of his observations, often writing notes to himself on the backs of bar napkins or restaurant place mats. One such note was penned in red ink on a piece of stationery from the Sheraton Stockholm Hotel in 1977. At the time, Eagleson was threatening to remove himself from his role as international hockey negotiator for Hockey Canada. Carl knew it was all a ploy to conceal his backroom attempts to weasel his way into replacing Guenther Sabetzki as head of the International Ice Hockey Federation. Carl knew that this was his ultimate goal and understood the motive: money.

> *Oh Gawd — He's done it!*
> *I didn't for one minute believe that he had missed a step. I didn't for one minute believe that he had conceded his exit.*
> *He hadn't... but while the world slept, the Great One had just pulled off another one of his great ploys. Perhaps his greatest. But only because of its international implications. Because he makes the impossible appear mundane and the improbable seem commonplace.*

Carl went on to explain his observations:

> *The subtlety of his latest ploy is even more unbelievable... His reasons for resigning? He cited harassment from the C.A.H.A. objecting to his high-handed methods. Some ploy! Bullshit! Eagleson walking away from a fight? He was publicly acknowledging his defeat by the C.A.H.A. but it was a seat on the Board of the IIHF that Eagleson actually coveted and was unable to get through conventional means. What the hell did he ever get through conventional means? It was Eagleson's unannounced goal to replace Guenther Sabetzki as head of the IIHF and to control hockey worldwide with his partners in the NHL. Controlling hockey worldwide meant power and millions upon millions of dollars for which there would be no accounting.*

Now, in the 1980s, Carl was more determined than ever that Eagleson had to be stopped. However, he didn't know what to do. Neither of us did. Consequently, our efforts were focused on fact-finding. Over a number of years, Carl and I had lunch regularly with Bill Watters, who had split with Eagleson and was now running his own agency, Branada Sports. When Watters left Eagleson's company, he was subject to a confidentiality agreement, and he seemed very nervous about saying anything to breach it. I kept notes of those meetings, and while he didn't get into specifics, Bill was a great source for us, providing us with ideas of what to investigate, and we enjoyed listening to his thoughts on issues close to our hearts. Carl thought Watters was many things, but cheap was high on the list! As Carl often said over the years, for all the times we met with Bill for lunch, he never once picked up the tab, even though he was financially very successful and we were struggling along by the seats of our pants.

Carl and I were both left shaking our heads in 1991 when Bill Watters was hired by Maple Leaf Gardens as assistant general manager and he announced at a press conference that he finally had the job he'd always wanted. The thought came to both our minds: if he always had his heart set on a career in management, what kind of independent advice and direction had his clients been paying him for? Why is it that pro hockey is so rife with such conflicts?

Carl continued to talk with players and agents about their experiences with arbitration. The results were predictable: it was not a forum in which players could expect to win. The NHL's insistence on secrecy meant that, for a player headed to arbitration, there were not even any precedents available to show how other similar grievances had been decided. The debacles surrounding free agency — or the lack thereof — were always close to Carl's heart; he followed with keen interest, and dismay, the cases of Dale McCourt and Pat Hickey. Carl found it despicable that there was no movement for players unless the team decided to initiate a change.

He clipped newspaper articles and followed events with great interest. We'd frequently go to the Press Club for lunch or drinks in the late afternoon and chat with reporters. Invariably, Carl would steer the conversations to the subject Eagleson. There was, however, little support or interest in Carl's complaints and concerns. Over time, we learned exactly why the reporters ignored us: most had been compromised, in one way or another, by Eagleson. He was always available to them. They could always call him up for a story. They got favours from him; one sports reporter for *The Globe and Mail*, Malcolm Gray, was the recipient of a mortgage on his house, in the amount of $27,000, from NHLPA monies. Another reporter's kids had jobs provided by Eagleson. Others enthused about how much fun it was to be around him. Later, as the Eagleson investigation grew and got legs, some reporters attempted to report on the issues, only to find that certain publishers close to Eagleson would not permit the publication of their stories.

On one occasion that stands out in my mind, Carl and I were about to drive down to upstate New York for a few days of rest and relaxation, when we got a phone call from a young reporter, James Deacon, of *Maclean's* magazine. He expressed a serious interest in writing a column for an upcoming edition about the Eagleson issues. We postponed our departure for several hours to assemble material for him, photocopy all of the documentation and deliver it to him. When the article appeared, we were shocked to read, not the story we'd been told was in the works, but more of an apologia for Eagleson. A few weeks, later our friend Bruce Dowbiggin, the CBC sportscaster, reported back to us that he'd been golfing with Deacon, and Deacon had told Bruce that he thought Carl was "off the wall" and that no one was going to listen to him!

Carl was not only hurt, he was angry. Carl had known Deacon's parents and remembered a time when they were terribly concerned about their son and what he was going to do in life. Carl, in his typically caring way, had gone out of his way to offer them his help and give them some suggestions. Situations like this made Carl increasingly cynical. He frequently chastised himself about his constant eagerness to help others, saying, "No good deed goes unpunished."

Despite the stories we documented, the people we talked to and the notes we took, we really weren't getting anywhere. Reporters dismissed us as "crazies" — and Carl as "obsessed." However, during 1989 there was a development that excited Carl: an uprising among the current players, who were becoming concerned about Eagleson's stewardship of the Players' Association. The original organizers of the movement were player agents Ron Salcer and Ritch Winter. The two men were dramatically different from one another. Salcer, located in California, was a small, earnest, quiet man, whereas Winter, a young lawyer from Edmonton, was a much more open, emotional, type who didn't exude a lot of self-confidence but whose heart was always in the right place. Salcer and Winter had become aware of a rising tide of discontent among their clients, and they could see the animosity towards Eagleson becoming a groundswell. There was a growing suspicion that Eagleson was not doing much to protect their interests. Players saw salaries in other pro sports escalating rapidly while theirs languished.

Salcer and Winter approached Ed Garvey, a lawyer from Madison, Wisconsin, who had been head of the National Football League's players' union, and retained his services, funded by "good faith" financial contributions of $100 made by close to 200 players. Garvey was a tough, hard-nosed fellow who was never known to back down from a fight. He had a deep dislike for sports owners, and he had a real dislike for Alan Eagleson. Garvey spoke of his agreeing to get involved: "I told them I'd be interested in getting involved in trying to clean up the Players' Association. I felt the association was a disgrace for a long time." Carl noted with interest that the core group of supporters — Jim Korn and Mark Johnson, for example — were Americans. Carl had a theory as to the reason for this: "They had the Boston Tea Party in the States; we haven't had our tea party yet here in Canada."

Salcer and Winter spent months making the rounds of the teams to solicit support and talk to the players about the problems. Then the trio of Garvey, Winter and Salcer advised the entire Players' Association that they would make a presentation at the player meetings in Florida in June 1989. Garvey started a newsletter that he called the *Players' Voice*, which he used to get information to the players. He started by pointing out small details that everyone could grasp. For example, he drew attention to Gordie Howe's 26 years of service in the NHL and his resulting pension of $875 a month (in Canadian funds), and compared that with Eagleson's pension of $50,000 (U.S.).

On June 2, 1989, some 80 players assembled in Florida for the player meetings. The dissident group booked into a modest Hilton hotel whereas Eagleson and his loyal cronies were in the luxurious and expensive Breakers Hotel. When the meeting came to order, some of the players worried about the consequences should this confrontation fail. However, they were in for a treat. "I wasn't nervous, but I wondered: 'Okay, what's Ed going to do?'" Winter recalled. "And it got very, very good from that moment on. It was like a shootout. Ed got up, he got the puck and I'm thinking, 'My goodness, I hope he scores' — and boy, did he ever!" It was the first time anyone in the room had ever seen Eagleson verbally outmatched. He was always the one intimidating others with his loud mouth and foul language.

The first order of business for Ed Garvey that morning was to question Toronto lawyer Edgar Sexton, who was there with Eagleson. He asked Sexton whom he was representing, and Sexton replied, "Mr. Eagleson."

"In what capacity?" Garvey asked. Sexton replied that Ritch Winter had threatened to sue Eagleson. Garvey hit right back, telling him that he was correct, that Winter had threatened to sue — the NHLPA, not Alan Eagleson. And he reminded Sexton that no writ had been issued. Garvey wasn't finished — he asked why Sexton was in Florida when the threat of an action was from someone in Edmonton, Alberta, against someone in Toronto. "Why did you have to be here, and at whose expense?" There was no reply.

Later that morning, Ritch was in the men's room and found himself standing at the urinal beside Sexton, and remembers asking him: "What does it feel like to be totally and completely embarrassed in front of your client?" Attaboy, Ritch!

Garvey outlined numerous complaints and findings that had surfaced from his study of the NHLPA. Among others, these included:

1. *With the exception of a few players handpicked by Alan Eagleson, players have little or no voice in the operations of the NHLPA. The NHLPA is the least democratic labour organization in sport.*

2. *Players have virtually no ability to get detailed information about the operations of their union, their pension, international hockey, decision-making in the NHL, salaries, the economics of the NHL, or any other important matter [affecting] their careers.*

3. *No benefits of any significance have been achieved in the entire decade of the 1980s through collective bargaining. In fact, the organization has gone backward while sports unions in all other sports have made major gains. [Hockey players] are last in salaries, benefits, percentage of gross and in information.*

4. *The NHLPA staff provides little or no help to players or their agents in the negotiation of individual contracts because the staff is small. Alan Eagleson is a part-time director who does not reach out to help his competitors — other agents.*

5. *The NHLPA provides few services to players despite high dues and other revenues.*

6. *Alan Eagleson's conflicts of interest negatively impact on almost every aspect of your profession.*

7. *Alan Eagleson refuses to provide information that is required by law to be made available to all union members. The deliberate decision to avoid United States labour law requirements regarding filing of financial statements is a major error in judgment.*

8. *In practice, the officers are appointed, not elected; the collective bargaining agreements have never been approved by secret ballot...*

9. *Finally, Alan Eagleson may well be the most overpaid executive in the labour movement in North America. Not even the president of the two-million-member Teamsters union comes close to Alan in wages, benefits, pension and expense accounts.*

Garvey's report went on to state: "What we found can only be described as a scandal. Frankly, if any other union leader did what Alan Eagleson has done over the past 22 years, the news media would be screaming for an investigation. The conflicts of interest are shocking, but even more shocking is a pattern of sweetheart agreements with the NHL over all these years. It may sound harsh, but he has not pursued player interests at critical times in your history as a union."

Later, Garvey addressed Eagleson's coziness with management: "Alan Eagleson is a brilliant attorney and politician. He admits that John Ziegler is one of his best friends and Bill Wirtz, who lives near him in Florida, is an extremely close friend despite the fact that Wirtz is the chief negotiator for the NHL. Given his brilliance, there is really no excuse for the lack of preparation for bargaining, except one: he does not take bargaining seriously because he is comfortable with the cozy relationship that has been so good for him."

Garvey also made his points in a way players could really understand — by comparing Eagleson's benefits with those the players received. For example, Eagleson's contract was guaranteed for six years; no player in the league had a six-year guaranteed contract. Alan was a free agent at any time of his choosing, while for players there was no free agency unless the club decided to move a player. Alan had the most generous pension in the history of the NHL, and it was guaranteed. The players' contributions to their pensions were not guaranteed after 1986. Players' pensions were in Canadian dollars, while Eagleson's were in U.S. dollars. Fees for the administration of the players' pensions were $261,000 in 1987 and $415,993 in 1988 and paid by the players from the fund (even though the NHL Pension Plan stated that these costs were not to decrease the value of the fund).

About international tournaments such as the Canada Cup, Garvey said, "You get precious little for your participation… Alan publicly announces that each new international event … will mean a million dollars in the player pension fund. Unquestioning players have participated for years in international hockey to help the pension fund. Only now do we understand that the money goes to *reduce the clubs' contribution to the pension plan*." In other words, the proceeds of international hockey were indirectly enriching the owners, not the pension plan. The report continued for page after page, outlining exorbitant expenses charged to the NHLPA by Eagleson with no supporting documents — $168,000 for promotions, $32,000 for international hockey meetings, and so on.

True to his bullying nature, Eagleson tried to deflect attention from these allegations by verbally assailing Garvey (allegations of wife-beating were his usual comeback). Garvey stood his ground. He revealed that, since 1982, approximately $3 million of association funds had been lent out to clients and associates of Eagleson. Although Eagleson tried to say he didn't charge fees for these transactions, it was proven that his law firm most certainly charged fees.

After all was said and done, the players voted to allow Eagleson to stay on as executive director. However, he did so only by the skin of his teeth, and only because he promised to produce a number of relevant statements, including income tax returns, financial statements from the NHLPA, a copy of the lease for the offices at 37 Maitland Street, details of $483,000 spent on meetings over two years, and to cease representing players as their personal agent.

Every morning, Carl rushed out to buy the newspaper for updates on this showdown. He was extremely hopeful that something earth-shattering was about to unfold. It was his intense desire that there would be a seismic shift and Eagleson would be dismissed. The morning he learned that Eagleson had managed to cling to his position as executive director, Carl was thunderstruck! He said right off the bat that there was absolutely no way Eagleson would ever live up to the agreements he'd made. He felt that Garvey, Winter and Salcer were so close to putting Eagleson on ice, but they had let him slip out of their grasp.

One morning, shortly after we heard this news, Carl said, "Let's go to Edmonton and meet Ritch Winter." We flew to Edmonton a few days later and met with Ritch at his office, then he took us to dinner. Ritch remembers getting the phone call from Carl and thinking, "There *is* hope; people *do* care!" We had a great chat, and the chemistry among us was excellent. Ritch is a tall man with eyes like those of a sad mongrel; he has a huge heart and is very emotional and passionate about the people and things he cares about. What he lacks in self-assurance he more than makes up for in courage and an old-fashioned sense of integrity and devotion to what is right. Over a pleasant meal, we commiserated about the events in Florida in June. He filled us in on all the drama. Needless to say, he had loved the way Garvey made mincemeat out of Eagleson. Carl told Ritch how desperately disappointed he was that they had not kept Eagleson's feet to the fire.

Towards the end of dinner, Carl urged Ritch to stay involved with the Eagleson fight. We brought Ritch up to date on our efforts over the past eight years, and then Carl promised, "Sue and I will get on board with you, and we're committed to help you in every possible way." Ritch really had to think about that one! His main worry was how his wife, Cindy, would react to the news that he was thinking about continuing this campaign. "I had promised Cindy that I would never do anything this stupid again," he told me. "Sue, we had death threats! I promised Cindy: no more crusading." Ritch had already devoted a huge amount of time to this cause and was concerned about the impact on his family's finances and his business. At the same time, Ritch's outrage at Eagleson's abuse of power was not subsiding. However reluctantly, Ritch agreed to come on board with us. "How am I going to explain this to Cindy?" he worried. We agreed to press on together and get the word out — this time, to the retired players, too. "After meeting you and Carl, I knew that we were going to be entangled in something important, something successful and something not very lucrative!" Ritch told me. For Carl and me, this was a turning point. Our private battle, plotted by a team of two, was about to transform itself into a broader and, we hoped, more purposeful effort.

Shortly after returning from Edmonton, Carl suggested that we drive down to Madison to meet with Ed Garvey. We did, in what Carl called "a 20-minute audience" at the Holiday Inn downtown. Ed is a no-nonsense type of man who loves a fight and cannot be intimidated. He, too, agreed to help us. We were all in constant touch from then on. The groundwork would soon be laid for actions that would rock the hockey world and impact players' lives in very substantial ways. We were all very close and committed; Ed Garvey called one day after Carl and I had been away for a few days, and when I answered the phone, Ed said to me: "You're there! I get nervous when I don't talk to you for a few days."

It didn't take long for Eagleson to start wriggling out of the commitments he'd made in Florida. The first to fall by the wayside was his agreement to stop representing clients. Just a few weeks later, he was saying that he couldn't drop the clients unless they wanted him to do so. In August, at a follow-up meeting in Toronto, Eagleson loyalists made up the bulk of those in attendance, and he managed to win a bigger vote of support.

Alan Eagleson may have hung onto his position by the skin of his teeth during the summer of 1989. However, he had been humiliated and defeated psychologically by Ed Garvey. Eagleson, the master intimidator himself, the self-proclaimed "czar of hockey," had turned turtle in the face of his opponents for the first time. It wouldn't be the last time.

CHAPTER 10

LAWYERS, LAWYERS, LAWYERS: THE PENSION SAGA

"We knew something was wrong with the pension. At best, we knew a pension so bad, with so little benefit for the participants could at least stand some serious scrutiny."

When Carl went to Maple Leaf Gardens in 1960 to collect the $100 they owed him because he'd been hospitalized at the end of the previous hockey season, they told him to get lost. Now, in 1986, when he asked for the pension benefits arising from his successful arbitration case, he was again told to get lost. Carl didn't back down in the first instance, and he certainly didn't intend to now.

The NHL Pension Society's bylaws were clear about the benefits Carl was entitled to. They defined a player as "any person who is party to an agreement with a Member Club under which he will or may play hockey for a Member Club." Of particular interest was a stipulation that a player didn't have to play any games to be eligible for the benefit, if the team was preventing him from playing.

However, when Allan Dick wrote to the Pension Society on Carl's behalf, requesting the pension credits he was entitled to as a result of his arbitration case, the letter was forwarded to the Toronto Maple Leafs, who in turn referred it to their legal counsel, who turned the request down flat. This surprised us, but we weren't about to accept it as the final answer. To find out where we stood, we consulted a number of player agents. To our amazement and chagrin, we quickly discovered that none of them had any familiarity with the terms of the standard player's contract, nor the bylaws, and certainly not pension matters. These were all areas of extreme importance to their clients and they were uninformed!

Allan continued to write to both the NHL Pension Society and the NHL Players' Association requesting the benefits for Carl. The result was always the same: refusal, accompanied by flimsy excuses — Carl didn't play any games, Carl had retired, and on and on. Not one of these arguments was valid or in keeping with the Pension Society's bylaws. And, the replies always came from various law firms representing Maple Leaf Gardens, which made us highly aware of the conflict of interest between the NHL Pension Society and the league. In essence, they were one and the same. The key issue was that the Pension Society was set up to be an independent trust with a fiduciary responsibility to those who paid into the plan and drew benefits; we felt the society ought to be taking responsibility for this matter and not passing it off to the Maple Leafs.

Because of this standoff, we found ourselves focusing more and more on the pension plan. For years, Carl had harboured uncomfortable feelings about it, and from time to time we wrote letters seeking information. The problem was, we really had no idea where to begin, so the whole system remained a mystery, and those replies we did get left us more confused than enlightened.

Among the issues that bothered us, we wondered what had happened to all the money from international hockey tournaments that had been promised to the players to enhance their pensions. Nor could we understand the death benefit, or how the values of pensions were determined. Players were eligible to begin drawing their pensions at age 45, but Carl had not yet done so and he wondered how the benefits were accumulating.

We weren't alone in thinking there were problems. In 1980, Bob Baun worked with Lorraine Mahoney, a pension benefits expert with the firm Allan Smart Services in Toronto, to look into his pension. Lorraine was shocked at what she found out about how poorly the players' contributions were managed. "I could have walked Bob's pension across the street and turned his $11,000 annual NHL pension into $55,000 because of the aberration of [high] interest rates at that time," she said, "but the NHL wouldn't permit him to transfer his pension out." Bob tried to get the players on board with him, organizing a meeting at which Lorraine spoke about her findings. Bob was bitter when the guys wouldn't even ante up 50 bucks a head to pursue the matter.

"I was gobsmacked by the cynical, cryptic attitude of the players at that meeting," said Lorraine. "They sat there with very suspicious looks on their faces and were more concerned with questions like 'What's in it for Bob?' than the unbelievably pathetic state of their pensions."

Meanwhile, we became aware of the efforts of other players who were looking for answers about their pensions. Carl remembered: "Bob Goldham had an ongoing correspondence with the Pension Society — in particular, Brian O'Neill — in his efforts to get improvements to the pitiful pensions. Goldham got replies in the form of obfuscations, usually extolling the wonderful benefits that [former NHL president] Clarence Campbell had acquired for the players in 'the best pension in sport.'"

Goldham's correspondence dated back to the late 1970s, and he shared his files with Carl. Indeed, Bob made a point of forwarding copies of his letters to other former players. What moved Carl so profoundly when he read these letters was Goldham's politeness and respectfulness. Bob — an outstanding player, a member of five Stanley Cup–winning teams, and a respected television analyst — was a true gentleman. How could anyone not want to help him? we wondered.

Goldham received pleasant, cordial replies from Campbell and O'Neill, but their answers never betrayed a sincere interest in addressing his concerns or helping the players. For instance, on February 26, 1980, Goldham wrote:

> *I have for a long time felt that some of the people who were involved in the earlier stages have not been accorded some of the privileges and benefits that the present players are enjoying. I am referring to, specifically, the pension as it stands with respect to the 1947–1957 era.*
>
> *Brian, this letter is written in the hope that perhaps in some way people who were associated in the past with the NHL are not forgotten by those who now have something to do with its operation.*

O'Neill's reply, dated March 7, stated:

> *I, too, share your concerns with regard to the matter of the status of the Pension Plan. Bob, we have been working on*

the basis of a fully funded plan, which means that as to the League's contribution there is no surplus which would allow us to make any allocation for back seasons. Believe me, if there was some way that we could improve the pension benefits of the players, particularly in the era that you mentioned, we would be most happy to do so.

Carl, of course, was well aware of the efforts in 1957 by Ted Lindsay and others to get information on the pension. Back then, Lindsay was convinced that contributions that had been promised were not being made. When simple answers to straightforward questions were not forthcoming, Lindsay and his group tried to organize a players' association. Every time Carl was reminded of the fact that the Toronto Maple Leaf players had, to a man, been courageous enough to stand up and support Lindsay's efforts to organize the players, tears came to his eyes and he was overcome with emotion.

At this stage, Carl knew, and was adamant, that the only way to deal with these pension concerns was in the courts. Anything else would simply be a further waste of time.

A pivotal moment in this saga was reached when Carl, along with hundreds of other retired players, received a letter in November 1988. The letter was jointly signed by John Ziegler and Alan Eagleson — that alone was enough to make Carl sit up and take notice. It read: "We are pleased to be able to advise of an increase in your pension. Although the agreement was reached in August of 1986, it has only been in the last 90 days that approvals from all government authorities (Canada, Ontario and the United States) have been obtained. We hope this makes your Christmas even merrier." This letter, which came to be known as the "Merry Christmas" letter, drove Carl crazy — he wanted to know what authority Eagleson had to negotiate *anything* for retired players, as well as how large the surplus was, how long it had existed, and in what manner this money had been accumulating.

As Carl's frustration mounted, we were introduced to a Toronto lawyer who specialized in pension matters. The process started when we were looking for help with a real estate matter. Ed Tonello, a lawyer we knew, owned a neighbouring property on the Danforth, and he introduced us to a friend of his, Sheldon Kirsh. During a meeting with Shelly, Carl mentioned that he was disturbed about his pension. Shelly suggested that we meet a friend of his, Mark Zigler, with the Toronto law firm Koskie and Minsky. He felt Mark was a perfect contact because he was a pension expert. Furthermore, his firm represented the interests of employees: Mark had recently been involved in a successful and highly publicized case on behalf of Dominion Stores employees against Conrad Black, as a result of which Black was prevented from stripping the employees of their pension benefits.

We first met with Mark in 1988. As Carl said so often, "It was an interesting meeting, but I had no idea what questions to ask." We spent the next year continuing to search for answers on our own. In that time, we had discussions with Alison Griffiths and David Cruise about their research for their book *Net Worth*, and we learned that they'd discovered irregularities about surplus monies that went back decades. We discussed these matters with Allan Dick on an ongoing basis, and finally, in 1989, Allan suggested that we go back to Mark Zigler and hire him to write a very simple letter of opinion — only one page, Allan insisted, so that it could be presented to the players and they would get it immediately. At that point we took a huge leap of faith and hired Mark, at our personal expense, to investigate the pension and prepare this letter for us. When our report was ready, we discussed it with Mark. His research clearly showed two scandalous results. Firstly, some $24 million in surplus monies had accumulated, and only $4.4 million of those funds had been used for the benefit of the retired players. It was Mark's opinion that the NHL had used these monies improperly. Secondly, he confirmed to us that not a dime from international hockey had ever been paid into the pension plan over the years.

Over the next several weeks, Carl set up daily meetings with four or five former players; they'd get together for coffee, and Carl would show them the documentation. However, at the end of each day he would return home frustrated and discouraged because, for the most part, although the guys enjoyed seeing him for a coffee, few seemed interested in what he had to tell them, nor did they support his desire to do something about it. We travelled to Montreal for an oldtimers' hockey game and distributed copies of Mark Zigler's report and the Garvey Report to the retired players, hoping they'd read the material. On another occasion, we drove down to Detroit to speak at a monthly meeting of the Red Wings alumni. They seemed more enthusiastic and interested in what Carl had to say. At least, we felt, we were planting seeds that might pique their curiosity as time went on.

The morning after the Detroit meeting, we were invited to Bill and Edna Gadsby's home for breakfast. We had a great visit, and Carl talked passionately about the pension problems. Edna is a delightfully warm and friendly woman and I enjoyed her company. At one point during breakfast, Bill got up from the table and meandered over to the kitchen counter. He leaned on it, looking at us wistfully, and said: "If, when I played, anyone had ever told me that Carl Brewer would be sitting at my table having breakfast in my home, I'd have told them they were crazy!" It was a wonderful comment that reminded us just how intense the rivalry between players of opposing teams had been and how thoroughly ingrained the "hatred" for their opponents was.

Eventually, seeing Carl get more and more worn down and discouraged from his efforts to rally the guys, I became increasingly worried about how it was affecting him. One morning as I was filing some papers, I picked up Mark's opinion letter and, in a quiet moment, re-read it. To me, the facts were crystal clear. I got angry, and when Carl came home later, I told him that I thought we should forget about trying to convince the players and just go ahead and proceed by ourselves. I had no idea how we would possibly finance a lawsuit, but I believed it was the right thing to do and that we would somehow find the resources we needed.

Mark Zigler advised us that our case stood a better chance of succeeding if a group of plaintiffs was assembled, so, armed with his information, we decided to bring the players together. Carl and I planned a meeting of retired players on October 24, 1990. The meeting was held in the basement of Hector's Restaurant, a folksy bar near Yonge Street and Eglinton Avenue. The date was chosen to coincide with a business trip to Toronto by Ritch Winter. About 20 former players showed up that afternoon, including Harry Watson, Bob Davidson, Bob Goldham, Red Kelly, Norm Ullman, Jim Dorey (with his lawyer from Kingston), Wayne Dillon, Wayne Carleton, Tod Sloan, Ed Shack and Billy Harris. Our friend and lawyer, Allan Dick, attended also.

Ritch Winter, the lawyer/player agent from Edmonton, spoke to the players about his involvement with Ron Salcer and Ed Garvey on behalf of the current players when they questioned Alan Eagleson's leadership. Ritch laid out the results of their inquiry, especially that the NHL Pension Society had violated all normal practice with respect to its management and accounting of the pension fund.

Zigler's facts were explained to everybody. They learned that from a surplus of some $24 million, approximately $140,000 had been used for administration costs, about $4.5 million had been allocated to the benefit of former players, a whopping $12 million had been appropriated to fund that was known as a "senior player benefit" for current players, while a residue of approximately $7 million remained. The latter amount had been used since 1988 to provide "contribution holidays" for the NHL owners. It was our clear understanding that the NHL Pension Society's charter and regulations mandated that *all* monies were to be used for the benefit of the former players — *not* the current players, and most certainly not the NHL owners.

Ritch informed the group that there had been overwhelming support by the current players to have Eagleson account for the vast sums of money he received, directly or indirectly, from international hockey tournaments. He reported that Eagleson had routinely charged legal fees for the lion's share of the profits from these tournaments. Mark Zigler's report gave further credence to this statement, because it indicated that not a dime of money from international hockey since 1972 had made its way into the pension fund.

At the conclusion of the meeting, Carl addressed the group. He thanked Ritch and reminded the players why they were there: "Because of hockey — and because hockey does not belong to the likes of Clarence Campbell or Harold Ballard, or an Alan Eagleson. The game of hockey belongs to the Bob Davidsons and Tod Sloans, the Harry Watsons, the Allan Stanleys, to me, and to each and every player in the room and to each and every player ever to play the game."

It was a start. The attendance was encouraging, but I couldn't help feeling that most players sat through the meeting with their arms folded across their chests and doubting expressions on their faces. Still, the information, the evidence, was mounting, and it was damning. At the very least, our suspicions of so many years were being confirmed for us.

Carl and I both felt that we were on the brink of a long, hard battle. There would be no looking back.

***

After the October meeting, our interest in the pension scandals grew into a full-time commitment for both of us. We had been able to gain a small band of supporters in the persons of Ed and Norma Shack, Allan Stanley and Frank and Marie Mahovlich. We had informal gatherings to strategize. Soon, David Forbes arrived on the scene. A former Boston Bruin, and by this time a financial planner on the west coast, Forbes was one of the brighter lights on the marquee. David had a lot to offer in terms of expertise and insights, and we were in constant communication.

We decided to plan another meeting of players, and this time to reach out to a much broader spectrum of NHL alumni (our first meeting had been attended only by retired fellows living in or near the Toronto area). Carl was also anxious to make sure that the "distaff side" be included in all of our activities. He felt that the real strength of our cause would lie with the wives and partners of the players; he remembered that early on, when the guys were eager to get Eagleson involved, all the wives told their husbands he was bad news. He knew that, if we got the information into their hands, they'd read it and want to help.

Norma Shack was instrumental in getting a lot of the players to the meeting. Ed Garvey, Ritch Winter, Mark Zigler and our personal lawyer, Allan Dick, were all on board and ready and willing to make presentations from their individual areas of experience. Allan, of course, had been involved in Vaclav Nedomansky's suit against Alan Eagleson and had successfully handled Carl's arbitration. His familiarity and experience with hockey matters were vital to our efforts.

On December 10, 1990, a snowy, wintry night, a Who's Who of hockey gathered at a small, nondescript Ramada Inn at Highways 400 and 401 in Downsview. The turnout, made up of players who travelled from near and far, was extraordinary: Bobby Hull, Bobby Orr, Gordie and Colleen Howe, Johnny Bower, Billy Harris, Glen Harmon, Ed and Norma Shack, David Forbes, Allan Stanley, Rene Robert, Fred Stanfield, Frank and Marie Mahovlich, referee Bruce Hood, Red and Andra Kelly — Jim Harrison flew from Kelowna. In all, there were 93 former players, wives and partners in the room that night.

Numerous bombshells were dropped throughout the evening, and they left many stunned and angry. The first came just a few moments before the meeting was called to order. A young man, delivering a large parcel, came bustling into the meeting room and handed a large box of printed material to Ritch Winter. Lo and behold, it was from Alan Eagleson. He had got wind of this meeting and was on the defensive. The material, in the form of an

18-page — that's right, 18-page! — document was addressed to "All Retired Players of the NHL." In his missive, he condemned Winter and Garvey, saying their information was unfounded and inflammatory. He included documents, many never before seen by anyone — including statements of pension monies, letters and other information that was unbelievable and became fuel for our side as our research continued.

Carl called the meeting to order by welcoming everyone and introducing the guests. Mark Zigler, in his usual direct, clear, concise manner, outlined the details of his investigation into the NHL pension plan. It was the first that many of these players had heard about the surplus money being used to give contribution holidays to the owners, or about the fact that not one dime of international hockey proceeds had made their way into the pension fund. The next bombshell Zigler dropped was equally enraging, particularly to the more senior retirees present. It was a letter he had received from Ken Sawyer, secretary/treasurer of the NHL Pension Society: "All-Star game proceeds are not contributed to the Pension Society. Rather, such proceeds are used to pay a portion of pension administration costs incurred by the Plan sponsors [i.e., the NHL owners]."

The general feeling was one of betrayal. For decades, the players had participated in the NHL's annual All-Star game — for free — under the understanding that the monies raised were being contributed to their pension fund. That's what they had been told. Ralph Backstrom, who had played in six All-Star games as a Canadien, was very clear about this point. "There's no question in my mind that we were told that all the net proceeds were going to our pension; that's why we played for no compensation." I recall that when Carl and I informed Ralph that we had discovered this fact, he was visibly stunned and annoyed. It was clear that he, too, felt betrayed. What was worse, there was no accounting for such hefty expenses.

Ed Garvey and Ritch Winter both outlined their investigative work on behalf of the current players in the attempted 1989 coup against Alan Eagleson. When Garvey got up to speak, he began by jokingly telling the players, "This must be the first meeting when you haven't been screamed at and called 'stupid.'" The information that Garvey and Winter provided was infuriating to those who were hearing it for the first time. One of the more dramatic reactions came from Bobby Hull, who raised his thumb in the air, yelling "Eagleson," then pointing to his backside and yelling "NHL," as he bent over, pretending to ram the thumb into his backside.

At the outset of the meeting, some of the players joked about who among them might be a spy for Eagleson and Ziegler. Young lawyer Shayne Kukulowicz signed in as a representative of his dad, Aggie, the former New York Ranger and a close pal of Eagleson's. Shortly afterward, we got wind of the fact that he had really been an Eagleson emissary; he wrote a four-page memo to Eagleson, marked "personal and confidential," describing the meeting, identifying the attendees and advising that the players wouldn't have any entitlement to the surplus. Shayne did not disclose that he was acting in his capacity as a lawyer and was actually representing Eagleson that night, so Carl and I filed a complaint against him with the Law Society of Upper Canada. The Law Society took our complaint seriously, and we had several meetings with officials to discuss our concerns about his conduct. In the end, no punitive action was taken against him, but we were gratified insomuch as it is never pleasant for a lawyer to have a complaint against him on record with the Society. Many years later, I ran into Aggie Kukulowicz and he told me that he never knew what Eagleson was up to and that he felt terrible that his son had been dragged into it. He spoke to me in a tone of regret and apology.

Not everyone present that night was on side when the talk turned to uniting to take action. Some saw Ritch Winter as a loose cannon, a trouble-maker; others suspected he had an agenda to use retired players to curry favour with the current players. We, however, had the greatest respect and admiration for Ritch and his integrity and courage. His analysis of the ways Alan Eagleson and the NHL had been ripping players off for decades was refreshing. Carl spoke for both of us when he said: "They have no idea how hard and unselfishly he has worked for us. Whatever he gets out of this, if anything, will never compensate for what he has done."

Uniting the group to take some action about the issues presented so convincingly this night was a daunting task, but there was a tremendous amount of enthusiasm for the idea. Bobby Hull was among the most vocal in that regard. At the end of the evening, a steering committee was formed that included Carl, of course, along with Mr. Hockey, Gordie Howe, Dennis Owchar, Fred Stanfield, Andy Bathgate, David Forbes and others. The committee was to investigate what action ought to be taken and, especially, how to finance any legal action that might be contemplated.

A little after midnight, Carl and I made our way to the bar for a drink to try to unwind. The evening had been a success; there could be no question that momentum was building. Our minds were dizzy with all the ideas, facts, opinions, energy, anger, disappointments, disillusionment and sheer disbelief that had been on display in the meeting room. Our minds were also racing with thoughts of all the work that lay ahead of us. We tried to allow the exhaustion to dissolve over a couple of drinks before heading home.

Alison Griffiths was with us that night — she and her husband, David Cruise, were just completing what would become a landmark book about the business of the NHL and of Alan Eagleson: *Net Worth*. Upon learning of our meeting, Alison flew from Vancouver to attend. After experiencing the evening, she and David restructured their book and wrote about the meeting in the opening chapter. When it hit the stores, *Net Worth* was a huge source of support for us because it laid out for the public at large, in excellent style and detail, the lengthy history of abuse and questionable business ethics in hockey. In many ways, this book laid the groundwork for everything that was to follow.

A few days after the meeting, Carl sent out a memorandum to all the attendees. "It was certainly gratifying for me to see such a turnout," he wrote. "Your support and enthusiasm are greatly appreciated. The energies in that room bespeak incredible power potential for all of us — speaking with a unanimous voice — to continue to make a positive contribution to our game — hockey. It is important that you understand that the issues leading up to this gathering were not born yesterday. I, for my part alone, have been following the course of these matters for decades and have devoted my energies full time over the past six months to assembling information, obtaining legal input, and informing former players." Carl concluded by saying: "I believe that you will agree that we all deserve a better fate. There is no reason for us to have been stripped of our dignity and it is a sincere desire to restore that dignity — both to the game and to the wonderful men who have made hockey the great institution it has been over the years."

Ritch Winter had filed a comprehensive written complaint about Alan Eagleson with the RCMP and the Law Society of Upper Canada in January 1990. A couple of days after the big meeting of December 10, 1990, Carl, along with Ritch Winter, Bobby Orr, Dennis Owchar, David Forbes and Jim Harrison, met with Toronto lawyer Tom Lockwood, who was acting as the Law Society's senior counsel in charge of discipline and was investigating the complaint against Eagleson. The players came away from the meeting optimistic and encouraged after Lockwood assured them that the matter would be thoroughly and objectively investigated and that player input was not only welcome but essential.

In January 1991 we travelled to Chicago for the All-Star weekend, to continue spreading the word of our mission. Bob Nevin, Ed Litzenberger and Dennis Owchar joined Carl and me, while others — including Red Kelly, Gordie Howe and Bobby Hull — were in Chicago as guests of the NHL. We were snubbed by one and all. Some of the group hoped to address a meeting of current players to explain our concerns and intentions, but Bob Goodenow of the NHLPA ruled out that possibility, telling us that the players had voted against having the retired players address their meeting. We did learn, however, that many current players did support us — among them, Marty McSorley, Ed Mio and Brett Hull.

Ed Garvey set up a meeting at the Holiday Inn, where he and the Toronto contingent were staying, to discuss our goals and options. Serious discussions took place about commencing legal action to recover the pension monies. We decided to hire Mark Zigler to prepare a more detailed report for us, and Mark estimated what kind of money it would take to get the ball rolling. At the meeting, an article by Russ Conway, sports editor of the *Eagle-Tribune* in Lawrence, Massachusetts, was circulated. The article took the form of a letter to John Ziegler, and it drew attention to the retired players' concerns. Carl was quoted: "There was a $24 million surplus in 1986 and $4 million was allocated in 1988 to the older players. Another $14 million was put aside to pay $250,000 lump sum bonuses at age 55 to current players who play 400 games. Then, if you can believe, $1.7 million was set aside for exorbitant administration costs. The $24 million came from the activity of players prior to 1986, and yet the owners are using it for current players." The NHL Pension Society ignored its fiduciary responsibility to protect the interests of the plan members by going along with this scheme that robbed the membership of their benefits. The Conway article also mentioned that the NHL had refused to recognize the group of retired players in Chicago. "They want us to go away," said Carl. "It's ironic, they're playing a Heroes of Hockey game as part of their All-Star game package, a sellout at $75 a ticket with national sponsorship. They say it helps the players' pension plan, but it's the same old story...

"Sure, just like all the international hockey games. This fall, NHL players will play in the Canada Cup series. They're always told it benefits the players' pension plan. Yet they'll play and not know what the receipts are at the end of the series. People ask, but neither Alan Eagleson nor the league will give them out."

Addressing Ziegler, Conway wrote: "You and your buddy Alan Eagleson have left retired players in the Twilight Zone for years when it comes to their pension plan.... You say you want to honour players who 'have contributed so significantly to the excellence of NHL hockey,' and yet you give the cold shoulder to Gordie Howe. Remember him? Highest goal scorer in the NHL? How about Bobby Hull? Carl Brewer?" It encouraged us to know that the public was getting a sense of what we were fighting for.

Meetings continued back in Toronto, and eventually we agreed collectively to retain Mark Zigler and proceed with a lawsuit. Before long, we had a group of seven applicants for the case: Carl Brewer, Andy Bathgate, Ed Shack, Allan Stanley, Leo Reise, Gordie Howe and Bobby Hull. To get started, we put up a $25,000 retainer, made up of $5,000 contributions from Carl and me, the Shacks, Allan Stanley, Bobby Orr and others.

***

"An integral reason for Sue and me to initiate the lawsuit was to draw attention to the stewardship of R. Alan Eagleson and the ongoing history of fraud, theft, misdirection and collusion."

April 26, 1991, was a momentous day for us, as we filed our lawsuit, naming the National Hockey League, its member clubs and the Pension Society as defendants, with the Ontario courts. It was a relief to take this step and to be moving forward; on the other hand, it was intimidating for all of us, especially because each of the seven applicants was squarely on the hook for costs if the action failed. As Carl so often said, "Any time you go to court it's a crap shoot." We knew the action would be defended vigorously by the NHL.

We had two reasons to celebrate on this date: it was also my 47th birthday. Carl took Norma Shack and me for a birthday luncheon at the Library Bar in the Royal York Hotel.

Public support for the lawsuit was strong and immediate. It helped that heavy hitters like Hull and Howe had signed on as applicants. Also the players involved in the suit played in an era — that of the six-team NHL — that defined hockey for fans of a certain age. Strangers approached us to express their support and their disgust at the conduct of the NHL, or to ask how they could help. Many shared their personal memories of Saturday nights spent watching *Hockey Night in Canada* with their families or of special outings to Maple Leaf Gardens with a parent for a Leafs game. Fans rose in unison to champion the cause of their old heroes.

Carl was especially pleased that the lawsuit had been filed. Finally, he felt that he had something tangible through which to focus attention on the misdeeds of Alan Eagleson.

The NHL's response was immediate and fierce, as it tried to deflect attention away from the court case. The first step it took was to distribute a notice of libel and slander against Bobby Orr and David Forbes. The two ex-Bruins had been quoted in an article by Les Munson of the now-defunct sports newspaper *The National* when the lawsuit was announced. "Our money is being used to pay pensions for current players," Orr said. "We have lost money from our pension fund, and we are still losing interest on that money, and now they're using our money to pay what they owe to today's players," Forbes charged. The NHL's motive in attacking one of the game's greatest stars was clear: it expected that everyone else would back down. Hockey players were, after all, known for their tendency to be easily intimidated by their bosses. Carl responded at once in a letter to John Ziegler: "It is regrettable that the NHL and the member clubs would resort to such treatment of one of our game's icons, Bobby Orr," he wrote, adding: "And isn't it interesting that baseball players who started their pension plan in 1947, as did the NHL, have assets in their plan of some $500 million while we, as far as we can understand, have $31.9 million. Yet, for years, persons occupying your office and others have been representing to hockey players that they had the best pension in all of major league sport." Hundreds of players clearly remembered being told every year at the annual All-Star weekend that theirs was the best pension.

What developed over the course of this litigation could only be described as a public-relations disaster for the NHL.

Shortly after our lawsuit was launched in Toronto, Colleen and Gordie Howe introduced us to a lawyer in Philadelphia — Ed Ferren, who was involved with the Philadelphia Flyers alumni. Ed and his team — David Ferguson, Joe Kearney and Phil Kirchner — were preparing to launch a similar pension suit in the United States, spearheaded by ex-Flyers Bob Dailey and Reggie Leach.

Carl, Allan Dick and I travelled to Philadelphia for an information meeting that Ferren and his team organized on May 21, 1991. Many of the Flyer alumni, including Dailey and Bill Barber, were in attendance, and so were Gordie Howe and Bryan "Bugsy" Watson. Carl and I were tremendously impressed by what we heard and learned, and we really took to the lawyers as well. They proposed that a lawsuit under ERISA (the U.S. federal Employee Retirement Income Security Act) would be much stronger than under the comparable Ontario laws. For one thing, even if pension plan documents permit employers to take monies out of surplus funds, ERISA forbids it. There was no such legislation governing the use of pension surpluses in Ontario, and this issue was the main focus of our Ontario action. Further, even though the NHL Pension Society was registered in Ontario, the legal team was certain that filing the suit in a U.S. jurisdiction was appropriate, since a large percentage of the plan's members were either citizens or residents of the United States.

Ed Ferren and his group proposed filing suit in Camden, New Jersey, across the Delaware River from Philadelphia. They planned to operate on a contingency basis, charging only for out-of-pocket expenses during the course of the action. (In our suit, the seven applicants were required to pay all their lawyers' costs, with the worrisome possibility that, if the action failed, they would also be liable for the defense's costs.) Finally — and this was of great interest to Carl and me — Ferren and his colleagues would be able to subpoena all sorts of documents and address a multitude of other concerns that were not being addressed in the Ontario suit. The rules of civil procedure in the States provided a wide-open scope for discovery. Also, if the Philadelphia group won the case, the damage award could be tripled. Carl was also enthusiastic because the U.S. suit would name Alan Eagleson as one of the co-defendants. Carl and I were brimming with excitement and optimism for the possibilities the U.S. action offered, and we quietly hoped that the Ontario suit would work its way slowly through the courts so that this one could get established.

To meet our legal bills, we had to conduct fund-raising activities, something none of us had ever done before. Our very first fund-raiser was a golf tournament at the Shacks' golf course in Vaughan, north of Toronto. Organizing the day took an enormous amount of planning and hard work — selling the foursomes, lining up prizes and volunteers to help out, buying food for the dinner. We got a lot of support and many generous donations. The day of the event, we were crazed with all the work, much of it last-minute, setting things up. Carl brought one of his sons along to help; however, he decided not to help, but rather sit back and mock the efforts of everyone else. He went so far as to try to dissuade, albeit it unsuccessfully, some of the other helpers from working. Well, this absolutely infuriated some of the team, and everyone was watching Carl to see what he was going to do about it. Fortunately for us, a friend of my daughter's, Joe Freitas, jumped right in and cooked all the steaks that night for well over a hundred people. Carl didn't handle the matter of his son; he came back having accepted some flimsy excuse. This sent a message to the group that Carl was weak and ineffective when it came to the tough calls. I knew this was going to be a huge problem.

***

Carl and I met regularly with Ed Ferren and his associates in the States, and they also came to Toronto to meet with us on occasion. They filed suit in June 1991, and Carl and I flew down several times to show our support. After several court dates, the NHL succeeded in convincing the American court that the Ontario action, filed just prior to the U.S. one, should take precedence, and the court terminated the action. We were greatly disappointed, but it had, nonetheless, been a very edifying experience getting to know the team of lawyers. Allan Dick took the well-reasoned position that the strongest possible situation for the retired players would have been a jointly orchestrated proceeding involving both sets of lawyers in both jurisdictions. Allan Stanley, the Howes, and Carl and I felt strongly that this was a worthwhile option, whereas the others were vehemently opposed.

Research by Ferren's group supported our conviction that many additional irregularities in the NHL Pension Plan were not being addressed in the Ontario suit. There was the matter of matching contributions — the players initially contributed $900 per season, and the NHL teams were supposed to match. But the numbers didn't add up. Had the appropriate contributions actually been made, player pensions ought to have been significantly higher. Remember, these contributions were paid out of salaries in the range of $7,000 to $9,000 per season — in other words, they represented a huge chunk of pre-tax salary that ought to have resulted in the Cadillac of pensions. Instead, Tod Sloan was receiving a pension of $4,176 a year based on a career that spanned some 13 years; while Gordie Howe was only entitled to $13,000 a year after a 32-year playing career.

Moreover, revenues from international hockey tournaments had not been accounted for to anyone's satisfaction, other than Eagleson's. Back in 1982, Phil Esposito, who had figured prominently in the 1972 series and who had served as president of the Players' Association, publicly questioned the whereabouts of all the money from international hockey. Carl enthusiastically applauded his stance and hoped it would lead to something worthwhile. However, Phil quickly gave up the chase, only to land a series of influential jobs in the NHL. Speaking to the Empire Club in Toronto on April 6, 1989, John Ziegler, the president of the NHL, said: "All of the profits go to the players' pensions, not only regular pension but also supplemental pension. This partnership has produced for players more than $10 million over the last 11 years."

This was an outright lie. Players had been duped — playing in those tournaments, extending their season, often purchasing their own insurance, and none of the money went towards improved pensions. Eventually, Carl and I got verification of this from Gary Bettman. We wrote to Bettman shortly after his appointment as commissioner of the NHL, asking for confirmation of the $10 million figure quoted by Ziegler, as well as how it was invested and for whom. Bettman's response of May 24, 1993, confirmed our deepest suspicions: "The NHL member clubs' share of international hockey proceeds are distributed annually among the NHL clubs for their general use." A pot of the money derived from international hockey remained with the NHL Players' Association and was identified to the players as a "bonus pension." Later, this term was changed to "employee benefit fund."

Carl and I spent considerable time and effort attempting to force the Pension Commission of Ontario (PCO) to make a declaration that these monies held by the NHLPA were in fact pension monies. It seemed like a no-brainer: pension benefits are what the players had been promised all along, and the funds were reported to players as a "bonus pension." A pension adviser who'd worked for the PCO for many years, Linda Ellis of Allan Smart Services in Toronto, helped us from time to time. She was adamant, after reviewing our documentation, that these were absolutely pension monies. At any rate, an investigation by Ed Garvey, Ritch Winter and Ron

Salcer in 1989 turned up evidence that Eagleson had for years been handling these monies as his own personal bank. Cash from this fund was routinely lent out to business associates and friends of his for deals that were highly questionable. Real estate development projects were a favourite — loans advanced without proper appraisals, without security and at rates of interest far below market rates for such high-risk projects. Some of these loans were reported as bad loans to the players and not repaid at all. Continuing research that Carl and I conducted revealed that Eagleson had an undisclosed personal interest in some of these transactions.

Linda Ellis firmly believed that the PCO had an obligation to declare the funds as pension moneys. From our point of view, it was imperative that this declaration be made because the ways in which Eagleson had been handling the monies violated the Pension Benefits Act. In February 1993, Carl and I met with a functionary at the Pension Commission's office in downtown Toronto and discussed the details with him. I followed up by documenting our information in a 16-page brief that we forwarded, under Carl's name, to Ross Peebles, Superintendent of Pensions. The brief set out certain facts:

> *I am a member of the NHL Pension Plan registered with the PCO and with Revenue Canada taxation.*
>
> *I am a member also of the NHLPA "Employee Benefit Fund," a.k.a. "The Canadian Pension Plan," a.k.a. "Bonus Pension Plan."*
>
> *I am writing to you to seek clarification of these funds, as my intelligence reports to me that, irrespective of the fact that the "Bonus Pension Plan" was never registered with the Pension Commission of Ontario, the monies in the fund ought to have been invested in accordance with the rules and regulations of the Pension Benefits Act of Ontario. I emphasize to you the fact that we were consistently informed that these were "pension" monies by the Executive Director of the NHLPA, Alan Eagleson.*
>
> *Subject to your ruling in this matter, and I respectfully submit that the PCO would have great difficulty justifying to those players who participated in these international hockey series at various times for minimal or nil remuner-*

The Brewer brothers — Frank,
Jack and Carl — Vancouver,
circa 1947

"Did the Maple Leaf jerseys
disported by Frank and me
presage an NHL career for
me?" Carl mused

Carl Brewer, circa 1952

Carl's parents —
Elizabeth "Tote" McAvoy,
and Carl Brewer, Sr.

—credit Authors' Collection

Front Row: Elizabeth
McAvoy and Carl
Oldshwager Brewer,
on their wedding day,
April 27, 1929.

—credit Authors' Collection

Carl at Lakewood Camp, an Easter Seals Camp, with two young campers, summer 1957 —*credit Authors' Collection*

Carl Brewer, Conn Smythe (Director of Easter Seals Camps) and Bob McAleese at Lakewood Camp, summer 1957 —*credit Authors' Collection*

March 1963 — Carl Brewer and Susan Foster meet — the beginning of a lifelong journey together —*credit Authors' Collection*

Carl shakes hands "dutifully" with his coach George "Punch" Imlach

—credit Hockey Hall of Fame

Carl and defense partner Bob Baun savour the Leafs' Stanley Cup victory, April, 1962

—credit Billy Harris - courtesy Harris family

Carl Brewer, bare hands controlling his hockey stick, scores on Chicago Blackhawks' "Mr. Goalie" Glenn Hall   —credit Hockey Hall of Fame

Left to right: Carl Brewer, Alan Eagleson (future Players' Association leader), Billy Harris and Bob Tindall, circa 1961

—credit Authors' Collection

Left to right: Carl Brewer, Dick Duff and Billy Harris on their way to class at McMaster University, Summer 1963

—credit Authors' Collection

Toronto Maple Leafs hamming it up as barbershop singers.
Left to Right: George Armstrong, Don Simmons, Carl Brewer, Bob Nevin
Ron Stewart and Bob Pulford   —*credit Authors' Collection*

Carl and Frank Mahovlich, 1962   —*credit courtesy Senator Frank Mahovlich*

Carl Brewer (background) and
Frank Mahovlich enjoying the beach
in Nassau, 1959

—credit courtesy Senator Frank Mahovlich

Carl Brewer, a member of
Father David Bauer's National
Team, 1966–67. Ah, the intensity!

—credit Authors' Collection

Muskegon, Michigan, 1968 — Carl and his young son, Christopher, and
Carl's mom —credit Authors' Collection

Muskegon Mohawks, IHL, 1967–68 League champions with Carl Brewer as player/coach. —*credit Authors' Collection*

Left to Right: Bob Baun, Frank Mahovlich and Carl Brewer reunited as Detroit Red Wings, 1969–70

—*credit courtesy Senator Frank Mahovlich*

George Donaldson, former Managing Partner, Clarkson Gordon, B.A., C.A., ASA Officer of the Court — a delightful man and cherished friend who was most generous and of invaluable help to us with the Pension fight

—*credit courtesy Lorraine Mahoney*

April 4, 1997 — NHHL Old-timers' Luncheon tribute to Carl for the Pension victory. Left to right: Gary Aldcorn, Tod Sloan, "Chief" George Armstrong, Carl Brewer, Dick Duff and Mark Zigler, of Koskie and Minsky, the players' pension lawyer —*credit courtesy Bob McNeil*

Peter Conacher (left) and
John McCormack present
Carl with a beautiful soap
stone carving depicting Carl
as a Toronto Maple Leaf, on
behalf of all the players

—*credit courtesy Bob McNeil*

Carl and Sue celebrate
the Ontario Court
of Appeal victory in
the Pension Litigation

—*credit Sun Media Corp.*

January 6, 1998 —
A celebration!
Carl and Sue share
laughs with friends
at "The Fours" in
Boston following the
sentencing of Alan
Eagleson in Boston
Federal Court

*—credit courtesy Russ Conway,
Lawrence Eagle Tribune*

A happy group in Boston, January 6, 1998. Left to right: Bobby Orr, Rick
Smith, Sue Foster, Russ Conway and Tom Lockwood

—credit courtesy Russ Conway, Lawrence Eagle Tribune

May 1997 — "Legends of Hockey" celebration, Helsinki Finland.
Left to right: Ulf Nilsson, Paul Henderson and Carl Brewer
—*credit courtesy Ari-Veikko Peltonen*

February 13, 1999 — MEMORIES! Nostalgic Leafs Jim Pappin, Carl
Brewer, Ed Litzenberger (Bob Baun in background) await a final hockey
hurrah at Maple Leaf Gardens —*credit CP(Frank Gunn)*

Carl congratulates the Honourable Frank Mahovlich at his investiture into the Senate of Canada, Ottawa, June 15, 1998. We were Frank's guests at this special occasion —*credit courtesy Senator Frank Mahovlich*

Left to Right: Carl Brewer, Dr. Tom Pashby and Susan Foster at a Dr. Tom Pashby Sports Safety Dinner —*credit courtesy Dr. Tom Pashby*

Fun on a legends of hockey cruise;
Back Row, left to right: Eddie Shack, Ron Sutter and Bill Clement
Front Row: left to right: Carl Brewer, Lorne "Gump" Worsley, Ralph Backstrom

—credit Susan Foster

Carl and "Mr. Hockey" Gordie Howe

—credit Authors' Collection

Our happiest times — in France! Carl and Sue enjoy Sunday lunch in the Beaujolais Villages town of Beaujeu —credit Authors' Collection

October 21, 2000, a joyous Carl Brewer celebrates his birthday at Cashel House in Connemara, Ireland, his ancestral homeland —credit Susan Foster

*ation and for the specific gain and benefit of having "en-
hanced" pension benefits, that these monies are anything
but pension monies.*

After a considerable length of time, during which Ross Peebles communicated with lawyers for the NHL and the NHLPA, we got his decision. To put
it bluntly, the PCO did not — and this opinion was shared by the experts
monitoring the situation on our behalf — do the honourable thing. Rather,
they chose not to assume any jurisdiction over the matter and declined to
make a determination about the status of the monies. Carl and I would find
over the years that the PCO was consistently not prepared to make the
tough calls. Player interests were certainly not well served by this result.

Another Canada Cup was confirmed for August 1991. By this time, we
knew that the profits from international hockey were not being used to enhance the players' pensions, so it was unbelievable when Mike Keenan, the
coach and general manager of Team Canada — and an Eagleson client —
was quoted in the press as saying, "The thing the players have to remember
is all these monies are for the pension plan." Carl wrote Keenan to straighten
him out: "In fact, no monies whatsoever from international hockey have
ever been contributed to the plan to improve or enhance the pension benefits of players. Indeed, monies from international hockey — i.e., the Canada
Cup series — that have found their way into the pension plan have been
used to fund the owners' contributions that they were obliged to fund from
their own resources whether or not there was such a series..."

The reply to Carl's letter came from none other than Alan Eagleson. He
accused Carl of making defamatory allegations and stating an outrageous,
malicious lie.

Wayne Gretzky, the "Great One," was one player who could have made
a difference, not only for the retired players who were fighting to regain
their pension monies but also for those players agreeing to play in the
Canada Cup under false pretences. All Gretzky had to do was ask Eagleson
to produce the financial statements for the earlier tournaments before
agreeing to play. David Forbes had requested the information from Hockey
Canada, only to be told to ask Eagleson. Ritch Winter wrote to Gretzky,
asking him to take a position in this matter by asking to see the financial
statements of the previous Canada Cups before committing to play in the
1991 tournament. Gretzky had also assured Gordie Howe earlier in the year

that he'd help him get the answers he sought about his pension. In the end, Gretzky backed down, and in so doing he let all retired players down. Gretzky let Alan Eagleson speak for him, and Eagleson told the press that Gretzky had told him: "I feel bad for Gordie Howe and the others who aren't getting the type of pension I'm getting. But I'll feel badly for myself because I won't have near the pension that Eric Lindros will have. That's part of life." What naïveté! What a team player!

***

Although the U.S. lawsuit had been stopped, we continued to stay in touch with Ed Ferren. For several summers in the early 1990s, we went to Cherry Hill, New Jersey, to attend the Anne Ferren Golf Tournament, a charity event in support of head injuries named in honour of Ed's daughter, who had suffered a life-altering head injury. Mark Howe was the chair of the event, and we met Gordie and Colleen there and enjoyed spending time with them. One year, at the dinner, I was seated at a table with people I didn't know; Carl was up working the room. All of a sudden, I felt a large presence come up behind me and plant a big kiss squarely on my lips. It was none other than Gordie Howe. I glanced at the people seated at the table and all of them were gobsmacked, looking at me in shocked disbelief — not only because Gordie was at the table but because of the familiarity between us. It was quite comical. Carl and I admired Ed's dedication to worthwhile causes, and the feeling was mutual — Ed often said, "In my next life, I want to come back as Carl Brewer!"

***

During the course of the investigation into the NHL Pension Plan, a particularly disturbing letter surfaced from the files at the Pension Commission of Ontario.

In 1987, the Commission had revised its regulations to require that participants in all multi-employer pension plans be represented on the pension plan's board. Of course, the players had not had a seat on their own pension board since 1969, when Eagleson negotiated it away in exchange for the NHL taking over "the full funding of the plan." It had been a very bad deal all around for retired NHLers.

The letter in question was written by Alan Eagleson. Without the knowledge or consent of the NHLPA player representatives or the retired players, he sent a letter to the Honourable Murray Elston, chair of the province's Management Board of Cabinet, supporting the NHL Pension Society's application for an exemption from this regulation. In the letter, he claimed falsely that he represented "all players who participate in the National Hockey League Club Pension Plan." He assured Elston, "In our view, this [exemption] is in the best interests of our membership." Interestingly, the letter was dated August 1, 1989, right around the time that Ed Garvey, Ritch Winter and Ron Salcer were questioning his conduct. At the end of the letter, Eagleson added a handwritten notation that read, "Murray, Personal regards, Alan."

The letter provided concrete evidence that Eagleson was working in concert with NHL management and not in the best interests of the players. Journalist Russ Conway learned through his investigative work that Ken Sawyer, the NHL's vice-president and head of the NHL Pension Society, asked Eagleson to write the letter. Eagleson could blatantly lie about whom he had the authority to represent because the retired players would never know about it. The word "collusion" was beginning to be whispered, and this letter certainly pointed in that direction.

Elston forwarded Eagleson's letter to the Pension Commission, which granted the exemption. After a complaint was filed with the Ontario Ministry of Finance by the "Group of Seven" — the name Allan Stanley came up with for the seven applicants — Floyd Laughren, the province's minister of finance, repealed the exemption. This was done on July 26, 1993. This step was encouraging, but the NHL continued to ignore the government's mandate. Carl and I kept up a letter-writing campaign for years, lobbying various ministers of finance to force the NHL into line, but the government seemed reluctant to press the matter. Mike Gartner, a former NHLPA president, told me in 2006 that joint trusteeship of the pension plan had only recently been restored.

CHAPTER 11

VINDICATION

"I didn't foresee any of this happening. The pension, I was hoping it would work out. My feeling was Alan Eagleson had to be stopped. He was stopped."

In October 1992, Carl and I had decided to take a break — and take advantage of an airline seat sale — and head to Europe to spend a few days with friends in Austria. We also looked forward to a few more days relaxing, just the two of us, at some place yet to be determined. We never planned ahead when we travelled!

October 21 was Carl's 54th birthday, and on that day we took the train from Innsbruck, Austria, to Lucerne, Switzerland, arriving late on a damp, rainy, dreary afternoon. Carl stayed with our bags in the station while I went out to look for a hotel. Right at the top of the escalator, as I exited the station, I saw a lovely old hotel — Le Monopol. They had a room and I registered us, relieved to find something so close by. After resting for a while in our room and freshening up, we headed out to celebrate Carl's special day. We walked across the bridge into Lucerne's old town and enjoyed wandering through the winding streets. Eventually, Carl spotted the restaurant where he wanted to have his birthday dinner: the Ristorante Pizzeria al Forno, on the ground floor of Hotel zum Weissen Kruz, an elegant old hotel along the river.

It was a comfortable, homey Italian eatery with lots of atmosphere, and we quickly immersed ourselves in the coziness and warmth of the dining room. We ordered a bottle of white wine and, over a wonderful meal of salad and pasta with a delectable sauce of cream and wild mushrooms, we spent several hours enjoying one another's company. We weren't forgetting the months of hard work and strife that had just passed, but it wasn't foremost in our minds. We were just enjoying the moment. The waiter was jovial and convivial. Patrons sitting around us chatted amiably with us — Carl conversing in fluent German as we ordered another bottle of wine. All I could understand of the conversation were his periodic references to me, as he'd look at me or touch my arm and say, "*mein frau*." We prolonged our happy evening with dessert — a memorable tiramisu — and cappuccinos. The waiter gave us celebratory grappa. It was obvious that Carl enjoyed the evening immensely and was in a happy and unusually relaxed mood.

The next morning, we had breakfast at our hotel. Carl felt that, at $75 a night, the hotel was pricey, so we started out on foot to look for a less expensive place. We walked for several hours — and into and out of a dozen or more hotels. Finally, we stopped for a coffee and I pointed out to Carl that many of the hotels we'd seen were more expensive than ours, while some of those that cost less were rather dingy, and it seemed to me that the most we could save was about $10 a night. I asked him if $20 was worth our wasting any more of our day looking at hotels. He looked at me, his eyes wide with amazement, and said, "Of course not. You're right: let's go back and tell them we want to stay." The rest of the day, he kept remarking to me how much he admired the way I made things so simple while he made everything so complicated.

On the 23rd, we went on an excursion up to Mount Pilatus — 7,000 feet above sea level. The views were breathtaking, both at the top and on the journey up in the funicular — the steepest railway anywhere! When we arrived back in Lucerne in the late afternoon, I phoned my 16-year-son Daniel in Toronto. By now, Carl and I were giving no thought at all to the pension decision. Dan immediately exclaimed, "You won!"

"What did we win?" I asked. Excitedly, he replied: "Your lawsuit. There are hundreds of messages here. Every reporter in the country wants to talk to you guys." At this point, Carl had come up beside me and I told him the news. He was speechless, and tears filled his eyes. We put in a call to Mark Zigler to get further details and learned that it was a solid victory for the players. Mr. Justice George Adams had handed down a 120-page judgment — "appeal-proof," Mark told us. (Sometime later, Carl heard from a fellow he ran into from time to time at the Balmy Beach Club, a friend of Justice Adams, that the judge had taken the mountain of documentation with him to his cottage over the summer and read every page of it.)

I think we were both completely numb. Carl suggested that we go for a drink, and we walked over to the outdoor terrace at the Hotel des Alpes along the river and had a few glasses of wine, saying little. By dinnertime, the news was starting to sink in and we certainly raised a glass or two to one another as we reflected on more than a decade of struggling. We'd been right all along, and the confirmation was sweet. Nevertheless, there was no sense of finality: we knew that the NHL would appeal; we were still determined to get Carl his rightful pension credits arising from his successful arbitration case in 1986; and, of course, there was the huge issue of R. Alan Eagleson. Over the years, Carl had made no secret of the fact that the pension battle was, for him, most importantly one way of focusing attention on the stewardship of Alan Eagleson.

In Toronto, the media jumped on the news with a vengeance. The newspaper headlines screamed, "NHL Acted Reprehensively Towards Players." *Net Worth*, the exposé by investigative reporters David Cruise and Alison Griffiths, had become a best seller and had helped educate the general public to the fact that, throughout history, all was not as it might have seemed in the business of pro hockey. Now, with this decision, it was clear to one and all that hockey's greatest legends had been ripped off and cheated by the NHL — and the NHL Pension Society. Justice Adams made two comments of interest. One of these read: "Had the NHLPA been representing the applicants, and had it been a trade union subject to the duty of fair representation under the Ontario Labour Relations Act, I fail to see how it would have honoured its duty in the circumstances." Secondly, Judge Adams took aim squarely at Alan Eagleson by writing, "Apparent moral shortcomings of the NHLPA's handling of pension matters was captured in the November 21, 1988, 'Merry Christmas' letter to former players."

Right on cue and as expected, on November 19, 1992, the NHL's legal representatives filed a notice of appeal with the Ontario Court of Appeal. We knew the fight was a long way from over.

Shortly after we received the wonderful news of the Adams decision, Lorraine Mahoney introduced Carl and me to a most incredible gentleman, George Donaldson. George turned out to be an invaluable resource for us, and he became a very close and dear friend. George was well into his 80s when we met — a large, portly, jovial man with a great head of grey hair and a warm, mischievous smile. He had been head of the accounting firm Clarkson Gordon for years, and was still very active doing consulting work around the world for numerous multinational corporations. Over the next few years, George provided us with a great deal of pertinent information and guidance. After our first meeting, he volunteered to review the lengthy decision of Justice Adams and all the annual financial statements of the NHL Pension Society.

We met with George after the weekend he devoted to his review. His findings and facts, which he related in his typically colourful fashion, were alarming and disconcerting. For starters, he told us point blank that all of the audited financial statements of the Pension Society were unacceptable and would never have been accepted had they ever come across his desk for approval. For one thing, there were no accompanying notes, as required by proper accounting procedures, to clarify and support the numbers and the conclusions drawn. His synopsis: "These statements aren't worth a pinch of 'coon shit."

Next, he pointed out that the 1981 financial statement was reporting on the years 1976 and 1977 — *four and five years in arrears.* He said this was absolutely unacceptable. Apparently, Clarence Campbell had been ill and the NHL Pension Society just sat in limbo all that time.

George fervently denounced James Ford's acting as auditor for both the NHL and the Pension Society. This, he advised, was a blatant conflict of interest. He questioned why a professional chartered accountant would ever have allowed himself to be in such a conflicting role.

George pointed out that that it was scandalous and completely inappropriate that the costs of administering the Pension Plan were reducing the benefits to the players. This really irritated him. His advice to us: "Stick the harpoon in and put an outboard on the end of it." The costs, in the amount of $808,000, were not only excessive in George's opinion, but he indicated to us the passage in the text of the plan where it clearly stated that the costs of administering the plan were to be borne by the member clubs and were not to deplete the value of the plan. (At other times, the owners had paid the costs out of the All-Star game revenues.)

He also informed us that the NHL Pension Society ought to have required verification of the number of games each player was credited with towards his pension. Without such certification, George felt there were too many loopholes for favoured players to be accorded credits they were not entitled to receive, while other other players, less in favour, could be cheated out of their full entitlements.

George felt that circumstances surrounding the 1969 agreement whereby the NHLPA gave up its seat on the Pension Society board was tremendously significant. We were pleased to hear George confirm to us what we had suspected for a long time. The concession, one of Alan Eagleson's first acts as executive director of the newly formed Players' Association, had resulted in the NHL contributing only about $1,300 to $1,400 per player per season. Prior to this agreement, each player had been contributing $1,500 per season, and this was supposed to have been matched by the member clubs for a total annual contribution of $3,000 per player. This clearly was the understanding the players were under when they were told about this change. Players remembered well how onerous it had been to come up with that contribution of $1,500 in an era when salaries were not much more than average wages. George concluded that, over all the intervening years, the shortfall amounted to "megabucks," and he felt this money was still owed to the players.

George Donaldson was impressed with the Adams decision, but cautioned us that it was good "only as far as it went." He advised us that what was missing was some provision to recover the money not paid into the pension fund by the clubs. He explained that once a determination was made about the surplus monies that belonged back in the fund, one then had to look at the contractual agreement regarding the funding of the plan and calculate the amount still owing. He called this "double liability" and advised that this, too, amounted to "megabucks."

George's information lit a fire under us. We knew that the Ontario lawsuit had focused on only a very narrow slice of the what was at stake: the surplus monies. We regretted that the U.S. action had not continued, because Ed Ferren had spoken of things like "double liability" and clearly intended to go after much more than our lawsuit sought. George, being an astute, brilliant businessman and professional accountant, advised that the entire pension plan needed to be subjected to a forensic audit. He considered his findings offensive, not only to the players, but also to his profession; like us, George couldn't comprehend the problems we'd had in getting the players to agree to do something about these issues.

George Donaldson passed away in 1999. Carl and I mourned the loss of a dear friend, a tremendous ally and a mentor.

There are basically two types of pension plans: "defined benefit" and "defined contribution." In the former, monies are contributed that will guarantee a specified, predetermined benefit at retirement. The employer (or trustee) bears the risk, and must pay the fixed amount, no matter how successfully (or unsuccessfully) the contributions are invested. In the latter, the contributions grow and accumulate in the plan in accordance with market conditions and the investment success of the trustee. The amount the employee draws upon retirement is not pre-determined; in other words, the burden of investment risk falls on the employee.

The NHL pension plan, historically, was represented as a defined benefit plan, and players were entitled to a specified figure once they started drawing their pension. From 1958 to 1964, each player contributed $900 per year and the benefit was $180 per year of service. The kicker was that the member clubs agreed to match the $900 per player. In 1964, the player's contribution increased to $1,500 a year, which was also to be matched by the team. The benefit was increased to $300 per year of service. However, although the Pension Society told the players it was administering a defined benefit plan, it was representing the plan to all regulatory authorities as a *defined contribution plan*. In Justice Adams's 1992 decision, he wrote, "The plan is reasonably characterized as a 'defined contribution plan.' The contributions were fixed by the plan and trust." He added: "From its inception, the club pension plan and trust was registered with Revenue Canada as a 'defined contribution plan.' The respondent has argued that this was a matter of form only and that the plan was a defined benefit plan. In effect the Court is being asked to ignore the formal characterization of the plan to two important regulatory bodies." Adams refused to do so.

Judge Adams commented on the 1969 deal whereby the players gave up their seat on the pension board in exchange for what was characterized as the full funding of the plan (expected to be the combined contribution of $3,000 per player per year). Adams wrote: "The cost to the clubs of their contributions, I might note, was not the $1,500 each player had been contributing." He also spoke directly about the Players' Association: "The NHLPA had no authority to act for retired players in the 1969 'deal.'"

***

It would have been hopelessly naïve to expect the "Group of Seven" to get along for any length of time. Early on in the proceedings, a schism began to develop in the wake of vehement disagreements over a number of issues. Keith McCreary, although not a signatory to the lawsuit, had become more and more involved with the group. McCreary had the admiration and respect of Andy Bathgate and the Shacks, particularly Norma. Carl was cautioned early on by several of the older retired players to steer clear of McCreary, but he didn't pay attention.

Originally, Carl's dream was to set up a not-for-profit corporation for retired players for fraternal purposes, but more specifically as a resource centre to offer advice and support for the traditional problems of pensions and disability insurance. Carl always talked of this, but at the same time said that he didn't want to run it. It was part of Carl's nature not to seek the leadership roles in life, mainly because he didn't see himself having leadership abilities. The problem was, in order for his vision to be realized, he had to be the leader.

The split within the ranks began over legal fees. Initially, we were quoted a range between $75,000 and $150,000 for the lawsuit — after a retainer of $25,000. When this amount had been raised, Carl felt strongly that the group should hold the lawyers to the quote and let them wait until the action was over for payment of any additional costs. The way Carl saw it, after the victory in the lower court, the NHL was on the hook for all the legal fees on a solicitor-client basis and would have to cough up the money anyway. The others weren't comfortable with this idea. When McCreary asked Carl what they'd do if the law firm didn't go along with this proposal, Carl's answer was typical: "We'll change lawyers." That idea was absolutely shocked the others, most of whom had little experience with lawyers and lawsuits and who were already feeling traumatized just being involved in this action. Carl, for his part, had been embroiled in legal and quasi-legal entanglements for years, and in his arbitration case he used 22 lawyers before we finally found Allan Dick!

By late 1992, the McCreary faction had basically ousted Carl and me and taken over. I was disappointed at the way this happened. I could see it coming, and I encouraged Carl to assert his role more forcefully because it had all begun with him, but he was unable to do so. I told him that if he wanted to see things done right, he had to take the reins and be in charge, because if any sign of weakness is shown, there are always others waiting in the wings, most of whom never had an original idea of their own, to barge in and take control. I personally didn't trust McCreary, but on the day of the Shack golf tournament my suspicions were confirmed when I saw him help himself to one of the prizes that had been donated: some choice seats for a Blue Jays baseball game (these were the days when the Toronto Blue Jays were a hot ticket).

Around this time, McCreary sent out a letter soliciting more funds for the lawsuit. Carl went ballistic and fired off his own letter in the form of a "Memorandum to All Retired Players Involved in the Pension Lawsuit":

> As the initiator of this lawsuit,… I feel a responsibility and an obligation to point out to you my very serious misgivings about… McCreary's plea to you for funds. McCreary claims to have raised about $450,000. The total legal and actuarial fees billed total approximately $303,142.98, of which [we have] paid about $170,928.09. Obviously, gentlemen, the facts do not add up.

Carl pointed out that McCreary had never made a financial contribution towards the fees, yet he was asking others to do so. It was important to Carl that all the players understand the NHL's liability:

> The decision of Mr. Justice Adams provided that all costs incurred by the players in this action are to be repaid by the league owners on a solicitor-client basis. I would ask you gentlemen why in the world you would even consider advancing funds when all the bills have not been paid with the money already raised and there has been no accounting to you for the funds raised.

So that there could be no mistaking his reason for writing the memorandum, Carl added:

> Keith McCreary, working in concert with Norma Shack and others, wanted to have control of this organization and do things his way, and I was unceremoniously pushed aside. My interest had been in seeing this association work to support the interests of all players, not just a few self-serving ones.

***

The appeal proceedings were heard at Osgoode Hall before Chief Justice John Morden and Justices Allan Goodman and Lloyd Houlden over three and a half days, September 21–24, 1993. During these hearings, many hockey legends sat in the Toronto courtroom. In the initial proceedings in the lower court, many former players, mostly from the Toronto area, showed up as a sign of solidarity and support for the seven applicants. At the appeal stage, there was a broader and more powerful presence. We saw the likes of Montreal Canadiens greats Dickie Moore, Dollard St. Laurent, Emile "Butch" Bouchard and Henri Richard. Gordie and Colleen Howe were on hand for the entire three and a half days. Chicago's Stan Mikita was there, as were David Keon and many others. One day, in the corridor, David approached me and thanked me most sincerely for all the work I had contributed. I really appreciated his gesture and his thoughtful remarks. Carl often mentioned with awe the fact that David had stayed clear of Eagleson and the NHLPA from the outset — when none of the other guys did — and that his wife, Lola, recognized Eagleson for what he was.

Once again, our lawyer, Mark Zigler, was brilliant. If he'd done an impressive and extraordinary job for us before Justice Adams in the lower court, he awed us even more at this crucial juncture with his knowledge and courtroom presence.

On the afternoon of September 24, the three-judge panel adjourned the proceedings with the statement, "Judgment reserved."

Speaking to *Globe and Mail* reporter Kevin McGran after the proceedings, Carl was upbeat and enthused as he stated: "We did it! Eagleson is no longer part of the game. John Ziegler is no longer part of the game [he had been replaced by Gil Stein and then Gary Bettman] and Bill Wirtz has a diminished interest in the game [he was no longer chair of the NHL Board of Governors]." Gordie Howe was a little more philosophical in speaking to the *Toronto Star*'s reporter Gary Oakes. Commenting on the multimillion dollar contract awarded to Wayne Gretzky, Gordie stated, "Well, there's a ton of us who've done the same thing and with very little compensation."

On September 28, I faxed a letter to Colleen Howe. "Last night, Carl was thinking about the week in court and he said that he felt the suit would be successful for three reasons: 1) because we are right; 2) because Mark Zigler was brilliant; and 3) because Gordie Howe, the greatest in the game, sat in court for the entire three and a half days of the hearings — and that that spoke volumes for the players and the situation."

In my letter, I shared a moment I had found very touching. "One day last week when we were all having lunch at the court, someone came up and asked Gordie how he liked being on the road so much. Gordie replied that it wasn't too bad, that he's used to it. Then his face lit up and his eyes glistened and he added, 'And, we're together; that's what's important.'"

At about 11 o'clock on the morning of February 16, 1994, I was busy organizing some documents when Colleen phoned — it was good to hear from her. From the first time I met Colleen, I knew she was my friend, and she was also a mentor to me. Throughout all of the trials and tribulations of the pension proceedings, Gordie and Colleen Howe had been solid supporters. Gordie described the friendship we shared: "Colleen and I spent many, many hours with Carl and Sue with the pension battle. We both had a great deal of respect for them and their hard work and dedication." We chatted about a number of things that morning — conversations with Colleen were never short! She informed me that, the day before, she'd had a lengthy discussion with U.S. justice authorities about the fact that Gordie had been named to the board of the NHL Pension Society but was never informed of it by the league — so he was never present at any meetings.

It was during this conversation that Colleen talked to me about Gordie; she spoke of how so very unlike Carl he was. "Carl is tough and outspoken and a man to stand up for his principles. Gordie, on the other hand, has always been at the other extreme — Gordie was always subservient, quiet and afraid to make waves." She told me of her pride in Gordie for standing up and putting his name on the lawsuit and being able to follow Carl's example. "There have been two occasions in Gordie's life when he has stood up for himself," she told me. "Putting his name on the pension lawsuit was one instance; and years earlier, when he learned that the Red Wings were paying both Bob Baun and Carl much more than him, he stood up and went to Bruce Norris and demanded to be paid accordingly."

In midafternoon, another phone call, this time from CBC reporter Dwight Smith, completely changed the face of my day. Dwight informed me that it was just coming across the Canadian Press wire that the Ontario Court of Appeal would release its decision the following day. He wanted to arrange an interview with Carl at that time. *WOW!* Immediately I phoned Bruce Dowbiggin and asked if he had heard anything. He hadn't. Next, I called Mark Zigler's office, and Dana, the receptionist, was very excited — "You've heard something too!" she said. Mark was out of the office, and no one had been able to locate him; Ron Davis, Mark's very able assistant, was in Sudbury for an arbitration hearing and Roberto, the student involved in the case, was nowhere to be found! We agreed to keep in touch.

Shortly, Bruce called back, saying, "Yeah, the word is out." My phone's call-waiting beep went off and Dwight Smith was on the line again to inform me that the decision would be released at ten-thirty in the front offices of Osgoode Hall. He requested an interview with Carl at that time and I confirmed it. I returned to Bruce and told him of the schedule. Bruce asked if he could drive down to the court with us, and I told him we'd pick him up.

At this point, Carl knew nothing. I had noticed his car at the Chick 'n' Deli, his brother's bar down the street, about an hour and a half earlier, so I put a call in to him. Carl sounded very subdued — he became very quiet when I told him the news. He said he really appreciated my calling him and said, "This is great news — one way or the other."

Finally, Mark Zigler called me late in the afternoon, and he was very upbeat. He told me that they'd get a copy of the decision at nine o'clock and suggested that we meet in their boardroom shortly after nine. I talked to Russ Conway of the *Lawrence Eagle-Tribune*, who was beside himself with anticipation. Russ went to great lengths to prepare me for a possible negative decision. He told me if, for any reason, the Adams decision was overturned, we shouldn't be upset because the FBI and U.S. Department of Justice had it all covered with their ongoing investigation into Alan Eagleson (more about this in Chapter 12). During the conversation, I mentioned that I had heard rumblings that things might not be going as smoothly as we had hoped with respect to the investigation. "Quite the opposite!" Russ shot back. He described at length the timing of the release of this decision, referring to it as "a drawing of lines in the sand between Canada and the States," and he said that we would one day have a good laugh about the "coincidence" of this announcement.

Despite Russ's assurances and the generally upbeat mood, I had little peace of mind. Carl was in a very contemplative mood, a little overwhelmed by the magnitude and the implications of what lay ahead of us. Consequently, I didn't sleep well. One thought kept running through my mind: if the Court of Appeal were going to overturn the lower court's decision, they wouldn't make a public announcement in advance of the release. Things somehow seemed positive.

Next morning, we got off the elevator at the offices of Koskie and Minsky and the receptionist, Dana, was beaming. She told us that there were a lot of excited people around and it was "all thumbs-up." When we walked into the boardroom, Mark Zigler rose to his feet and announced, "There he is!" We both shook hands with Mark, who informed us that it was victory all the way. Leo Reise, one of the applicants, and Norma Shack and Keith McCreary were already in the room. We discussed the need to prepare a press release on behalf of the seven applicants. Other partners in the law firm wandered in to offer their congratulations. There was a wonderful joyous spirit of accomplishment and success in the air.

Mark had scheduled a conference call for nine-thirty — Gordie and Colleen called in from Traverse City, Michigan, and Gordie reminded us that it was Colleen's birthday. Andy Bathgate called from Whistler, British Columbia; Bobby Hull called from — only he knows where! When Bobby heard the verdict, he let out a whoop and a holler: "It's better than winning the Stanley Cup!" he yelled. Eddie Shack called from Hamilton. Everyone was celebrating the victory as if it were the end of the road. However, I happened to read a press release from the NHL that came in while we were sitting there, and I noticed the line, "The NHL will abide by the higher court rulings." It hadn't yet occurred to the other applicants that there was still a higher court: the Supreme Court of Canada. But Carl and I recognized immediately that this was where we were headed next.

Andy Bathgate, showing no class, announced that there were three people in the room who had made it all happen: Mark, Norma Shack and Keith McCreary. Mark immediately jumped in to correct him. When Colleen Howe started to speak about the victory, Leo Reise began to mock her rudely and laugh at her in a catty and unkind manner, as if she had no right to comment. His chauvinistic disrespect was disgusting and ignorant, and it was not the first time we had seen him behave so rudely towards Colleen. I gave him a stern glare and he straightened up. Carl later said that if he could change anything, it would have been not to have Bathgate and Reise as part of the action. There were constant disagreements and power plays going on, and I give Mark Zigler full marks for keeping this action together throughout. He wasn't only a genius in his knowledge of pensions, he was a virtuoso in the area of human relations, too!

Mark began drafting a press release, and Carl and I were amused when some of the guys started telling him what to say and how to say it. "The world's great orators," Carl whispered to me. Mark prevailed and composed a succinct statement that all agreed served them well.

From Mark's office, I phoned our friend Ralph Backstrom in Colorado to tell him of the victory. I think I woke him up, but he sounded genuinely pleased and excited. Ralph had come to be a good friend and was supportive throughout the lengthy struggles. Next, I phoned Jim Roberts in St. Louis to share the news. His daughter Vicky answered. Her parents were in Florida, but when I told her the news she shouted, "You mean WE WON?!" Vicky told me she'd pass on the message, adding, "Dad will be thrilled." Her comment made me realize that the players weren't the only ones affected by this case; their families were interested and excited, too.

Bruce Dowbiggin, Carl and I left to walk to Osgoode Hall. It was a splendid, mild sunny morning. As we rounded the corner past the Law Society, I was amazed by what I saw. The media were there in droves — television cameramen, reporters and photographers. Bruce immediately introduced us to Paul Hunter of CBC television, and Dwight Smith introduced himself. Everyone converged on Carl and crowded around with microphones pressed towards him. Carl answered question after question in a warm, relaxed and articulate manner. The picture-taking persisted. As a Christmas gift, I had given Carl an Irish woollen cap that he was wearing. Everyone loved it on him and it became his signature look. It was a rare hat that fit his large head! We had to be back at Mark's office for 11 o'clock for a satellite hit with Dave Hodge back at the studio. Congratulatory comments were directed at us from everyone and everywhere. As Carl and I made our way back over to University Avenue, the press followed us all the way out to the street, cameras rolling. It didn't seem real. Back at home, dozens of messages were waiting from reporters who wanted a comment or to send a photographer to the house. One of these was our dear friend and loyal supporter, Rafe Mair of radio station CKNW in Vancouver, who wanted some time with us for his Monday show.

Ritch Winter phoned from Edmonton and asked me, "How does it feel?" I replied, "GREAT!" Ritch talked about the victory and told me, "Sue, make sure that you and Carl take time to enjoy this, because there are very few days this significant in anyone's lifetime."

That night, every local television channel profiled this story front and centre. Carl went to the CBC's Toronto broadcast centre to appear on the national program *Petrie in Prime*. Kathleen Petty was subbing for Anne

Petrie that night, and she was thoroughly informed about the issues and was an outstanding host for the call-in show. Carl was relaxed, funny, gracious and superbly articulate, as always. The first caller was from Kelowna, B.C. — our friend Liz Harrison, Jimmy's wife, offering her congratulations. Liz had phoned me earlier in the day to say "thank you" and told me Jim was in hospital. As the show was ending, Stevie Cameron called the house. She began talking immediately, saying that she was not calling as a journalist but as our friend. She said that what she had just seen on CBC was awesome, and expressed the hope that Carl realized what a personal tribute this was to him. "Every caller, from coast to coast, knew [Carl's] role in this victory and supported the story," she pointed out. "Carl is so inclined to think that people think of him as 'off the wall,' but after this he must surely know that people do understand him and respect him." She went on to say that she had never seen anything like it before on TV, and admired Carl for acknowledging Bruce Dowbiggin and his new book, *The Defense Never Rests*, which told the story of our pension battle. I was deeply moved by Stevie's comments.

On Friday morning, the press demands continued. Carl went to Maple Leaf Gardens to do a spot for CBC's *Midday*. After lunch, he left to drive up north to Sutton to his son Chris's home to look after their dogs, Max and Duffus, whom Carl adored. Carl was happy to just get away and be able to do some cross-country skiing, walk the dogs and decompress.

Roy MacGregor phoned me. He wanted to know how we had celebrated — we hadn't, really — and he asked a lot of questions aimed at learning the step-by-step details. Mary Ormsby of the *Toronto Star*, one of the very special people in the Toronto media, called to congratulate us. There were calls from radio stations from New York City to Antigonish, Nova Scotia, all wanting a comment from Carl.

On Friday afternoon, there was a very unexpected call — one that shocked and flattered Carl enormously. *Hockey Night in Canada* wanted him to do a spot with Ron MacLean for the following night's broadcast! Carl would pre-record the interview at three o'clock Saturday afternoon, after which he would do an hour-long show with Ted Woloshyn on CFRB. The Fan 590 in Toronto wanted Carl to do the Bob McCown show on Monday morning and Rafe Mair was scheduled for one-thirty on Monday.

We had breakfast on Saturday morning at the Detroit Eatery on the Danforth, our old stomping grounds, with the local member of Parliament, Dennis Mills, who was very excited for us. Carl was busy all afternoon with the media responsibilities, after which we went to Giacomin's, a neighbourhood restaurant on Mount Pleasant Road, for dinner. We hoped to unwind and have a quiet, relaxing time together; instead, it was mayhem as all of the other diners came by to offer congratulations or buy us a drink. Everyone was happy and truly excited for us. After dinner, Carl drove back up north to dog-sit again and to watch his *HNIC* appearance. "I feel great for all of us," he told MacLean. "The dignity, esteem and self-respect of all hockey players, not only the guys of my vintage but the players of today, because this will give them the courage to know that they can fight the good fight."

Just as the *Hockey Night in Canada* interview was ending, an enthusiastic Bruce Dowbiggin called me. "It was a perfect, perfect hit," he said. "Carl was intelligent, he looked great, he was loquacious, he made short, punchy statements and succinctly got his points across." He went on to say: "I'm just so proud of you — what you've accomplished. I'm so proud to know you, to be with you — although I'm a Johnny-come-lately. You two have been barking at the moon for years and you kept barking for all of us. That Carl was on *HNIC* is astounding in and of itself — it's the first indication I've seen that anything has changed at *Hockey Night in Canada*."

Later, just before turning in for the night, Carl phoned me from Sutton. I related to him what Bruce had said. There was silence, then Carl said, "Tell me again what Bruce said." He was deeply, deeply moved and added, "For Bruce to say those things … *wow!*" Carl admitted that he had been nervous, anxious and a little apprehensive about the interview. As usual, everyone who saw it thought he had done an excellent job.

Shortly thereafter, we learned that the NHL was again appealing, this time to the Supreme Court of Canada. That didn't bother Carl; we expected it. What did trouble him was that there were many aging former players, and he feared that some wouldn't live to see or enjoy the benefits they were supposed to receive.

Simultaneously, we got word that the NHL's commissioner, Gary Bettman, wanted to speak personally with Carl. A couple of days later, we called Gary from Allan Dick's office. It was an affable conversation during which Gary wanted to make it perfectly clear to Carl that the appeal was not intended as a slight towards the retired players. He explained that it was necessary for the NHL to exhaust every single option of appeal in order to sue the law firm of Baker & McKenzie, on whose advice the NHL had relied in reverting surplus monies to their own use. Carl assured Gary that he felt no animosity towards Gary or the league and that we had expected this move. Both men seemed lighthearted throughout the conversation, which lasted about 10 minutes.

At this juncture, Carl and I felt a tremendous sense of relief. Certainly there was vindication and a huge sense of accomplishment. However, our work was far from over. Over the years, people have asked us how we celebrated "milestones" such as this along the way. I would have to say that it was really only in retrospect that we could even identify certain moments as milestones. At the time, it seemed like we had just leapt over the latest hurdle, with an endless row of hurdles still ahead.

***

The Supreme Court of Canada refused to hear the NHL's appeal, a decision it released on July 28, 1994. Now, finally, there were no further avenues of appeal left for the league to pursue. It would be a couple more years before the pension monies began to flow to the players, and each time Carl heard of the death of another player, like Jean-Claude Tremblay in 1994, he was sad that the player hadn't lived to enjoy the moment of receiving his money.

There was still much work to be done by the actuaries for both sides, and by the lawyers working with Revenue Canada and the U.S. Internal Revenue Service to clarify the tax implications in both Canada and the U.S. Also ahead were discussions about the various options for distributing the individual entitlements. Many issues had to be put before a Master in the Courts for rulings; in this regard, Allan Dick cautioned us that the process would be frustrating for us because he didn't feel there was any master with the requisite expertise in business or pension matters to effectively and properly make some of the necessary decisions.

When a disagreement arose between the NHL and the players' legal team about whether simple or compound interest ought to be applied to the monies owing, Carl and I strongly believed that the lawyers should go back to Justice Adams and ask him to clarify his intentions before taking the matter to Master Linton. It seemed clear to us that Justice Adams's strongly worded decision indicated that he intended for the players to get the maximum award possible. We made Mark Zigler aware of these feelings. Also, of course, we were thinking of Allan Dick's comments. However, the matter proceeded directly to Master Linton, and the result was not favourable for the players. Finding the results computed using compound interest to be too rich, the Master ruled in favour of simple interest. Our pension advisor found this reprehensible — unfair and certainly not reflective of industry practice. Zigler proposed to the applicants that the Master's decision be appealed. Now, after the ruling by Master Linton, lawyers for both sides appeared before Justice Adams to request his input. Adams declined to intervene and imparted the message that the lawyers ought to have thought about seeking his clarification *before* the courts had made a ruling. Carl and I couldn't argue with his decision — it was fair and reasoned.

Although Justice Adams refused to get involved, Mark still left the notion of an appeal open. On November 2, 1995, Carl and I sent a note to Mark saying: "Please be advised that we do not wish that this matter be appealed. Having read the decision of Justice Adams, we agree he made the most logical decision in supporting the master. We do note, however, his comments that neither party found his original decision so vague as to seek his interpretation in advance of the reference proceedings."

In June 1996, the months of discussions and negotiations were finally complete, and players were first informed of their entitlements. When Carl received his information package, it informed him that he was entitled to $87,000 from the surplus award. An accompanying letter advised that the NHL Pension Society had had these amounts audited for accuracy and directed him to sign an enclosed form to indicate that he agreed with the figure provided. The form was to be returned within seven days.

Immediately, I was suspicious. By this point, we knew only too well how liberally terms like "audit" had been thrown around, especially by Alan Eagleson, over the years. How many players would understand the distinction between a true audit and a limited review? We replied to the NHL Pension Society that we neither confirmed nor questioned the amount allocated to Carl and requested a copy of the employment record upon which the amount was calculated.

When we received the material, we immediately discovered errors. First, Carl had played the better part of two seasons with St. Louis Blues in the early 1970s, and he had been credited with only *five games* for pension purposes. Fortunately, Carl had retained his documents over the years. I wrote to the NHL Pension Society, pointing out the shortfall, and requested a correction. The reply was swift: they concurred with our position and corrected their records.

Secondly, and of great interest to us, there was a problem with the terms of Carl's employment with the Detroit Red Wings in 1969–70. One of the terms the Red Wings had agreed to in order to entice Carl to sign with them was to buy up his pension credits for the preceding four years while he was out of pro hockey. The agreement was very specific and called for the Red Wings either to match Carl's contributions for that period ($6,000) or pay the matching amount into an annuity for Carl. We knew from his old income tax papers that Carl had paid his $6,000, but he had never been able to get a straight answer about the Red Wings' contribution. This issue went right to the heart of our suspicion that, although the NHL had promised to match players' contributions over the years, they had not done so — because in most cases, the player contribution alone more than paid for the benefit the NHL Pension Society was actually providing. In Carl's case, he had also not been paid the dividends that were distributed to players over that four-year period. Eventually, the Pension Society agreed to apply these entitlements, as well as additional credits Carl had been awarded. When all was said and done, Carl's entitlement was increased from $87,000 to $156,000. Several players close to the scene — Frank Mahovlich, for example — asked Carl how on earth his entitlement was raised so significantly. Each time, Carl answered "because of Sue."

On September 15, 1995, the first interim payments were sent out to players already receiving their pensions. Those who had not yet retired their pensions would wait approximately two more years to receive any money. When packages finally arrived from the NHL Pension Society, the paperwork was voluminous and probably overwhelming for the guys. There were many forms to complete, and decisions had to be made about the various options for receiving the payout. Generally, there were three options: they could take a fully taxable lump sum cash payment; they could transfer the funds to an RRSP; they could use the money to purchase an annuity. Or, they could take any combination of the three. Of course, another very important decision for families was the selection of a joint and survivor option so that payments would continue for the lifetimes of both the plan member and his spouse. We were extremely fortunate to have Lorraine Mahoney helping Carl to understand his options and to carry out his desire to retire his pension and purchase an annuity on a joint and survivor basis so that it would be payable for both of our lifetimes. We heard that, of the approximate 1,300 retired players, roughly two-thirds did not deal with the massive paperwork and so they automatically received an annuity by default.

Over all the years that Carl and I worked on this issue, there were many naysayers. One exchange with NHL vice-president Jim Gregory was particularly infuriating for Carl. At the All-Star weekend in Chicago in 1991, Gregory told Carl in a very defiant and condescending tone that he was crazy, that the players would never win. At the end of the day, when we were successful, Carl ran into him again. This time, Gregory tried to congratulate Carl and portray an attitude of having had confidence in the result all along. Carl spoke up and reminded Jim of what he had said years ago in Chicago, and Gregory tried to deny having said those things. Carl was enraged and told him in no uncertain terms, "Jim, I know exactly what the fuck you said!"

Another ex-player who not only angered but disappointed Carl was Bob Pulford, his old teammate with the Leafs and roommate at McMaster University when they took summer courses in the early 1960s. At the outset of the litigation, Pulford, the longtime general manager of the Chicago Blackhawks, submitted an affidavit supporting, not the players, but the NHL owners. To Carl, this was the ultimate betrayal. Pulford's statements contradicted the fundamental tenets of the trust, which specified that all the monies in the NHL pension plan were to be used for the exclusive benefit of the plan members — i.e., the players.

Over time, we dealt with many players who, because they were employed by the NHL, could not openly support our cause. None of us expected these men to do so. Most, nevertheless, found ways to show their support. Many quietly contributed money for the legal fees. But Pulford was one former player who assumed an active role in trying to weaken the players' position.

After the courts and interested parties had finally agreed upon on all the details, and the determinations had been made as to what each club owed, Chicago — Pulford's team — held back on its payment until the very last minute.

It should be noted that the former players weren't the only ones who won big as a result of this lawsuit. Everyone else who was a plan member benefited: coaches, referees, general managers, scouts — even the commissioner of the NHL — automatically received significant increases to their pensions without the long, costly fight.

We received numerous letters of thanks after the success of the lawsuit at the Court of Appeal level. One of these came from Carl's old teammate, Bert Olmstead: "Thank you Carl, and congratulations for your efforts and perseverance during the NHL pension litigation. If in Calgary please call and we'll have lunch or whatever fits." Carl was really touched by the note, and I believe that from that point on he felt much more warmly towards Bert than when they were teammates years before. Another note arrived from Bruce Hood, who as a former NHL referee had received additional pension benefits thanks to our efforts. "Carl — what a super job!" he wrote. "Words cannot convey my thoughts of appreciation for the efforts you and Sue have (and are) put forth in all this. But certainly a big THANK YOU is in order!" Ritch Winter wrote: "Remember when the three of us were the lone beacons on this issue? It was lonely in our pension lighthouse. I have watched all of the national coverage on this and been so pleased to see the two of you standing together on the steps of Osgoode Hall. It was a thrill to see how far the two of you brought this case, but most important to see Carl solely recognized by his peers and the media as the player catalyst. Credit where credit is due, finally. I am proud to say you are my friends."

***

While the pension litigation went ahead, we continued to work at getting Carl the pension entitlements he was owed from his Leaf arbitration — the issue that had been responsible for giving rise to the pension suit in the first place. Lorraine Mahoney helped us a great deal along the way and became a dear friend to Carl and me. By the time she picked up the ball and commenced a letter-writing campaign of her own in an attempt to help us get the issue resolved, it had been going on for seven years! Initially, Lorraine's letters got the same cold shoulder that our efforts had. On November 28, 1994, Lorraine again wrote to the NHL Pension Society administrator and said, in part:

> *Accordingly, at the heart of my November 17 letter is not the issue of your level of service, but instead the blatant conflict of interest and collusion issues that continue to*

exist within the NHL and the NHL Pension Society.... You must be aware that [Carl] was in fact (as a result of legal proceedings) given credit and awarded compensation for the period in question. The compensation was considered to be pensionable compensation. At the core of our concern of the "conflict of interest" is the practice of the NHL Pension Society referring matters relating to the determination of a plan member's entitlement to the owner clubs and their outside legal counsel. It appears to the writer that the NHL Pension Society and the clubs routinely spend hundreds of thousands of dollars of legal fees in their attempts to disenfranchise or deny claims for legitimate benefit entitlements. In the case of Mr. Brewer, the cost of establishing the benefit entitlement in question at the time would [have been] $6,000 to $7,500 tops. However, the Society, in concert with the owner club, spent tens of thousands of dollars in legal charges to avoid recognizing a period of service for which Mr. Brewer was granted pensionable compensation and for which he clearly met the definition of "player."

The dreadful legacy of Mr. Eagleson aside, it does not help the players' confidence or increase their comfort level to learn that Mr. Bruce McNall, the former Chairman of the Board of Governors and a trustee of the NHL Pension Society, has been charged and will soon be convicted of fraud and embezzlement.

Around the same time that Lorraine wrote her letter to the Pension Society, Carl and I wrote to NHL Commissioner Gary Bettman, outlining our frustrations with this matter. We raised some serious concerns about the conflicts of interest we perceived between the league and the Pension Society. Jeffrey Pash, the NHL's general counsel and a senior vice-president of the league, wrote us on December 23 to advise us that our letter was the first indication the league had had of Carl's claim. He added that Dr. David Johnston, the former principal of McGill University, would evaluate it. "As Chairman of the Board of the Pension Society," Pash wrote, "I give you my assurance that we will follow Dr. Johnston's advice on this matter." The appointment of Dr. Johnston to the board of the Pension Society (as vice-president of special matters) seemed to indicate to us that someone was paying attention to our concerns. We were delighted with the appointment. We felt that Dr. Johnston was a most appropriate choice for such a role, as he is a Canadian of impeccable reputation and integrity.

Shortly after receiving this news, I received a letter addressed to all alumni of McGill University concerning the Alma Mater Fund. The letter bore Dr. Johnston's signature. I telephoned his office to discuss arrangements for a hearing about Carl's pension. When I introduced myself, I told him I was calling on two counts — one being that I had received his letter about McGill and secondly to discuss a date for Carl's hearing. There was a lengthy pause. I began to feel uncomfortable. Then he spoke: "Susan, I am so proud of you! I am so proud of you. I have followed this story all along and I really admire all that you and Carl have done." I knew that things would be different from here on in.

On April 11, 1995, Carl and I went to dinner at La Bettola on Bayview Avenue, which was our favourite restaurant at the time. John, the Calabrian maitre d', seated us at our favourite table: a round one at the front, with a semicircular banquette built into the wall — comfortable and private. Here we had celebrated birthdays and successes; we'd come here to comfort ourselves in the discouraging times as well. On this evening, it seemed appropriate that we were getting special treatment, as it was time to unwind, relax and commemorate a milestone. Carl's bid for two additional years of pension benefits, in keeping with his arbitration ruling, had been reviewed that morning by Dr. Johnston.

Mark Zigler and Allan Dick, our lawyers, attended with us and addressed the legal implications of the issue. Our friend and staunch ally, Lorrraine Mahoney, was with us and she outlined the pension aspects. Carl and I basically directed the meeting, adding details and indicating relevant points. Dr. Johnston showed keen interest and was attentive and efficient throughout. It was immediately apparent that he had reviewed all the material I had assembled and sent to him in advance of this appointment.

After the evidence had been presented and the long history summarized, it was Carl's turn to speak. The final words — the summation, if you will — were left to him. He spoke eloquently and passionately as he described our lengthy battle. He spoke about the historical lack of dignity suffered by all NHL hockey players, the collusion and the so-called stewardship of Alan Eagleson. He mentioned some of the players so badly disadvantaged by Eagleson — the likes of Ed Kea, Jim Harrison, Blair Chapman and Pat Hickey. Carl went on to talk about the "kangaroo courts" of the past — but was quick to interject "Not this, this is a joy," referring to the professionalism of Dr. Johnston. Carl read the "godfather letter" Eagleson had written him. He spoke of the years of effort we had invested in remedying some of these wrongs. He told Dr. Johnston about my voluminous research that had been so helpful to the FBI in its investigation of Eagleson, and that many high-profile Canadians who had contributed to the hockey establishment's abuses of power would soon be exposed. Throughout, Dr. Johnston kept his head down, writing feverishly. When Carl concluded — and by now he was breaking down emotionally and tears were streaming down his face — Dr. Johnston looked up at him with his warm, expressive eyes, and in a very sincere and sympathetic tone of voice thanked Carl and said, "It has been a long struggle." He promised to have his decision to us no later than three months hence.

As we relaxed that night, enjoying each other's company, the togetherness that was our world, enjoying the wine, the penne alla vodka — Carl's favourite and usual meal here — we felt tremendously relieved and encouraged. Our nine years of persistence and dogged, unrelenting determination, aided by Allan Dick and Lorraine Mahoney, had brought us to this moment.

Dr. David Johnston was obviously not a man who was about to sell his soul to the NHL or anybody else. He was an honourable man of outstanding reputation and impeccable character. Win, lose or draw, we knew our struggles had brought us to the best possible situation and that the matter could not rest in better hands. To have accomplished this was already a huge victory for us. If this was what we could expect from the new commissioner, Gary Bettman, we were encouraged.

As August arrived, Carl was beginning to get anxious. We were checking our mailbox daily. Eventually, we contacted Dr. Johnston to inquire about the delay and we received an apologetic, understanding reply — he guaranteed we would have his decision by the end of August. The decision was dated August 31; that day, we were advised by his office at McGill that it had been sent to us by priority mail, but it didn't arrive before the Labour Day weekend, so we were left hanging for three additional days. By now, we were both impatient to know the fate of this matter.

The decision from Dr. Johnston was a straightforward and reasoned analysis. He concluded: "I find that Mr. Brewer is entitled to service under the Club Plan in respect of league games played by the Toronto Maple Leafs during the 1980–81 season and during 15 days of the 1981–82 season. It is my view that the NHL Pension Society should implement my decision in accordance with applicable legislation."

Not only were we thrilled with his decision, but we were deeply touched by a comment in his covering letter: "This entire process of reconstituting a history of the NHL Pension Society and establishing the appropriate level of pensions has been a singularly arduous and difficult one for you. I appreciate your patience and tenacity over many years and I especially admire the fact that your own efforts have done so much for so many others in establishing their fair entitlement."

We felt tremendously proud and especially vindicated. We had struggled for nine years to convince the league to acknowledge our entitlement to a pension adjustment that Dr. Johnston clearly understood and endorsed as Carl's. Perseverance had paid off, but we felt that no player should ever have to fight so long and hard over such a simple matter. The upside to our battle was that, in addition to Carl, all of his peers got benefits they were entitled to — something we both felt was destined to happen.

At the end of the day, it is impossible to get over the irony of our case. As Lorraine Mahoney had written in her letter to the NHL Pension Society, it would have cost the Toronto Maple Leafs somewhere in the neighbourhood of $6,000 to $7,500 to fund Carl's benefit at the outset. And, had the issue been settled properly in the first place, it is entirely possible that the pension litigation, which ended up costing the league around $100 million dollars, might never have happened! Beyond the additional benefits, the NHL was liable for all costs of the action on a solicitor-client basis, and of course the league had its own huge legal bills, as well.

On one occasion, early on in the action, Carl and I showed up in court for the simple matter of setting a date. We noticed that there were half a dozen lawyers there that day representing the NHL. When we left the courtroom, Carl and I were leading the way; the troop of NHL lawyers followed. Carl turned around and said to them mockingly, "Did any of you sons of bitches ever think of *thanking* me for the largesse I have brought to you?" When we got home, we couldn't help ourselves; we sent a fax to Gary Bettman, remarking slyly that it was good to see that jurisprudence was alive and well and needling him about the battery of lawyers the league had dispatched just to set a date. The next time we went to court, Mark Zigler told us that the NHL's lawyer asked him to make sure that Carl realized that there was only one lawyer in attendance for the NHL that day!

***

A few months after the Court of Appeal upheld the pension case, Carl and I were back in Europe for a brief vacation. After spending a week with old friends in Innsbruck, we were passing through Zurich on our way home. Werner Schwarz was the archetypal Swiss banker, very serious and professional; Carl was first introduced to him through player agent Derek Holmes years earlier. Werner had spent many years working in New York for a Swiss bank in his younger days, and he was an avid hockey fan, having followed NHL hockey while living in the States. In Switzerland, he followed all the teams, attended games and knew all about the Canadian players who were playing for Swiss teams. Werner loved nothing better than to talk hockey with Carl, and he always was up for taking us someplace for a really nice lunch whenever we were in town. He was enthralled by the inside stories that Carl always had to tell him.

Although we had heard rumours for years that Alan Eagleson might be one of Werner's clients, one would never hear any indication of this from him. But we had received a phone call from him once when he showed up in Toronto as a guest of Al's for one of the Canada Cup tournaments, and we met him for lunch.

During this stopover, we were sitting in Werner's office, chatting with him as a prelude to going out to lunch in Zurich's old town. He was no longer with Cambio Valoren Bank, as it had been sold; he was now with Union Bancaire Suisse. Carl was relating — in very animated fashion — the lengthy saga of the pension litigation and describing for Werner the various ways the monies had been handled. Werner was intrigued by our story, but we could also see from his expression that he was offended by the blatant abuse of trust. He outlined for us his practice in dealing with pension monies: first of all, he said, the trustees are obliged to determine the total amount of the contribution to be made; secondly, they have to certify that the monies have been received; and finally, they must invest the monies in accordance with the trustees' guidelines. We all agreed: straightforward and simple. Then, in a priceless moment that we both savoured, Werner asked us, "How much does the NHL owe you?"

Carl answered, "Approximately $50 million."

With that, Werner sat back in his chair and I noticed a slight smile creep across his face. He looked at both of us and said, "Carl and Susan, you just might own my bank."

***

THE GREATEST STORY EVER TOLD

The accolades we received in the wake of the final victory were all very nice, but Carl and I felt very strongly that Gordie Howe deserved a huge share of the credit. Gordie played a tremendously important role in the lawsuit. He had taken a lot of flak over the years for caving in to management when Ted Lindsay tried to organize the players back in 1957; Carl understood why Gordie did what he did back then, and he believed that Gordie had more than made up for it now. He wrote a little story explaining why. He called it "The Greatest Story Ever Told."

> *Redemption. Reconciliation. Vindication. Validation.*
>
> *The pension battle by the upstart players against the league and the NHL Pension Society (one and the same thing) was a long and arduous battle, and ultimately a successful one. It seemed odd to many observers that the players had been able to band together to see this court fight through to its conclusion, even with the massive egos and petty jealousies. Yet, out of this morass emerged the inestimable Gordie Howe to seal one final victory.*
>
> *Gordie, the Greatest of Them All, had always prevailed on the ice. Between the dashers, he was a brute. He hurt and maimed a lot of players. A simple, uncomplicated farm boy from the prairies of Saskatchewan, whose brute of a father, a noted barroom fighter, called Gordie "backward" and provided his son with his own credo: "Never take any dirt from nobody, because if you do, they'll just keep throwing it at you — that's the way life is." That not-untrue credo is what*

carried the powerful Gordie Howe to unparalleled stardom in the NHL … nay, in the world of sport!

That was on the ice… between the dashers. Off the ice, it was a different story.

Gordie, in civvies, was quiet and self-deprecating, shy and unassuming — a country bumpkin. He would've played the game he loved for nothing and Jolly Jack Adams — surrogate father and prototypical NHL panjandrum — would have seen to it that he did. On the shoulders of Gordie Howe, the Detroit Red Wings grew into one of North America's wealthiest sports franchises. The credulous Howe was barely paid a living wage. Gordie trusted Jack Adams.

A sad indictment of Jack Adams. A sad testimony to the Detroit Red Wings. A sad legacy for the NHL.

Colleen Howe recalls raising their four children and scrimping along. "I made clothes for the kids, cut their hair, and used the skate exchange. Life was no-frills."

Near what the lamentable cognoscenti in Detroit determined was the end of his career (how wrong they were!), Gordie approached making monies commensurate with his abilities and his contribution to the team. Brewer and Baun helped set the standard for him in 1969. But the idiot Red Wing organization forced Howe into premature retirement. What a mistake!

That fledgling upstart called the WHA (the World Hockey Association) not only resurrected Gordie but also signed his sons, Mark and Marty. A dream fulfilled for Gordie to play with his sons. A public relations coup for the WHA! A strategy that is only heresy to the obtuse NHL. Not only did they play together in the WHA, but later, in a return to the NHL when the two leagues merged. Alas, the reluctant suitor, the NHL, is dragged kicking and screaming out of the dark ages, but only for a brief moment. Gordie Howe starred again in the NHL until he was 52 years of age. The Red Wings organization under the pathetic Bruce Norris was now bankrupt.

Yes, Gordie has always starred between the dashers,

but off the ice? Well, that was a different story. In the book Net Worth *and its subsequent movie adaptation, a different Gordie Howe was portrayed. Whom should he trust? Jolly Jack Adams — by the bye, if there ever was a misnomer, this was it. Jolly Jack, indeed. This jolly one had been a father figure ... trusted, blindly trusted. It had been the same for Red Kelly. Red had a different education, yet he was no less seduced by Jolly Jack. Kelly had graduated from St. Michael's College in the cosmopolitan city of Toronto but he was no less duped than was Howe.*

Nevertheless, as the book and movie Net Worth *reveal, in 1957, when Ted Lindsay et al. were leading the organizing of the NHL players into a union to secure more realistic benefits, it was Gordie Howe and Red Kelly who unwittingly sold out the players. They were management dupes. The combined pressures of Jolly Jack Adams, Big Jim Norris, Major Conn Smythe and Frank Selke succeeded in destroying the ill-fated attempts to unionize.*

The members of the Toronto Maple Leafs, to their everlasting credit, stared down the intimidating and unforgiving Smythe, and to a man voted 100 percent in favour of a union. Nonetheless, the guile and wile of Jolly Jack prevailed, and any plans for a players' union were thwarted.

The hockey lives of Ted Lindsay, Tod Sloan, Jim Thomson, Doug Harvey and Dollard St. Laurent were destroyed. The careers of Red Kelly and Gordie Howe flourished, for the moment. But that's another story!

In 1991, a meeting was convened at the 400/401 Ramada Hotel in Toronto. Over 100 players attended, among them the greatest names and vintage Hall of Famers. Obviously, the prevailing attitude was one of bitterness — still smarting from the earlier and continued abuses and disdain of management. The stage was now set to sue the NHL and the NHL Pension Society over the last 30 years.

Out of the gathering of the clan, a different Gordie Howe emerged. When it was roll call time, Gordie walked to the front of the room and signed up to serve on the organizing committee. Colleen was surprised at his actions. Later, he signed his name to the lawsuit as one of the applicants. On this subject, Colleen was to remark to Susan Foster: "I was surprised and proud of Gordie. That was only the second time I'd seen him stand up for himself."

In my estimation, he played a pivotal role in the eventual outcome of the court case. Gordie's presence and commitment were highly profiled. Judge George Adams's favourable decision in this case before the Ontario Courts of Justice was a solid victory for the players... fairness and equity had prevailed, justice was served.

As expected, the NHL... that public relations giant — harrumph! — carried the action to every level of appeal and lost. But for me, the real story took place at the Ontario Court of Appeal. The case was heard before a three-judge tribunal. Obviously erudite and imposing, these three judges presided with customary aplomb as befits senior, competent jurists. In the courtroom at Osgoode Hall, a scattering of curious and interested parties came and went. The judges were not judging, but being judged ... by the Greatest of Them All! And they knew it! For the three and a half days of the appeal hearings, Gordie Howe, with Colleen, sat quietly the entire time at centre court, following the proceedings carefully. His presence alone was awesome. His presence and attention were appreciated. The three judges did not want to come up short: they were fans; they were human; they were contemporaries; they knew their work was being assessed by the Greatest of Them All.

This day, once again, fairness and equity prevailed. The three-judge panel upheld the lower court decision of Judge Adams. The league was denied leave to appeal. The hockey players would get their pound of flesh ... some 45 million dollars.

Approximately 1,400 hockey players owe to Gordie Howe, the Greatest of Them All, an incredible debt of gratitude.

CHAPTER 12

SYNCHRONICITY

"From 1989 there was a synchronicity of events that brought people together. There was Sue and myself in Toronto, Ritch Winter in Edmonton and Ed Garvey in Madison, Wisconsin. Russ Conway came on board next, and then Bruce Dowbiggin, who has been with us and worked with us and has done some remarkable work."

While Carl was hailed by players and fans alike for the pension victory, the lawsuit had become, for him, a means to focus attention on the dubious stewardship of Alan Eagleson. "The lawsuit is of limited interest to me," Carl told Bruce Dowbiggin. "I was more interested in what it meant in providing an avenue for cleansing hockey, and that meant getting rid of Eagleson." We had succeeded in getting players together to get the pension litigation underway. And, having watched Eagleson from the get-go, Carl had accumulated a great deal of information and background on him. The work done by Ed Garvey, Ron Salcer and Ritch Winter gave us concrete proof that Carl's concerns about Eagleson had merit. However, Eagleson's power remained such that the players grew extremely reticent whenever Carl mentioned his name. Many players wrote Carl off as "obsessed" over Eagleson, and for various reasons they preferred not to criticize him.

It was just as tough for Carl to interest the press in his worries that something was rotten in the NHLPA. Don Ramsay, of course, had written the occasional scathing report in the *Toronto Sun* on his own initiative, but for the most part the media were solidly behind Eagleson. If we were going to make any headway, we'd need to find someone who wasn't interested in currying favour with him. Carl and I had had numerous phone conversations with a reporter from the Boston area, Russ Conway, and we seemed to have a meeting of the minds on many issues. In early April of 1991, we got a phone call from Russ, telling us he was coming to Toronto and asking us to meet with him. Russ is a pleasant man, a few years younger than Carl and I, with a delightful Bostonian accent. We met in the lobby bar of the Westin Harbour Castle Hotel. Sitting in a secluded back corner of the bar, we had a lengthy, animated, and very informative chat. Right away, Russ could see Carl's cynicism about reporters. He remembers Carl asking him point blank: "Russ, why are you interested in this?"

Russ explained to us that for years he had been hearing rumblings from retired members of the Boston Bruins about their lousy pensions and their concerns about Alan Eagleson. Lately, he was hearing those complaints much more frequently. Bobby Hull had also been telling Russ that he was unable to get information about his pension. Russ was beginning to think it might be time to take a serious look at these complaints. But Carl was not easily convinced. "Quite frankly, Russ — don't take this personally, but I don't trust people in the media," he said.

Russ wasn't discouraged. "I knew immediately Carl's burning desire to find someone to take this seriously enough to carry it out," he later said. We talked about pensions, international hockey, free agency and Carl's arbitration, among many other subjects, that night. After a few drinks, we adjourned to Russ's hotel room to go over some files he had brought along and was working on. One of these involved pension matters, and Russ had been authorized by both Brad Park and Ray Bourque to represent them at the Pension Commission of Ontario to look at the records. Russ chain-smoked, and the only displeasure I felt about spending time with him was that my eyes were soon watering and my nose running nonstop. Before the evening was over, Russ said something that would turn out to be critical: "I have a publisher who is supporting me, and I wouldn't commit to anything unless we can finish it — and we are committed to finishing this." Carl replied, still not convinced: "That's good. We'll see if you are."

It was well after midnight when Carl and I finally took our leave that night. Russ remembers with fond lightheartedness: "When Carl left the Harbour Castle that night he was smiling, but I knew he was somewhat cautious. He wanted to see if Russ was there for a quick story or the long haul." He was right. On the way home we talked about what a tremendously interesting evening it had been, but Carl had trouble getting his cynicism out of the way and he wondered aloud if this was just another experience with a reporter like all the rest to date. Meanwhile, after we left, Russ said he was thinking, "These people are committed and I don't want to let them down."

The following day, Carl picked Russ up at his hotel "in his old buggy," as Russ described the car — Carl always drove old or secondhand cars. Russ wanted to go to Eagleson's office at 37 Maitland Street, near Maple Leaf Gardens, so Carl dropped him off there. Russ recalled waiting in the foyer and hearing the receptionist answer the phone "Eagleson, Ungerman" — before correcting herself and saying "NHLPA." Russ asked her if she ever got mixed up, and she answered, "All the time." Bob Goodenow, the deputy executive director of the Players' Association, was in the office, and he came down and ushered Russ to a seat in Ungerman's office. According to Russ, the first thing Bob did was put a finger to his lips. "We whispered all through the meeting and he told me what was going on there," Russ jokingly remembered.

It was well known that in 1988 Eagleson had moved the NHLPA's office from 65 Queen Street West to 37 Maitland. What he neglected to disclose to the PA's members, however, was that the owner of this building was Jialson Holdings, a company of which Eagleson himself was president. Jialson was a contraction of Jill (Eagleson's daughter), Alan, and "son," for Alan's son, Trevor. The NHLPA was paying rent to Eagleson. Although this move was presented to the players as a cost-cutting move, in fact, the rent increased. The players were not only not informed about the ownership of the premises, they were not told that the building was also the office of the Eagleson, Ungerman law firm as well as the Toronto base for Hockey Canada.

After his chat with Bob Goodenow, Russ spent the remainder of the day at the offices of the Pension Commission of Ontario, where he paid $387 for photocopies. He returned to the PCO the following day for additional papers, only to be told that there was a gag order on the file because of our lawsuit, and he couldn't have access to the material.

Still wondering if Russ was for real, Carl put in a call to Bobby Orr a few days after our meeting. "Don't worry about Russ," Bobby told him. "Russ is a horse." That was all Carl needed to hear to be convinced that Russ was on the case for the long haul. From that time on, our lives were fully involved in helping Russ with the investigation of our lifetimes. Russ was masterful at gaining the trust of everyone, and information flowed to him in a torrent, leads often showing up in unmarked brown envelopes from a wide range of surprising and important sources. Russ co-ordinated everything from his home in the small New England town of Haverhill, Massachusetts. Reflecting back on this time, Russ told me: "There was never a doubt, never a thought that we couldn't do this. It took extraordinary efforts on your part." Every morning — early — the phone would ring and Russ would be on the line giving me a list of names, corporations or real estate transactions to investigate. I would drop everything and head downtown to City Hall, the land registry office at the Atrium on Bay or the Corporations Branch at Yonge and Wellesley and spend hours checking files, copying documents and often shipping them out by FedEx to Russ that night.

I was aware that all the information I sent to Russ would be subpoenaed by the FBI for an ongoing investigation in the U.S. Not infrequently, I would get calls directly from Tom Daly, the special FBI agent, or from Paul Kelly, the Assistant U.S. Attorney, requesting help with documents or seeking additional input. Stevie Cameron wrote about this scenario in *The Globe and Mail* on February 23, 1993: "When journalists needed documents, [Susan Foster] had them. Hockey sources say that the U.S. Federal Bureau of Investigation has based much of its probe on files she originally developed." With every parcel of information I dispatched to him, Russ promised me a bigger and bigger lobster dinner when Carl and I came down to see him in the summer! Carl and I were always more than happy to help the journalists by sharing material or explaining things to them. Stevie Cameron quoted Alison Griffiths as saying: "This was a woman who saw everything with those large, deep eyes and absorbed everything. She has an extraordinary capacity to analyze and boil things down. She has been a great resource for all of us."

One of the details I tracked was Eagleson's transfer of the title to his home at 110 Park Road to his wife, Nancy, in early 1992. At the same time as the transfer, he mortgaged it — for pretty much full market value — in the amount of $1,125,000. This coincided with the timing of the announcement of the FBI's investigation, and it indicated to us that Eagleson was feeling the heat. Russ also learned from one of his sources that Eagleson was indeed concerned about his assets and had consulted his advisers about asset protection at this time.

Soon after we became involved with Russ, confident that he was indeed for real, I was contacted by another journalist. This time it was Bruce Dowbiggin, a sports reporter with CBC television, who called me up one day out of the blue and expressed an interest in our story. He said he was amazed that no one else — in Canada — had picked up on the story. Bruce didn't realize that this was a loaded observation, and I couldn't contain my laughter at his remark. Bruce dropped by the house a few days later. He remembered getting the same icy reception from Carl that Russ had experienced. Carl answered the door, and when Bruce told him he wanted to cover our story, Carl asked him dryly, "Why?"

"My knees felt like jelly and I wished the ground would just swallow me up," Bruce said, "but Sue came to the door and she said, 'Oh, Bruce, don't pay any attention to Carl. Come on in and have some pie." Bruce felt relieved. "At that moment," he said, "I knew I was at home with Carl and Sue." We felt comfortable enough to have a follow-up meeting with Bruce and bring him some copies of information shortly after. We met at Bigliardi's Restaurant, close to the CBC's Church Street studios. Over drinks one afternoon, Bruce was even more excited by what we had to say and by the material we shared with him.

Bruce, a good-looking man, poised and erudite, articulate and a quick study, "got" the story immediately and he was eager to get involved. Very quickly, Carl came to enjoy and appreciate our discussions with Bruce. We both respected him, and it was obvious to us that he was not going to jump ship on us the way all the other Canadian journalists had done. Bruce and his wife, Meredith, and their children, Evan, Rhys and Clare, lived close to us. Many a morning, Carl would suggest to me that we drop over to Bruce's for a chat. Since Bruce did the late-night news, he was home most mornings. We used to sit around the Dowbiggins' kitchen table and, over a large pot of tea with brown sugar, discussed the developments. I phoned Russ Conway and told him about Bruce and insisted that he absolutely must meet him. Russ was very circumspect, preferring to keep everything close to the chest. He saw everyone, especially in the Toronto scene, as a potential spy or pipeline for Eagleson and his cronies in the NHL, and he was very nervous about discussing his project with any outsiders. It was quite cloak-and-dagger!

A few days later, however, Russ got back to me about Bruce. He told me that he'd checked him out with his "sources," and "he's a terrific guy." I put them in touch with one another and the rest is history. Russ was really enthused about connecting with Bruce, and they worked very closely together, developing the story on both sides of the border. Russ at one point characterized Bruce as "the gutsiest reporter in Canada." This turn of events was truly exciting for Carl and me.

In 1993 we were introduced to another highly regarded Canadian journalist in the person of Stevie Cameron. We met Stevie through our MP on the Danforth, Dennis Mills. Stevie was the first to admit that she had no interest when Dennis first contacted her and suggested we should meet. "I said, 'Sports? I don't follow sports. Hockey? Forget it! Get a sports reporter.'" When she learned it involved crimes, fraud and cronyism, well, these things were right up her alley. Stevie, one of the country's most accomplished investigative journalists, was working for *The Globe and Mail* at the time and had been asked to contribute to a series about Alan Eagleson. Carl and I met her at a McDonald's restaurant for coffee one morning. She was, and is, a clever, warm, insightful, caring, gracious woman. She understood and sympathized with our cynicism about reporters, and she was very respectful of our story and appreciative of our support. It was remarkable and reassuring to have three excellent journalists in our corner — and I must not overlook Rafe Mair, who bravely championed us and our issues.

Our relationships with all three transcended the story and became close friendships. Carl was enthralled with Bruce's brilliance, and we both adored his wife, Meredith. She is funny, warm and a real straight shooter. I recall one particular afternoon, after we had met someone at Original's Bar on Bayview Avenue. As we were returning to the car, the Dowbiggin children were walking home from school. They spotted us, and I heard them say "There's Carl and Sue" and all three came running up to us to give us hugs. I said to Carl on the drive home, "Life just doesn't get any better than that!"

Stevie has always been the kind of friend who will drop whatever she's doing to help, and she has many incredible resources with which she generously helps her friends. Stevie and her husband, David, are dear friends. Stevie, a Cordon Bleu–trained chef, has devoted a huge amount of her time to feeding the homeless each week at her church, St. Andrew's Presbyterian in downtown Toronto. Never have I known a kinder, more generous person, and she and I share many common interests — including a love of cooking, antiques and France.

Russ Conway — well, he is a first-class friend. He will set aside anything to help out a friend. An outstanding journalist of absolute integrity, he is considerate, diplomatic, fun, fascinating, a workaholic and a fabulous host when we got to spend time in Boston or at Hampton Beach for lobster at Le Bec Rouge. And Tom Lockwood, the lawyer who investigated Alan Eagleson for the Law Society of Upper Canada, told me recently that the best thing for him out of his work was that we are friends.

Stevie invited me to use her computer and taught me many tricks of the investigating trade. One of her tips paid off in a big way for all of us. She told me that an excellent way to find out who is linked up with whom, to connect the cronies and associates, is to check out the society pages — in Toronto, that meant Zena Cherry in *The Globe and Mail*. One of Zena's columns mentioned Alan Eagleson, and my interest was piqued when I noticed a company name, Doneagle Investments. (One thing about Eagleson — his company names weren't terribly subtle!) I searched the provincial government's corporate records and found out that this company had been incorporated by Alan Eagleson and Norman Donaldson back in 1980. The directors listed: R. Alan Eagleson and Norman Donaldson. The officers of the corporation: R. Alan Eagleson, Norman Donaldson and Marvin Goldblatt (the latter was the accountant in Eagleson's office and a close personal friend of his).

This was a significant find; for years, NHL players participated in international hockey tournaments for no pay — sometimes even paying for their own insurance — on Eagleson's promise that all the profits went towards improving the players' pensions. By now it had been confirmed for us that no money whatsoever had ever been used to increase benefits, and that any money that did go into the pension fund was done in lieu of the owners' contributions.

A pot of international hockey money had remained with the NHLPA and was referred to as a "bonus pension"; this was always represented to the players as pension money. It was discovered that Eagleson had been using this fund as his personal bank for years. I first became aware that Eagleson was lending out money he managed on behalf of his clients when I watched the Vaclav Nedomansky trial back in the early 1980s, but I had no idea he had been doing so — liberally — with the bonus pension funds. The work Ed Garvey did in 1989 revealed that Eagleson had routinely and systematically lent those monies, to the tune of approximately $2 million, to friends, family and clients of his law firm over many years. In doing so, he was in a blatant conflict of interest: he was acting for the lender — the NHLPA, which was the rightful owner of the funds and which paid him to look after its interests — and he was acting on behalf of the borrowers, who were invariably clients of Eagleson, Ungerman. We tracked scores of such deals.

With the information I'd found about Doneagle, we had evidence that these were not arm's-length loans; rather, Eagleson had a business relationship with the borrower or was, in some cases, a silent partner. In his autobiography *Powerplay: The Memoirs of Hockey Czar Alan Eagleson*, co-written by Scott Young, Eagleson referred to Donaldson as his "tennis partner"; now we knew that Donaldson was also his client, friend and *business* partner. Why was this relevant? Donaldson, or companies controlled by him, received hundreds of thousands of dollars from the NHLPA without the knowledge or consent of the players. Donaldson was the principal of two companies, New Leaf Florists and Tessen Developments, that received loans. He was also a client of Eagleson, Ungerman.

The loans, advanced on undeveloped land, were interest-only — making them riskier — and at interest rates lower than what the borrower would have paid at a conventional lending institution (in an era when the money could have earned double-digit interest simply by sitting safely in a bank). Moreover, Eagleson lent these monies without the necessary due diligence; loans fell into arrears and were renewed or extended with no penalty — one-year loans took four or five years to be repaid. In similar fashion, Eagleson also lent $27,000 from this account to another client of his law firm, former *Globe and Mail* sportswriter Malcolm Gray, as a mortgage. There were dozens of similar loans over the years. Until the player meeting in 1989, when they heard about these loans from Garvey, the players had been kept in the dark about the way in which Eagleson was using their "pension" money. This did not escape the scrutiny of the Law Society when Eagleson was investigated for professional misconduct.

***

Hockey Canada, a federal not-for-profit corporation through which Eagleson co-ordinated the Canada Cup tournaments, was another focus of our attention. However, our requests for information about revenues and income from international hockey went unanswered. Ian MacDonald, the chairman, passed the buck, telling us to ask Eagleson — who, of course, had no intention of disclosing the details of his personal fiefdom. Dennis Mills tried to get the information by bringing it up on the floor of the House of Commons in Ottawa — resulting in nothing but a closing of ranks. It was shocking how the veil of secrecy descended over a corporation that received taxpayers' money and had the ability to issue charitable tax receipts. Later on, Russ Conway succeeded in obtaining the financial records of Hockey Canada, but not from conventional sources.

Russ was able to confirm what Don Ramsay had written in 1981 about Eagleson's use of Hockey Canada to subsidize his employees' salaries. Rick Curran, a former employee of Eagleson's, had been on Sports Management Ltd.'s payroll at $12,500, but Eagleson lent his services to Hockey Canada for $115,000. Curran got to keep his Sports Management salary but had to sign the Hockey Canada payment over to Eagleson. Bill Watters's situation was similar, except that he kept his cheque from Hockey Canada while Eagleson didn't pay him his Sports Management salary.

When Russ got the chance to examine Hockey Canada's financial records, he discovered the general one-way direction in which money flowed. For the three Canada Cup tournaments of the 1980s, the gross revenues were reported as $24 million, of which three-quarters were paid out for operating expenses. This suggested that Eagleson had his own gold mine in Hockey Canada, but it wasn't possible to determine exactly how much money he was directing to himself. For instance, for the period of 1987 and 1988, Hockey Canada's international committee — chaired by Alan Eagleson — billed $1.9 million for administration and expenses, but there was no breakdown as to who received how much. Of the $1.9 million, close to $800,000 was allocated to "salaries."

The information and documentation I tracked down for Russ was used by him and by others to piece together the bigger picture that eventually led to criminal charges. At one point, Russ told Carl that he had learned from his good friend Bill Shaheen, a former U.S. attorney, that memoranda distributed widely by Eagleson announcing that neither he nor any member of his family or corporation in which he held an interest had ever profited directly or indirectly from revenues from international hockey was grounds to get him for both mail fraud and racketeering. "I thought Carl was going to come right through the phone, he was so excited," Russ said.

Hockey fans who followed the 1991 Canada Cup will remember that Team Canada held its training camp near Collingwood, Ontario, near

Georgian Bay, and players were seen golfing on the nearby Monterra Golf Course. Eagleson suggested this came about as a result of a chance meeting with the mayor of the town. That wasn't true. What the players didn't know at the time was that Eagleson had a large financial stake in the very resort property they were advertising for him nationwide. Nor had they been told that their money, controlled by the NHLPA, was lent out to purchase of the land.

Several times, Carl and I drove up to Collingwood to look into real estate activity involving Eagleson. We'd book a room at the Holiday Inn in Owen Sound and spend hours looking at documents in the land registry office there and in the municipal office in nearby Thornbury. We found that people working in these offices were more than willing to assist us in our searches. Everyone seemed to be aware that Alan Eagleson was a big mover and shaker in local real estate.

The Monterra project was one of the many that Carl and I researched. Eagleson owned a 25 percent interest in Monterra Properties, half of it personally and half through a family trust. Initially, Monterra Properties sold the land to Howard Ungerman (the other half of the law firm Eagleson, Ungerman) in trust — supposedly for his father, Irving Ungerman, the boxing promoter, who was also a close personal friend and business associate of Eagleson's. A $500,000 loan from the NHLPA had financed part of the purchase. Take a moment to think about that: the players' money was used to finance a purchase by Eagleson's law partner, from a company in which Eagleson had a one-quarter interest. About a year and a half later, Ungerman sold the property back to Monterra Properties for $1.9 million. The same day as this transaction took place, deals totaling $900,000 conveyed lots at Blue Mountain to associates, friends and family members of Eagleson. An RCMP search warrant, issued in July 1995, captured the essence of the problem: "Eagleson's dishonesty in obtaining this loan (material non-disclosure) and the circumstances surrounding the nature of the loan (risk of prejudice) imperiled the economic interests of the NHLPA, and I verily believe that his actions constitute fraud."

In spite of assertions that neither he nor any members of his family had ever benefited from international hockey tournaments, Eagleson proceeded with business as usual when he hired his son, Trevor, to help out with the 1991 Canada Cup at a salary of $95,000. Bruce Dowbiggin broke this story in Canada, much to the chagrin of the younger Eagleson, who sued Bruce and the CBC. Trevor Eagleson's case was so weak that it was dismissed with costs before the CBC even had the chance to submit a counterargument.

On September 21, 1991, Russ Conway's series, entitled "Cracking the Ice: Intrigue and Conflicts in the World of Big-Time Hockey," began running in the *Lawrence Eagle-Tribune*. Carl and I were in awe of the voluminous coverage and the information that came to light. We were also very amused that Alan Eagleson, a larger-than-life presence in Toronto and across Canada, had never been challenged to any serious extent in the Canadian media, but was now the subject of a huge exposé in the United States. Moreover, while Lawrence is only about 25 miles north of hockey-mad Boston, we pictured the residents opening their Sunday papers to find the entire front page devoted to Alan Eagleson and wondering who the hell he was! The subtitle blazed, "Did union chief Alan Eagleson help the players or himself?" The story ran over onto four full pages inside. The series continued in equal depth on the following day as well as Tuesday and Wednesday.

Just over three months later, on December 27, the U.S. Federal Bureau of Investigation publicly announced that it was conducting an investigation into the affairs and conduct of R. Alan Eagleson. Bruce Dowbiggin called me late that afternoon to break the news to us. It was a momentous day for all of us. Then, just four days later, on December 31, Alan Eagleson stepped down as executive director of the NHLPA and Bob Goodenow succeeded him.

It became more and more apparent, when we looked into all the schemes and scams Eagleson perpetrated, that it didn't matter how large or small the deal was, he had to have a piece of it. Russ called me one day specifically to ask me to check out certain zoning bylaws with the City of Toronto. Russ had figured that Eagleson was collecting rents for 10 parking spaces at 37 Maitland; four were rented to the NHLPA (the association paid $500 per month for three spaces and got one gratis); six more were leased to Hockey Canada at $600 per month. I found out from city officials that the building was only licensed for four parking spaces! As one city official told me, "To get 10 cars on that lot, he'd have had to stack them one on top of the other."

We were delighted that the FBI was diligently investigating the history of Eagleson and his handling of the Players' Association, and we were supremely confident that the agents were committed to seeing it through.

However, we never stopped wondering about the status of the formal complaints Ritch Winter had filed back in January 1990, with the RCMP and the Law Society of Upper Canada. The RCMP quickly washed its hands of Ritch's complaint and handed it off to the Metropolitan Toronto Police fraud squad in February 1990. There, the complaint sat on a back burner, and there appeared to be no will whatsoever to take a serious look into the matter. We grew ever more concerned that Eagleson was simply too well connected in Canada for any investigation to ever take place. After all, over the years he had insulated himself extremely well by courting friendships with prime ministers, provincial premiers, cabinet ministers, Supreme Court justices, chiefs of police, media moguls and prominent businessmen. And he had done it all using the players as a lure. Every year, he hosted a gala for the premier of Ontario (regardless of which political party), and naturally, the guest list included his high-profile hockey clients, such as Darryl Sittler. And, of course, the event was paid for with Players' Association funds. Over a three-year period, Eagleson charged back expenses for promotion and gifts in excess of $52,000, plus more than $30,000 for "special meetings." The costs he racked up were absolutely mind-boggling; his brash arrogance and self-assured confidence infuriating.

Finally, on June 28, 1993, by which time the FBI had been investigating Eagleson for well over a year, the RCMP finally announced that it had launched a formal investigation into the complaints about Alan Eagleson. John Beer and Glen Harloff were in charge. Shortly after this announcement, Beer was in touch with Carl and me, asking us to meet with them and requesting our documents. Carl never did meet with them, and I did so only when the Assistant U.S. Attorney, Paul Kelly, gave me the green light. Although I liked these two men very much — I heard all the right things from them about their commitment and interest — none of us was fully convinced that the Mounties would really take their investigation seriously, given Eagleson's clout in Canada.

The RCMP probe did move at a snail's pace, but I felt this had less to do with Beer and Harloff's dedication to their assignment than with the limited resources their superiors provided them, plus an otherwise heavy case load. One thing I learned from John Beer was that there were very few officers in the RCMP with the knowledge and expertise to understand the intricacies of white-collar crime. The satirical magazine *Frank* summed up the RCMP involvement with great candour:

Sychronicity

It took the RCMP several years to make up their minds about investigating hockey megalomaniac Alan Eagleson (O.C., Q.C., B.A., LL.B., R.I.P.), despite well-documented complaints filed some four years ago about how he was ripping off taxpayers and hockey players. The public humiliation by massive media reports last spring that the FBI and a Boston grand jury were actively investigating Eagleson finally prodded the reluctant Mounties into action. They even assigned a good cop to look into Al's adventures — Sgt. John Beer, an expert in white-collar crime — and they gave him an assistant. However, given that the investigation involves several U.S. cops examining 20 years of files and grilling dozens of witnesses, wasn't the RCMP once again doing that voodoo that they do so well — i.e. making certain that Beer and his assistant will be so overwhelmed by their task that they can't possibly ever dig their way out and damage someone who has so many powerful connections?

On July 27, 1993, Russ Conway phoned me in the afternoon. He was quite agitated, and he asked me to get in touch with "my friend with the computer" — I knew he meant Stevie Cameron. Russ needed information on a Timothy J. Lemay, a lawyer with the Canadian Justice Department. Russ had been tipped off that he was the brother of Trevor Eagleson's wife, and he may have worked at the Toronto law office of Eagleson, Ungerman. Russ felt they were on to something significant in Boston and he wanted me to track down the date of his employment with the Department of Justice.

The next morning, Carl and I left home early and headed down to see Dennis Mills, arriving at his office right at nine o'clock. We asked Dennis to get confirmation of Lemay's employment; he immediately phoned Ottawa and asked his assistant, Diane, to check it out and get back to him as soon as possible. A short time later, Diane called back and told Dennis that no information was available. Dennis picked up the phone and called Ottawa himself. He, too, got a pat answer: no information could be given out unless Lemay agreed to it. Dennis was shocked. Not one to be easily deterred, he tried another tack, this time calling the Toronto office of the Department of Justice. During this call, he learned that Lemay was with the RCMP and was working out of the Newmarket Division — the exact same division where John Beer and Glen Harloff were heading up the Eagleson investigation! Russ was indeed on to something — an Eagleson mole working in the very office of the RCMP that was supposedly investigating him! I had been in that office to meet with Beer and Harloff, and I knew that it was very small and offered no privacy for the men working there.

Dennis Mills had Lemay paged and left a message for him to call. At this point, Carl and I left Mills's office. We put in a call to Russ Conway and reached him. By now, Russ had spoken to Lemay and told us that Lemay, in a very abusive tone, refused to confirm anything to Russ. Apparently, Lemay asked Russ, "What are you going to do, write an article about me?" Lemay added that he didn't have to give Russ any information. Russ replied that he was right about that, but that he had neglected to tell a number of people something very important — that he was related by marriage to R. Alan Eagleson. I checked the Toronto phone directory while Russ was on the phone and found a listing for a Timothy J. Lemay at 37 Maitland Street — the address of the NHLPA and the law offices of Eagleson, Ungerman! Russ went ballistic with this latest bit of news. They hadn't even tried to cover their tracks.

After our conversation with Russ, we phoned Dennis Mills again. He reported to us that he had heard back from Lemay, who told him that if he was an agent for a reporter, Lemay wouldn't give him any information other than that he was a member of the Ontario Bar. Lemay gave Dennis a message: "Tell the reporter to call me." I told Dennis about my conversation with Russ and about the phone directory listing for Lemay. Mills was stunned. He said: "Susan, this is big — this is really serious. I don't know how to respond to you. I am overwhelmed. I am shocked. I have to sleep on this."

Carl and I needed a break, too, so we drove downtown to Rodney's Oyster House for a late lunch. It was fun to be there. It was my first visit, although Carl had met the owners at several hockey-related functions. Carl had oysters; mussels were more to my liking. We had a few glasses of wine and tried to settle down and absorb the information that had just hit us. What a powerful confirmation of Carl's oft-repeated statement, "Alan Eagleson is the most powerful man in Canada." We barbecued steaks for dinner that night and were grateful to have one another to share this latest unfolding drama.

The following day, Glen Harloff phoned and asked if he could drop by the house; he had some papers to return to me. I knew Glen's timing was not a coincidence, and when he came in and sat down, he asked me if there was anything on my mind. Of course there was, I told him; the Lemay situation was simply incomprehensible. He tried his best to convince me that there really was nothing to it. With this, Carl and I were more grateful than ever for the FBI and the U.S. Department of Justice. Again, *Frank* magazine picked up on this story.

> *The latest developments show just how hard the Mounties are trying to keep Eagleson out of jail. Beer and his assistant work in the Newmarket Division of RCMP Headquarters in Toronto. A third gentleman shares the room with them, sitting at his own desk. He's been seconded temporarily from a Toronto law firm to help police on a drug investigation. His name? Timothy Lemay. His former law firm? Eagleson, Ungerman.*

In the final week of 1993, we went to Davos, Switzerland, for the Spengler Cup. We'd been there before, but this year one of Carl's sons was playing for Team Canada. Carl always respected the history of this tournament, and we loved the venue. The Spengler Cup, the oldest tournament in which European club teams participate, dates back to 1923. Canada didn't officially send a team until 1984, but was represented at the inception: the first champions were a group of Canadian students playing for Oxford University. Davos was a winter wonderland when we arrived: mounds of freshly fallen, white snow covered the town — and everything as far as one could see, off into the mountains. The sun shone brilliantly and the skies were a deep, clear blue. The gigantic fir trees on the mountains were also covered with many inches of new snow. We stayed in the Sporthotel, where Team Canada was housed, and we enjoyed the games as well as the postgame parties held in huge tents outdoors next to the arena.

Carl, of course, ran into old hockey friends from all over the world. Future NHLers Manny Legace and Chris Pronger were playing for Team Canada, and we enjoyed chats with Chris's parents and Manny's mum, Margaret. On New Year's Eve, we had a sumptuous dinner at the hotel with the entire team and family members, and we marked the arrival of 1994 with champagne poured generously and freely from the magnums that were offered around as a finale to the evening. The next day we went tobogganing on the mountains and had dinner at night with former NHL player Bob Murdoch (from Kirkland Lake, Ontario) and his wife, Bev. We thoroughly enjoyed our visit to Davos, after which we made quick stops in Innsbruck and Rome before coming home. We had no idea what the year ahead would hold for us, but we remained hopeful.

***

When I spoke to Russ Conway on February 17, I asked him about the Eagleson matter and the talk I'd heard that things in Boston weren't as rosy as we'd hoped. Russ couldn't have contradicted me more emphatically. "Quite the opposite!" he assured me. "But just let everyone think that way. If you were to ask me on a scale of 1 to 10, I'd answer 25!"

A mid-morning phone call on March 1 set Carl and me off on a frantic scramble. The message, relayed to us by Bruce Dowbiggin, told us that something big was about to break in Boston. We were advised that, although an announcement might not be forthcoming for a couple of days, we should get to Boston as soon as possible — no later than suppertime, as a huge Nor'easter was expected to hit Boston late in the day and there was a real possibility that Logan Airport could be closed down for several days.

Immediately, I sprang into action. I was able to redeem some Aeroplan points for tickets, and arranged to pick them up at the airport. I phoned Boston to reserve a room at the Parker House Hotel — the closest hotel to the federal courthouse, we'd been told. Next, I baked a birthday cake for my daughter, Melanie, who would be celebrating her 24th birthday on March 3. It looked as though I was about to miss her birthday for the first time ever, and I hurriedly made arrangements for her dad and his wife, Beverley, to host her birthday party. We packed our bags and rushed to Pearson to catch the three o'clock flight to Boston.

With the news coming so unexpectedly and being so rushed all day, we didn't have a moment to reflect on what was probably about to transpire. No doubt we were excited, but also somewhat anxious and overwhelmed about what lay ahead of us. From the moment we knew we were headed to Boston, Carl told me we were going to have a very special dinner at Loch Obers — an old Boston landmark that Carl remembered fondly from an earlier lifetime, that of a hockey player. Bruce Dowbiggin arrived in Boston shortly after us, and we invited him to join us for dinner.

The weather was ominous, and it seemed as though everyone had long since left the downtown core to get home ahead of the coming storm. On such a cold, windy night, we were glad that it was only a short walk through the deserted streets to the restaurant. At Loch Obers, the staff was neither friendly nor helpful and our meals were very disappointing overall. The saving graces were the company and a particularly lovely bottle of French red wine that Bruce offered as a celebratory treat. Bruce is very knowledgeable about wines, and this bottle was memorable. So, we were still able to enjoy ourselves and use the time to relax and unwind a little. Carl was enthralled by Bruce's insights and points of view and was always very spirited when we sat down to talk and spend time with him.

At one o'clock in the morning, Carl and I were awakened by the ferocious winds. Looking out of the window of our room, we could see nothing but white sheets of blowing snow whipping past the windows, the street lights barely visible beyond. The Nor'easter had arrived right on schedule. We marvelled at how it was that, in Toronto, the weather forecasts were so unreliable or just plain wrong, yet here in New England they seemed to be able to predict a storm to the minute.

The following day, the weather continued to be unrelentingly nasty. We went to Quincy Market and had lunch at the Olde Union Oyster House, then wandered into Brookstones — anyplace to keep dry and warm — and sat in the wonderful massage chairs that Carl had learned how to use to adjust his back. When we returned to the hotel at midafternoon, dozens of messages were awaiting us. By now, word was leaking out back home that breaking news in the Eagleson affair was imminent. When members of the media learned that Carl and I were not in Toronto, it further raised their excitement and piqued their curiosity. It was ironic: with the exception of Stevie Cameron, the callers were mostly reporters who had shunned us for years and chosen to ignore our pleas to sit up and take notice of the facts we had assembled. The calls continued nonstop as Carl tried to take an afternoon nap, so he instructed the hotel reception to hold our calls.

As evening set in, we got word to be at the federal courthouse at nine-thirty the following morning, March 3. Carl and I started the morning off on the wrong foot and went to the wrong courthouse! When we finally found out where we were supposed to be, we had to walk several blocks through blistering wind and sleet. By now, Carl was upset and anxious — terribly uptight and very intense. He was frustrated and annoyed that we made the wrong turn, but it was about much more than that. He was consumed with the frustrations, anger, resentment and agitation of all the years — decades, even — that Eagleson's schemes, scams and side deals had taken the players to the cleaners.

When we finally reached the correct courthouse, we were drenched and windblown beyond recovery. The first person we met was Russ Conway, with whom we exchanged hugs and pleasantries. As more members of the press corps arrived, the buzz in the air quickly escalated. A box containing copies of the indictment was opened, and the documents were made available. There was a mad dash for them; I reached for a copy and found myself on the other end of a tug of war. After a brief struggle, I looked up and locked eyes with Russ. We both laughed heartily as we realized we were struggling for the same paper. Always the gentleman, Russ let me have that copy and I carried it into the courtroom as Carl and I took our seats. Across the front of the 62-page indictment, it read, "United States of America v. R. Alan Eagleson." We both expressed the same thought: we regretted that it did not say, "*Canada* v R. Alan Eagleson."

The whopping size of the document, and the specific charges we saw at first glance, spoke volumes for the work done by the FBI and the U.S. Department of Justice. Our eyes were drawn to sentences like, "From in or about 1976 through 1992, Eagleson did obtain money and property of the NHLPA and its members and Hockey Canada by means of fraud, conversion and embezzlement.... From in or about February 1981 through 1991, Eagleson fraudulently expended NHLPA assets by lending NHLPA funds in the form of private mortgages, on terms quite favourable to the borrowers, to clients of his law firm, and to other personal and business associates without the knowledge or approval of his membership.... From in or about 1975 through July, 1991, Eagleson did obtain money and property from the NHLPA and its members by means of fraud and by causing the payment of fees, benefits and expenses to Gregory Britz as a payback for years of friendship and free airline travel (on American Airlines) and while knowing that Britz was not substantially performing the duties and responsibilities for which he was allegedly retained."

As we scanned the small courtroom, we noticed that a surprisingly large contingent was covering the story for the French-language networks in Quebec. The television lights were turned on and U.S. Attorney Donald Stern took his place at the lectern, flanked by his assistant, Paul Kelly, and others from his department. Stern spoke precisely and plainly as he outlined the charges against Eagleson. "At the heart of the indictment, he breached his responsibilities. It's a misuse of trust that can't always be measured in dollars," he said. "Eagleson used his position of power for purposes of personal wealth and profit." As Stern spoke, tears began streaming down Carl's face. All the feelings he'd harboured for years were coming to the surface. There was the pent-up anger, resentment and disappointment, followed by the discouragement he felt when he tried to get someone — anyone — to pay attention. Then there was the guilt, the feeling of personal responsibility for the rise of Alan Eagleson. We held hands and tried to let it all just sink in.

At the end of the briefing, we spent a good hour with the reporters and journalists. Carl had promised the Montreal reporters that I would speak to them in French for their coverage, and I did so. Speaking to *Toronto Sun* reporter Jack Saunders, Carl said: "I wish it had been the Canadian government doing this, but the powers that be didn't want to do it. Alan Eagleson was the most powerful man in Canada, including the Prime Minister, and he still was, until recently."

In the midst of the melee, Paul Kelly caught my eye and invited Carl and me to join him for lunch. We arranged to meet in the restaurant at the Parker House Hotel in half an hour. We had a great chat, and Paul asked me more specific questions about some of my research. As the afternoon progressed, we frequently had to add additional tables as alumni from the Boston Bruins and others joined in what developed into a celebration and a time for reminiscing and expressing our gratitude to all — especially Russ Conway, Paul Kelly and Tom Daly.

We came away from the luncheon with the understanding — in our minds, at any rate — that the FBI and U.S. Justice Department were by no means finished with their investigation. It seemed that more and more players who had been ripped off with their disability insurance claims were coming forward.

We stayed in Boston for another day — we always enjoyed the opportunity to spend a few days there. The next morning, we were invited over to Bobby Orr's office for coffee and a chat. There was jubilation and hugs and a lot of back-slapping all around, and Carl and Bobby rehashed their histories and their observations about the now criminally charged Alan Eagleson.

Carl had been, in a significant way, responsible for Eagleson's securing Bobby as a client many years ago — before Bobby had even turned pro, in fact. Carl had become well aware, in retrospect, of the degree to which Eagleson had, time and again, used the senior, more established players like himself to impress the parents of young, up-and-coming stars — and potential clients — of the future. Carl told me that on many occasions he'd get a call from Al, in the middle of dinner, asking him to rush out and meet him someplace where he'd be with a junior prospect and his family. Carl would drop everything and run. Now, he realized what a fool he'd been and how he'd been used. Years later, Carl tried to warn Bobby about Eagleson — he remembered trying to talk to him at a charity dinner one night — but Bobby would hear none of what Carl had to say at the time. On this day, we were all in agreement.

We couldn't have been more impressed with the industry, hard work, dedication and commitment of the U.S. officials, and we felt an immense debt of gratitude for their unrelenting efforts. Above all, Russ Conway of the *Eagle-Tribune*, who with the support of his wonderful publisher, Irving Rogers, was absolutely amazing and was by now a dearly cherished and devoted friend to all of us who gathered at Bobby's that morning.

Later in the afternoon, we dropped in to see Paul Kelly at his office. After clearing the very stringent security, the likes of which we'd never encountered in Toronto, we spent about an hour chatting with Paul. We had come to know him as a compassionate, caring man. We respected his integrity and his intent to see justice prevail throughout this long struggle.

The phone in our hotel room remained disconnected, but I did write a detailed account of our experience in court and faxed it to Stevie Cameron so she'd have an account from our perspective for her coverage for *Maclean's*. Throughout this long, drawn-out saga, Stevie had frequently expressed her respect for the position Carl took about Eagleson. In her story, which appeared in the March 14 edition, she began with a mention of the most emotional detail: "Tears ran down Carl Brewer's face as he stood in the drab press room of the federal courthouse in Boston, listening to a U.S. official read a grand jury indictment against Eagleson, the most powerful man in Canadian hockey for almost a quarter of a century."

To rid hockey of Eagleson's sinister presence had become Carl's top priority, his mission in life. Nevertheless, it was neither a vindictive nor a malicious mission. In fact, Carl always applauded Alan Eagleson's brilliance; he just felt sad and betrayed that Alan hadn't used his brilliance for the benefit of the players whose interests he was supposed to have been protecting over all the years. Stevie understood that very special aspect of Carl right from the outset. She chose to highlight it in her article by including the following quote from Carl: "It's not that I'd be happy to see him go to jail; it's just that I wanted him stopped." That was always Carl's interest, and he was never hesitant to admit it. Stevie clearly understood Carl when she described him in the closing paragraph of her account: "But it was thinking of Ritch Winter's determination and of the plight of comrades like Jimmy Harrison that made Brewer so tearful in the courtroom. 'Ritch was maligned and pilloried in the press for years,' said Brewer. 'And, Jimmy Harrison was cheated out of his disability insurance. He's crippled today and he got nothing.' Now, ironically, he and hundreds of others who devoted their lives to Canada's sport will have to await the verdict of an American court."

On the morning of March 4, listeners to radio station CKNW in Vancouver heard Rafe Mair, the outspoken radio host, begin his morning commentary:

> *Alan Eagleson has been charged with 32 counts of offences in the state of Massachusetts...*
>
> *The first question one must ask is, "Where were the Royal Canadian Mounted Police?" These charges were not hastily drafted by some Boston district attorney on the make — they were the result of two years of deliberations by a Boston grand jury. The events — or at least, many of them — took place in Canada as much as in the United States. Certainly, many of the allegations involve Canadian citizens. Could it be that the RCMP deliberately went slow? If so, on whose orders? If they didn't go slow on orders from on high, surely, then, it must follow that they were derelict in their duty. An explanation, while not expected, would be refreshing.*
>
> *All of a sudden, people who were kooks aren't kooks anymore. Ritch Winter, the player agent from Edmonton to whom Carl Brewer gives the highest praise, was a kook. He was pilloried, stonewalled and God knows what because of*

his persistence for the players against Eagleson. As of yes-
terday morning, Mr. Winter is no longer a kook. Carl
Brewer and his indomitable lady, Sue Foster, were kooks,
too. Pains in the butt. Johnny and Janey One-Note. No one
except idiots like Rafe Mair would listen to them. Well, Carl
Brewer and Sue Foster stopped being kooks yesterday
morning at nine-thirty our time.

Whatever the result of the United States of America v.
Alan Eagleson court case, it has been known for years that
Alan Eagleson had conflicts of interest which boggled the
imagination. While he was supposed to be representing the
players' union, he also acted for about 350 players. He in-
vested their money in some terrible schemes, including ones
in which he and his family had strong interests. He was so
close to the owners that it is impossible to conclude that he
could fairly be said to be on the players' side, who, after all,
were paying him.

It's a long story and a sad and hurtful one. Our sports
heroes cried out for someone to listen to them instead of
Alan Eagleson. No one — at least, very few — would give
them the time of day. The players gave Eagleson their trust
and their money. He betrayed the former and mismanaged
(at best) the latter.

The release of the indictment in Boston was a significant milestone, but it
clearly was not the end of this story. Eagleson, who had actually been in
U.S. territory when the indictment was opened in Boston, had agreed to
appear to face the charges. Instead, he caught a plane back to Canada and
was declared a fugitive from U.S. justice on March 12, 1994. He would remain so for the next four years. Meanwhile, the RCMP investigation
remained active and the Law Society of Upper Canada continued to delve
into the complaints of professional misconduct.

***

In 1994, Harry Watson was inducted into the Hockey Hall of Fame in the
Veterans' category. Harry was a much-loved oldtimer. He played 14 seasons

on four teams between 1941 and 1957. He won a Stanley Cup in Detroit in 1943, and four more in a five-year span with the Leafs. When traded to Toronto, Harry was partnered with Bill Ezinicki and Syl Apps on one of the great scoring lines in the NHL. He made a name for himself as the player who got the assist on Bill Barilko's Stanley Cup–winning goal in 1951.

The induction ceremony took place on November 15, and John McCormack reserved a table for some of the NHL Oldtimers and invited Carl to join them. I received two phone calls from Carl during the course of that evening. The first came early on, shortly after his arrival, telling me in a most disgusted tone: "You won't believe this — Eagleson is here. The son of a bitch knows no shame." He was even more annoyed that Eagleson's escorts that night were Bob Pulford and Bill Wirtz, along with Toronto Maple Leaf general manager Cliff Fletcher. Later in the evening, at about nine-thirty, Carl phoned me again. This time, I immediately sensed that he was extremely unnerved and asked him what was wrong. He told me he'd just had a nasty encounter with Jill Eagleson — Al's daughter and Carl's goddaughter. "This small, short woman just walked right up to me," he told me. "I had no idea who she was; she looked me straight in the eye and said to me, 'Now look what you've done. No one is going to want to marry me now!' And then she turned and stormed away." Carl kept repeating that he had absolutely no idea who it was until after when she walked away from him.

The next day, I just happened to be talking to Mary Ormsby of the *Toronto Star* and I mentioned Carl's episode the night before with Jill. Immediately, without a moment's hesitation, Mary exclaimed, "Fuck her!" Mary went on to say that Jill was no innocent victim; as a lawyer, she must have clearly understood what her father was doing all those years. Mary reminded me that both Jill and her brother had benefited significantly from their father's largesse — all of which actually belonged to the players he was supposed to be representing. When I told Carl about my conversation with Mary, he was very relieved and it helped him put the situation in perspective. Typically, the sensitive Carl had been suffering pangs of guilt about Jill's plight ever since the confrontation.

And Mary was right. Jill and her brother, Trevor, and his wife had travelled free on airline tickets provided by Air Canada in exchange for rink-board advertising at international hockey tournaments. This scheme, too, was mentioned in the U.S. indictment. Authorities had identified some $60,000 worth of airline tickets given in exchange for rink-board ads at the

1984 Canada Cup alone. The same arrangement existed for the 1987 tournament, this time to the tune of $84,000. The indictment alleged that Eagleson didn't inform Hockey Canada of this benefit, that it was he who exercised complete control over the passes and that they were used by "his wife, son, daughter, friends and business associates for personal travel unrelated to the business of Hockey Canada."

According to the Law Society complaint, Jill Eagleson enjoyed $9,000 worth of airline travel to Paris, Bombay, Vancouver and New York. Moreover, Jill and Trevor both had received expensive clothing from Cam Natale, a Toronto clothier who outfitted Team Canada. Natale revealed: "I would regularly provide Eagleson personally with suits and other merchandise for free which we would bill through the Canada Cup, Labatt's or somebody else. From time to time, we also provided clothing to Eagleson's wife, son or daughter on the same basis."

***

A couple of days after the big player meeting of December 10, 1990, Carl, along with Ritch Winter, Bobby Orr, David Forbes, Dennis Owchar and Jim Harrison paid a visit to Toronto lawyer, Thomas Lockwood. Lockwood was the outside counsel engaged by the Law Society of Upper Canada to investigate the complaint Ritch Winter had filed in January 1990, alleging professional misconduct on the part of Alan Eagleson.

Everyone came away from the meeting optimistic and encouraged by Lockwood's reassurances that the matter would be thoroughly and objectively investigated and that player input was not only welcome but necessary. By 1993, however, with no communication or announcements whatsoever from either the Law Society or Tom Lockwood, Carl and the others were becoming increasingly troubled. The immediate concern, of course, was that the Law Society was treating this matter the same way that the RCMP and the Metro Toronto Police fraud squad had handled the complaints about Eagleson. The fraud squad had told Ritch Winter that they were waiting for the Law Society to complete its investigation before making a move. Ritch responded that this was akin to a lawyer killing someone and the police not charging him until the Law Society investigated him. By this time, of course, the Law Society — set up by lawyers to police their own — was suspect in our eyes as well.

Carl was not one just to sit back and stew over these concerns. We wrote letters — lengthy and strongly worded ones. Our skepticism was evident in a letter to Lockwood dated May 5, 1993:

> I am again writing to you to inquire about the status of your supposed investigation into the conduct and affairs of R. Alan Eagleson. Unfortunately, the entire matter of the Law Society investigation has come to be about as controversial as the Eagleson saga. It is further disconcerting to many of us to learn that a number of key figures, persons adversely affected by Mr. Eagleson's activities, have yet to be interviewed by you. Be assured that we will not be snowed by anyone's attempts to make light of our allegations or to whitewash this investigation.

Even Russ Conway was having serious doubts about the Law Society. Russ was in possession of important information and documents that would have been very helpful to Tom Lockwood, but by the time Lockwood went to Boston, those documents had been turned over to the grand jury.

Eventually, we did hear from Lockwood and met with him and his staff on a number of occasions to supply information and documentation. A formal outline of Carl's eventual involvement in the prosecution of his complaint was prepared, and we all expected fully that Carl would one day testify along with many other former players. We were now much more assured and confident that something worthwhile would come of this inquiry. Still, until we saw something concrete, we did not feel entirely comfortable.

On November 11, 1994, the Law Society of Upper Canada issued a communiqué announcing a formal complaint against Eagleson, accusing him of professional misconduct and conduct unbecoming a solicitor. The report contained 44 allegations of professional misconduct, among them the lending of trust monies without the consent or knowledge of his clients; failing to serve the interests of numerous individual hockey players, including Bobby Orr, Andre Savard, Jim Harrison and Mike Gillis; misleading Mike Gillis and causing him to pay more than $40,000 (U.S.) to a company related to Eagleson; co-operating with the NHL Pension Society without the knowledge of authorization of the NHLPA membership or of retired players in a request for an exemption from pension legislation; and taking kickbacks and undisclosed benefits from the Canada Cup and other international hockey tournaments. This report, outlining Lockwood's findings, was comprehensive, direct, hard-hitting and thoroughly detailed. After the release of the complaint, we were greatly relieved and tremendously impressed. We wrote to Lockwood:

> *Friday, November 11, 1994 was a very important day for hockey and for hockey players, particularly all those seriously disadvantaged by R. Alan Eagleson. It is also a great day for all Canadians. I would like to commend you, wholeheartedly, on your outstanding research and efforts as evidenced in the thorough and comprehensive complaint by the Law Society of Upper Canada against R. Alan Eagleson. It is sad and unfortunate that the conduct of Alan Eagleson was [allowed] to go on for so long unchecked, but the results that were made public on Friday are conclusive and all-embracing and have addressed our concerns in a forthright and admirable fashion.... You have done a fine job and we thank you.*

In 1995, at the age of 56, Carl again played hockey internationally, this time as a member of the Balmy Beach Oldtimers hockey team, which toured several European cities. Carl skated and worked out to get in shape for the games. One night, while out skating, he caught an edge on some rough ice and had a nasty, awkward fall. A few weeks before, while playing with the NHL Oldtimers in a charity game, he'd had another bad fall. Peter Conacher called me at the time to enquire about Carl, fearing that he had hurt himself badly that time, too. Carl played in games in Varese, Italy; Innsbruck and Villach, Austria; and Bled, Slovenia, and enjoyed himself thoroughly. While in Europe, Carl's back began to give him a great deal of difficulty and discomfort, and it interfered with his sleep. It seemed to bother him particularly at night and he had trouble getting comfortable. In Slovenia, we found a large, heavy-set therapist who was able to manipulate Carl's back and relieve his distress somewhat. Each night, I'd massage Carl's back, and I could see that the muscles on the left side of his entire back were as hard as a rock and about an inch and a half higher than those on the right.

Sychronicity

After travelling through Italy, Austria and Slovenia, the Balmy Beach group scheduled a week in Malta for sun and relaxation. We found it disappointing — the weather was cold, it was terribly expensive and, unlike every other place in the world we had visited, the people were not very friendly or helpful. After a few days there, we left the group and flew to Rome to continue our travels on our own. We took a train from Rome to Innsbruck to visit friends, before returning to Rome for a couple of days prior to our return flight to Canada.

A sunny day in Rome: Saturday, March 25, 1995. We awoke early in our room at the Hotel Diana in downtown Rome, a few blocks from the train station. Carl got up first and opened the shutters and exclaimed, "Well, Sue, we have a sunny day in Rome!" He sounded very upbeat and excited. We showered and dressed quickly and had an excellent cappuccino and a typical Italian jam-filled croissant in the breakfast room before setting out for a full day of exploring. Armed with a McDonald's map of the city, we walked along the Via Nazionale towards the Trevi Fountain. It was truly a splendid day for walking and absorbing the magnificent sights and beauty of Rome. The sky was blue and crystal clear, the forsythia bushes were vibrant with yellow blossoms and the fruit trees everywhere were gorgeous with pink blooms.

We walked along the Via Quattro Fontane and stopped at the intersection where each of the four corners features a beautifully sculptured ancient fountain. It was a beautiful, intriguing sight. We continued our walk until we arrived at the palace of the president. Guards stood at attention at the front gate and tour groups from Britain fussed with their cameras. We had walked this same route a year earlier, after the Spengler Cup, but it had been cold and grey and devoid of the charming appeal we were experiencing today. We walked down the stairs to the Trevi Fountain. A short walk ahead, and there it was: clean and gleaming white. "Three Coins in the Fountain." It is interesting how some sights, even if you've seen them before, will just stop you in your tracks. Carl and I were happy just to stand and gaze. I passed Carl a coin, and he reflected for a moment before tossing it down into the fountain. With my coin, I walked down beside the fountain, partly because I didn't want to embarrass myself by missing the fountain with my throw! I could sense the most extraordinary energy — of the ages — surrounding me as I stood there.

After doing a little shopping in the nearby stores, we headed towards the Vatican and St. Peter's. As we walked, I noticed, as I glanced down a tiny side street, a scene that looked like a picture on a postcard. It turned out to be a charming little square, the Piazza delle Coppelle. There was a small market on the square, and we bought some luscious strawberries and an orange. The aromas wafting out of a quaint restaurant nearby were intoxicating. We continued our walk towards the Vatican, and next thing we knew we were standing at the Tiber River — the Tiber of our Latin studies! We crossed the bridge over the Tiber, facing the Tribunale, or courthouse — with the dome of St. Peter's off to the left. It was a glorious view.

We stopped for a break at the Universal Bar on the Via Conciliazione and chose a table outside. I went in and bought a cappuccino for Carl and a glass of *vino bianco* for myself. We sat comfortably, enjoying our drinks and the truly succulent strawberries from the market, bathed in the hot sun. I said to Carl, "Sipping wine and eating strawberries in the shadow of St. Peter's on a glorious day — it doesn't get any better than this." Carl smiled warmly and lifted his cup to me. We stayed there for quite some time, reading the *International Herald Tribune* — Carl's favourite newspaper when we travelled — enjoying this moment in our lives. A trio of young men speaking English, having noticed our McDonald's map, came to our table and, in a lively chorus, asked, "*McDONALD'S*! Where's there a McDonald's?" They looked at our map, feverishly trying to locate the nearest restaurant. It turned out that these fellows were from Georgia in the United States. They walked off towards St. Peter's, but just a few minutes later hurried past us — going the opposite way, off to find McDonald's! Carl rolled his eyes and we laughed aloud at the idea that McDonald's would win out over St. Peter's on such a glorious day in Rome!

Reluctantly, we left our table and started walking towards St. Peter's. The interior of the basilica and dome was awesome — every magnificent inch. I was remembering how exciting it had been for Carl the year before, in January, when we came into the basilica and the Pope happened to be celebrating the first Mass of the new year. We left St. Peter's and crossed back over the Tiber. At the far end of the bridge, Carl stopped and leaned against it. It was lunchtime. We could go either to Al Fontanone in Trastevere, or back to the little restaurant we had found earlier on the Piazza delle Coppelle.

Carl mused.

I waited.

Sychronicity

Finally, Carl said, "You know how hard it is for me to make decisions!" I told him that I *did* know and reminded him that it was because he was a Libra. We both laughed, and he continued to deliberate for several more minutes. Finally, he decided upon Al Fontanone in Trastevere — "unless you prefer something else?" I knew we were in for a memorable meal. After a long walk along the edge of the Tiber, we reached our quaint little trattoria built into the hill. We were welcomed warmly and seated — at the very same table for two we had had the year before.

We ordered a bottle of the same white wine — Villa Antinori. It was icy cold, crisp, absolutely delicious. We toasted each other and our beautiful day in Rome. For the *primi piatti*, Carl chose *zuppa de verdura* (vegetable soup) and I had the *linguini al pesto*. Both were sensational. I loved the pesto; it was particularly fragrant and richly flavoured. I shared a bite with Carl, who paid me a lovely compliment by telling me that the pesto wasn't any better than what I made at home for us. There was a very large platter of grilled vegetables sitting on a side table and we watched the chef, a man about four feet tall and four feet wide decked out in an enormous, tall white chef's hat, retrieve his leg of lamb from a wood-fired oven. Carl wanted to be certain we got some of the vegetables and he chose his favourite: artichokes. My *secondi piatti* was an excellent *vitello limone* (lemon veal), and Carl chose the lamb. He shared a taste of his lamb with me, saying, "I can't say I've never had better lamb — this is the best *ever!*"

We lingered over our fabulous meal, thoroughly enjoying every moment, every mouthful of the food, every sip of our wine, and the conversation was intimate and easy. I told Carl how much I was loving every moment of the day, and what a joy the past few days had been. I mentioned our favourite room at the Gasthof Sailer in Innsbruck and the good meals there. "And the bathtub!" Carl added. And now we were having this spectacular day in Rome. "I feel so happy," I told Carl. "I'm loving every moment of this — every step, every view, but mostly, I love just being with you, wherever that might be. I love going to bed with you at night and waking up with you in the morning. Thank you — thank you for being such a special part of my life." Immediately Carl's eyes welled up with tears that began streaming down his face. His eyes locked with mine and he said, "Thank *you*, Sue. You are all those things for me, too."

The owner, sensing a very emotional moment, came to our table carrying his offering of a special digestif — a somewhat sweet concoction, like a sweet red wine. "For cleansing the system before dessert," he told us. We had tiramisu and *zuppa inglese* (trifle, although the name literally translates as "English soup") for dessert, and cappuccinos brought the meal to an end. The owner bade us farewell and wished us a good vacation, saying he hoped to see us again the next year. And we truly hoped we would return one day.

CHAPTER 13

CARL AND SUE

> *"Sue, is it right for me to say that without you and me and all the work we did, Alan Eagleson would never have gone to jail; Bob Goodenow wouldn't have his job; John Ziegler would still be around; Ken Sawyer would still be there; the players wouldn't have neutral arbitration; and player salaries would be nowhere where they are today? Am I right to think that?"*

As Carl's battles became more and more public in the mid to late 1980s, we were being seen together more and more frequently. Then, as the pension litigation unfolded and Carl's outspoken criticism of Alan Eagleson became the subject of discussion in the media, attention was focused on Carl Brewer and Susan Foster as a couple, as crusaders, as an inseparable team. I was increasingly asked to appear with Carl, or by myself, on national television or radio programs to discuss the issues. Reporters were calling me for help with their stories. Carl usually threw all the credit for our efforts and accomplishments my way. He'd say, "Sue does all the work," or "Sue writes the letters; I just sign them." Many times, he was heard to say, "Alison Griffiths and David Cruise or Russ Conway — they don't want to talk to me; they want to talk to Sue," or "I'm just a pretty face; it's Sue who does it all."

It was flattering, but it wasn't the case, of course. None of the work that the two of us did — which resulted in the return of millions of dollars in pension monies to their rightful recipients, and the removal of Alan Eagleson as executive director of the NHL Players' Association — could ever have been accomplished by either of us alone. We each brought different and complementary qualities to the cause.

Dr. Tom Pashby, reflecting on our relationship, observed: "The best thing that ever happened to Carl Brewer, in my estimation, was when he found Susan Foster. They just seemed to be a pair that worked well together. I knew Susan a lot better and longer than Carl, but Susan not only picked up on the enthusiasm Carl had to go here and there, do this and do that, she had the ability to stick at one thing and see it through. Carl might think it a great idea this year, and next year he'd have another idea. Susan focused in on what Carl felt was the thing to do. That was a great combination."

Bruce Dowbiggin told Roy MacGregor: "If Carl was the heart of the thing, Sue was the brains. Carl does the act; Sue books the hall, drives the bus, sells the tickets and makes sure the costumes get laundered — and does it all cheerfully, too."

Carl understood his strengths and weaknesses well, and he did depend on me for support and strength. At the end of many a day, he'd refer to some words of reassurance I'd offered, and say, "Thanks, Sue. If you hadn't said that to me this morning, I don't think I would have made it through the day."

Carl was very public in admitting that I was his strength; others saw it, too. After Eagleson pled guilty in Boston and Toronto courts, Carl spoke with Roy MacGregor for a column he wrote entitled "The players' unsung hero."

All through the most incredible week, she was at the centre of every scene. When Carl Brewer stood up in that tiny Boston courtroom and all but shouted out, "Thank God for the United States of America because none of this would have occurred in Canada," she was the one reaching up to offer quiet support. And when the fallen czar of hockey, Alan Eagleson, was dragged off to jail, she was the one whom those on the other side hugged and kissed before heading out to face the cameras and microphones that never once took notice of her. Small, with warm, sympathetic eyes and a constant smile, Susan Foster, retired school teacher, companion of Brewer, is the unsung hero of the players' long battle to get back some of what they have lost.

Carl had a brilliant mind. He was insightful and could see situations developing and understand them long before others caught on — if they ever did. He knew there were serious problems with the NHL pension from his discussions with other players and from his own unanswered questions. He also had a sincere desire to rid hockey of the sinister presence of Alan Eagleson and restore "dignity and respect" to hockey players. He saw himself as a players' rights advocate. Allan Dick, our friend and lawyer, once remarked to me, "Carl, for all his ideas, was always right, but he was just about two years ahead of everyone else."

I, on the other hand, took care of details and tried to sift through all the commingling and conflicting ideas Carl had racing through his mind at all times. Relying on my teacher's skills — studying and recording information in such a way that it was clearly understood — I researched all his issues and put the documentation together. It meant several hours every day — for weeks at a time and eventually years — spent in public offices, tracking real estate transactions, copying documents, following the flow of money. Similarly, I spent months researching Carl's personal battles — studying collective bargaining agreements, NHL bylaws, contracts and contract law. This work was an important part of Carl's arbitration hearing in the 1980s, and much of the research was helpful to the FBI in their investigation into Eagleson. I was at an advantage in tracking down these leads because for years Carl had been discussing all of his concerns with me. As a result, every person, company, crony, event or activity that bothered Carl was well known to me. That certainly helped me know where to look and what needed to be checked out. After we began helping Russ Conway, I'd get documents, copy them and ship them via FedEx. In turn, the FBI would subpoena the material, with Russ's co-operation, for their own investigation. Russ and I had a great mutual admiration. Russ told Roy MacGregor about my contributions: "Sue was incredible. You'd give her a lead and two or three days later she'd be back to you with everything. She's a very, very bright woman."

I've been asked numerous times how it was that Carl became the squeaky wheel who spearheaded the pension lawsuit and took up the challenge of going after Alan Eagleson and what that was like for him. Carl also asked himself why and how he found the courage to stand up for his rights when others didn't. When one considers Carl's hockey background, he was very much his own man — he had a history of making decisions that his peers didn't dare to make, or didn't understand that they could make. Early in his career with the Leafs, when he felt he wasn't being treated with dignity and respect, he quit. When the pressure of dealing with Imlach grew too burdensome and was destroying him psychologically, he retired from professional hockey. Carl was never beholden to the system. He was a man who marched to his own drummer. Many players longed to have a lifelong career with their team; it worked out for a few, but not many. Carl possessed a marvellous capacity to understand that there was always someplace else to go and something new to try. Unquestionably, some of his peers resented his moves — thought he was a quitter, that he let his team down. It was a stigma he carried around for a long time. For Carl's part, he'd comment, "I've been tilting at windmills all my life."

So, it was not uncharacteristic for Carl to become the whistle blower in the pension and Eagleson matters. It takes a great deal of courage to play that role — very few people will take it on because, invariably, it invites isolation, resentment, criticism, jealousy and just a lot of people who will dismiss you as a wacko. Carl experienced all of those reactions, and he was most definitely not immune to the hurt. Carl was an extremely sensitive individual with very deep feelings. Mostly, he couldn't fathom why others couldn't see what he saw so clearly, and he couldn't for the life of him understand why others were so reluctant to stand up and be counted.

None of these issues would ever have been my issues without Carl. They weren't relevant to my life. Carl was my cause. For decades, it had troubled me that Carl didn't get the respect I felt he deserved within the hockey community. He was quickly labelled or dismissed as a quitter, a flake, unstable. To my mind, this was grossly unfair and shortsighted. Countless times over the years, Carl told me that I knew him better than anyone had ever known him. And, knowing him so well, so intimately, I knew there was so much more to this man than such superficial, insensitive labels. I saw his beauty, his wonderful spirit, his talents, his warmth and his generosity. He cared deeply for others, especially the disadvantaged and downtrodden. I knew of his brilliance, his intellect and his resourcefulness. Stevie Cameron interviewed me for a feature article in *The Globe and Mail* in 1993 and asked, "Why did she do it?" My answer: "Out of my respect, admiration and love for Carl." An important aspect to my commitment to all of these struggles was to help Carl accomplish his dreams and to help him reach a place of respect within the community that mattered so much to him — professional hockey.

Some saw my role as gatekeeper to Carl Brewer. Our friend Bruce

Dowbiggin expressed this idea in his book about the pension battle, *The Defense Never Rests*. He wrote: "Sue Foster, who sees beyond Brewer's Teutonic fierceness and channels his energies, is the gatekeeper to Brewer and his alter ego. Strangers and lazy journalists alike get weeded out by the ebullient, middle-aged Foster. Together, Brewer and Foster make an unusual pair of revolutionaries when they enter a room, but it would be wrong to mistake their commitment."

Naturally, there were many ups and downs along the way for Carl and me during our crusades — moments of great joy and exhilaration as well as moments of disappointment or discouragement. I recall being upset at one point about certain attitudes and developments among the "Group of Seven" applicants in the pension suit. My son, Dan, said something to me at the time that shocked me: "Mum, you've got to understand there are a lot of jealous people around you and Carl." Such a thought had never occurred to me, and at the same time I was amazed by this insight. Jealous? Of what? All the work, the struggle, getting along on a wing and a prayer — what was there for others to envy?

But it did come out that certain people resented the fact that the public spotlight was focused almost exclusively on Carl — he was the player who was sought out to speak on radio or television or to add his comments for a newspaper article. Andy Bathgate, one of the applicants, told *The Globe and Mail*: "When the television cameras were around, Carl and Susan were always around." Well, if we were around, it was because we were asked to be. Almost daily, I fielded calls from reporters, journalists and producers asking for information, interviews or comments about the ongoing efforts. Mary Ormsby of the *Toronto Star* explained why she sought Carl out frequently to contribute something to the stories she was working on: "Carl was honest to a fault. He would scold me and tell me I was lazy if I hadn't done enough research on the Eagleson matter, and that always made me feel bad because he was usually right. On other days, he would be delightful — just like a little kid when he'd come up with news in the *Star* or if I was working diligently on a tip or an angle, even if it didn't pan out. But because he was so brutally honest, I knew I could rely on him to comment on any matter concerning the Eagleson case because he was informed, intelligent and always had an opinion."

Within a couple of weeks of that revelation from my son, Colleen Howe phoned to chat. During the conversation, Colleen ventured onto the subject of my relationship with Carl. "Do you realize that the relationship you and Carl have — the strong, incredible bond, the way you support each other and share the same ideals and care so much for one another — is a real inspiration for everyone, especially in the hockey community?" she asked. "People are very much aware of the two of you. But Sue, be careful never to overlook the fact that as much as you are a wonderful inspiration, there are those who are envious of what the two of you share." Same message, different source — nonetheless, a source I respected and appreciated very much.

What intrigued others was that Carl and I were equal partners in everything in life. In the male-dominated world of hockey, Carl did not hesitate to let everyone know that he respected me and considered me his equal in all things. He'd often tell people, "Sue speaks for me." Sometimes, Carl felt insecure about his understanding of the facts that were coming to light in our investigative work. Mary Ormsby noticed this: "Carl was a man who, rightly or wrongly, felt he had some limitations in the Eagleson matter. Whenever it came to reviewing the painstaking detective work that revealed so much detail over the years of following paper trails, Carl would hand the phone to Sue. Sue was not only an equal partner in the pursuit of Eagleson, she was his anchor when I think Carl was unsure of an answer or an issue. He was very proud of his brainy girlfriend and had no problem deferring questions to her."

In 1994, Carl and I went out to Olds, Alberta, where Carl was guest speaker at the Italian Club's 32nd Annual Sports Dinner. Allan Maki of the *Calgary Herald* interviewed Carl and asked the question, "Why was it left to Brewer to take on the NHL kingpins?" "Me? This has dominated my life for 20 years," Carl replied. "It has been a thread there for 20 years. I had something no other hockey player had — a brain — and the brain's name is Susan Foster. I was hoping it would work out. My feeling was that Alan Eagleson had to be stopped. He was stopped. Now there are so many things if it all comes out, it'll make *The Pelican Brief* look like a Sunday in church."

Surprisingly, Carl was conflicted over what was playing out with Eagleson. Despite the satisfaction of knowing justice had been served, he felt sad and a little uncomfortable about Eagleson's fate. Mary Ormsby saw this and remembered: "One time Carl just materialized in the newsroom, at my desk, like a phantom. I don't know how he got past security, but he did, and he had Sue with him. I'll never forget the conversation. Eagleson had not yet entered a two-country plea agreement, but Carl was feeling guilty. He said something along the lines of, 'How can you celebrate the destruction of another human being?' Carl was in a state of personal anguish over what would happen to Eagleson — and to the NHL — and Sue's eyes were so full of empathy as she listened to him. She knew what a toll this case was taking on Carl, and without her constant support, I'm not sure Carl would have made it to that Boston courtroom."

Although hockey-related issues dominated our lives for years, that wasn't all there was to our lives together. We shared such a deep bond that the communication was often unspoken but undeniable, and it defied description. The two of us were so closely aligned that when we ate in a restaurant, no matter how long or complicated the menu, we'd invariably end up choosing the exact same meal. We were very fortunate to share many common interests.

One of these was a passion for travel, and we saw the world together. France was a special love for both of us, and we had some truly memorable trips. Carl used to tell our friends, "Sue used to live in France … in her past lives." In 1994, we were in Normandy after the 50th anniversary of D-Day. We were deeply moved by the presence of Canadian flags everywhere we went, in every town and village. We walked through the seaside towns of Courseulles-sur-Mer and Arromanches, on whose beaches the Canadians had landed, and enjoyed the beautiful fishing village of Honfleur. The most deeply emotional time during this trip was when we stood in the Canadian war cemetery at Beny-sur-Mer, stopped in our tracks by the sight of the white crosses, row upon row — commemorating young men, children really. The 23- and 24-year-olds were the elder statesmen. The cemetery itself was beautifully maintained. Bruce Dowbiggin once said it is a pilgrimage every Canadian should make. The experience left us both overcome with tear-filled eyes. We drove around the countryside the rest of that day, saying little.

We went from there to Avignon, in the south of France. Every morning, we drove a short distance to what quickly became a cherished spot: the village of Châteauneuf-du-Pape, home of some of the choicest wine in the world. It's a surprisingly tiny town, and although it was summer there were no tourists. We went to the town square each morning — to the locals' bar — for breakfast. This was an experience that Carl never ever tired of talking about! The meal included a glass of red wine, a glass of white wine and a choice of several food items like *tarte aux oignons* or croissants and coffee.

While we sat on the patio enjoying this unbelievable experience each morning, the elderly men of the village sat on an old stone bench under a huge olive tree, their dogs at their feet, engaged in animated conversation. It was a classic French country scene and it delighted both of us.

On another visit to France, in the fall of 1999, we enjoyed Brittany, which boasts miles and miles of coastline with both sandy beaches and dramatic rugged coastlines. In the tiny fishing village of Le Pouliguen, Carl had six oysters at the extraordinary Sunday-morning market. These were shucked for him on the spot by Phil Marais, a village fisherman — the cost: $2.50! Carl said, "These are so good, I'm never eating another oyster at home again. People in Toronto don't even know what an oyster is!" While we enjoyed a lovely lunch in Quiberon, at a tiny restaurant called La Chaumine, a local resident overheard our conversation and came over and invited us to her home for coffee. She was a charming woman, an artist, and the walls of her little village house were adorned with her lovely paintings. She was a delight and we had a lovely visit.

On other trips, we went to Hong Kong and Thailand (on Aeroplan points!), Greece and Austria (frequently). Italy was also a favourite. We met and made friends all over the world.

We both loved to read. Carl always enjoyed reading anything written by Father Andrew M. Greeley, who was famous for his Bishop Blackie Ryan mysteries. He called it "escapism" and each time he reached the end of one, he'd invariably say, "God, I enjoyed that!" He also re-read the Agatha Christie novels because they were his mum's favourite. Carl, of course, had read *The Search for Bridey Murphy* in Grade 10 and it tweaked his interest in many concepts like ESP, thought transference or reincarnation. Carl learned self-hypnosis early in his hockey career to try to alleviate stress, and he taught me what he had learned. Together we were intrigued to learn more about these things.

After I read Shirley MacLaine's *Out on a Limb*, Carl also read it and we attended her seminars. Carl felt that the meditations she did, when she had everyone visualize the white light and see it spreading all over the troubled spots in the world, were a factor in the fall of the Berlin Wall shortly afterwards. I introduced Carl to Louise Hay's work and he referred to her book *You Can Heal Your Life* as his bible; we both identified with her teachings and did the meditations together almost daily. We attended her seminars in Toronto and Los Angeles. When Carl encountered problems with his health, we meditated together before going to bed every night, and it helped him sleep.

***

Over the years, people have frequently asked me, "What was Carl really like?" Everyone tried to figure him out over the years, to understand what made him tick. This frustrated Carl, who would ask me: "How would you feel if people were always trying to psychoanalyze you?" More often than not, they failed to get a handle on him, so reporters and others wrote him off as an "enigma" or a "mystery man." He hated that. And the description "smart, for a hockey player" drove him nuts! In all the years that I knew Carl, he told me time and time again: "You know me better than anyone has ever known me." I'm sure that was true, but even I had my moments! Ralph Backstrom picked up on that, and he laughingly remarked, "Sue, even you had trouble figuring him out sometimes!" Touché!

Carl was always the first to admit he was complicated. "There's no one more complicated than me," he'd say. He freely admitted, "I have a lot of hang-ups." I would say that the best way to describe Carl is as a man of many paradoxes — by his very nature, a study in dramatic contradictions. Physically, he was a large, intimidating presence with his broad shoulders and bald head. And he was bombastic and highly opinionated. He never backed away from expressing his opinions, and if you didn't agree with him, you probably got shot down with his classic line, "You're entitled to your opinion, no matter how wrong you are."

People who were most acquainted with this Carl have a very hard time believing that he was actually very shy, retiring and terribly modest. Whenever he was faced with the prospect of attending a social function, he had to work hard to psych himself up just to get there. When he was invited to be a guest speaker at some event or other, he'd suffer extreme anguish; he feared he wouldn't be accepted or that he'd mess up. Yet the moment he entered a room, he was like a magnet; people were invariably drawn to him, interested in him and intrigued by what he had to say. He could be warm, funny and delightful. He was interested in other people, too. I noticed how he often interrogated people — asking an endless string of questions. He was truly interested in their answers, but I used to wonder sometimes if this was a defense mechanism to keep others from getting too close to him or asking him the same type of probing questions. He always was more concerned about others than himself.

Mark Askin, the producer at Leafs TV, was close to Carl, who trusted and liked him. Mark said to me: "People didn't know Carl. They saw the bombastic Carl, but he genuinely cared deeply about people. He was interested in you, and if you had his attention he wasn't thinking about the next conversation like most people."

Belying his imposing form, he was probably the most sensitive individual I have ever known. He had deep feelings and cared passionately about people and situations. His eyes filled with tears at the slightest provocation. He'd invariably cry in movies, and on Sunday evenings when we watched *Touched by an Angel* on television, he'd sob at the stories of redemption. Every time he watched the movie version of *Net Worth*, the story of Ted Lindsay's efforts to organize the players in 1957, on television, he wept. The morning he learned that his son Chris's dog Max had died, he was devastated. He came downstairs looking ghostlike and crying and he mumbled to me, "Max died." Carl adored that dog, and when Max got old, Carl used to have me bake dog biscuits to take to him because they were soft enough for him to chew. As I tried to console Carl, he said through his tears, "Max knew how much I loved him."

Carl was extremely generous and kind. If someone needed help, he'd be the first to jump in to do whatever he could. At times, he could be overly eager to help, going beyond appropriate boundaries, and this sometimes caused people to back away. This confused Carl and oftentimes left him feeling underappreciated. He'd say, "I frighten people," and the very idea was hurtful to him. He had an enormous capacity for compassion, but from one moment to the next, he could explode — like a volcano, setting people back on their heels in shock. No one ever knew when Carl was just going to lose it, and that was a very disquieting experience for anyone.

Some have said they felt they were walking on eggshells around him. (There were times when I felt that way, too.) As an example, Carl had a keen interest in building and real estate development. He dreamed of buying a bungalow in Leaside and building a second storey on it, as was the trend for a number of years. One day, we stopped by a site our friend Ralph Gallinger, a real estate broker and builder, was constructing. During our brief visit, Carl sketched out for Ralph the costs he thought were representative of the project he hoped to undertake. When Carl left the room momentarily, Ralph said to me, "His numbers are ridiculous; they're not realistic at all."

"Tell him, *please!*" I replied.

"I'm not going to tell him nothin," Ralph said. "He'll just take it personally and he won't talk to me for the next five years."

Despite all his accomplishments, Carl always felt inadequate, never good enough. He was very critical of himself, and he frequently made disparaging comments about himself. "You'd think a 62-year-old man would be able to keep track of something," he angrily remarked while looking for some stock certificates. As much as Carl always impressed me with his generosity of spirit and tendency to see the good in everybody, he was also often critical of others, too, and impatient if they didn't agree with him or see his point of view. He admitted to me that he was critical of others because it was his way of trying to make himself look good; he needed to do that because, deep down, he didn't really feel that he was.

Carl was always my biggest fan. One of the nicest things anyone ever said to me was when Carl told me, "Usually, the longer you know someone the more you see their faults, their weaknesses — with you, every day that I know you, I am more and more in awe of you, of your brilliance, your strengths, your abilities."

For much of his life, Carl felt like an outsider. When he played with the Leafs, he felt estranged socially from teammates who called him "Skitz" and "Psycho." Jim Roberts once said to me, "Carl was always a lone ranger." Once, when he was trying desperately to make something work out that clearly wasn't, I asked him why it was so important to him. His answer saddened me: "Sue, I've always just wanted to belong." I gently suggested that I didn't think there was anything there to belong to. Almost in tears, he said, "I think I understand that now, too, Sue." He often said to me, "I don't have friends; I have only one friend, and that's you." Many found it hard to get to know Carl. One childhood friend and Midget teammate, Bill Agnew, remembered telling Carl he couldn't be Carl's friend. "You're too high maintenance for me, Carl," he said. Gordie Howe, described his friendship with Carl to Randy Starkman of the *Toronto Star*: "With friendship, you've got to work on it. I don't think many people wanted to work on it with Carl. Once you get to know him, he's really a very nice man." Gordie told me, "Carl was hard to get to know, but once I got to know him, I could say with pride that he was a true friend."

Carl was unrelentingly intense; he was well aware of this characteristic, and the toll it took on him and others. He realized that it had been a double-edged sword when he played hockey. His hero in his hockey-playing days was his old friend and teammate, Bob Nevin. He admired Nevvie's laid-back approach to hockey — and life in general — and he used to joke to Bob, "If I'd been more like you and you'd been more like me, we both would have been great!"

Carl was very cerebral. He was a real intellectual who was very well-spoken and informed about all areas of life. I used to be amazed how often, during the first years I knew Carl, I'd find myself looking up the meaning of a word he'd used in his normal conversation. I'd have a general idea what his word meant, but was compelled to check out the complete inference. I felt very relieved one night while having dinner with Brit and Sally Selby when Brit brought up the same thing. He told Sally and me that he considered himself well-educated and well-read, but every time he talked with Carl, he'd go home and get out his dictionary to check the exact meaning of some word Carl had used! And Brit and I were both high school teachers! Carl had studied hard as a student and was interested in learning new things all through his life. He had a very curious mind and was insightful.

On the other hand, he was also very gullible and easily led — especially by those with the biggest stories and promises of great wealth and success. People selling snake oil or its equivalent — like gold mines in Costa Rica — had Carl's full and undivided attention. He had a history of getting himself — and that always meant both of us — involved with shysters in dubious business activities. Invariably such deals fell through, the partners took off and Carl was left holding the empty bag. If there was an area where we had disagreements, it was here. He was very stubborn, as Johnny Bower pointed out, and he often refused to listen to reason, even when Allan Dick looked into the background of a proposal and explained to him that there was no merit or substance.

Once, I asked John Beer of the RCMP about a boiler-room deal someone was coaxing Carl into. John guided me in the necessary steps to get Carl extricated from this web before he got into trouble. The instigator of the plot was already well known to the RCMP. The problem was, Carl had no idea whom he could trust. This was a fairly common trait among hockey players in general — one of the reasons Eagleson lasted as long as he did! For the most part, they'd been immersed in hockey from a very young age and had missed out on some important life learning along the way.

Carl was very focused and determined. Yet he had a mind-set that always expected the worst to happen. On one of our trips to France, there was a mix-up over our rental car and we had to return to Nice Airport the following day to get it. As we approached the rental counter, the attendant wasn't there, but within seconds he showed up and couldn't have been more helpful. As Carl drove the car out of the parking space, he heaved a huge sigh of relief and said: "Thank God we got a car! I was so sure all morning that there wouldn't be a car here for us." For me, it was akin to going to Loblaws for butter and being sure they wouldn't have any. I was really taken aback by the intensity of his comment and asked him if he was inclined to think that way about a lot of things. After a moment of reflection, he said, "Yeah, I guess if I'm honest about it, I do — all the time."

In the summer of 1988, we went to Austria to visit friends and took my son, Dan, with us. Dan was 12 at the time and he and Rene, our friends' grandson, hit it off immediately and became friends. On a hot day, Carl and I walked downtown to have a glass of wine and some private time. Carl decided to phone back to check on the boys. There was no answer, and immediately Carl got very upset and began to fret. He was convinced they'd gone swimming and suffered a terrible mishap. We raced back to find the boys tinkering with their bikes — all was well.

At the same time, he had a delightful sense of humour. He'd laugh uproariously at the reruns of his favourite television show, *Cheers*, no matter how many times he'd seen the episode. He'd also fall off his chair laughing at Dennis Hull's jokes. Dennis told me that the last time he saw Carl, at a charity golf event, he couldn't even look at Carl because Carl was laughing so hard it was cracking him up. Afterwards, Dennis asked Carl why he was laughing so hard at the jokes when he'd already heard them all, and Carl said, "but they're so funny, Dennis."

Sometimes, people weren't sure whether Carl was pulling their leg. His humour could go over their heads. In a restaurant, if the cutlery was missing, he'd call a waiter over and say, "I can't eat this." The waiter, thinking the food had been improperly prepared, would immediately apologize and offer to remove his plate. Then Carl would indicate the absence of cutlery, reducing the waiter to howls of laughter — an immediate stress release. I can recall another time, when the waitress came to our table as soon as we sat down. "What took you so long?" Carl asked, feigning impatience. When she left, Carl said to me, "I hope she knows I was kidding." When she returned, he asked her if she realized he was joking. Her answer set Carl back: "No, I didn't know you were kidding me — I didn't know what you meant."

Although Carl had a charming lighter side, the opposite was also true: he was a man with a great many insecurities. It is very sad for me to recall that Carl left many little hand-scribbled notes in books or on note pads: "I'm afraid of not being good enough... I fear failure... I fear disapproval... I am fearful, anxious and antisocial... I have no self-love... I have no strength of character." He was fearful — "I'm afraid of everything," he'd tell me. He was constantly, at the core of his being, tormented by negative, self-defeating thoughts of self-loathing. To add to that, he was guilt-ridden and felt shame. He attributed this to his Catholic upbringing, but I always felt it came from someplace more personal. One night just before he died, Carl, unexpectedly, told me for the first time: "My dad didn't die the way everyone thinks he did; he died on top of some broad and it wasn't my mother". The deep shame Carl had felt all those intervening years was clearly evident on his face. I really cannot recall any reasonable length of time when Carl's mind was not filled with dozens of thoughts, ideas and plans, all racing around in his mind at the same time — ranging from bank mergers to the way the Toronto Maple Leaf Alumni was being managed and the treatment of former players by staff at the NHL Pension Society; from his divorce, his relationship with his brother, and his son's building business to his inability to manage his finances and business associates who took advantage of him. It seemed that Carl was rarely in the moment. Countless times, we'd be driving and he'd start talking to me, and I'd have no idea what he was talking about. That was because he'd already carried on the first half of the conversation silently in his mind. When I'd ask for clarification, he'd shake his head, smile, say "sorry" and start again from the beginning. This constant stream of thoughts, many of which were negative, was a source of angst and torment, not to mention pain, both mental and physical. This was a very heavy cross for him to bear. Nothing over the years managed to release him from it.

It troubled Carl greatly that it was so difficult for him to speak up for himself. The idea of having to confront someone terrified him. Being a Libra, he sought to keep the peace at all costs. It was always left to me to fight his personal battles, to stick up for him and get him his due. This stands in stark contrast to the fact that it was Carl who, alone amongst his peers, stood up and spoke up for all retired players in the lead-up to the pension lawsuit. Moreover, it was Carl who stood up and challenged some of the most powerful and influential people in the country as he fought for decades to bring Alan Eagleson to justice. On both counts, Carl was successful. Whistle-blowers are never applauded; indeed, they're generally denounced as crazies or troublemakers. Carl experienced those jibes, but he remained undeterred.

The Celtic philosopher John O'Donoghue writes, "There is no force that I know that can so quickly destroy the happiness and tranquility of life as negative thinking." This could easily have been written to describe Carl. He was afraid to speak up for himself, afraid of confrontation, afraid of others' opinions, afraid to answer the phone, to open the mail. O'Donoghue continued: "Even in their solitude, they remain afraid of meeting themselves. Negativity is an addiction to a bleak shadow around every human form. The negativity holds you outside in exile from your own love and warmth."

Carl's complexities and troubled nature aside, he was a special presence, a wonderful man. He was the essence of goodness, of kindness, of generosity, always grateful for the blessings he had in life. He said "thank you" often. He enjoyed simple things in life, like going to Wal-Mart (always his idea, not mine), fish and chips on Friday nights, watching an old movie on television, and having friends and family in for dinner. He loved my cooking, and when guests commented on the meal, he'd proudly interject: "You think this is gourmet? What you don't understand is that I eat like this every night!" He had a sweet tooth and enjoyed the fresh cherry pies I baked each year when sour cherries arrived in the market. As he pushed his plate towards me for another piece of pie, he'd say: "Anything this good can't be bad for me." He realized that he was stressful and he worried about the pressure he placed on me. Before he died, he said to me more often than usual, "You must be a saint to put up with me" or, "what did I ever do to deserve your love?"

People have asked me if Carl was a happy person. I would have to answer that he probably wasn't, not fundamentally. He himself said to me, during the time he was struggling with his health and trying to prepare me for the possibility of his not being around: "Sue, you'll be fine. You're a happy person. You're not like me — I'm morose. You're happy and upbeat." He went on to mention that Al Shaw, who organizes the oldtimers' luncheons, had recently told him, "When I call your place, I don't want to talk to you. I only want to talk to Sue, because she is so relaxed and uplifting when I talk to her, it makes my day." Certainly Carl had many happy moments — travelling, enjoying a nice meal, visiting with good friends, walking through the markets or old towns of France or Italy, driving around the countryside looking at real estate anywhere we were, especially Florida. He was especially happy when he went to the monthly luncheons with the NHL Oldtimers. He would come home, bursting with stories about whom he'd seen, all about Wally Stanowski's fishing trips to Mexico or Ron Hurst's jokes, and he'd tell me the name of every person who had sent their greetings to me. He felt accepted with this group of men. Al Shaw told me that he was such a presence when he arrived for the luncheons, everyone seemed to stop talking and the room fell silent when he walked in.

Over the years, many have suggested that Carl must have wanted to give up the pension and Eagleson battles on a regular basis. In fact, there never was a point when Carl wanted to give up — or even expressed such a possibility to me. He'd sometimes ask, "what are we doing?" when we were overwhelmed or when I'd get anxious about the expenses we were constantly incurring, but we always remained fixed on our goal. Discussing Carl's legacy recently, David Keon said to me: "Well, he was a great player, a great skater, he could handle the puck and he certainly helped our team. After, well, *you*, what you did with the pension — I know how much work you did.

"But the worst thing that anyone could wish for was for Carl to get interested in something and put his teeth into it, because he wasn't going to let it go. When he got his teeth into it, it didn't matter to him what happened, good, bad or indifferent. He was going to get results that he wanted."

CHAPTER 14

CANADIAN HOCKEY PSHAW!

"Canada always has had difficulty growing up, and diehard hockey fans still insist that Canada's best is superior to the Russians, the Czechs and the Swedes."

From the moment Carl first learned that the World Championships were to be held in Vienna, Austria, in April 1996, he was determined that we'd be there, no matter what. He considered this tournament a special one, because it was just one year shy of 30 since he had played in the same tournament in Vienna as a member of Father David Bauer's National team.

We flew to Zurich in April a few days in advance of the tournament; as we had some free time, we took a short train ride to Geneva. It was Carl who found us a hotel — Hotel Moderne, a small, family-run establishment on a side street not far from the railway station. It was a perfect location, and we spent three nights there, enjoying Geneva. We loved the light, upbeat atmosphere — the French influence that was noticeable everywhere was a stark contrast to the more austere, Germanic atmosphere of Zurich.

Spring had arrived fully: the sun shone brilliantly each day, the trees and flowers were all in full bloom and the *Jet d'Eau* sparkled in the middle of Lac Léman (Lake Geneva). We walked for miles, strolling through Old Town, took a boat ride on the lake and enjoyed good meals and a perfect relaxed holiday.

On April 21, we got on a train again, this time back to Zurich, where we caught the Transalpine Express bound for Austria. Initially, our plan was to get off the train in Feldkirch and visit old friends. However, this train was extraordinary: it was brand new, spotless, comfortable, and furthermore, it had a dome car! Carl loved trains. Also, it was a picture-perfect day. When we arrived in Buchs, on the Swiss border with Liechtenstein, Carl looked at me, shook his head and said, "Let's stay on and go to Innsbruck."

A short time later, at our original destination of Feldkirch, the conductor helped us out by validating our passes instead of requiring us to get off and have them validated inside the station, as is the norm. The trip from Feldkirch to Innsbruck takes approximately two hours and is truly a fantastic route. Carl had taken me on this journey for the first time back in July of 1985, when we made our first trip to Europe together. The views are breathtaking, and they were at their very best on this day. We made a habit of sitting in the dining car when we travelled by train because we could share a couple of carafes of *weise wein*, chat and enjoy the countryside through the huge panoramic windows of the car. We changed seats frequently between the dome car and the dining car on this trip, trying to decide which offered the more spectacular views of the forests, the green valleys alive with their first crops, the baby animals hanging close to their mothers, grazing on the new grass, the powerful mountain torrents cascading down from the still snow-capped mountains — all wondrous to behold. As we approached Innsbruck, we were enjoying the train and the trip so much that, again, Carl looked at me and said, "Sue, let's just stay on and go right to Vienna."

We reached Vienna's Westbahnhof station very late at night. Shortly before the train pulled into the station, the only other remaining passenger, an American, began chatting with us. He asked where we were staying. When Carl told him that we had to find a place, he looked alarmed and told us, "Good luck finding a place tonight — the World Championships are on and there are no hotel rooms in Vienna." He was booked in a hotel outside of town.

After our glorious day, we were brought crashing back to earth. Neither of us had given a second thought to the fact we had no reservation — we never did plan ahead. Carl left me in the station with our bags, asked a newspaper vendor to look out for me, and went out to look for accommodation. In about 20 minutes he returned, having found a room for us at the Ambassador Hotel just across the road from the station. This was an occasion when his command of German came to the rescue! We were certainly relieved and grateful as we registered and found our way to the room.

The next morning, we went down for breakfast. Carl had said that there were two people he wanted to meet up with during our stay in Vienna. One was his old friend from Finland, Goran Stubb, a European scout for the NHL's central scouting bureau, and the other Gord Renwick, a businessman from Cambridge who had served as president of the Canadian Amateur Hockey Association and vice-president of the IIHF. Carl greatly admired Gord for keeping Alan Eagleson at least a little accountable within the sphere of international hockey.

As we ate breakfast and read the *Herald Tribune*, a man approached quietly from behind Carl and smiled broadly at me. Although we had not yet met, I recognized Goran right away. He put his hand on Carl's shoulder, and Carl immediately jumped to his feet, delighted and surprised to see his old friend. For years to come, Carl expressed his amazement at the coincidence of our being in the same hotel as Goran, especially when rooms were so scarce.

Our days in Vienna were wonderful. We attended several of the hockey games and were given VIP passes that allowed us into the hospitality suites, where we visited with old friends. We had breakfast each morning with Gord and Maggie Renwick at the Inter-Continental Hotel, where Team Canada was staying. Rene Fasel, Murray Costello, Bob Goodenow and many others came by to say hello. We had supper one night with Alan Adams and Roy MacGregor from the Canadian media. We walked for hours along the Ringstrasse, which encircles the old town, attended a performance at the famed Vienna Opera House and enjoyed the famous *Sachertorte* on the terrace of the Hotel Sacher. We took the train out to Schoenbrunn Castle and spent a most enjoyable sunny afternoon touring the castle and walking around the grounds. We saw the Lipizzaner horses at the famous Spanish riding school and took in a Mozart concert.

We spent time with the Stubbs, and one night we drove out of Vienna with them for a traditional Austrian meal in a small town, along with a number of the Finns who were in Vienna for the tournament. Carl was completely enthralled by each and every moment of this special "return visit to Vienna." Throughout the entire trip, Carl appeared to have the same youthful energy and enthusiasm he'd had almost 30 years prior when he'd been there as part of Canada's National team. He was unusually relaxed and extremely happy. The immense pleasure he was having in every moment couldn't have been more apparent.

In the tournament, Canada won the silver medal, while the Czech Republic won the gold and the U.S. went home with the bronze. Back in 1967, Canada won the bronze medal and Carl was selected the outstanding defenseman of the tournament.

We took a side trip to Budapest, where we celebrated my birthday; on another day we travelled to Prague and spent a night. Soon, we were re-tracing our steps from Vienna to Zurich — this time, stopping to visit our friends in Innsbruck and Feldkirch en route.

As we flew home, we were listening to the same channel on the music system when John Berry's song "Your Love Amazes Me" began to play. Carl turned to me and took hold of my hand in his. Tears were streaming down his face. Throughout the song, Carl's eyes were focused intently on mine and he sobbed uncontrollably. My wonderful Carl, my "*anam cara*," who often choked on his emotions, unable to articulate his deepest feelings, let the lyrics be his words of gratitude and love. To this day, these words and this song bring peace and love to my heart and a beautiful memory to my mind.

***

It was a thrill for Carl to return to Vienna for several reasons. He had been a strong devotee of European hockey ever since he played with Canada's National team back in 1967, and again two years later as playing coach of Helsinki IFK. Years later, Carl was still observing, with keen appreciation, the progress and success of the Europeans. We were in France in February 1998 when we watched the Olympic gold medal hockey game from Nagano, Japan. Carl put pen to paper to express his opinions about the su-periority of European hockey and the thrill he had watching the Czech Republic beat Russia 1–0 for gold.

EUROPEAN HOCKEY DOMINANCE

So near and yet so far! As with any intense hockey game, the winning score can go either way. As Punch Imlach always said, "I'd rather be lucky than good." Team NHL/Canada, "the dream team," did the unthinkable and lost. So did Team USA — the Olympic tourney's co-favourites — down and out. And once and for all, the technical and tac-tical dominance of Teams Europe is obvious to all. For

Canada and Canadians, a sad admission, but true. What has been obvious to me for some 30 years, the superiority of European hockey, is now obvious fact. That's the good news! The bad news is that we will never catch up. No matter how many "task forces" or inquiries there are into hockey, nothing will change.

Yes, Canada, with its insane will to win, will bring back World and Olympic gold in the future. But the technical and tactical superiority and dominance of Europe will still be obvious. The cultural differences are vast. Canada and the U.S. are young countries, and their vigour and motivation to win are insatiable. Remember Bobby Clarke and Valeri Kharlamov? North American players will die to win — at any cost.

Europeans, on the other hand, would prefer to play well and enjoy their game while expecting to live and enjoy a beer and other pleasantries for another day. Europeans all move the puck with dexterity and skill — to a man; whereas Canadians are more laboured in this task. Nothing is going to change this.

CANADIAN HOCKEY — PSHAW!

Canada's emotional victories in the World Championships of long ago remind us of the halcyon days of the Whitby Dunlops and the Trail Smoke Eaters. It was always said that our NHL players would really show them how the game was played. The stage was set for the memorable Canada–Russia series of 1972. We all remember that fateful day in Canadian history when Paul Henderson scored that last-minute goal that gave Canada a "victory" in that first-ever "open" tournament — no amateurs, just pure professionals.

Yes, Canada won on the scoreboard, but in every meaningful aspect of the game of hockey, the Russians were superior. As a result, Canada and Canadians learned nothing. Since then, the Canadian game has stagnated in its own self-satisfaction.

Anatoli Tarasov, a charismatic bear of a man and the

architect of the formidable Russian machine, outlined to me the future course of hockey. His prescient logic was not incorrect.

The scene was a bleak, dark and cold night in Helsinki in November 1968. I was the playing coach of Helsinki IFK in the Finnish league. Both teams assembled for the traditional postgame dinner after my team, in spite of a valiant effort, had been humiliated 12–3 by the Red Army team in an exhibition game. The Soviet teams, at the time, loved any excuse to get out of Russia and savour Western goodies. Mercifully, Tarasov had sat out his first line of Anatoli Firsov, Venyamin Alexandrov and Viktor Polupanov after the first period.

Towards the end of the dinner, Tarasov wanted to hold court, as he usually did. I was the focal point of his lecture; I sat directly across the table from him. Tarasov had a tray of black bread in front of him. Tarasov and the translator went to work. With a piece of black bread in his raised hand, he said, "Brever (he couldn't pronounce Brewer), in team conditioning, the Soviets are number one." Dramatically, he placed the black bread in front of himself. Raising a second piece of black bread, he said, "Brever, in team tactics and team techniques, the Soviets are number one." Again, the black bread was placed on his side of the table. Continuing, a third piece of black bread was raised. "Brever, in the ability to produce the individual superstars, the Soviets have not been able to equal the Canadians."

What would one expect from a collective? Hell, what would you want me to say? We had just lost by nine goals!

The slice of black bread was placed in front of me; I breathed a little easier. Finally, a fourth piece of black bread: "Brever, I will never be able to teach my players to hate to lose the way Canadians hate to lose." The final slice of bread was added to my pile.

Ergo, the thesis of Canadian hockey: "Try Harder." Canadians play with emotion and passion, and sometimes individual brilliance. The Russians/Europeans play with skill and tactics and technique. Canadians will die to win; Europeans are not stupid — they prefer to play the sport and have a few beers. And, *for Russian hockey, the emergence of* perestroika *and* glasnost *did what Tarasov was never able to do: money — greed and avarice — the great motivators... and now, individual superstars!*

At the World Championships in Zurich in 1998, the play of the Canadians and Americans has been abominable. The national team project of Father Bauer could be resurrected, and that team would perform as well as the NHL worthies. The Olympics in Japan involved early exits for Canada and the U.S. The World Cup of Hockey was won by the U.S. Canada's superstars were not good enough. Of course, Canada's juniors did not fare so well this year, either [they came in eighth].

Have you looked around the NHL recently? Effectively, there is not one European coach there. Obviously, Canada/North America has nothing to learn.

The embodiment of Canadian hockey is Don Cherry. Not necessarily a bad thing. I personally admire all his work and the impact he has had. It is not simply for me to say, but I believe him to be the most recognizable and most listened to personality in Canada. I look forward to his Hockey Night in Canada *diatribes and to his repartee with his "handsome" partner (I'd give up* my *husband for Ron MacLean!). But Cherry, as a hockey player, was distinguished by his combativeness rather than his style and skill. As a further Cherry accolade, were I to coach against Cherry, his goons would never beat my goons; the result: a hockey game!*

My experience in international hockey began in 1966 with Father Bauer's national team. This was the finest system of hockey I have ever encountered, and that premise exists even to this "modern" era. At that time, I was quickly made aware that Russia and Czechoslovakia were equal in calibre to the NHL. And this is where I am diametrically opposed to Cherry's thinking. At the time of the World

Championships in Vienna in 1967, the Swedes soundly defeated us 5–1. They were brilliant. That and subsequent games played against Swedish club teams have left me with a lasting impression that the Swedes were the best and most talented players I was ever to see. That impression lasts to this day. The Swedes are the smartest and best hockey players extant.

To condemn the Swedes, as Cherry has, because they wouldn't fight Stan Jonathan is absurd. Hell, I wouldn't fight Stan Jonathan! But, even more important, Don Cherry wouldn't fight Stan Jonathan!

I would agree with Tarasov that his Russian system of hockey, now adopted by the whole of Europe, is superior to the style of game played in Canada and the U.S. It is suggested here that there are two styles of hockey. First, the "try harder" system of Canada. This is the game I played and that is played in Canada today. Before the game, the coach comes into the dressing room and encourages the boys to "try harder." At the end of the first period with the score tied, the coach expounds that "you guys have to try harder." At the end of the second period, with the team down 2–0, the coach comes in and says, "You assholes have to TRY HARDER." After losing the game 4–0, the coach comes into the dressing room and screams, "You sons of bitches didn't try hard enough!" So much for the science of Canadian hockey.

Second: Tarasov's Russian system, adapted from the work of Eddie Shore, one of the game's great talents and surely one of the game's few teachers — and, of course, from soccer. The passing and circling and control game of the Russians is the system of hockey developed by Father Bauer, who is acknowledged as one of hockey's great creators. His style was defensive. He taught unique defensive techniques to combat the Russians. He liked to win games 1–0. His followers are legion. I played for him in 1966–67. Then and now, it was the most adaptable and preferred system I have encountered.

In August 1998, when the Toronto Maple Leafs announced that Alpo Suhonen had been hired as assistant coach, no one was more excited and pleased than Carl. Alpo, a Finn, was an old friend of Carl's, and Carl regarded him as a hockey genius. Alpo is a unique and fascinating man who brought much more to hockey than most. His background was very diverse — sports, of course, and also politics, theatre, acting and music. He treated his players with respect. The power of the mental aspect of hockey was particularly important to Alpo. He once said that a hockey player isn't always a hockey player — he is only one when he's on the ice. Alpo always paid attention to a player's emotional state to determine what impediments were preventing the player from achieving his full potential. He encouraged his players to investigate the bigger questions in life — what they wanted to get out of the game, who they were. This, of course, was very near and dear to Carl's heart.

I first met Alpo in 1989 with Carl when we were in Los Angeles to attend a workshop given by Kevin Ryerson (the psychic — or more specifically, channeller — who is well known from Shirley MacLaine's book *Out on a Limb*). At the time, Alpo was an assistant coach with the Winnipeg Jets and was enjoying a successful year. The Jets were in L.A. to play the Kings, and Carl and I met Alpo for lunch at the Sheraton Hotel in Redondo Beach. Carl and Alpo thoroughly enjoyed reconnecting with one another; their conversation was animated and happy. Alpo's intellect was impressive and his attitudes about hockey refreshing. Carl told Alpo during this lunch that he believed that Alpo would one day be the first European-trained head coach in the NHL. Years later, in May 2000, Alpo was hired as head coach of the Chicago Blackhawks, fulfilling Carl's prediction. Alpo proudly told Carl that he never forgot what Carl had told him at our luncheon.

While he was with the Leafs, Alpo and his sons, Markus and Heinrich, came to our home for dinner several times. On other occasions, Carl and I enjoyed spending time with Alpo and his partner, Sinikka, a warm, vivacious, attractive Finnish actress.

Carl continued to follow the goings-on in the hockey world with the keenest of interest. Time and again, he lamented that "nothing has changed!" It frustrated Carl that he, in his mind, no longer had a forum through which to make his views about the game known. In fact, Carl could have had any forum he wanted. Until the day he died, he continued to get calls from reporters seeking his input or wanting him to appear on radio or television. I can't count the number of times Mary Ormsby would call for Carl, telling me she needed "an intelligent comment" for something she was writing about. "Even after Alan Eagleson went to jail, I'd call Carl on other hockey stories," she said. "He'd always speak from the heart, and whenever he could, he'd tweak the hockey establishment because he loved to be cheeky."

***

We came home from Vienna in 1996 to more good news: the actuarial exercises had finally been completed and pension monies were soon to be paid to the players. In the latter part of June, the retired players who had been victorious in the pension litigation received their packages from the NHL Pension Society, setting out the amount of money from the surplus each was to receive. "After the oldtimers finally receive the funds from the NHL Pension Society they may pay tribute to Carl Brewer, without whom the windfall would not have been possible," Marty York wrote in *The Globe and Mail* on July 13, 1996. "In 1991, Brewer almost singlehandedly launched the legal battle to reclaim the pension money that the NHL had misappropriated. He began the fight with his own money and often did not receive any co-operation from his former colleagues and counterparts. 'What Brewer did was heroic,' a source said, 'and some of the men who will flash the largest smiles when they open their cheques will be the very ones who did their best to prevent Brewer from winning the case by not co-operating. Most of the former players, in fact, never co-operated at all."

***

If it had been difficult for Carl to convince many retired players to speak up and actively support the pension litigation, it was virtually impossible for him to get them to support his challenge of Alan Eagleson. The majority of former players seemed to prefer to remain silent when his name came up, and many of Carl's peers suggested that he was obsessed with Eagleson. Some felt Carl had an agenda, that he viewed the pension lawsuit as a means of getting at Eagleson. Of course, Carl never denied that.

One skeptic was Mike Gillis, a former Boston Bruin and Eagleson client, who went on to become a lawyer and player agent based in Kingston, Ontario. When Carl and I discussed our concerns about Eagleson with our

MP, Dennis Mills, he contacted Mike shortly afterward. It seemed to me that Dennis wanted to run our allegations past someone he could trust. At that time, Mike stood behind his friend and former agent; he couldn't imagine that there was any veracity to our concerns. Mike's wife, Diane, was less comfortable, however, and we later learned that she'd had a lingering uneasiness about Eagleson and his business associate, Marvin Goldblatt, for some time.

At the Bruins' training camp in September 1984, Gillis broke his leg, and it was deemed a career-ending injury. He was insured against such a mishap under three policies: one from the NHL, for $100,000; one from the Players' Association, for $75,000; and a third, optional, policy he'd taken out, for an additional $100,000 (all three were in U.S. dollars). At first, the insurance adjuster refused to pay. In May 1986, Eagleson told Gillis that the insurance company had refused to pay Mike's claim, and it would be necessary to hire lawyers to fight them on his behalf. Gillis was told that Eagleson would pursue his claim, in exchange for 15 percent of whatever was extracted from the insurance companies. In June, he informed Gillis that the companies had agreed to pay $175,000.

On July 23, 1986, Eagleson wrote to Mike: "All OK with your claim — when I was in London spent lot of time with underwriters — I told them your lawyer had been instructed to sue them for $275,000 U.S. — no lesser amount acceptable." In September, Gillis cut a cheque to Kingsmar Holdings — an Eagleson company — for the agreed-upon contingency fee of $41,250 (which was 15 percent of the full amount).

That's where the matter rested until early 1992, when Eagleson was beginning to feel the heat in a rather serious way. His office returned Mike's files to him, and in 1994 another batch was returned. Many believed that the sudden decision to return files to players was prompted by a concern that the RCMP was about to raid Eagleson's offices.

Diane Gillis began going over the documents, and she discovered a letter that indicated that Lloyd's of London had agreed to pay the full amounts of the NHL and NHLPA policies — $175,000 — ten days before the meeting at which Eagleson told Gillis that they would have to fight fight the Insurance company. Eagleson and NHL vice-president Gil Stein had both been informed of this settlement, but Eagleson did not tell his client, Gillis. Nor did he inform Gillis that the $100,000 from the optional policy would have been a *fait accompli*, since it was a mirror policy written by the same company as the other two. Eagleson had also blatantly lied about needing to hire outside lawyers to fight the insurance company.

When Mike realized what had happened to him, he felt betrayed — and angry enough to go after his former agent through the courts. In May 1994, he sued Eagleson and two of his companies, Rae-Con (which had managed Gillis's finances) and Jialson Holdings (formerly known as Kingsmar). True to form, Eagleson countersued.

The case was heard by Mr. Justice Joseph O'Brien, beginning on September 24, 1996 and continued for seven weeks. I sat through the entire proceedings and found them fascinating. I also became close to and tremendously fond of Mike and Diane Gillis. I admired their courage and determination in taking on this struggle.

Mike didn't just have a strong case; he also had the perfect lawyer in Charles Scott. Scott is a brilliant litigator, completely unpretentious, and tough as nails. As usual, Eagleson approached this situation as if it were a mere inconvenience and he was above it all. He was represented by a friendly lawyer, Charles Wagman, while his own son, Trevor Eagleson, served as co-counsel. Simply put, he misgauged the situation and was about to experience one huge comeuppance. Scott cut Eagleson down time and again, calling him on his double talk and self-contradictory answers, and he responded sternly to Eagleson's habitual glibness. On more than one occasion, I watched with amazement and delight as Scott turned on his heel in response to some inappropriate outburst of laughter or snarkiness on Eagleson's part and stared him down. I began to think that this was probably only the second time in his life, after Ed Garvey in 1989, that Eagleson had found himself so completely outsmarted and outfoxed.

It quickly became apparent that the judge understood the gist of the case. A small, older gentleman, O'Brien was tough, direct and serious. He immediately saw through Eagleson, as well as the convenient lapses of memory displayed by witnesses such as Marvin Goldblatt.

There were times when I felt frustrated or irritated, thinking that the judge had been too lenient or accommodating towards Eagleson's lawyer's demands, such as when he agreed to allow Eagleson to amend his counter-claim from $100,000 to $244,038. Mike Gillis, however, is a very quick study, and he'd explain to me during the recesses that the judge's action indicated that he really wasn't giving any credence to Eagleson's countersuit. During several breaks in the proceedings, Mike would give me a signal and we'd go out onto the street behind the courthouse so he could have a smoke and we'd discuss what had transpired in court. I learned a lot during the trial.

A fascinating cast of characters spent time in the courtroom. Mary Ormsby was covering the story for the *Toronto Star*; Andrea Lockwood, the daughter of Tom Lockwood — the outside legal counsel who was investigating the Law Society complaint against Eagleson — took notes for her dad; James Christie of *The Globe and Mail* was also there, as were many other regulars from the media. We all sat together, saved seats for one another and ate lunch together throughout the seven weeks.

By this time, Eagleson had been a fugitive from U.S. justice for more than two and a half years. There was an active warrant out for his arrest, and the U.S. Department of Justice had filed an extradition request with the Canadian government. Consequently, there was interest in this trial south of the border. Russ Conway came up for a day, and his presence in the courtroom did not evade the notice of Eagleson's defense team. Trevor Eagleson dropped hints that they might serve Russ with a subpoena to testify. Russ had no problem with this, other than that it would prolong the trial and potentially increase Mike Gillis's court costs. At the afternoon break, Russ and I quietly slipped out of the courthouse and arranged his airline ticket back to Boston. On another occasion, on October 15, Assistant U.S. Attorney Paul Kelly showed up. I had prior knowledge that he would attend that day, because he had contacted us a few days earlier to tell me he wanted to entrust some papers to me that might be needed during the trial.

Kelly was interested in the trial because the Gillis situation was one of the charges in the American indictment against Eagleson that had been opened back in March of 1994. During his visit, he entrusted to me a large, sealed dossier of sensitive legal papers that I was to present to Mike's legal counsel if, as had been rumoured for weeks, certain parties happened to come to court to testify on Eagleson's behalf. For the rest of the trial, it was necessary for me to be in court every day, should the material be required. I carried the documents with me in a common plastic grocery bag that attracted the attention of no one. The material never was needed, and I returned it to Kelly at the end of the trial.

Paul's presence caused quite a stir. Eagleson and his lawyers were well aware of him, and Mary Ormsby captured the significance of his visit: "An American Eagle was sizing up the Canadian one — one was the hunter, one the prey. His stalker was a lean, young Assistant U.S. Attorney named Paul Kelly, who sat at the back of a downtown Toronto courtroom, sending a silent message that screamed one purpose: 'Uncle Sam wants you — or more precisely, Uncle Sam still wants you.'" Paul took a seat in the courtroom where he had an unobstructed view of Eagleson, who was in the witness box being cross-examined by Charles Scott. Eagleson was undeniably more subdued, was not his usual boisterous, combative self, on this occasion.

At the end of the day, Paul Kelly told James Christie, "I'm here because the United States has a continuing interest in Mr. Eagleson. Contrary to some media reports that we have lost interest, we are pursuing it vigorously." To Stephen Brunt of *The Globe and Mail*, he said, "It's unusual, being seated 25 feet from a person who is a fugitive from justice in the United States and not being able to take action."

This was the second time I had watched Alan Eagleson testify in court. The first had been during the Vaclav Nedomansky trial in the early 1980s, and he hadn't changed his act at all since then. He traded barbs with Charles Scott about wording. When Scott claimed, "It's false," Eagleson countered, "It's incorrect." When Scott said, "It's deception," Eagleson countered, "Bargaining ploy." This went on for days. (The trial, which was supposed to last a few days, dragged out for weeks because of Eagleson's countersuit, which he'd brought as a stink bid and which was being tried simultaneously.)

I had an amusing encounter with Eagleson. He was well aware of everyone sitting at the back of the courtroom day after day, and he seemed to know practically everyone except me. Many times, I noticed him looking at me curiously, including once when Paul Kelly and I were huddled in a whispered conversation in a back hallway of the courthouse and he passed by on his way to the men's room. Finally, one day, he wandered over and stood in front of me, smiling. "Do you work for *The Globe*?" he asked. "The *Star*?" I politely answered "no" to each of his questions, knowing that I was driving him crazy. Finally, none the wiser, he left and returned to his seat. It was unfortunate that Carl didn't feel comfortable about attending the trial — he didn't want to be up close with Eagleson — because it was actually a real treat to watch. Carl would have found the entire process extremely fascinating and validating. He certainly looked forward to my updates every evening!

Right near the end of the proceedings, Dr. Chuck Bull, a friend of

Eagleson's for more than 40 years and a doctor to whom players had frequently been referred for orthopedic assessments, was called to testify. Bull had been Mike Gillis's doctor and had played a role in determining the status of his disability. When Gillis requested his medical files, Bull, knowing full well there was a lawsuit at issue, sent the Gillis files to Eagleson's lawyer — namely, Trevor — and not to his patient, Gillis. Charles Scott tore a wide strip out of Bull over this breach of professional conduct, reminding him that this was not the first case in which he had done exactly the same thing. At the end of Scott's questioning, Bull was obviously traumatized; I saw his hands trembling to the point that he had trouble picking up the various papers he had spread out in front of him before he walked uneasily out of the courtroom.

The trial concluded on November 7, and the judge said his decision would take about a month. Those of us sitting in the back of the courtroom all those weeks had bonded very closely during this trial. Afterwards, we all felt disconnected and missed one another.

On December 3, 1996 — almost three years after the United States charged Eagleson with 34 counts of fraud, racketeering and embezzlement — the RCMP finally laid charges of its own. Surprisingly, only eight charges were laid, and these dealt almost exclusively with rink-board advertising and fraud against Labatt's (a Canada Cup sponsor). We were disappointed and not very proud of Canada's law enforcement agencies. The players, the real victims of all of the scams, schemes and frauds committed by Eagleson over the years, were left completely out in the cold by the Mounties. It seemed like a slap in the face.

Two days later, Carl and I were in a Boston hotel room when we got an early-morning phone call from Russ Conway, telling us that Justice O'Brien's judgment had been handed down. He filled us in on the results, and we were ecstatic. Justice O'Brien found entirely in favour of Mike Gillis, ordering Eagleson to repay him the $41,250 as well as punitive damages and costs.

Several Toronto radio stations tracked us down in Boston to get comments from Carl, and he held nothing back. I couldn't believe my ears as I heard Carl exclaim, "Now it's official — the whole world knows that Alan Eagleson is a crook, a liar, a fraud and a cheat!" He went on and on, absolutely relishing every moment now that he was free to say the things he had suspected for decades. It seemed to be very cathartic for Carl to scream these facts — unfettered — into the phone, knowing that his remarks were hitting the airwaves back home in Toronto. Even Russ Conway was taken aback at how forcefully Carl expressed his feelings over this verdict.

One of the very first things we did when we got back to Toronto was go to Charles Scott's office to pick up our copy of the O'Brien judgment. It made for very informative reading.

> *I accept submissions of Gillis's counsel that the evidence demonstrates [Eagleson's] ability to mislead and lie with documents and in his testimony.... I am troubled by Goldblatt's alleged memory failure about these events. I accept submissions of Gillis's counsel that there is an element of intentional failure to recall events hurtful to Eagleson's case.... At the very least this illustrated Eagleson's willingness to use misleading documents to accomplish his purpose.... Eagleson engaged in a devious plan to obtain payment of fees in this case.*

Justice O'Brien dismissed Eagleson's counterclaim, describing it as "vexatious." He noted that it was a ploy by Eagleson to try and frighten Gillis into dropping his claim and that it had prolonged the trial considerably.

Mike Gillis was by no means the only player who was caught up in such a pattern of deceit and dishonesty. Others who were entitled to disability insurance, such as Glen Sharpley, Bob Dailey and Andre Savard, also paid hefty fees to get their insurance payments. The indictment issued by the U.S. Department of Justice classified Eagleson's scheme as racketeering. He had received unlawful payments, kickbacks and other benefits from the insurance companies as payback.

The Gillis case was significant in that, for the first time, Alan Eagleson was successfully sued by a former member of the NHLPA and brought to his knees in a court of law for his years of scams and dishonesty. It set the stage for more that would eventually come to pass, and gave tremendous credibility to the U.S. charges. Most importantly for us, it vindicated everything Carl had been trying so hard to make his peers aware of for so many years.

CHAPTER 15

THE STARS SHINE MORE BRIGHTLY

"Alan Eagleson was the most powerful man in Canada. People always write 'the most powerful man in hockey,' but he really was the most powerful man in Canada with his connections. He was unbelievably connected."

Although the Gillis verdict had delivered a small amount of retribution, in early 1997 the fact remained that Alan Eagleson was a fugitive from U.S. justice. And, despite the recent RCMP charges, there was no sense that he would ever be called to accounts in Canada for his activities. Indeed, more than a year had passed since the U.S. Department of Justice had applied for Eagleson's extradition. In mid-December 1995, the American authorities filed some 800 pages of documentation with their counterparts in Ottawa; since then, not only had the federal government not co-operated, but we were being made aware that Canadian officials were exerting considerable pressure on U.S. Attorney General Janet Reno to dispose of the charges.

There were moments when even the lead investigators were worried. Tom Daly, the FBI special agent in charge of the Eagleson investigation, told us later that extradition proceedings between the U.S. and Canada are a regular and routine exercise for all kinds of crimes — drugs, smuggling, murder — and there is always complete co-operation on both sides. The FBI, according to Daly, had never before encountered a stalemate such as this one. What kept our spirits up was the knowledge that there was only one person who could revoke the charges contained in the U.S. indictment: Paul Kelly.

For years, Carl had told everyone that Alan Eagleson was "the most powerful man in Canada." To a person, they would try to correct him, suggesting that he must surely mean the most powerful man in *hockey* — and each time, Carl would bristle and reply, "I speak the Queen's English very well and I said he is the most powerful man in *Canada*."

***

On April 4, 1997, the NHL Oldtimers, a fraternal group made up mostly of long-retired NHL players — the majority of whose careers predated Carl's by five to ten years — held a special luncheon to honour Carl and me for all the work done on the pension lawsuit. This coincided with their regular monthly luncheon. Originally, Frank Mahovlich, Brian McFarlane, Peter Conacher and John McCormack had approached Carl with their idea to hold a dinner in his honour. Although he was deeply touched by the gesture, Carl declined — not because he didn't appreciate their thoughtfulness, but because, as he said, "I was afraid nobody would show up." Sadly, I know that this is how he did indeed feel, even though he always knew he was accepted and appreciated unconditionally among this group.

Undaunted, Conacher and McCormack, the key organizers of the luncheon, decided to surprise Carl. Peter was in regular communication with me — usually seeking my reassurance that we would in fact be in town on the appointed day and not off travelling somewhere! I think poor Peter fretted until the moment he saw us arrive that afternoon.

Despite Carl's misgivings, many of the guys did show up for this luncheon — about a hundred, in fact. Quite a few travelled considerable distances to be there: Kent Douglas and Leo Labine drove down from North Bay, while Jim Dorey came from Kingston, to name but a few. Harry Watson and Tod Sloan were on hand, along with Billy Harris, Sid Smith, Wally Stanowski, Mike Walton, Brit Selby, Gary Aldcorn, Cal Gardner, Pierre Pilote, Gary Collins, Dick Duff, Frank Mahovlich and many more. One former player we missed was Jerry Toppazzini, who normally would have driven down with Leo Labine. For me, the sad part of the day was learning that Jerry's wife, Dolly, had died suddenly a few days earlier. Dolly Toppazzini was one of the kindest, wisest women I'd ever met, and I felt that I had lost someone very dear to me, even though I was just getting to know her.

Many tributes were offered up to Carl that day. Brian McFarlane spoke for the group in commending the huge effort, the success, and the impact of the victory on so many former players. Peter and John presented Carl with a magnificent soapstone carving depicting a young Carl Brewer in his Leaf uniform. I was presented with a beautiful Royal Doulton figurine. Other players, including Jim McKenny and Bob Baun, stepped forward to offer their thanks and praise and to add a few notes of levity. Bob Stellick spoke on behalf of the Toronto Maple Leaf organization. Mark Zigler presented Carl with a pair of Law Society cuff links as a humorous gesture, in recognition of the many hours Carl had spent with lawyers and in courtrooms over the years!

After all the tributes had been paid, it was Carl's turn to acknowledge them. He spoke from the heart and off the cuff, and everyone enjoyed his message and applauded him loudly, especially when he broke down sobbing on more than one occasion. Former New York Ranger Ivan Irwin was seated at our table. Ivan has always been very active with the Oldtimers' group, and he is a great friend. Carl began his speech with a story about Ivan:

> I've never met anyone who enjoyed life more, laughed better, or played the game better or harder than Ivan Irwin. When I think back to the dressing room stories, the guys talk about Ivan playing in the old Quebec league, playing for New York, playing wherever he was — but always laughing!
>
> We play on Sunday mornings now, and nothing has changed. Ivan's out there with those goddamn feet — you can't get by them. The hands — he doesn't have hands, he has paws! The odd time during the course of the morning, he'll sneak up to the front of the net, thinking he should get a goal. He never has! But what I notice, he's always laughing. He enjoys life and he makes life better for everybody.
>
> And Ivan's still laughing.
>
> And me, being kind of the complex individual that I am, I make life very complex. And I'd prefer to go through life smiling, but I haven't succeeded in doing that. But as we came into this battle [the pension lawsuit], and if you think of Net Worth, we were in a battle yesterday — Ted Lindsay was a hero; Tod Sloan was my hero. It was a battle yesterday, it is a battle today and it will be a battle tomorrow because nothing has changed.
>
> But when you think about what happened in the past,

when Sue and I started this, we were searching our way around, trying to figure out what to do. And, of course, monies were required. And lo and behold, we got a cheque — for $500 — from Ivan Irwin. First cheque, very first money in — and no one had yet asked! That was interesting, and his gesture of support meant a great deal to us personally.

And the struggle goes on for many years, and as the years go on, we find ourselves in a little predicament — there's a bill unpaid, and we don't like to leave bills unpaid. So, a request went out for some more money. However in doing so, I made a mistake. Nevertheless, once again, oddly enough, the first cheque comes in from "Ivan the Terrible."

What's really interesting is that my mistake was in including Ivan's name on the list of players I asked to help out.

You see, Ivan Irwin doesn't get a pension. He is not a member of the NHL Pension Society. He had taken his money out. There was no money from this lawsuit for Ivan Irwin.

However, the class gentleman that he is, he wanted to help the guys — and he did so generously and without hesitation.

I will always have the greatest respect and admiration for Ivan the Terrible.

I watched Ivan as Carl told his story, and I could see that he was laughing — in part because he was embarrassed, but mostly because he was very moved by Carl's expression of appreciation for his generosity and support. Carl continued:

In telling the story of how this all came about, it's not very complicated. Bobby Baun did the work with this lovely blonde here, Lorraine Mahoney. Sue and I have worked with her for many, many years, and she's not only good at what she does, she's a dear, dear personal friend and has become such. We feel all the richer for it.

It was Bobby who, with Lorraine in 1980, discovered the discrepancies in our pension. But it wasn't only 1980. Ted Lindsay and his boys were aware in 1957 that there were discrepancies, there were problems. *Frankly, they were stealing our goddamned pension money. I don't ever want to be accused of being a nice guy, because otherwise I never would have been able to do what happened. But looking back at that time, Bobby, through his own efforts and with Lorraine Mahoney — they knew something was wrong. I sat on a note for several years — Lorraine had prepared it all. There was something in that note called "experience rate credits." Well, I don't know about you guys, but I don't think I ever grasped what the hell it meant.*

It was in the early 1980s when I was on another gambit, and one night I said to Sue, "I want to do something. Will you help me?" Silly girl, she said okay, she'd help. But anyway, it was the work of Lorraine with Bobby that set the stage.

In 1989, we had a lawyer friend by the name of Sheldon Kirsh and we went to him and we said we have to do something about our pension concerns, and asked him, "What do we do?" He said to us: "There's a friend of mine by the name of Mark Zigler. I want to introduce you to him. He's a pension expert."

So Sue and I met with him and with Shelly and we enjoyed meeting him; it was a very nice meeting, but not a goddamned thing came of it because I still didn't know what questions to ask. So it sat for a year, and almost a year to the day we went back to Mark Zigler, and this time we asked a couple of questions. It was decided to have Mark do a report for us. And that report became the basis for the lawsuit that we fought and eventually won.

So when you think in terms of what we've got to be thankful for — that little guy over there with the beard, quiet little guy, nice guy, he's one hell of a lawyer. He's a little guy — I happen to be a lot bigger than I'd like to be — but if there is a giant in this room, the giant is Mark Zigler. Sue and I worked with him over a period of time. I watched his work in court, in cross-examination, and let me tell you, gentlemen, he's impressive. We had a good case, but fortunately we had a better lawyer, and it worked out favourably for us.

And any of you who happened to have the good fortune to see the appeal saw the work that he did for us in making all this possible. I've got to tell you, over a period of time, I got to know the lawyers on the other side and I felt sorry for them because his encyclopedic knowledge of our pension was the reason that we won and why we're here today celebrating. And we can never really express to him the thanks that we owe him.

Over the course of the past couple of years, I've asked myself a couple of questions. "Carl, would you do it again?" I had to think about that one, but, yeah, I'd do it again. "Is there anything you'd change, Carl?" Yeah, there are some things I'd change. But there's one thing I wouldn't even think of changing, and that is the presence of Mark Zigler, because I'm not sure anyone else could have handled it the way he handled it and got the results that we got. He was absolutely incredible.

When you watched the movie Net Worth *last night, you understand how we were treated as hockey players — how we were serfs, how we really didn't have any dignity. But through Mark Zigler and people like him, we benefit.*

I really don't want to forget Lorraine Mahoney and Bobby Baun — because that's where it all started. Of course, it all started with Ted Lindsay and Tod Sloan and it was a worthwhile passage.

During the course of all that time, I have a friend, my best friend. I couldn't have accomplished anything if I hadn't had Sue with me.

Carl broke down sobbing at this moment and struggled to compose himself.

I want to get this out… Sue is my best friend, my helpmate, my partner for life. I get a lot of credit, or it seems people would like to think I get a lot of the credit — I don't take any of it. I doff it off to Bobby Baun and everybody else who

needs to be acknowledged. But let me tell you, there's no
way, there is NO WAY we have anything to celebrate today
if it hadn't been for Sue.

At this point, Carl completely broke down sobbing and had to sit down. It had been a tremendously emotional afternoon for him and a very long haul in getting to this point. I took the microphone and expressed our heartfelt thanks to everyone for coming, and especially to Peter Conacher and John McCormack for their unrelenting friendship and for organizing such a lovely tribute. There had indeed been many ups and downs, and Carl and I both were deeply appreciative of this wonderful afternoon of acknowledgement organized by some very dear and loyal friends. After all was said and done, perhaps the most special moment for me personally came when Dr. Tom Pashby, the highly regarded ophthalmologist and a dear friend, commented: "Why am I not surprised? I knew both of their parents."

***

On a personal note, Carl at this time was being dragged down by financial difficulties. It frustrated him that, although his career aptitude test in high school indicated that he ought to be an accountant, he could not keep track of money. Carl, in his heart of hearts, did not feel that he deserved his share, his good in life, and this applied to money as well. In the absence of healthy boundaries, he would have given his money to others for their ventures and neglected his own needs. A year earlier, we were in the ironic position of having to ward off creditors attempting to attach Carl's pension increase after *The Globe and Mail* published a list of the amounts of surplus monies attributed to each of the former players. Carl was not the only player in this situation by any means.

In July 1997, Carl was forced to declare personal bankruptcy. This was not a situation that developed from the pension and Eagleson pursuits. Carl had advanced monies to a family member for a venture whose revenues just weren't what they were expected to be. Carl was generous to a fault and had trouble learning that it was important to look after his own needs above those of others. This was a very difficult time for Carl. He suffered terribly with anxiety and shame. The associated stresses certainly did not help his health.

THE POWER OF TWO

***

Carl was, is, and always will be a national hero in Finland. This dates back to 1968–69, the year he spent in Finland as playing coach of the Helsinki IFK team. Carl left his mark on Finnish ice hockey and taught the Finns a great deal about the game. For several summers in the early 1970s, he held summer hockey schools in Finland. He is considered the father of hockey in this small, fascinating country. His friend Tommi Salmelainen, who played for Carl in 1968–69, has said: "The Finns all thought that they were no good as hockey players. Then Carl came along and made us believe we were all capable of playing in the NHL."

So, in May 1997, when Carl and I were invited to Finland as guests of the Finnish Ice Hockey Federation, it was a welcome respite. Carl was proud to take part in the "Legends of the World" hockey game being played in Helsinki. Paul Henderson and his wife, Eleanor, were other Canadian invitees, and we enjoyed getting to know them at the various functions held that weekend.

I revelled in watching Carl's absolute delight and exhilaration in being on the ice alongside so many legends of the hockey world, as well as his old Finnish confreres, and talking with them joyfully at the functions. Several of the Russian and Czech players he remembered from the 1967 World Championships in Vienna were there, including Alexander Ragulin (the same "Rags" Ragulin whom Carl had flattened in the Nats' game against the Soviets in Montreal), as well as the generation of Russians who came to prominence in the 1972 Summit Series: Alexander Maltsev, Boris Mikhailov, Valeri Vasiliev, Alexander Gusev and Vladimir Shadrin. All were players whose careers Carl had followed over the years. Carl had tremendous admiration for them.

In our hotel, the Ramada Presidentii in downtown Helsinki, Carl couldn't make his way from the elevator to our room without being squired into a succession of rooms occupied by the Russians and given a friendly shot of vodka. Carl was delighted by their warm reception and acceptance of him, but a little overwhelmed by all the vodka being offered to him morning, afternoon and night! The morning after the big game and postgame party, we watched with utter amazement as two of the Russian players sat in the hotel lobby in a drunken stupor. They would struggle to their feet, only to slump down again in their seats. We wondered how long

278

they would stay there in such a state.

After these fun-filled days, we stayed on in Helsinki with old friends Tommi and Sirpa Salmelainen and their boys Tomas, Tony and Tobias. Tommi had played for Carl, and was actually the first Finn to be chosen in the NHL draft, by St. Louis in 1969. He played for the Blues' farm team in Kansas City, but never did make it to the NHL. His son Tony was drafted by the Edmonton Oilers and played briefly with them. We stayed at their home had a great time, especially at a dinner party attended by Alpo Suhonen and his companion, Sinikka.

The visit was a homecoming of sorts for Carl. When not visiting friends, we spent our time strolling together along the beautiful tree-lined Esplanade, lined with interesting shops selling crystal and all sorts of wooden gadgets and decorations, as well as some pleasant cafes. This walk took us directly to the harbour. It was intriguing to watch the fishermen from the far north or the islands selling a wide variety of freshly caught fish directly from their boats. The fishers' wives, most dressed in traditional garments, were offering colourful hand-knits and homemade preserves for sale along with the fish and delicious pickled herring. In the market, stalls were colourfully bedecked with canvas to protect against the wind and rain, and here we found furs — pelts, hats, mitts — wooden brushes with natural bristles for sauna use, socks made of hemp fibre, and other fascinating items. The food stalls sold salmon in every imaginable mode of preparation, as well as delicate pastries and coffee. The food was beautifully prepared and delicious; Carl particularly enjoyed the poached salmon served with baby potatoes tossed in butter and dill — a local specialty. There were all varieties of homemade soups, and buns filled with any fish you chose. On a sunny day, one could enjoy a marvellous feast sitting on a wooden chair alongside the vendors on the edge of the sea. Carl was equally fascinated with the huge ocean liners in various stages of construction at the Helsinki shipyards.

The following year, in 1998, we were invited back to Finland again, this time for Matti Hagman's 50th birthday celebration. Matti was drafted by the Boston Bruins in 1975, and he played 290 games in the NHL and WHA (with Boston, Quebec and Edmonton) between 1976 and 1982. Matti was the very first Finnish hockey player to play in the Stanley Cup finals. Carl's friend Goran Stubb and his wife, Citte, hosted a lovely dinner party for everyone one evening; another night, we partied with friends at Jari Kurri's bar in downtown Helsinki.

All his life, Carl was very proud of what he had been able to accomplish in Finland — and what he learned about hockey from the Finns. He remarked many times that winning the Finnish league championship with Helsinki IFK was as much of a thrill for him as the Stanley Cup victories. During this visit, Carl was stunned and deeply moved when he was shown a large corner in the Helsingen Jäähalli that had been dedicated to him. This area features a gigantic likeness of Carl in his IFK uniform and is named "Brewer's Corner." Carl was very proud and most appreciative of this incredibly special acknowledgement.

On another occasion, Carl and I were sitting in the Air Canada departure lounge at Heathrow, waiting to board our flight to Toronto. Two young men wearing suits were seated opposite us, and they were talking on their cellphones. At the time, cellphones were not a common sight in North America. Carl nudged me and whispered, "They're Finns." When the Finnair flight to Helsinki was called, the young men gathered up their belongings and walked over to Carl. They both shook hands with him, and one of them did the talking: "We know who you are, Mr. Brewer, and we are very proud to meet you."

***

It was in 1997 that Carl began to experience serious health problems. He was increasingly plagued by back pain, especially on the upper-left side of his back. He called the spells "attacks." Also, he still had constant stress that he had been unable to learn to mitigate over the years. Our naturopath, Dr. Bill Cheng, described Carl's problems as his "overly dominant autonomic nervous system." Examining Carl one day, Dr. Cheng looked at me in shocked disbelief and said, "I am alarmed at how little oxygen he is getting into his lungs." He sent Carl for X-rays, but there was no indication of fibrosis. Carl practised some prescribed breathing exercises and added yoga to his exercise regimen. Dr. Cheng was quick to point out to me that Carl shouldn't be doing any strenuous exercise unless he was breathing properly. Dr. Cheng was one of many people we encountered over the years who sometimes found Carl too intimidating to tell him things directly; it fell to me to be the messenger.

Around this time, Carl told me that when he played hockey, making all those long, end-to-end rushes, he didn't breathe — he held his breath the entire time!

Carl and I shared an enthusiasm and preference for holistic health care. Over the years, Carl sought out many different therapies. He had chelation therapy, a process whereby an intravenous solution helps clear out the arteries, with Dr. Paul Cutler in Niagara Falls, New York. He tried prolotherapy treatments with Jim Dorey's therapist, Dr. Blazer, in Kingston and a Dr. Kidd in Renfrew, Ontario. Dr. George Roth in Caledon, an exceptional osteopath, treated Carl, and he also had cranial sacral treatments. Each night, he'd gather all the cushions onto the couch, stretch out and ask me to "mobilize" his back as I had been taught to do by Dr. Blazer.

Carl had been a voracious reader all his life. We were both charmed by Peter Mayle's *A Year in Provence*, and in mid-November 1997 we had our "Month in Provence." We travelled to Pont-Royal, a village between Aix-en-Provence and Cavaillon, and stayed at a property built to resemble a typical Provençal village. It was situated on a fabulous golf course. The cost for one month, including Air France travel from Toronto to Marseille Provence airport: $900 Canadian per person! It was absolutely beautiful in the Luberon Hills in November. The clarity of the vistas and the stars at night were a joy. During our stay, we got to experience the full force of the mistral winds, and some nights we were kept awake by the smashing of loose shutters against the outside walls.

We enjoyed walking around the property, feeding the ducks and swans on the small lake and hitting golf balls at the practice range. One morning, when out for a drive, we were stopped by police conducting the French version of our RIDE program. It was hilarious because the spot check was set up at 11:30 a.m. — before lunch! The gendarme handed Carl some sort of puffer and told him jovially, "*Soufflez, Monsieur!*" Carl blew into the hand-held device, and the policeman laughed, said "Canada," smiled and wished us "*bonnes vacances.*"

Each day, we drove to some local village to explore, visit the markets to buy some of the local produce for meals at home, and often to have lunch. We visited all the charming towns of Peter Mayle's book — Ménerbes, Bonnieux, Lourmarin, Apt, Lauris and many more. We bought bread at the *boulangeries* he wrote about, ate in the same village cafes where, on return visits, we were greeted warmly with a welcome drink, usually a kir. During this adventure, we kept a travel journal. On November 25, Carl wrote:

Leisurely morning, breakfast in our apartment. Cloudy, windy day. A 30-minute drive into Aix-en-Provence. Quelle surprise! *This town is a miniature Paris without the chaos... wide boulevards (treed), and wandering, narrow streets — all with interesting shops and ancient architecture. And the restaurants and bakeries — for me, a paradise. We walked through the delightful markets with their fresh fruits and vegetables and dry goods. Then we had a sensational lunch at a boulevard café... yes, outside! The weather is still good. Forgot to mention the bottle of* rosé *— PERFECT!*

The following day, Carl continued:

Strong winds howled and weather was dull and overcast. After a light breakfast we walked to the small lake to feed the ducks and swans. Then we walked to the practice range where I played the night before. Our walk continued and took us to our car, at which point we decided to drive nine kilometres to Lambesc, a nearby village, for coffee and sightseeing. But we didn't make it there until after a humongous and delightful lunch in the village of St. Canat, some 10 kilometres farther.

To retrace, we stopped first at a winery for a taste (dégustation) and purchased a bottle of rosé; a half a mile farther, and another stop — a nicer winery, good taste, same result: bought another bottle. At this point we decided to visit St. Canat — no reason — we don't need one! En route, the plane trees, planted by Napoleon, periodically line both sides of the highway — incredibly spectacular... A good afternoon, a quiet evening at home — no need for supper — just a glass of wine.

On November 27, Carl was writing again: "Turned out to be a beautiful, sunny day about 60–68 degrees. The golf course looked beautiful. Unfortunately, back woes kept me in bed for the morning. Sue made a delicious leek soup for lunch. Then we drove to two small villages — La

Roque d'Anthéron and Rognes. My back has laid me low and have not even done my yoga exercises. Tomorrow will be a better day."

As predicted, Carl was feeling better the next day:

> *Sunny day to start. Did my yoga and stretching exercises minus the back miseries that laid me low yesterday. Put magnets on my back last night. What ho, the witch doctor! Nevertheless, it is nice to be free of pain. We started the morning at Mallemort market. It was special, and I do enjoy markets! One stall was selling paella; it looked fabulous, but today we didn't try it. Bought myself a toque.*
>
> *From there, we continued to the other side of the Luberon Hills to Mérindol — just drove through it to Lauris, another hill village, which we walked through and enjoyed the views and buildings. Then, on to Lourmarin — a beautiful village and an artist colony — very special! This village had another market, and much superior. We walked through town and then had a long, leisurely and delightful lunch at Bistro Lourmarin. From here we had an excellent drive up and down through the Luberon Hills to Bonnieux — another picturesque village built on the side of a mountain. We then drove back to Pont-Royal, with one stop for a drink at Peter Mayle's famous Gare de Bonnieux. Just a delightful day. Rain in the afternoon. Every village is a joy and different. A quiet night at home, reading and CNN.*

His last entry in our journal was December 4: "We have just returned from another very interesting day. Right now, it is 6:00 p.m. and we are sitting in our lovely, cozy, warm apartment. Outside it is very dark, and tonight there is a chill in the air. But, the sky is very clear, and for some reason the stars shine more brightly here. Sue is starting dinner and we plan to stay in tonight."

When we returned to Toronto in mid-December, Carl's first annuity cheque from the pension litigation had arrived. And Alan Eagleson was still a fugitive from justice in the United States.

CHAPTER 16

"GUILTY... GUILTY... GUILTY"

"Eagleson was popularly viewed as the Abraham Lincoln who freed the hockey slaves, but in reality he was the Benedict Arnold who betrayed his sacred trust and did more to enslave the hockey serfs than any other event or person. This is now a proven fact."

A few days before Christmas 1997, we got word from Russ Conway to be in Boston on January 6. Arrangements had already been made with the Westin Hotel in downtown Boston for Carl and others to stay there at the NHLPA's special rate. We also learned that we would be needed back in Toronto at the end of the week. I made our travel plans and allowed for a couple of extra days in Boston, a city we both loved. During the Eagleson investigation, we had occasion to visit Boston many times, and we both looked forward to these visits. The spirit, the history and antiquity in the old buildings, so well preserved and maintained — Boston Common, Faneuil Hall, Quincy Market and Little Italy — all appealed to us and enriched and lightened our spirits.

Carl had fond memories of Boston from his playing days — especially the seafood. His favourite spot was the Boston landmark The Olde Union Oyster House on Union Street, and it was always our first stop. We would take a cab there directly from the airport, or else have the cab stop at our hotel so we could check our bags with the concierge and carry on to the restaurant. The Olde Union Oyster House was established in 1826 and is the oldest restaurant in Boston. However, the real appeal for Carl was the old oyster bar at the front of the restaurant. Carl loved to sit on a stool there and eat a plate of oysters, washed down with a glass of white wine. The legend of Daniel Webster inspired and intrigued him. Webster was the great advocate of American nationalism, a leading lawyer and outstanding orator who became the U.S. Secretary of State. As the story goes, he sat at this same oyster bar every day and drank a tumbler of brandy with each plate of half a dozen oysters he consumed — and he never had fewer than six plates of oysters! Carl didn't eat quite so many oysters, but somehow he seemed to feel a connection.

We got to know the oyster shucker, John, who was an older gentleman with a wry sense of humour, a heavy Bostonian accent and a bald head. He remembered us and treated us well, bringing us extra corn bread or refilling our glasses with wine, every time we returned. One particular day stands out. We were seated at the oyster bar early on a sunny autumn afternoon. We both noticed Barry Melrose, the coach of the Los Angeles Kings, walking into the restaurant with his hockey team in tow. They moved swiftly into a back room of the restaurant. A short while later, one of the team's rookies walked right up to John, the oyster shucker, who happened to be standing right in front of where Carl was sitting. Looking John straight in the eye, the young man said, "Barry Melrose and the Los Angeles Kings want to thank you for all the work you did for the retired players and their pensions." With that, he turned, embarrassed, and retreated. John's face was expressionless, but he rolled his eyes at us as if to say, "We get all kinds in here!" Carl couldn't contain himself, and he let out a loud, hysterical roar of laughter that seemed to come right from his gut. Through the laughter, he blurted out, "Don't worry, John, he just had the wrong bald head!"

Most summers during the years of the Eagleson investigation, we'd head to Boston and Carl would join Russ Conway, Bruce Dowbiggin and some of the Bruins alumni for what came to be known as "The Alan Eagleson Memorial Golf Tournament." We loved these get-togethers, and especially going to Markey's or Le Bec Rouge at Hampton Beach afterwards with everyone for lobster — the most extraordinary lobster — and plenty of laughs.

On January 5, 1998, we flew to Boston. The lobby bar at the Westin Hotel was the place where everyone congregated, and the excitement and noise level rose dramatically over the course of the evening as more and more former players and reporters joined in, discussing the events that were about to unfold and sharing memories of bygone days. Mike and

Diane Gillis arrived, as did Rick Smith, Glen Sharpley and Ulf Nilsson. Roy MacGregor from the *Ottawa Citizen* and Bruce Dowbiggin of the CBC also joined us. During the evening, we learned that there had been a change in plans and the Toronto court proceedings had been rescheduled for the day after the Boston court date. I suddenly had to make a couple of phone calls and change our travel plans. Later in the evening, with the lobby bar filled to capacity, the room suddenly fell absolutely silent as none other than Alan Eagleson, his son, Trevor, and his lawyer, Brian Greenspan, walked quickly past us en route to their rooms. Later, the scuttlebutt in hockey circles reported that Eagleson's room that night had been paid for by the Philadelphia Flyers. This fact was never denied by Flyers general manager Bobby Clarke when the question was put to him.

Later, after chatting and visiting with everyone, Carl and I accompanied Mike and Diane Gillis, Bruce Dowbiggin, Rick Smith and Ulf Nilsson for a wonderful dinner. We had a most enjoyable evening and a fabulous meal. Mike had chosen the restaurant — the Capital Grille, a classy establishment on Newbury Street. We were seated around a large round table, and it was a perfect spot for a celebratory dinner.

Early the next morning, after a quick breakfast, Carl and I made our way to the federal courthouse. We left our hotel room so excitedly that Carl forgot his prized Irish cap in the room, and Russ Conway had to go fetch it for him a week later.

As we reached the courthouse, there was an obvious flurry of excitement and activity. Carl ushered me in through a back door so he could avoid the media crush. Inside, the mood was unbelievably tense and sombre. The atmosphere was surreal; after all these years, it was impossible for Carl and me to accept that what we were witnessing was really unfolding! Rick Smith had the same problem: "I had a hard time getting my feet on the ground. I'd never been in an environment like that before. Just to be in the presence of all those great players — Bobby Orr, Frank Mahovlich — it was like I had to tell myself, 'Give yourself a pinch,' to believe it all. I'd never been in a courtroom until that day, and I was thinking, 'This is important; I'd better pay attention.'"

Admission to the tiny courtroom was tightly controlled and was orchestrated by Paul Kelly. A mob of people waited outside, hoping to get a seat. Certain people were to be assured seats before the general public would be allowed in. Carl was the first of the players to be admitted, then he and Paul Kelly immediately came out to usher Diane Gillis and me to our seats. The members of the press, somewhat ironically, were sequestered in the jury box. As the proceedings were about to unfold, the tiny court-room was filled to capacity with such former players as Bruins legends Brad Park and Bobby Orr. David Forbes was there, as was longtime Bruins player and coach Milt Schmidt. So were Rick Smith, John Bucyk, Rick Middleton, Terry O'Reilly and Dallas Smith. Frank Mahovlich arrived late and ended up watching through a window in the door at the rear of the courtroom.

Then came the moment we were all waiting for: the doors opened and Alan Eagleson walked into the courtroom — in handcuffs, escorted by Special Agent Tom Daly of the FBI on one side and Tom's son, Tom Daly Jr., also of the FBI, on the other. You could have heard a pin drop at that moment, and then a voice, that of Dallas Smith, could be heard: "There's the son of a bitch." Tom Daly told us sometime later that the entire time they were walking Eagleson down from the holding area to the courtroom, he was chirping away at them, threatening them with repercussions and hurling insults at them.

Eagleson took his place in court before Judge Nathaniel Gorton. He wore his Order of Canada pin in his lapel and assumed a posture of supe-riority, arrogance and defiance.

Ben Clements, the Assistant U.S. Attorney who had succeeded Paul Kelly a few months earlier, began to brief the court. I felt anxious; I worried that Ben might not be as familiar with the case, or as committed to it, as his predecessor. There was no need for concern. Ben may have been new to his position, but he had a thorough and comprehensive knowledge and under-standing of the case. He knew every fact and detail, and the implications of every charge against Eagleson. His presentation was nothing short of bril-liant. He had command of the courtroom and spoke strongly, clearly, emphatically and precisely. There were three general charges against Eagleson — fraud, embezzlement and racketeering. However, within each of those three general charges, the numerous counts were read out, effec-tively requiring Eagleson to plead guilty to everything — to all of the individual charges within the body of the indictment. Initially, Eagleson, displaying his arrogance and lack of respect for the court, had to be re-minded that his one-word answers were not appropriate and that he was to answer the judge by saying, "Yes, Your Honour."

Once all of the charges had been read, there was complete silence and

anxious anticipation as everyone waited to hear Alan Eagleson plead —
"Guilty... guilty... guilty" — to the three charges.

Clement then invited David Forbes to present the victim impact statement on behalf of all players. As Carl put it: "David Forbes, ex–Boston
Bruin, ex-friend of Henry Boucha, college grad, an eloquent spokesperson
for all downtrodden and ill-informed hockey players, rose to his feet to deliver a victim impact statement." David's statement was powerful, deliberate
and very moving: "Closure? No. The harm that has been caused to hundreds
and hundreds of hockey players, in my opinion, far exceeds what I have
heard today by way of restitution." When David Forbes finished speaking,
Ben asked if anyone else had anything to say to the court. It was at this moment that Carl rose to his feet. Ben, noticeably surprised, acknowledged
Carl, saying, "Mr. Brewer, I believe, would like to address the court."

Carl, gripping the polished oak railing in front of us, spoke firmly,
clearly and gratefully. I put my hand on his arm to steady him, to support
him. "I just want to thank God for the United States of America, because
none of this would have occurred in Canada." He sat down beside me,
his eyes filled with tears. Later, Carl mused: "Wow! How the hell did I do
that? It was uncharacteristic of me, but I had to say something!" This, in
my opinion, may very well have been Carl Brewer's finest and proudest
moment, not only for his courage in standing up and speaking from the
heart in this very formal setting, but for the moment of vindication that it
represented for him personally. He had been cast aside as the flake, the
troublemaker obsessed with Alan Eagleson, for decades. Today, he demonstrated that wasn't true.

Jane O'Hara of *Maclean's* was sitting with other members of the press
in the jury box, and she told us that when Carl spoke, Eagleson smirked
and laughed.

We later learned from the U.S. justice officials that their Canadian
counterparts, including Crown attorney Susan Ficek and the RCMP investigators sitting in court that morning, were furious when Carl made his
statement. Somehow, they presumed that it had been scripted. It had not:
neither Carl nor I knew beforehand that he was going to say anything. It
was entirely spontaneous.

After Carl took his seat, the judge proceeded with the sentencing. It
was a highlight, and a source of sheer affirmation, for Carl and me to hear
Judge Gorton speak directly to Alan Eagleson: "Mr. Eagleson, before I im-

pose a sentence, I want to say that the charges to which you have pled guilty are very serious felony charges. You have defrauded and stolen money and benefits from them, which they earned and to which they are entitled. But for the unusual international character of this case, the court would not depart from the sentencing guidelines and would sentence you to serve a substantial prison term in this country." Jane O'Hara's subsequent article in *Maclean's* reported that the U.S. charges would have been punishable by 15 years in prison; instead, Eagleson was fined $1 million. (This money was divided among the affected players. Carl received a cheque for $117. He told everyone that he took me out to dinner with his "windfall.")

When we left the courtroom, members of the Toronto media rushed to Carl for his comments. Carl told Alan Adams of the *Toronto Star*: "If it wasn't for Russ Conway, none of this would have happened. We would not be here." He told the *Star*'s Dave Perkins that his cause was about two things: he wanted Eagleson out of hockey and he wanted the world to know what he always sensed was true. Rick Smith laughs when he recalls that Carl, as he exited the courtroom, asked him, "What did I say in there?" For Carl, all of this seemed on some level like a dream.

We all adjourned for a celebratory get-together at The Four's restaurant, a favourite gathering spot of the Bruins and a place where Carl and I had often met with Russ Conway. The scene was joyous and noisy. It was a private party in the upstairs reception room; the press was not invited and the location was deliberately kept under wraps. However, Christie Blatchford of the *Toronto Sun* somehow found out about the gathering and showed up. She was on the verge of tears. I chatted with her and she told me about the deep regret she felt for not having supported this story over the years. We knew that Christie was sincere. Years earlier, as a young journalist with *The Globe and Mail*, she had tried to expose Eagleson's questionable practices. When she left the *Globe*, the circumstances were never made public, but Carl was certain that her career had been hijacked as a result of her interest in the Eagleson story. Christie asked if she could buy a round of drinks for the guys — or do anything to express her feelings about what had happened to them. Her offer was declined because the entire party, organized by Russ Conway, was courtesy of the owners of The Four's. Ray Bourque, then the captain of the Bruins, also dropped by to say hello.

There were many broad smiles in the room and, for the first time in a couple of days we were able to unwind and really relax and enjoy the upbeat mood and visit with old friends. This was most definitely a day for celebration.

Russ Conway remembers going up to Carl at one point. "I put my arm around those great, huge shoulders of his and I asked him, 'So, Carl, what do you think of the media now?'" Carl answered him: "Well, most of them are just sycophants for Eagleson, but you did it, Russ!"

After a hectic afternoon, it was time to head to Logan Airport for our return flight to Toronto. At the Air Canada check-in counter, the agent told us she was glad we were headed to Toronto because our flight would be departing on time. However, those destined for Montreal and points east would not be flying — this was the night of the great ice storm of 1998.

Back home in Toronto, Carl and I were still pretty buzzed after a long, emotional day and we didn't get much sleep. However, we were at the University Avenue Courthouse early on the morning of January 7. This promised to be another very busy and emotionally charged day for us. After the court proceedings, we had media interviews scheduled for pretty much of the rest of the day and evening; all the Boston officials and friends would be in town as well, and we also wanted to spend time with them.

The courthouse was already a mob scene when we arrived. People were crowding about, anxious to secure a seat inside the courtroom when the doors opened. Stevie Cameron arrived — we hugged so tightly that my glasses broke! Jill Eagleson, Alan's daughter, was standing close to us. In spite of everything, I felt sad for her, for the embarrassment she would have felt.

The contrast between the energy in Toronto and in Boston the day before was dramatic. In Boston, the atmosphere had been very serious and tense; in Toronto, it could be best described as chaotic. Mr. Justice Patrick LeSage, well known at this time as the judge in the Paul Bernardo case, presided. There was another contrast between the proceedings in Toronto and Boston: on this day, Eagleson was ushered into court — without handcuffs! Everyone was stunned.

As in Boston, the courtroom was packed. Eagleson pleaded guilty to the eight criminal charges brought by the RCMP. Justice LeSage said little, but chastised him, telling him that someone in his position ought to have known full well that he couldn't wear all those hats without it catching up with him eventually. The proceedings were over quickly, and they ended with Eagleson being sentenced to 18 months in a medium-security prison — with the possibility of parole in six months. As Carl told *Maclean's*, "Al being Al, he managed to cut himself a good deal."

Eagleson was then led out of the courtroom — again without handcuffs. Christie Blatchford remarked on this in the *Toronto Sun*.

> *When R. Alan Eagleson was led from Courtroom 2–7 yesterday, against all tradition of the court, in shocking defiance of the process that is part of the punishment for all offenders who are in custody and heading off to jail, in a breach that left Crown attorneys with their mouths agape, he was not in handcuffs. As it was in the beginning so it was in the end. Special treatment, special rules for a special sort of thief. Heads ought to roll.*

That day, there could be no doubting Carl's contention that Alan Eagleson had indeed been the most powerful man in Canada. Approximately 30 letters, written by many of Canada's most prominent citizens, were presented by Eagleson's lawyer as character references. Those who wrote the letters included former Prime Minister John Turner, former Supreme Court Justice Willard "Bud" Estey (a frequent member of Eagleson's entourage at international hockey tournaments), former Ontario cabinet ministers Tom Wells and Darcy McKeough, the son of the late Supreme Court Justice John Sopinka, *Toronto Sun* president and former Metropolitan Toronto Chairman Paul Godfrey, and journalists such as George Gross, Bill Stephenson and Douglas Fisher.

The content of these letters was shocking to everyone — especially given the severity of the criminal charges to which he had pleaded guilty and the harm done to so many. Bob Pulford wrote that Eagleson had always represented the players first and never let their friendship affect his decisions. Others characterized Eagleson as "honest" and "a distinguished legislator." Paul Godfrey called him "a good citizen, but most of all a great individual." What a shameful commentary on the leaders of Canadian society! Carl was quick to give his take. "Alan Eagleson never had friends," he said. "All he had were dupes and stooges."

Paul Kelly, who had conducted the investigation stateside for years, echoed Carl's comments when he told the press that the people submitting them "were either fooled or co-opted by Eagleson." Indeed. Yet Alan Eagleson had systematically, over some 20 years, insulated himself extraordinarily well by surrounding himself with prime ministers, provincial premiers, Supreme Court justices, chiefs of police and media moguls. No wonder he believed he was untouchable and invincible.

Carl had absolutely no patience for the ever-faithful band of loyal Eagleson supporters, especially the hockey players, who continued to stand by him. It was bad enough that Bobby Clarke flaunted his friendship by having Al at his side in the press box at Maple Leaf Gardens (and later, at the Air Canada Centre) at the same time that he was a fugitive. But now, even after Eagleson had pleaded guilty to criminal charges in two countries, there were still players who defended him. Carl could only shake his head in response to the stupidity or naïveté of former players like Darryl Sittler, Paul Henderson and Lanny McDonald when they declared that Eagleson had never done anything to hurt them. "Are they so fucking stupid that they can't get that if he stole monies from international hockey, he stole from them?!" he thundered. It disappointed Carl that certain players preferred to show their true colours (and support their own personal interests) by defending Alan Eagleson instead of standing by their abused brotherhood.

After the Toronto proceedings, Paul Kelly spoke about the hockey players he had met during his lengthy investigation. "They are the most honest group of professional athletes with the highest level of integrity. There isn't a better group, a more likeable, more honest, and probably more gullible group."

Carl always remembered that his friend, Toronto lawyer Bill McMurtry, once told him way back in the 1970s that someone could stop Eagleson, but it would take him 24 hours a day, seven days a week to do so. From about this point on, Carl would emphasize, "Enter Russ Conway."

That night, after fulfilling numerous media commitments, we all converged at a pleasant Italian eatery on Yonge Street north of Lawrence where Bob Goodenow hosted a celebratory dinner before Paul Kelly and Tom Daly left for the airport to return to Boston. The following night, everyone involved with us in this lengthy saga — Carl and me, Russ Conway and his guest, Bruce Dowbiggin, Stevie Cameron and her husband, David, Lorraine Mahoney, Mark Zigler and Tom Lockwood — all gathered at Barberian's Steak House for a wonderful evening, sharing our stories and memories. Aaron Barberian and his father, Harry, made certain that we had the most memorable of evenings. It was this team and all its hard work, commitment and dedication that helped bring this long quest to its successful conclusion. As we left that night, Aaron said he hoped that we would consider his restaurant our second home. We have — it's a "happy memory place," and whenever Russ comes to town we always get together at Barberian's.

***

On January 22, 1998, the Law Society of Upper Canada disposed of the complaint against R. Alan Eagleson. Carl and I attended the formalities at Osgoode Hall. Eagleson received what the Law Society described as the "ultimate penalty," and he was disbarred. He initially sought permission to resign, but his request was vetoed. He did, however, plead guilty to a certain number of the 44 counts of professional misconduct he was charged with as a result of the thorough investigative work of the society's outside legal counsel, Tom Lockwood. "Because he pled guilty to some of the charges, we didn't prosecute them all," Lockwood explained to me. However, he added: "I wanted to have a hearing. I felt the players were entitled to a hearing — that it would have been best for the players to have a trial or a hearing. But the society argued that when he was getting the 'ultimate penalty,' what else would a hearing accomplish?

"I wanted to get all the facts on the table for everybody to get all the facts, so the world knew what all the facts are. I know what's in my files, but no one else knows. It was disappointing, but there was not much more you could do."

There is a provision in the Law Society's regulations that allows a disbarred lawyer to seek reinstatement at a future date. Tom Lockwood was very cognizant of this when he negotiated the terms of Eagleson's disbarment. "I insisted that there be a provision that if he ever sought to get back in, we had to have the ability to go ahead with [prosecuting] all of the allegations. This was terribly important to me, and I wouldn't sign off without this provision. It was the very first time that a provision of this nature was built in. I felt good about that."

Carl and I — and others — had hoped that the other professionals, especially lawyers, who had co-operated with Eagleson in the various criminal schemes over the years would also be subject to scrutiny. Eagleson didn't do everything alone, and it seemed that other heads ought to have rolled. However, the way in which the matter was handled at the Law

Society precluded any such inquiry. Although we were disappointed that all of the 44 counts were not prosecuted, we had the utmost respect for the work that Tom Lockwood did.

Tom and I recently reminisced about this time in our lives. He reminded me how hard Carl and I had been on him at the time, and he assured me that he was always intent on ignoring us and doing what he had to do. I replied that he must surely understand where we were coming from when, over the years, every authority figure in the country had refused to touch Alan Eagleson. We were fearful that the Law Society would whitewash its investigation, given his powerful and extensive connections. Tom admitted to me that it wasn't easy for him to deal with the Law Society: "There were some issues, some real difficulties I had with the Law Society. It doesn't bother me because I did what I thought was right. I have my values and others can have theirs."

Under intense pressure, Alan Eagleson resigned from the Hockey Hall of Fame, and he was stripped of his membership in the Order of Canada.

***

On a very high note, and a feeling of great relief at everything that had been accomplished, Carl and I left at the end of January for France. Since the autumn of 1995, when we spent six weeks at my cousin Anne Acland's home in the French countryside outside the university town of Poitiers, we had spent extended periods of time every February and March in the small coastal village of Villefranche-sur-Mer, just east of Nice on the Mediterranean. It was a very inexpensive "long-stay" package with Air France that worked beautifully for us. We both loved being settled into a small village like this and fitting in with the locals.

In Sanxay in 1995, it had been a pleasure to drive around the countryside each day, visiting the local towns and hamlets, exploring the local *châteaux* and markets, eating in tiny restaurants where there was no menu, just what they cooked that day — and a three-course meal with all the wine you could drink cost about $10. We went to La Rochelle on the Atlantic coast — the beautiful port city from which many French-Canadian immigrants left their homeland behind in the 17th and 18th centuries. We visited the Loire region, the Cognac region and, just north of us, found the Muscadet wine route — the best wrong turn that Carl ever made!

From 1996 to 2001, we spent four to six weeks every year in Villefranche-sur-Mer. These were our most special times of each year — sharing our days in a completely different and wonderful environment in one of the most beautiful parts of the world. One time, it turned out that Carl's childhood friend and Marlboro teammate Bob McAleese and his wife, Roz, were staying at the same residence at the same time. "I never saw Carl more relaxed and happy than he was in France that winter," Bob commented to me. "He was away from all the scrutiny in Toronto and he was like a different human being."

Our routine was fairly consistent. In the early mornings, we walked into Beaulieu-sur-Mer, a 10-minute walk, and had coffee — a grand café crème — and croissants (a *croissant aux amandes* for Carl) at La Boulangerie Calleri. Carl always sat so he could watch the baker preparing his baguettes — he was fascinated by the way he cut diagonal slashes along each loaf with a razor blade before they were rolled into the oven. The baker and Carl communicated throughout this process with smiles and nods, and when the fully baked croissants were rolled out of the oven, Carl would break into a huge smile and give the baker a big thumbs up! We'd buy a baguette to take home with us and head down the street to the daily market to buy our provisions — local leeks, carrots, tomatoes, roquette, *salade frisée*, asparagus from Provence, farm-fresh brown eggs, blood oranges from Italy for the best juice in the world, and home-pressed olive oil. On Saturday mornings there was a larger market in the village, where vendors sold honey, cheese, breads baked in big wooden ovens, and socca, a local delicacy made from chickpea flour. There were also clothes, soaps, and all sorts of locally produced items. Carl loved it all. One of the market vendors had two large dogs that were accustomed to sleeping in cardboard boxes close to their mistress. However, each morning when Carl showed up, they immediately left their boxes and went to him. He'd sit on the old stone wall that surrounded the market square, and the dogs would stay at his feet, leaning against him. Carl loved animals, and these fellows picked up on it right away.

Many days, we'd drive to one of the nearby villages, such as Vence, Gorbio or St. Agnes, or to the fascinating *villages perchés* like Peille — towns that cling to the sides of mountains — to admire the sights. Fridays, we made the 40-minute trip — sometimes driving, sometimes by train — to Ventimiglia in Italy for the huge weekly border market. Here you can find absolutely everything — fruits, walnuts, cured meats, all sorts of cheese (including huge slabs of parmigiano), shoes, woollens, suits, housewares, linens and all styles of espresso makers. Carl never tired of this ritual. And we'd always drop in to say *bongiorno* to Fernanda, our newfound friend, who owns a shoe store in town. Year after year we were always welcomed back and greeted with hugs and kisses. Fernanda would recommend a place where we should eat lunch, and call ahead to let the restaurateur know that her friends from Canada were coming by.

The other market that Carl particularly loved was at Cours Saleya in old Nice. Many a morning we'd drive the seven kilometres into Nice and stroll the market stalls, inhaling the wonderfully fragrant aromas of spices, cheese and flowers. After making our purchases, we'd sit on the outdoor patio at Les Ponchettes at the far easterly end of the market, sipping a *grand café crème* or, if later in the day, a glass or two of delicious local rosé wine, all the while appreciating the colourful old buildings, the energy and vibrancy of the marketplace, the beauty of it all, and being very grateful that we could have these moments together to enjoy. Sometimes we bought a *fougasse* (a flat French bread) and had a picnic on the beach.

In the afternoons, Carl liked to walk down to the beach at Beaulieu and read or meditate; or, we'd walk along the seashore into Villefranche and have a kir at Cosmos, a fabulous café. The time always passed far too quickly, and it was always with great reluctance that we packed up to leave. Routinely, as we drove away from the residence, Carl would slow the car down to a snail's pace as we passed the spectacular sight of the port of Villefranche and say to me, "Sue, have your last look for this year." There is no doubt in my mind that these were the happiest and most relaxed times in Carl's life.

***

With Alan Eagleson's imprisonment in 1998, there was a sense of closure for Carl — at least to the lengthy battle to "stop him" and "get him out of hockey."

Nonetheless, the business of hockey continued to dominate his thoughts. Shortly after the final chapter in the Eagleson saga drew to a close, Carl and I were having lunch one day when he presented to me a long list of further lawsuits he was convinced we had to undertake. It was obvious to me that he'd been thinking about these things for a long time and he was very focused and determined. First and foremost, he desperately wanted to continue legal proceedings to recover what we felt to be, conservatively, an additional $200 million shortfall in the NHL Pension Plan because of monies not contributed by the NHL, the promised monies from international hockey that the league had reneged on, and double liability concerns. The Adams decision had left the door open to examine other issues that weren't raised within our lawsuit — including matching contributions, the 1969 agreement that left the players without a seat on the Pension Society board, and the NHL's misrepresentation of the pension plan as a defined benefit plan. In addition, Carl wanted to sue the Toronto Maple Leaf Alumni Association for an accounting. It infuriated Carl that players still lined up to participate in all sorts of fund-raising events, but they never saw any financial statements. There had been a large sponsorship payment from Bell Canada, the details of which had never been made known to the members, so Bell Canada was also on Carl's list. He also spoke of an action against the NHL Players' Association for the damages Eagleson had caused to players and the association during his tenure. The list went on and on.

I listened to Carl and was well aware of his intensity and determination. Just hearing all this was fatiguing, and I knew what it entailed — the negativity, the battles... the costs! And after what we had just been through, I was burned out. I usually went along with what Carl wanted, but not this time. I told him that we simply could not devote any more of our lives to fighting these battles. By now, we had given 23 years to the pursuit of justice, both for Carl personally and all hockey players. This was in no way to diminish the reality of these obvious problems; it simply wasn't financially possible for us to embark on such a quest, and the thought of continuing to spend countless hours embroiled in all of it was unfathomable to me.

To simplify matters, I suggested that there were two areas that it made sense for us to pursue, because Carl might have a financial stake in them. On the one hand, I proposed that we continue to work on the pension question by presenting all of our evidence to the Pension Commission of Ontario. We had been informed by forensic investigators we'd met through Stevie Cameron that the PCO is empowered to order a forensic audit of any pension plan within its jurisdiction if there is evidence of fraud or mishandling of the money. We definitely had evidence of the latter: the successful lawsuit and our exchanges of correspondence with the NHL Pension Society over Carl's inaccurate record clearly proved the existence of irregularities.

Secondly, I suggested that we stay close to the collusion lawsuit that was being advanced in Philadelphia by Ed Garvey, representing David Forbes, Ulf Nilsson, Brad Park, Rick Middleton and Doug Smail — this was a class-action suit filed under the RICO (Racketeer Influenced and Corrupt Organization) Act on behalf of all former NHL players. In this action, they alleged that the NHL (President John Ziegler, Chairman Bill Wirtz and the owners) turned a blind eye to Eagleson's financial misconduct as head of the Players' Association, in return for which Eagleson negotiated collective bargaining agreements that benefited the league. The suit had been filed back in November 1995. Carl was an interested observer in this case: according to the collective-bargaining agreement that Eagleson had negotiated, arbitration cases were to be heard, not by an independent, neutral arbitrator but by the league president. (Carl's own claim for the unpaid salary the Leafs owed him was adjudicated by John Ziegler.) This could be considered an unfair practice. The suit also dealt with the matter of the monies from international hockey that had been promised to enhance players' pensions and had never found their way into the fund.

Carl knew that it was futile to expect the PCO to support us. However, to my way of thinking, it was worth a shot — it was our only option. To do so would involve hours of work on my part, putting the documentation together and corresponding with the Pension Commission, but there would be no significant outlay of money. With the collusion lawsuit, there was nothing to do except make certain that Ed Garvey was aware of which of the allegations were relevant to Carl.

After months of letters, materials and personal meetings with the Pension Commission, the final result was as Carl expected: they refused to take a position in these matters, and their excuse was that some of the documents were unsigned drafts. Yet these same documents had been satisfactory to Justice Adams to make his favourable judgment in the lawsuit.

The real travesty of justice came in August 1998, when the class-action suit was thrown out on the grounds that the plaintiffs hadn't filed it in a timely fashion. The district court pointed to the Garvey Report, presented in 1989, and Russ Conway's articles in the *Lawrence Eagle-Tribune*, beginning in 1991, and ruled that the players should have been aware of Eagleson's malfeasance and filed their complaint much sooner. The players appealed, saying that they didn't have enough evidence until the grand jury indicted Eagleson in 1994. They lost that appeal, and lost again at the U.S. Supreme Court.

Recently, David Keon spoke with me about the quality of leadership of the NHL Players' Association. "I don't know if Canadians are dupes or what, but to a certain extent I think the same thing went on in the last stoppage of play [the lockout of 2004–05, which caused the season to be cancelled]. The only people making the decisions were those making $30 or $40 million, and they weren't talking about the guys who were making half a million or whatever they were making. To me it was almost the same. At no time has anybody ever represented the players in a good manner."

CHAPTER 17

CARL BREWER: QUINTESSENTIAL HOCKEY MAN

> *"Bobby Clarke does not come to the table with clean hands.*
> *Leadership, pshaw! Does a leader of men sell out his team-*
> *mates? Bobby Clarke betrayed all the players who fought*
> *his battles and gave him the courage to play hockey. In*
> *essence, Bobby Clarke is a gutless fuck!"*

An important chapter in the history of the Toronto Maple Leafs — and of hockey in general — was due to draw to a close on February 13, 1999, when the last game was played at Maple Leaf Gardens. Carl was very emotional about this event. "They can never replicate the history and tradition of the Gardens," he said. He felt that the Gardens had been the bastion of Toronto hockey tradition for decades and should not be discarded but rather updated. However, practically every team in the National Hockey League had moved into new, more modern — and lucrative — facilities, so the Leafs were bound to follow suit.

We had fond memories of watching the closing of the Montreal Forum on television on March 11, 1996. The standing ovation the packed house gave Maurice "Rocket" Richard was unforgettable. But when the time came to say goodbye to the Gardens, Carl was ambivalent. We had booked our long-stay vacation in France months before there was any suggestion of special ceremonies, and Carl was vehemently opposed to interrupting our plans — that trip had become our most special and eagerly anticipated time of the year. Furthermore, Carl was miffed that the Leaf organization had been so late in confirming the dates and announcing the details of the closing festivities; this made him even more determined to take a pass.

However, it soon became apparent that the powers that be at Maple Leaf Gardens wanted Carl present. When they heard of his reluctance to return, they took care of bringing us back to Toronto. We travelled back from Nice to Toronto on Friday, February 12 and were put up at the Sutton Place Hotel on Bay Street. Our flight back to Toronto — Nice to Frankfurt on Lufthansa and Frankfurt to Toronto on Air Canada — had been comfortable, even for Carl, who was terrified of flying, and we felt less weary than usual after a lengthy international flight. The stewardess kept Carl supplied with vodka throughout the flight and was exceptionally attentive to us. He promised her that we would get some autographs for her young hockey-playing son.

At noon on Saturday, Carl left to meet with all the other players for a get-together and briefing about the agenda for the evening. At about two-thirty, he telephoned me from the Gardens. The sheer joy and delight in his voice made the whole trip back worth it for me. I knew then and there that Carl would never regret our decision to reconsider the Leafs' invitation. Carl was ecstatic; he sounded happier and more exuberant than I could remember him sounding in ages. He was thrilled to see old comrades, and especially thrilled to have met some of the older Leafs and 90-year-old Harold "Mush" Marsh of the Chicago Blackhawks. Carl said to me, "Sue, these men were my heroes when I was a kid and I have never met some of them before today."

Carl was incredulous at the commotion already building outside the Gardens — the police had already closed down Carlton Street and there were thousands of fans already assembling around the arena. Our plan had been that Carl would return to the room and we would go back down to the Gardens together at six o'clock, but now Carl was worried about not being able to get close to the building if we left it too late. "Sue, we'd better get down here much earlier, like pretty soon," he said. "Can you be ready by four?"

The game between the Leafs and Chicago Blackhawks that night was pretty uninspiring; the visitors beat the Leafs 6–2, and Chicago's Bob Probert scored the final goal in Maple Leaf Gardens. But the postgame celebrations were memorable indeed. For Carl and so many others, walking out onto the ice again to the roar of the fans represented a last hockey hurrah at Maple Leaf Gardens. Carl's introduction drew a tremendous ovation. "I was shocked that when the game ended that night the fans all stayed in their seats for the closing ceremonies," he often remarked. "I thought when I walked out on the ice, the building would be half-empty." This kind of thinking was typical of Carl, who had difficulty grasping the heroic status he and the other Maple Leaf players of his era had been afforded in this town. It was a most sentimental moment for Carl, and one of my favourite photos, which went over the Canadian Press wire, showed Carl waiting for his call to go out on the ice. The photograph clearly shows him being both reflective and emotional.

Later, after the ceremonies came to an end, the ice surface was transformed into a huge party scene for all the players, former players, their spouses, and everyone who had ever had a connection with the Gardens. John McDermott, the marvellous tenor who often sings the anthem at the hockey games, invited us to go to Ireland with him on his upcoming tour. Our friend Joe Freitas showed up and Carl was delighted. Everyone present was tremendously upbeat. At one point, Carl and I looked at one another and realized that it was one-thirty in the morning and we were still going strong and enjoying ourselves; normally, after a long international flight, we would have been hopelessly exhausted and in bed hours earlier. There was obviously a lot of adrenaline in our systems that night.

Not everyone was pleased with the way this historic event was handled. David Keon didn't attend for the same reasons that have kept him away from Leaf-related functions for years. Carl was disappointed not to see David, who he hoped would decide to come and enjoy this moment with his fellow teammates, but it was not to be. Bert Olmstead stayed home because he didn't think the Leafs handled the arrangements fairly, and there were several other players who voiced their complaints.

We spent the week in Toronto and attended several of the functions at the new Air Canada Centre. Carl participated in the grand parade from the Gardens to the new rink the following Friday. The entire city of Toronto seemed caught up in the excitement of the move. Immediately after the parade, we headed to the airport to return to France. At the Air Canada check-in counter, we were ushered aside and upgraded to business class for our return flight. We spent a restful night over the Atlantic, awash in wonderful memories. In the morning when the stewardess woke us for breakfast, she smiled as she told us: "You two have had a great night, a great sleep." It was the very first time I remember Carl ever sleeping on a plane!

Upon our return to France, Carl sent a letter to Ken and Linda Dryden:

> *Saturday, February 13, 1999, was truly one of the most wonderful days of my life. It was an absolute joy to have such a marvellous opportunity to meet old friends and reacquaint with colleagues, and visit with some much older players who had been my heroes and role models growing up. It was a thrill to participate in this milestone event. It was unbelievable to me that that all the fans that night stayed for all of the postgame program and activities. When I came out [on the ice] I expected the Gardens to be half-empty. It was a great honour and a pleasure indeed to be part of all the festivities.*

A few months later, Carl and other former Toronto Maple Leafs were asked to appear at Maple Leaf Gardens for the big auction at which all the fixtures were sold off. The building was being stripped, and the Leafs believed Carl and other former players would add some interest and attract bidders. Carl was reluctant to go; it was very sad for him to have to watch this dismemberment of his hockey shrine. Mark Askin, the producer from Leafs TV, ran into Carl at the Gardens that day and Carl asked him, "Mark, does this hurt you as badly as it hurts me?" Mark told me that all the pictures had been removed from the walls and were piled up to be auctioned off. He remembered Carl saying, "All those memories going out the door!" Mark saw how deeply Carl felt about this. He said, "Probably Carl was in a lot of the pictures in the pile and he was really emotional about what was happening to his past."

***

In November 1999, Carl's health took a serious turn. He had continued to have the "attacks" of pain in his back and breathing was becoming increasingly difficult. Doctors were unable to get a handle on his problems, and stress was cited as the most likely explanation. This time, however, he had an attack that he was unable to breathe through. He had gone out for a walk on a particularly cold, nasty day and when he returned I found him standing at the bottom of the stairs, looking terribly uncomfortable. I didn't like his colour and immediately gave him an Aspirin and suggested we go to Sunnybrook Hospital and have him checked out. He didn't resist, and when we got to the emergency room, the nurse took his blood pressure and said to me: "You take care of the paperwork; I'm taking him in right away."

His blood pressure was off the scale; we spent the entire day in the emergency ward while the doctors stabilized it. At first, the attending physician thought his pain was from arthritic deterioration in his spine. Later in the day, however, she returned to tell us that enzymes in his blood indicated he had suffered a heart attack. The doctors disagreed about his symptoms and the best treatment for him; all they could determine was that, sometime between 1997 and 1999, he'd had a heart attack. He was admitted immediately to the coronary intensive care unit, where he stayed for four days.

Carl found it tremendously stressful to be hospitalized. He was frightened and wanted me with him at all times. He'd call me at seven-thirty in the morning and ask if I was on my way over. I'd make him freshly squeezed carrot juice and orange juice and a sandwich and stay with him until late at night. He had trouble sleeping and insisted I stay, telling me, "I enjoy your company." It was an exhausting time; I was terribly worried about Carl, and even when I could get to sleep, I awoke feeling like I hadn't slept at all. One evening, Carl, seeing that I was worn out, told me to go home and get some rest. However, by the time I got home, he had already called and left a message, worried because I wasn't home yet and asking me to come back and bring him a salmon sandwich. One evening, he sounded almost desperate: "Sue, what are we going to do?" he asked. I tried to reassure him, saying: "Together we'll get through this." He breathed a sigh of relief and answered: "Thank you, Sue. You have no idea how much it means to me to hear that."

We were absolutely delighted, and very proud, when the Hockey Hall of Fame announced that Russ Conway had been chosen to receive the Elmer Ferguson Memorial Award. The selection is made each year by the Professional Hockey Writers' Association, and the recipient is honoured on a plaque that is displayed in the Hall of Fame. Russ was honoured for his extraordinary series of investigative reports, entitled "Cracking the Ice," in the *Lawrence Eagle-Tribune*. In this series, he exposed the details of Alan Eagleson's scams as well as the misdeeds of management. He was also runner-up for the Pulitzer Prize for his excellent reporting.

Carl checked himself out of hospital, having decided to follow a treatment plan with Dr. Cutler in Niagara Falls, just in time to attend Russ's Hall of Fame celebrations. We were able to show up for his big dinner at Barberian's Steak House as well as the luncheon on the Monday when Russ received his award. That night, we attended the induction ceremonies at the Hockey Hall of Fame. We didn't stay very long, because Carl needed plenty of rest, but he thoroughly enjoyed himself. We had a particularly lovely time visiting with Gordie and Colleen Howe. It turned out to be our last good visit with Colleen; soon afterwards, a degenerative neurological condition known as Pick's Disease took hold of her, causing drastic memory loss.

Carl worked diligently to regain his health. For many weeks, we travelled to Niagara Falls and stayed over one or two nights so he could have several consecutive chelation treatments. We read a book on back pain by Dr. John Sarno, in which he discussed his thesis that over 90 percent of back pain is caused by repressed emotions. When Carl read that, he immediately saw himself. "It's all here," he told me, referring to the theories in the book. Dr. Sarno described the personality profile of someone who typically suffers back pain: a perfectionist who has feelings of vulnerability, guilt, inadequacy and anger, and who takes on a lot of responsibility. According to Dr. Sarno, all of this results in tension that in turn causes the back pain. Carl worked with the treatment outlined in this book and felt encouraged. I asked him if we should cancel our reservations for our upcoming winter vacation in France. His answer was emphatic: "No, Sue, absolutely *not*. It's more important than ever that we go."

The NHL All-Star game was scheduled to be played in Toronto in early February 2000, so we postponed our annual sojourn to Villefranche-sur-Mer by a week in order to accept the NHL's invitation to this marvellous, once-in-our-lifetime, gala event. Carl had played in four All-Star games — three as a Leaf, and once as a member of the Detroit Red Wings. Much had changed since Carl's day. For one thing, the peripheral events and hoopla had grown exponentially. Ralph Backstrom played in six All-Star games, and he remembers that there was little activity outside of the game itself. "I don't remember any banquet or skills competitions," he told me. The format had changed, too. Back in the 1960s, the Stanley Cup champions faced off against a team of selected players from the other five clubs. In 2000, the competition was between the North American All-Stars and their counterparts from the rest of the hockey world.

The weekend was sensational. We enjoyed the comfort and luxury of the elegant and stately Royal York Hotel for the duration. The Territories Room was set up as a hospitality suite, available for the players and their guests to mingle and socialize, and we met old friends from far and wide and made many new ones.

On Thursday evening, February 3, within minutes of our arrival in the hospitality room, we were chatting with old friends. Gordie Howe, was there, and Bobby Orr came up behind me and grabbed me in a big bear hug. Bobby Hull floated through with greetings and hugs as he looked for the bar. There was also a particularly poignant moment for Carl and me, when Emile "Butch" Bouchard, the great Canadiens defenseman of the 1940s and '50s, approached us and thanked us for all we had done to help him and the others with the pension battle. Butch informed us that he had received $37,000 from the settlement, and this obviously meant a great deal to him. During our conversation, Sid Smith, who was standing nearby and had overheard us, interjected to let us know that, in the very beginning, when Clarence Campbell met the players at the All-Star break and told them they had the "richest pension" in pro sport, Butch spoke up and told Campbell he was wrong. Butch informed the league president that 3 percent per year was not such a good deal and that there were much better investment vehicles that would yield superior returns for the players. According to Sid, Campbell reacted sternly and angrily, telling Butch he didn't know what he was talking about — that this pension was "guaranteed!"

Frank Mahovlich shared a similar story with me about Campbell. Like Bouchard, Frank knew the money wasn't invested to get the best possible gains for the players. "They were investing the money in railway bonds," Frank told me. "They weren't earning a reasonable rate of interest and I stood up and asked him about it. Well, he laid me out! He asked me how many years I'd been in the league and asked me why I thought I should be questioning him!" In later years, when Frank attended charity golf tournaments and saw retired players from other pro sports arriving in chauffeured limos or driving their own Cadillacs, he figured something didn't add up! Over the years, we had heard so many similar stories; now, however, it had been proven that the NHL had been playing games with pension monies for decades.

I was particularly charmed that evening to meet Butch Bouchard's wife, Marie-Claire — we chatted in French, expressed our shared views about separatism and Canadian politics, French-Canadian cuisine and song. We amused ourselves singing French songs, such as Françoise Hardy's "Tous les Garcons et les Filles." Her husband was concerned and kept whispering to Marie-Claire, in French, that she shouldn't be saying such things to Susan — that I was English and might be offended. Marie-Claire told him that I shared their views — *"Elle pense exactement comme nous!"* I also assured Butch that he needn't be concerned about offending me.

After meeting and greeting for about an hour, Carl and I slipped away and went across the street to Bardi's Steak House for a quiet, relaxed dinner and evening together. We were exhilarated by our experiences so far — the friendships, the camaraderie — and we looked forward to the enjoyment that the next three days promised. This part of the evening was like most of our nights out — just the two of us, together, away from the crowds and confusion. It was where we were always most comfortable, safe and secure in each other's company.

Over the weekend, it was wonderful to observe so many old Leaf warriors — Harry Watson, Ed Litzenberger, Kent Douglas, Larry Hillman, Bob Nevin, John McCormack and many others — sitting together, sharing old hockey stories and memories. There is nothing that brings greater joy to these former players than an opportunity to get together and reminisce over a few beers.

What followed was a whirlwind of events that literally left us barely enough time to catch our breath between functions. On Saturday morning, the ladies were guests of Shelli Bettman, wife of NHL Commissioner Gary Bettman, and Sally Stavro, wife of Leafs owner Steve Stavro, for a function at the Art Gallery of Ontario. The morning began with a delicious brunch, followed by a captivating lecture by the renowned architect Frank Gehry. After Gehry's talk, we were feted at an elegant luncheon, once again at the AGO. On Saturday evening the NHL hosted the Heroes of Hockey dinner at the Four Seasons Hotel. Everyone was in attendance. It was an elegant evening, highly charged with exuberance and enthusiasm. Gary Bettman addressed the gathering. The league pulled out all the stops for this extravaganza, and it was truly a memorable evening. Later on, Roots hosted a post-dinner reception in the hotel.

After the dinner guests had pretty much dispersed, Carl and I wandered back into the dining room, seeking a quiet moment. We sat down and chatted with our old friend Susan Conacher, Brian's wife, for a few moments. At this time, Carl spotted Paul Martin, who was then the federal minister of Finance, accompanied by financier Gerry Schwartz. The two were wandering about the room together — dressed in jeans — slumming, basically. These two powerful men were — for this night, at least — just a couple of jock chasers! Carl really got a kick out of this — and it was very typical of him to have spotted them in the first place!

Carl was asked by the *Toronto Star* to reflect on the weekend and write a guest column. His article came out under the headline, "Things weren't always so good," although in the draft he submitted, he entitled it "Lest We Forget."

Ah, the changes in hockey don't really take place on the ice. This starry aggregation has an average salary of $5 million per man. I don't know about you, Grandma, but that sounds like a lot of chicken feed to me. Alice Snippersnapper and Nutsy Fagan would really turn over in their respective graves.

Do you think these fellows have any understanding or appreciation from whence this largesse came? Would they be aware of the forces of neutral arbitration, salary disclosure and a bona fide union boss which together make this largesse possible?

Of course, one should never forget the greed and duplicity of management. The likes of Tod Sloan and Jimmy Thomson — All-Stars, both — led the solidarity movement in the '50s. All the Leafs stood up to the tyrant Major Conn Smythe in their union struggle. Both Sloan and Thomson were ignominiously and unceremoniously dealt off to the then Siberia of hockey — the Chicago Blackhawks — a high price they were willing to pay.

In today's market, both Thomson and Sloan would be $6 million men, and not the paltry $15,000 per year they did earn. Hockey has come a long way, but do these diverse kids have any idea why?

Carl continued to follow hockey, and hockey-related events, all of his life. The removal of Alan Eagleson from the scene and the return of millions of dollars in pension monies to the retired players did little to assuage Carl's concerns about the unfair and undignified treatment of current players. He was especially anguished over the seemingly endless saga of Eric Lindros and the constant degradation he suffered at the hands of Flyers general manager Bobby Clarke. One day, to vent his frustrations, Carl scribbled a note about Clarke:

> *Bobby Clarke does not come to the table with clean hands. Leadership? Pshaw! Does a leader of men sell out his teammates? Bobby Clarke betrayed all the players who fought his battles and gave him the courage to play hockey.*
> *In essence, Bobby Clarke is a gutless fuck!*
> *Collusion? By his actions vis-à-vis his undisclosed, secret contract and his consorting with and his support of Alan Eagleson, the recalcitrant union boss and convicted felon, NHL salaries were artificially manipulated and remained low.*

The "secret contract" Carl referred to was something we found out about from the FBI's investigation of Alan Eagleson. Tom Daly, the FBI Special Agent, disclosed that in his playing days, "Mr. Clarke had a personal-services contract, which was good for the remainder of his lifetime, which would pay him a set sum of money. My best recollection was that it was $250,000 [U.S.] per year. It would be guaranteed for life." Carl was quick to point out to everyone that, when contract negotiations were taking place with Flyers management, it was Clarke's official contract that was used as the benchmark by which other players were paid. But the amount Clarke was actually earning was, unbenownst to him teammates, far greater.

Lindros's contract expired after the 1999–2000 season, but that didn't mean he was free to play wherever he wanted. He was a restricted free agent — meaning that the Flyers had the right to match any other team's offer and prevent him from leaving. Carl was always a champion of true free agency, going back to 1967, when he considered challenging the NHL's reserve clause.

On March 29, 2000, Carl and I went out for breakfast. We had all three newspapers and planned to spend a leisurely morning reading and having our breakfast. I began reading the *National Post*, and a front-page feature by Roy MacGregor under the headline "A team that has had its fill of the

Lindros legacy?" caught my eye. I read the article in disbelief. It was hostile and scathing — uncharacteristic of Roy, I thought, because in our experience he had always been pleasant, kind and polite. I handed the paper to Carl without saying a word. He read the article, and when he looked up at me, I immediately saw the fury in his eyes. "Sue, we have to respond to this," he said. He was livid.

The letter that was sent to Roy read in part:

> *Your writing credentials are superb, and deservedly so. Your ability as a words craftsman is unparalleled in the journalism industry. For this reason, I find it interesting how myopic and misguided your reasoned diatribe was in the above article. "'There's always something,' says Flyer teammate." Who the fuck said that? Another unattributable source? Sounds to me like this latter would be the cancer in the Flyer lineup.*
>
> *Contrary to your comment, this 27-year-old prize athlete is anything but an "enigma." Injuries have distorted the significance of his whole career. The collapsed lung of last year was almost fatal. Eric did nothing wrong; the medical staff did nothing right.... To listen to Bobby Clarke, one would think that Lindros was a malingerer. His teammates have never doubted Lindros's competitiveness game in and game out, but they may have been jealous of his status. Strange that only now one hears the silent whispers by his unseen and unidentified teammates, who are apparently displeased by his speaking out about his treatment at the hands of team management, trainers and medical staff.*
>
> *What is surprising is that it is only now that there have been some aspersions about the competence of the medical staff, the training staff and management as a whole. Is it not obvious that these various parties have been totally incompetent?*
>
> *Eric Lindros has always, above all, been a team player. He has always, in spite of being embroiled frequently in a flurry of controversy, taken the high road. In light of the*

belligerent, nasty and disrespectful treatment he has received from Bobby Clarke, one has to take a long, serious look at just who is not the team player: Bobby Clarke!

Bobby Clarke will be remembered on three levels for the sportsman that he is: (1) the slash that broke Kharlamov's ankle in the great Russia–Canada series; (2) for running Eric Lindros out of Philadelphia; and (3) his sellout of his fellow teammates during his playing days in Philadelphia.... Moreover, Bobby Clarke remained a loyal and steadfast supporter of deposed hockey czar Alan Eagleson. As the evidence mounted and some 34 charges were laid against Eagleson by the U.S. Department of Justice citing mail fraud, racketeering... Clarke continued to squire Eagleson around to hockey games and flaunt his presence with his friend in the face of all his peers. Again, a great team player? Eric Lindros still stands tall amongst his peers. Amazing it is to me that one so pilloried can continue to disport himself with so much class. No wonder he's envied.

In many respects, Carl saw himself in Eric's struggles. He anguished over Eric's decision to return to play; Carl was certain it was too soon after his concussions. Carl himself had rushed back to play and suffered because of it — after the Balfour incident, for example. He detested the way Eric was being treated by Flyers management and found it not dissimilar from what he and others experienced under Imlach. Almost daily, he expressed the wish that Eric would quit — play in Europe and get the hell away from the destructive, dark forces of the NHL. And for Roy MacGregor to call Eric an enigma infuriated Carl, who had had the same label applied to him many a time and had grown to hate it. (When we received a faxed copy of the Toronto Maple Leafs' current bio about Carl and it included his old nickname, "Skitz," he was livid!)

Carl did, however, find something in the modern era that impressed him. He was amazed by his friend Ralph Backstrom's creation of Roller Hockey International in the 1990s. Ralph had introduced the first in-line skates back when he played for the Los Angeles Kings in the early 1970s. He took Carl and me with him to watch his league's championship game in Buffalo in 1994. It was incredible. It wasn't just a hockey game played on in-line skates, it was a fabulous entertainment package. There were cheer-leaders, mascots and raucous music to get the crowd enthused during the game. The atmosphere around the rink was not unlike the midway at the Canadian National Exhibition — games, music, amusement for young and old. Ralph wrote the rules and redesigned the game of hockey in a way that Carl thought made sense for the NHL also. Carl outlined his thoughts:

> *Ralph Backstrom, NHL Calder Trophy winner in 1959 and a star centre for the dynastic Montreal Canadiens teams of the 1950s and 1960s, has developed what the NHL could use to make its game great again. Ralph is a very creative individual — he is commissioner of Roller Hockey International and one of the game's great creative geniuses. Backstrom custom-designed the entire game of roller hockey and the rules for the game. Think about his format! It is brilliant. A game divided into four quarters to appeal to the American audiences, and all games played in less than two hours to appeal to American television. There are no blue lines, which speeds up the game, and there are no offsides if the puck is carried over the centre line. ["This was the best rule we ever wrote," Ralph him-self commented, "because it opened up the game tremendously."] He has taken one player off the floor and now all players, especially the small, skilled players are back in the game.*

In response to the various rule changes discussed and debated in the NHL every year, Carl said, "My friend Ralph Backstrom's tenets improve on any of the NHL's proposed changes." Ralph saw tremendous potential for roller hockey because it could be played anywhere in any weather, and equipment cost much less.

***

Healthwise, Carl continued to struggle. We bought the book by Jose Silva, *You the Healer*, and worked together diligently to do the mental exercises the book advocated. Carl was always optimistic that things would get better.

He had been disappointed back in 1979 when he didn't manage to get a German passport. First of all, he was curious about the exercise, the process of obtaining a second passport and his possible eligibility. Also, he had a real fondness and affinity for Europe and never ruled out the possibility of working and/or living abroad.

Some time later, he made a discovery about his mother's family. He had always understood his mum to be Scottish, but he learned that her family had immigrated to Scotland from Ireland, and that he therefore had an extensive Irish background on his mother's side. During a visit to Ireland in 1995, we inquired about the possibility of his getting a Republic of Ireland passport. A helpful woman named Mary at the Justice Department in Dublin told us exactly what we needed and how to go about it. Among her tips, she advised us to take a bus to Newry, in Northern Ireland, assuring us that it was safe. She advised us to go into any local bar, look for the oldest man sitting there, and talk to him. She said that man would know plenty about Carl's family connections.

We followed Mary's advice and took the bus to Newry. Immediately, I could sense a very different energy than there was in the south. It was neither comfortable nor inviting. Nonetheless, we looked around, then engaged a taxi driver to take us out to the hamlets where Carl's ancestors had lived in the 1800s. We spent a couple of hours walking around the old cemeteries, looking for tombstones bearing the names McAvoy or O'Hare and driving around the region where his ancestors had lived and no doubt farmed. Back in Newry, we walked around the town. However, in midafternoon we walked out of a store and found the street full of young British troops rushing about with their guns drawn. Carl was horrified, particularly because, as he said, "These are just kids — they're no more than 17 years old." Then he said, "Let's get the fuck out of here!" We kept a very low profile in a pub until it was time to catch the bus back to Dublin. When the bus crossed the border — where there were armed guards and spikes in the road — back into the Republic of Ireland, Carl was enormously relieved.

Over the next year and a half, I worked diligently to collect documents from Irish public records. Soon we had all we needed to trace Carl's lineage, and we filled out his application and delivered it personally to the Irish Consulate in Ottawa. Shortly thereafter, Carl received his Irish/European Union passport. In the fall of 2000, we returned to Ireland and visited Galway, where his maternal ancestors were born. Now that Carl had his

E.U. passport, he could go through the fast line — for bearers of European travel documents — and he did so ever so cockily while I had to stand in the long line for those passengers with non-European passports! Of course, Carl always insisted that we both benefited, because he could go ahead and collect our bags off the carousel while I stood in line.

In July 2000, Carl read an article in my *Bon Appetit* magazine about a country hotel on Galway Bay called Cashel House. He put the magazine on the dining-room table and said, "I want to go there!" That autumn, we flew to Shannon Airport, then hopped a bus to Galway. The bus driver had us in stitches the whole trip! I've always said that the best entertainment in the world is a two-dollar ride on a local bus anywhere in Ireland. We found Galway absolutely delightful. We took bus tours around the mystic land of Connemara — Carl was hesitant to drive, considering they drive on the left. We also spent a night in the Aran Islands, which was like going back in time 300 years. It was magical. We celebrated Carl's birthday at Cashel House — that very weekend, the off-season rates kicked in — and it was a fabulous experience. Kay McEvilly, the owner, welcomed us with her warm smile and charming Irish greeting, "You are most welcome in our home." This would turn out to be Carl's last birthday, and at the time he said, "Sue, this has been the most wonderful birthday I've ever spent. Thank you!" It was another high point in our lives that has provided a lasting happy memory.

We went to France in the winter of 2001 to our favourite place, Villefranche-sur-Mer. This year, Carl's brother Frank and his wife, Ann, came with us and stayed in an apartment near us. They were terrific to be with and they enjoyed doing all the things and seeing all the beautiful spots that Carl and I had come to love over the past six years. Afterwards, Carl told me: "I feel really good that we were able to share this with my brother." During this stay, however, Carl was having great difficulty walking and was experiencing increasing shortness of breath.

***

Back home in Toronto in May, Carl was fixated on the Stanley Cup finals between the Colorado Avalanche and New Jersey Devils. The Devils had eliminated the Toronto Maple Leafs in the second round, and Carl had some pointed thoughts, specifically about Leaf captain Mats Sundin.

Consensus among Maple Leaf fans is that the Maple-O's have failed to provide Mats Sundin with proper and talented wingers that would allow him to attain the status of superstar. All great hockey players make the players around them better. Anybody who ever played with Stan Mikita in Chicago became All-Stars — Ab McDonald, Kenny Wharram, Doug Mohns, Cliff Koroll — and these were fringe players. Johnny Bucyk's line in Boston over 20 years was always the best line in hockey — no matter what linemates he had. Mats Sundin has never made anybody better. Steve "Stumpy" Thomas makes Mats look good!

This season it was the New Leafs, constructed specifically for the playoffs. They fared better — they got more than six shots on goal. New Jersey Devils were victorious again. Yet, what an immense contrast to the New Jersey series of a year ago. The powerful Devils murdered the Leafs, and our boy Mats was conspicuous by his disappearance. Bobby Holik kicked sand in his face. The Leafs went down without a whimper. Not so, this year. Totally out of character, Mats Sundin, the quiet pacifist of Swedish extraction, beat the crap out of Bobby Holik the entire series. Holik backed down, and this bully was totally ineffective. Holik comes by his surliness honestly — his father and uncle used to spit in my face in 1967. Mats Sundin became the bona fide superstar he'd promised to be. Remember Mats skating around the rink and rubbing his gloved hand in the face of Holik at every opportunity and pushing him over the boards at the players' bench — and the lack of surprise on Holik's face? Holik took it and didn't retaliate.

Mats in this series had his and everyone else's number as he passed and scored at will. Jonas Hoglund played well and Stumpy Thomas was a youthful and useful 38-year-old. Luck was not on the side of the inferior Leafs, who tried to steal the series like a thief in the night. Did the Maples ever recover from the deletion of the architect of the team's performance in the 1998–99 and 1999–2000 seasons? What deletion am I talking about? Alpo Suhonen! He made the Leafs' passes click. Their flow and motion, the speed, were all the design of this one man. Did his removal spell disaster?

And have you ever had the impression that the Leafs rid themselves of the wrong Swede? Fredrik Modin led his mates in Tampa Bay in scoring. Sundin did nothing for Modin. Now it's Jonas Hoglund who skates and plays effortlessly. Did Sundin make Hoglund credible, or was it the other way around? Then there is Eric Lindros — big in stature, big in talent. Would I make a trade for the multi-talented Lindros? Yeah! Why not? Because Mats Sundin is unlikely to play this well again!

In May 2001 we learned from our friend Lee MacDonald that a condition Carl had had for years had a name: sleep apnea. It is a serious affliction that is a precursor to heart attacks, asthma, high blood pressure and other problems. For years, I had been terrified when Carl stopped breathing in the night — for an alarming number of seconds each time. I would sit up in a panic, by which time he had either awakened or his body gone into spasm and he'd roll over — not awake, but no longer in a deep sleep. Lee, who for many years arranged appearances and signings for the players and saw that they were paid for their services, called me one day and described how his life had turned around now that he had been diagnosed with sleep apnea and was being treated. He told me he was no longer taking blood-pressure medication, he was digesting food much better and he didn't snore anymore — which meant he no longer had to sleep in the basement so his family could sleep.

Right away, I recognized Lee's symptoms as the same as Carl's. Lee arranged for us to see his internal specialist in Woodstock, Ontario, Dr. Gary Fullerton. When we went to see Gary, he asked me to describe Carl's condition. (He explained that it is only the partner, and not the patient, who can provide the necessary information to make a diagnosis.) After I described the symptoms, the doctor was absolutely certain that Carl had sleep apnea and arranged for him to go to the sleep clinic in Paris, Ontario, for assessment. For the first time in a long time, Carl was excited and confident that there was a solution at hand for him.

Unfortunately, he had difficulty at the sleep clinic, where he was supposed to spend a full night. At about one-thirty in the morning, he was home again, upset that it was impossible to sleep with a big box on his chest and amid the noise. A subsequent appointment didn't work out for him, either, and finally the doctor decided to get him a CPAP machine (which increases pressure in the throat so that the airway doesn't collapse when the user inhales) and have him work with a sleep apnea specialist.

Some have suggested that all the years of struggling on behalf of his fellow players took their toll on Carl's physical wellbeing. I'm not sure about that. The various battles were taxing, but they were all successful. On the other hand, Carl was unrelentingly intense; he had a great deal of anger buried deep inside, and he never seemed to be able to let go of his grievances.

We were able to cope and survive our years of struggle and hard work by taking frequent last-minute sell-off trips to Nassau, Jamaica, Mexico or Florida, where we could take it easy on a beach and regroup. We loved these times together. We were not particularly social people, and for the most part we went everywhere and did everything together. Carl really enjoyed having friends and family in for dinner. In the hockey world, Carl was close to Bob Nevin, his childhood friend and Leaf teammate, and to Kent Douglas, and he met Frank Mahovlich for lunch from time to time. Carl loved to go to the games at the Air Canada Centre and visit with the guys in the alumni lounge. He especially enjoyed the monthly luncheons with the NHL Oldtimers. He loved the camaraderie among the older players and came home every month happily telling me all about it.

He especially enjoyed any time we were able to get together with Ralph Backstrom and his wife, Janet. As much as we both loved Ralph, we adored Janet. She is from the southern states, and is sunny, warm and very friendly. We travelled together to Ralph's hometown of Kirkland Lake, where he took us to the chip truck on the main street to try what he insisted were "the best chips in the world." Ralph was right — neither of us had ever eaten better french fries!

When Carl played, the animosity between opposing players was often fierce. Such was not the case between Carl and Ralph. "As hard as Carl competed on the ice, he was as helpful and considerate off the ice," Ralph told me. "I mean, he set very high principles for himself, both on and off the ice, and you could really feel it. I really got to know him a lot better when we both retired and had a chance to become human beings again, and we became good friends." Carl had the greatest respect for Ralph, not only because he was a good friend, but because he accepted Carl. We had some really good times together. Carl and I met Ralph's friends, Alex and John Perron, in Kirkland Lake. They were operating the old Kerr-Addison gold mine at the time. On one visit, Alex took Carl and me down the mineshaft, more than a mile underground. If Carl was petrified to fly at 37,000 feet above the ground, he was equally terrified when we descended the shaft in the rickety elevator. He vowed never to do that again.

Carl liked "real" people, and he realized late in life that some of the people he had associated with away from the rink as a young adult were not really his friends. Now he spent more time with people he enjoyed and with whom he felt comfortable. Several times a year, he'd tell me not to make tea in the morning because he was going down to Queen Street to look up his old friend Ted Schmidt in his usual coffee shop and have a visit with him.

At the end of July 2001, Carl was invited to attend a charity golf tournament in the Windsor–Detroit area. Bobby Baun called to tell Carl that he was driving down and offered to take Carl along with him. Carl accepted the ride, and they had a great time during the drive down and back. On the return trip, Carl took Bob on a detour, to Caledon, to see our osteopath, George Roth, who checked out Bob's knee. This was the last time these old partners would see one another.

Late one afternoon in August, we were coming home and, as we were about to open the front door, Carl began saying to me, very excitedly, "Isn't that Shayne Corson and Darcy Tucker?" At first I couldn't tell where he was looking, but he had spotted them in front of the Sherwood Market a few doors away. When I caught on, I said, "Yeah, that's Shayne and Darcy — go and say hi to them." Carl, shy and embarrassed, said, "Oh, no, I can't do that." Yet, just the week before, as Carl and I were going into the same store, Steve Thomas was coming out. He immediately stopped, his face lit up, and he stood talking to us for several minutes. He was obviously delighted to talk with Carl. The current players respected and admired Carl, but he was shy and uncomfortable about approaching them, even though several of them lived in our neighbourhood.

***

On the morning of August 24, 2001, Carl awoke in great spirits. He looked terrific, had good colour and his eyes were clear and bright. He was extremely pleased and encouraged because his first night using the sleep apnea machine, the CPAP, had made an amazing difference. He had slept well. "God, I feel terrific," he said. "You know how I usually have to have a bath or shower in the morning to feel human? I feel great this morning!" He didn't want any breakfast, as he was going to have bloodwork done for Dr. Cutler. Then, he planned to drive up to Brian and Joan McFarlane's home to return a manuscript that Brian had asked him to read and give his feedback. Carl was in a happy mood when he walked in the door again at around four-thirty in the afternoon. He was swinging two bags of fresh vegetables that the McFarlanes had given him from their garden. He sat down and told me all about his visit with Brian and Joan. He spoke affectionately of Joan, saying, "Joan is American. That's why she's so friendly and outgoing!" He spoke of how they didn't want him to leave, but he knew they wanted to get away to their country home north of Grafton.

Carl asked me what we were going to do about supper. I suggested that we could have some of the lovely fresh vegetables he had brought home. He was silent. It was Friday night, so I knew what he was thinking. "Carl, I bet you're thinking fish and chips," I said. So, we decided to forego the vegetables and go out for his fish and chips.

We had a really good heart-to-heart chat over dinner that night. I mentioned something that continued to perplex me. "Carl, I feel there is one thing that I just cannot understand, one area where I feel that I have failed in our relationship over the years," I said. "For 38 years, I have told you repeatedly, from my heart, sincerely, how wonderful you are, how accomplished, how bright and how admired you are. Yet, in spite of everything, you have always chosen to believe that you are no good, not worthy." Carl looked into my eyes intently, and he replied very softly and lovingly: "Sue, I know what you mean, and believe me, I don't understand it, either. I do know that I'm tired of all the bullshit. I really just want for you and me to have a happy, peaceful life together."

Later in the evening, as we watched TV and relaxed, Carl asked me a question he had asked many times already. "Sue, is it right for me to say that without you and me and all the work we did, Alan Eagleson would never have gone to jail; Bob Goodenow wouldn't have his job; John Ziegler would still be around; Ken Sawyer would still be there; the players wouldn't have neutral arbitration; and player salaries would be nowhere where they are today? Am I right to think that?" We talked about this. We reminisced about our long years of lonely struggle as a team of two and how eventually, magically, all the pieces came together to help pull it all together — especially Russ Conway. Carl had a pleasant expression on his face that reflected a sense of satisfaction. He asked if I'd like to go with him early in the morning to his grandsons' soccer games, and I told him that I'd love to.

CHAPTER 18

THE FINALE

My world came to a crashing, brutal halt and life as I'd known it was, in an instant, forever shattered and changed when I awoke on the morning of August 25, 2001, to find that Carl had passed away. It was a shocking and horrible moment for me. At first, I wouldn't believe what I had to have known at some level. My son, Dan, was living at home and he had to confirm the dreaded fact to me: "Mum, I'm so sorry, but he's gone." It would be weeks before the full, harsh reality of his passing would even begin to sink in.

Carl's death instantly became a huge national news story. Bruce Dowbiggin pointed out to me that the day after his death it was the lead story on every CBC national newscast — not merely a hockey story, but a national news story. Because it was such a high-profile event, I responded — even though I was numb with shock — by doing what I had done for Carl for years: I handled the hundreds of phone calls from friends, acquaintances and the news media; I agreed to requests for interviews and helped journalists with details for their stories.

I encountered a problem with the priest at the church where Carl had attended Mass, where his mother had attended Mass, and where his mother's funeral had been held: he refused to come to the house for prayers because we didn't live in his parish! The last thing I expected that morning, in my shock and despair, was church politics. A young priest from the Catholic church down the street came immediately, even though Carl had never set foot in his church and didn't have any connection with the parish. Red and Andra Kelly were a tremendous help in this regard. Andra phoned just as I was dealing with the situation, and she said, "Sue, I know you haven't thought about this, but you're going to need a big church." She told me that she and Red were just leaving for Mass and they would ask their priest, Father Paul McGill at Holy Rosary, if he could help out. Father McGill, whom I had never met before, immediately offered his church and his services. He could not have been more supportive and welcoming, and he was a tremendous help with all the details of arranging the funeral — choosing the readings, and making the organist, choir, hall, and all of his church's resources available to us.

Many gestures of respect and kindness were extended in the days immediately after Carl's death. When Bruce Dowbiggin boarded his flight in Calgary, the flight attendant asked if he was going to Toronto for the Brewer funeral, and he was then ushered into business class. The flags at Maple Leaf Gardens were lowered to half-staff. The Toronto police advised that they would not ticket cars parked anywhere near the funeral home and told the staff that if anyone did get a ticket, it would be dismissed. NHL Commissioner Gary Bettman dispatched Jim Gregory to come and meet with me and inquire as to whether there was anything the NHL could do.

The funeral was held on August 29 — a glorious, sunny, late-summer morning. Time and time again, Carl had spoken fondly of his father's funeral in September 1961; the last time was two nights before he died, when we were having dinner at our favourite Greek restaurant on the Danforth, Mezes, with friends Roy Main and Sue Myers. Carl told them that his dad's was the biggest funeral and the longest procession he had ever seen. He added then, as he always had, "Nobody will come to mine." Sadly, he believed this.

Well, this was one time when Carl was wrong. People did come — by the hundreds. Old friends Tommi Salmelainen and Goran Stubb flew in from Finland and brought with them letters and cards from Alpo Suhonen and other friends in Finland. Senator Joyce Fairbairn flew a very long and complicated journey from Lethbridge, Alberta, to be present that morning. As I followed directly behind the coffin and passed through the main doors of the church, I immediately felt the energy of a full church! Out of the corner of my eye I could see that it was standing room only. Father McGill had told us that the church held a thousand people. Instantly, a feeling of joy flooded through me. The thought came to my mind, "Yes, Carl. They have come!"

The outpouring of tributes, affection, recognition and gratitude for Carl was tremendous, overwhelming and deeply moving. My only regret was that he had not experienced this in his lifetime, that he never understood the influence he'd had, nor did he comprehend the respect, admiration and high esteem people felt for him.

The funeral service was beautiful, and many of those in the church that day have since told me that it was the most beautiful funeral they ever attended. There was a very upbeat, joyful atmosphere throughout. John McDermott and Michael Burgess, two of Canada's best-loved and best-known singers, sang and their powerful, melodic voices filled the church majestically. Five priests shared the officiating. This was in itself astounding to our friend Lorraine Mahoney, who is Catholic. She told me that so many priests are normally seen only at the funerals of high-ranking clergy. Carl's friend Father Thomas Mohan gave a most fitting homily entitled "Everyman," in which he said it would have been far easier for Carl to do nothing, but he had instead gone to extraordinary lengths to serve his fellow man.

Following John McDermott's haunting rendition of "Danny Boy," appropriate for a man with Irish ancestry, Bruce Dowbiggin came forward to give the eulogy. He spoke magnificently, as I knew he would. He was sincere, but also lighthearted as he related humorous little stories about Carl and spoke of his struggles. Because Bruce knew Carl so well, he captured his essence and his multifaceted personality. As I listened to Bruce, the first tears came to my eyes and I didn't want him to stop talking. I knew that when Bruce stopped, I would have to face the difficult work of dealing with a life I didn't know how to live — a life without my precious life partner, Carl.

Cards, letters and flowers continued to arrive by the dozens, and every day there were phone calls. Bobby Orr called early one morning to chat and express his sorrow; David Keon phoned me from Florida, and "Big Gordie" called from Salt Lake City, where he was making a public appearance. Speaking of Carl and the pension litigation, Gordie said: "Carl did it all. The rest of us just put our names on the papers." In one of his many phone calls to me, Ritch Winter spoke about the belief in his Mormon religion that the spirits of our departed loved ones are always near us. He went on to say, "Sue, now he can't not get it!" He was referring to the respect and admiration Carl never felt he deserved. Invitations to lunch and dinner came by the dozens, and I accepted them all. It didn't take the pain away, but the distractions were definitely appreciated.

Carl's passing left many of his fellow hockey players shaken to the core. Billy Harris, his Leaf teammate, had been ill for several years with a rare form of leukemia called Waldenstrom's macroglobulinemia; he died two weeks after Carl. Bill's death was expected, but none of their peers ever imagined that Carl would go before him. Many former players felt a deep regret that they hadn't thanked Carl for what had been done, and so they showered me with gratitude. One especially moving phone call came from former Leaf Walter McKechnie, who phoned to explain why he hadn't attended the funeral. Then he went on to say how upset he was that people, himself included, do not take the time to say "thank you" and "I love you" to the people in their lives that mean the most. Walt said, "I didn't say thank you to Carl, so I'm calling today to say 'thank you' to you and Carl for all that you did for us." He reassured me that, just because Carl was no longer here, it didn't mean I wasn't welcome at the various hockey-related social functions. "You will always be welcome," Walt told me, "and that is what Carl would want also."

In November, I ran into Bobby Hull at the Hockey Hall of Fame game at the Air Canada Centre. Bobby came up and gave me a big hug and was visibly disturbed. "This has really shook me up," he said. "We're the same age, for God's sake." The same weekend in November, Russ Conway organized a tribute dinner at Barberian's. He invited Stevie and David Cameron, Tom and Donna Lockwood and their daughter Andrea, Brad Park and Todd Bailey — whose father, NHL scout Ace Bailey, had been killed in the 9/11 disaster a few weeks earlier — Bruce Dowbiggin, Lorraine Mahoney and Mark Zigler. As we left the restaurant that night, Brad Park came up to me and put his arm around my shoulder, giving me a comforting hug. He said to me: "When I was just breaking into hockey, I admired Carl — not only because he was such a superb athlete, but because he was an independent thinker and I knew that I wanted to be just like him." The first time I met Dave Hutchison at a charity golf event in Carl's memory, he literally jumped out of his seat to come and give me a hug. No words were spoken; the hug said it all.

Appreciative players continued, and continue, to express gratitude for the work Carl and I did on their behalf. In November, Frank Mahovlich rose in the Senate to pay tribute to Carl, as well as Billy Harris and Ace Bailey. "Carl Brewer: defender of the underdog," he began. "To take on the NHL, it was David against Goliath." He went on to call Carl "a man of vision with a mission, a believer in principles, a fighter for the NHL players' rights."

The Finale

In early December, I was attending a gala Maple Leaf function at the Royal York Hotel. Prior to the official proceedings, I was chatting with Jim Pappin and other Leaf teammates of Carl's, when a man bounded up to me and asked, "Are you Susan Foster?" He introduced himself: "I'm Vic Stasiuk." Vic had been a member of the Boston Bruins' legendary 'Uke' line, along with Bronco Horvath and Johnny Bucyk. He told me he had been at an autograph signing in Detroit when he heard about this evening's function. "I jumped in my car and drove to Toronto on the off chance that you might be here," he said, "because I wanted to meet you and thank you for all that you and Carl did for the pension." He had received a nice bonus, and it meant a great deal to him. It was terrific to meet this fine man and I was very moved by Vic's appreciation.

The finality of death is always difficult to accept. In retrospect, I recognize that for several months before his passing, Carl had been expecting to die, and he was trying to prepare me for that eventuality. In April, he had been unusually attentive to my birthday — my last with him. Normally, birthdays didn't mean much to Carl; this time, however, he told me he was taking me to Joso's Restaurant for dinner, and he made the reservation — a detail he had always left to me. Later, he told me that he very much wanted to get me something I'd really like for my birthday, but he didn't know what that would be — could I help him? I answered that I'd love to have Patricia Wells' *At Home in Provence* cookbook — and that he'd have no trouble finding it in Chapters, where I had picked it up so often my energy would be calling to him. He brought it back for me, beautifully wrapped and with a card enclosed in which he thanked me for my "prodigious support over the years" and expressed his love.

At various times, Carl said things to me, out of the blue, that seemed like non-sequiturs. One evening, as we sat relaxing together on the couch, he implored me to promise him that I'd pursue the pension shortfalls if anything happened to him. He reminded me, "If anything happens to me, the pension will be yours, and it would be entirely appropriate for you to do so." He told me that he had continued to pursue the pension matter with his friend, Sudbury lawyer Rennie Mastin, because he wanted to be sure that I'd be okay, that I would have enough. Another evening, again apropos of nothing, he said: "Tom Lockwood thinks the world of you. If you ever need anything, don't hesitate to ask Tom." He instructed me to finish this book — we had been working on it for years — telling me, "I'm not going to be able to."

In spite of all this, I refused to hear him. One afternoon in mid-July, I had a call from a friend, Cathy Callejous. Cathy is from Guatemala, and we met her when she worked for our naturopath, Bill Cheng. She is an amazing "healer" who operates in dimensions beyond the reach of an ordinary person — she has acute psychic powers. There was a sombre tone in her voice when she phoned and asked to drop by. She didn't stay long; we had a cup of herbal tea, but as she was leaving, she gave me her message. She took hold of my hands and said to me pointedly, "My dear, Carl will be leaving soon, and then it will be your time for your lessons." I heard Cathy's words, but they didn't register with me. I continued to refused to admit to myself that Carl, who went to bed with me at night and woke up with me each morning, with whom I spent most of my time, could ever just not be with me — that he could die.

Carl had been extremely tense and anxious the last few months of his life — worried about speeding up his sleep apnea assessment, getting his CPAP machine, cleaning up files and sorting his old clothes. One afternoon, he sat down at the dining room table with me and said, "Sue, you've always said that it didn't matter to you if we were married or not. I need to know: do you still feel that way or would you like to change that?" He exerted a great deal of energy trying to resolve everything and leave everyone content with him and his role in their lives.

Interestingly, in spite of Carl's anxiety and intensity as the end drew near, there seemed in those final summer weeks to be a definite peace within Carl — a real sense that he was at one with his connection to the Divine. That summer, it was a rare Sunday morning when he didn't go to Mass at St. Anselm's. In the mornings or late afternoons, he sat on the deck, excitedly observing the hummingbirds that were attracted to the flowers in the hanging baskets I'd planted. He said it had been years since he'd seen as many monarch butterflies as he saw that summer, and he pointed each and every one out to me. He had given me an Easter lily, which I planted in the garden when the blooms died; he took great joy in watching it grow and develop, and when the buds burst into bloom, he happily exclaimed, "It's even more beautiful than when I gave it to you."

He was absolutely thrilled to get a phone call from Alpo Suhonen in Finland just two mornings before he died. He had been trying to track down Alpo's number to call him, and then Alpo phoned him and they had a great chat. Alpo expressed his happiness for having had the inspiration to phone that morning.

One morning, as Carl was leaving the house to go up north to his son's, he stopped and read to me — slowly, in a very heartfelt manner — the words on a small wall hanging that was by the front door:

AN IRISH BLESSING
May the road rise up to meet you,
May the wind be always at your back,
May the sun shine warm upon your face,
And the rains fall soft upon your fields,
And, until we meet again,
May God hold you
in the hollow of His hand.

He gazed at me intently when he finished. I said to him, "You gave that to me." Still gazing at me reflectively, he quietly replied, "Uh-huh." He was giving me a message.

In spite of Carl's health problems, we spent a pleasant summer. In early June, we enjoyed the celebration of Dr. Tom and Helen Pashby's 60th wedding anniversary. In July, we went to Jim Dorey's golf tournament in Kingston, an event we both looked forward to every year because it was fun and we had a chance to meet up with so many old friends from hockey. This time, we travelled by train and Carl's grandson Jacob came along. In August, we spent a beautiful day at Brian and Joan McFarlane's country home on the occasion of Brian's 70th birthday. It was a beautiful party on a perfect summer day, and we enjoyed visiting with John McCormack, Red and Andra Kelly, Mike and Cathy Amodeo, and Gary Hull (brother of Bobby and Dennis) and his wife, Lois, and countless others.

The final weekend of Carl's life, we were guests at a garden party in the Thousand Islands for Bob Runciman, Ontario's Minister of Economic Development and Trade. We spent two nights at the beautiful Glen House Resort, and all we had to do was put in an appearance at the afternoon garden party, mingle with the guests and have dinner with the Minister. The morning of the event, however, Carl was dreadfully stressed. "Sue," he said, "I nearly woke you a half a dozen times in the night to tell you I just can't do this!" I did my best to calm him down and reassure him that he handled these things beautifully and he'd be fine. We went into Gananoque after breakfast, and he seemed happy. When he parked the car, he was quite excited. "Sue, look, it's my lucky day," he said. "Two dollar stores in one block, and a secondhand book store!" He rested that afternoon and, other than returning to our room midway through the party to rest, he seemed to have a great time.

***

When you lose a partner in life, all the moments — not only the milestones, but every small everyday experience — become sacred. The memories are vivid, the details indelibly imprinted in the mind with infinite clarity. Carl's "Let's go to Wal-Mart"; having breakfast on the back deck in the early morning as we watched the monarch butterflies and admired the flowers; walks in Sherwood Park together; Saturday mornings at St. Lawrence Market, where we would share a vegetarian frittata at Mustachio's; seeing the movie *Chocolat* twice because Carl loved it so much — all of these were as precious as watching the pressing of olive oil in the village co-operative in Maussane-les-Alpilles; breakfasts on several consecutive mornings at the local bar/tabac in Chateauneuf-du-Pape, where the daily meal included a glass of white wine and a glass of red wine; or preparing to fly, when I always had his Evian bottle handy for him, filled with a half-and-half mixture of water and vodka. All of these memories, each one more special than the last, were continuously occupying my mind.

I continued to go back to the same places we loved and did the same things we'd done because, after all, they represented my routine, my normal, part of what had defined me and my life. However, it was never the same. I returned to Villefranche-sur-mer in February, and everyone in the village was tremendously supportive. The first morning that I went to Boulangerie Calleri, they all broke out in big smiles, but then it hit everyone at the same moment and I watched the smiles fade and the colour drain from their cheeks. Everyone hugged me and asked me to bring Carl's picture with me next time. When I did, they passed it around, and each person paid his or her little moment of respect to him. When I had my coffee, Madame Calleri herself sat with me each morning and chatted, keeping me company.

When I went to Italy, to Ventimiglia, on market day, it took a lot of courage to go and see Fernanda at the shoe store. She, too, knew right away and gasped, "*Le monsieur?*" She immediately started to cry. Then she called everyone in the store — customers and employees — together around her and told them all in Italian about her friends from Canada, and especially *le monsieur*, because she and I communicated in French. Next thing I knew, everyone was crying and offering me their condolences. The only word I knew how to say to them was *grazie*. The scene was surreal. Only in Italy, I thought to myself.

The void, the emptiness, the coldness had replaced the warmth, the protection, the loving energy of my loved one. Not only was my life as I knew it shattered, but so was my whole sense of my identity. There were many days when I wondered who I was and what I was doing without Carl there to share nearly every moment. For weeks, I awoke in the morning thinking about what I'd prepare for Carl's breakfast; or I'd be out shopping and be hit with a moment of panic, thinking I should be home starting dinner for Carl, only to have the next thought hit me — he won't be home for dinner. I didn't know myself anymore — my thoughts and reactions were not like they used to be. I felt vulnerable, extremely vulnerable. Carl always told me that I was his strength. Often he told me that he wouldn't have made it through the day had it not been for my saying something re-assuring to him. Carl was notoriously indecisive, and it was always up to me to make decisions about our activities. After his death, without his constant presence, I found myself being indecisive. It was frightening to wake up and feel so unlike the person I used to be. The pain was so acute that I hardly knew how I would get through the day, let alone handle the things I always used to do routinely with little or no effort.

So many people, with their tremendous love and support, were an enormous help to me, and I will always be grateful to them for helping me through such a difficult passage by rallying around me with their exceptional kindness, frequent phone calls and by including me in their plans. These include my children, Melanie and Daniel, the Toronto Maple Leaf organization, the NHL Oldtimers group — and its leader, Al Shaw, and his wife, Lorraine and their family — Russ Conway, Bruce Dowbiggin and his entire family, Stevie Cameron and her family, Ritch Winter, and two very special reporters: Mary Ormsby of the *Star* and Mike Ulmer of the *Sun*.

Carl's Leaf teammate Kent Douglas grieved the loss of the man he affectionately called "my best friend." He undertook to establish a beautiful trophy that the Toronto Maple Leaf Alumni award each year in Carl's memory. The Carl Brewer Memorial Trophy goes to the Leaf alumnus who performs the greatest service to the community. I was truly honoured when the Leaf Alumni voted to make me the first recipient of the trophy. They presented it to me at a function in North Bay, and Carl's old friend and teammate Senator Frank Mahovlich was in attendance for the presentation.

Several months after Carl's death, John McCormack, who played with the Leafs and Habs in the late 1940s and early '50s, contacted me about a conversation he'd recently had with Terry Kelly. Terry is a lawyer in Oshawa, John's hometown, and formerly was a director of Maple Leaf Gardens. He was also on the selection committee for Canada's Sports Hall of Fame. John and Terry had discussed the idea of putting Carl's name forward as a candidate for induction into this prestigious Canadian institution. John brought the papers to me, I filled them out and Dr. Tom Pashby, himself an inductee, nominated Carl. A few months later, John phoned excitedly to tell me Carl's nomination had been accepted by the selection committee. He would be inducted posthumously in November 2002.

I felt very honoured again when Brian Conacher phoned me on behalf of Canada's Sports Hall of Fame to tell me they wanted me to accept for Carl at the induction ceremony. Brian explained that there were three reasons why they wanted me to accept: "First of all, you are the person who was closest to him; second, you're the reason he's being inducted; and finally, it's what Carl would want."

The induction ceremony was held on November 7 at the Royal York. A Who's Who of the political and sporting scenes was in attendance: Premier Mike Harris, former Lieutenant Governor Lincoln Alexander, Russ Jackson, Sandy Hawley, Marlene Stewart Streit and Dr. Tom Pashby. Ted Lindsay was also inducted that night, as was the late Tim Horton, another former teammate of Carl's. Tim's daughter, Jeri, accepted on behalf of her dad. Jeri and her husband, Ron Joyce Jr., were very kind and they looked out for me over the course of the evening. I was really impressed by what a considerate and kind woman she is, and I knew her father would have been immensely proud of her.

Carl's seems to be one of those deaths that people remember forever; they can recall exactly where they were and what they were doing when they heard about it. In late 2005, Jean Beliveau shared just such a memory with me. "I was in Windsor, at an event," he said. "I came down to breakfast in the morning and I heard about Carl. I was very sad. I couldn't believe it." Jean had spoken with Carl just a few weeks earlier, and he remembered the conversation: "He was telling me all about the time the two of you spent in the south of France each year. He looked so happy telling me about it. He told me, 'It's so beautiful, Jean — the sun shines every day!'"

It took some three and a half years before real healing took place, and when it did the transformation happened quickly. It was January 2005 when I finally understood just how much I was still living in the past, stuck in grief and loss and memories and holding on to Carl. Then, the right people came along at precisely the right moment to inspire me to move beyond the pain — as if Carl had orchestrated it for me!

It began with my "north star," Ralph Backstrom, who told me: "Sue, there's a lot of pain in life. We lose our parents, we lose our loved ones, we lose our friends, relationships go bad… but it's really important to look at what you've got left and make the most of it." For whatever reason, I really heard his words. Ralph also told me pointedly: "He's gone, Sue." To underscore the message, he made a decisive, cross-cutting motion with his hands — a gesture that conveyed finality. "He'll always be with you," he added, "but he's gone." It may seem irrational, but it was at that moment when I finally grasped it fully — that he wasn't coming back, and he wouldn't need the clothes, the toothbrush or the medications that I'd been saving all this time. He told me that I only had to make decisions for myself now. I immediately began to feel an enormous burst of energy and optimism that I couldn't remember feeling in a very long time.

A couple of days later, I went to Stevie Cameron's place with Jan Wong for tea. Stevie noticed a new vibrancy in me and she e-mailed me later that night: "My dear Susan — it did my heart good to see you so happy and excited about your life. You have been so brave and cheerful when you must have felt so lonely." But it was the following day, when Stevie and I were talking on the phone, that she said something that really grabbed my attention. She asked me if I'd ever thought about what a long, hard journey it had been for me with Carl. She said: "It was like being married to Mozart — because the two of you were married without the clergy." She continued: "Carl was very intimidating — people didn't know what to make of him, he frightened people — but he always had you with him, and you were always so kind and pleasant that you made him respectable. Because as much as people could be uncomfortable with him, they loved you." She explained that she personally didn't feel that way, and she had always gotten along well with Carl, but she did say, "And he was so utterly dependent on you — he came to you with his every little problem and dropped it in your lap to take care of. Did you ever stop to think just how stressful that was for you all those years?" Stevie is very astute, and I respect her insights. I really didn't answer her at the time, but she certainly gave me a lot to think about.

Stevie told me some time later that she had thought these things for years, but never would have dared say them to me because she knows that, in all relationships, you do what you have to do. That day, however, she told me, "I don't know why, but I just *had* to tell you those things that day!"

Over the next few days, the picture became crystal clear to me. A week later, the clincher to this process came from Allan Dick. From our first meeting, Allan has been such a good and loyal friend and adviser to Carl and me, and on this day we were having lunch together. It turned into a long, leisurely lunch and a really good chat. Near the end of the afternoon, I mentioned something to Allan that Ralph Backstrom had brought up. Years before, Ralph reminded me, I'd told him, "Carl has a lot of baggage." Allan looked right through me — he spoke directly and deliberately, as if he had rehearsed his words for a pivotal moment in a court case: "Carl *did* have a lot of baggage," he said. "But he didn't carry his baggage — *you* did. You carried all of his baggage for all of those years because he was not capable of doing it." Allan's eyes were penetrating, as if he was willing me to get this. Well, I did get it, in spades! I was speechless. I felt like I'd been hit by lightning. I could hear words going through my head: *This is not my work anymore; this is over.* To illustrate what an amazing epiphany this had been for me, my left shoulder had been aggravating me for months, and nothing would relieve it. By the time I got home that afternoon, my shoulder was better, and it's been fine ever since. My chiropractor, Dr. Paul Kennedy, told me that he sees this all the time: "When an emotional burden is lifted, all sorts of aches and pains simply vanish."

It was the most wonderful and welcome feeling to experience such a tremendous resurgence of energy, to feel a powerful new optimism, to be genuinely happy and excited about living and to have my power back. I suddenly felt that I was fully connected to life again. I am very grateful to these friends who just seemed to know what to say to me at the right time to help me move beyond grief. I knew I had not only survived but successfully moved into a new space in my life when former Maple Leaf Brian Glennie phoned me — one of his periodic "checking in on you" calls since Carl's death. Partway through our conversation, he stopped in mid-sentence, then exclaimed , "Oh my *gawd*, honey, you sound fantastic! You have moved from 'stuck in existence' to living again." My daughter, Melanie, also noticed that I was much happier, that I had so much more energy, that I had lost a lot of weight, and I looked much younger. Melanie said to me: "Mum, I am so proud of you! You know, I think that if Carl were to come back today, he wouldn't even recognize you."

Carl will always be with me, and his influence will always be an integral part of who I am. There will always be much love in my heart for Carl. Carl said so many times that our relationship transcends time and space, and I know that we will always be together in spirit.

His legacy lives on in many ways. Rick Smith once said to me: "Every month, about 1,800 people open a pension cheque and they must all say, 'Thank you, Carl and Sue.'" I've heard from people in other walks of life that they'd never given much thought to what kind of pension plan they were paying into, or how it was being managed. Now, they take note. At the Winter Olympics of 2006, in Turin, the Finns excelled in hockey and reached the gold medal game, where they lost to the Swedes by a single goal. To this day, the Finns look to Carl as the singular influence that ignited their ascent to prominence on the world hockey stage.

Carl left with me with some very precious gifts in the form of a most incredible circle of wonderful, caring and loving friends all over the world. He also left me with the words he spoke to me on coming home late one afternoon, just a few days before he died. I will treasure them always. He came in, said nothing — not even his usual announcement that he was home. I was preparing our dinner. Carl stood quietly, looking at me intently and reflectively, and said, "Sue, I don't want to go. I *really* don't want to go. But if I do go, it's perfectly all right. I've had a wonderful life. I've done it all."

INDEX

father, 8, 10–11, 11, 34, 62; relationship
with Imlach, 30–31, 35–36, 41–42, 45, 62;
relationship with mother, 8, 10; relationship
with Susan, 239–54; relationship with Susan
begins, 60–63, 93–95; relationship with
teammates, 29–30, 80, 85–89, 249, 317;
reliance on Susan, 33, 44–45, 61–63,
100–101, 248, 332; rookie season, 19–27;
seeks outstanding pension benefits, 139,
159–60, 199–204; self-doubt, 10, 22–23, 35,
68–69, 249, 252–53, 322–23; sues Leafs for
back pay, 107, 114–17, 127–29; travels with
Susan, 180–81, 204–5, 234–38, 245–46,
255–58, 278–83, 294–96, 301–3, 313–14,
317; tryout with Leafs, 17
Brewer, Carl Sr., 6–11, 20, 54, 62; death of, 33–34
Brewer, Christopher, 62, 93, 193, 248
Brewer, Elizabeth (McAvoy), 6, 8–10, 48, 313
Brewer, Elsie, 8
Brewer, Frank, 6, 9–11, 15
Brewer, Fred, 7–9
Brewer, Jack, 6, 65–66, 76, 99–100
Brewer, Marilyn (Rea), 13, 60, 62, 89, 93, 131
Brewer, Michael, 93
Brewer, Roy, 6
Brewer, Shirley, 7, 9, 11
Brewer, Willie "Wee," 6–9, 11, 54
Britz, Greg, 125, 133, 135, 142, 226
Broda, Turk, 15
Bucyk, John, 287, 315
Bull, Dr. Chuck, 268–69
Burnett, Red, 17, 23
Burns, Charlie, 11

C

California Seals, 47, 65, 121
Cameron, Stevie, 193, 212, 214–15, 225, 228–29,
242, 290, 292–93, 324, 329, 331
Campbell, Clarence, 55, 306
Campbell, Gordon, 17
Canada: doesn't co-operate with Eagleson
extradition, 271–72; national team, 51–65, 67,
70, 87–88, 258–62, 278
Canada Cup, 170–71, 177–78, 217–19, 231–32
Canadian Amateur Hockey Association
(CAHA), 55, 150
Carleton, Wayne, 164
Catzman, Justice Marvin, 129
Chapman, Blair, 202
Cheevers, Gerry, 88
Cherry, Don, 261–62
Chicago Blackhawks, 33, 34–35, 38, 40–41,
83, 198, 263

Clancy, King, 27–29, 46, 47, 103
Clarke, Bobby, 259, 286, 292, 300, 309, 311
Clements, Ben, 287–89
Cleveland Crusaders, 87–88
Conacher, Brian, 308, 330
Conacher, Charlie, 65
Conacher, Peter, 272–73, 277
Conacher, Susan, 308
Conway, Russ, 129, 170–71, 179, 190, 209–28,
233, 241, 267, 269, 284, 285, 289–93, 304–5,
324, 329
Cooper, Cliff, 13
Corbie, Gary, 10
Crosby, Bing, 65
Crozier, Joe, 103, 104
Cruise, David, 143, 163, 182, 207
Curran, Rick, 217
Cutler, Dr. Paul, 281, 305, 319

D

Dailey, Bob, 172–73, 270
Daly, Tom, 212, 227, 271, 287, 292, 309
Davidson, Bob, 164
Davis, Ron, 190
Day, Hap, 21
Deacon, James, 152
DeLise, Jerry, 66
Detroit Eatery, 193–94
Detroit Red Wings, 72–77, 129; buy up Carl's
pension benefits, 73, 197; sign Carl, 72–73;
underpay Howe, 75, 205
Dick, Allan, 110, 120, 131–37, 159–60, 163–66,
173, 174, 195, 201, 202, 241, 250, 332
Donaldson, George, 182–84
Donaldson, Norman, 215–16
Dorey, Jim, 164, 272, 281, 327
Douglas, Kent, 22, 25, 37, 43, 45–46, 272, 307,
317, 329
Dowbiggin, Bruce, 143, 189–94, 213–14, 218–19,
224, 240–45, 285, 286, 292–93, 321–24, 329
Duff, Dick, 27, 32, 35, 38, 42–44, 107, 272

E

Eagleson, Alan, 122, 140–58, 286; attempted
extradition, 267, 271–72; behaviour in court,
268, 288; bid for IIHF presidency, 150; bills
Carl for amateur reinstatement, 55–56; bills
Carl for Muskegon contract, 66; blamed for
Leaf revolt, 102–3, 106; Canadian fraud trial,
290–93; Canadian investigations, 169–70,
216–21, 229–34, 269; as Carl's agent, 35–36,
50, 51, 60, 65, 141; claims to represent retired
players, 162, 179, 185; coziness with NHL

Index

executives, 124, 146, 155–56, 162; disbarred, 293–94; "godfather" letter, 140–41, 202; influence over media, 151–52; involvement in WHA "merger," 89; kickbacks to and from Britz, 125, 133, 226; leases space to NHLPA, 211, 219; lends out players' money, 129–31, 152, 176, 215–16, 218; "Merry Christmas" letter, 162, 182; political connections, 129, 179, 220–23, 271–72, 291; profiteering from international hockey, 145, 147–48, 156, 165, 216–19, 231–32; represents coaches and managers, 81, 146; resigns as NHLPA executive director, 219; Salcer and Winter attempt to unseat, 152–54; sued by Mike Gillis, 264–70; token support for Carl's arbitration case, 125, 135, 141–42; tries to undercut Winter and Garvey, 158, 166–67; U.S. fraud trial, 287–89; U.S. indictment, 224–30; U.S. investigations, 190, 212, 219–21
Eagleson, Jill, 129, 140, 141, 211, 231–32, 290
Eagleson, Nancy, 129, 141, 212
Eagleson, Trevor, 211, 218–19, 231–32, 266, 267, 269, 286
Ehman, Gerry, 26
Ellis, Linda, 175–76
Ellis, Ron, 94
Elston, Murray, 179
Esposito, Phil, 175

F

Federal Bureau of Investigation (FBI), 190, 212, 219–21, 226, 227
Ferguson, David, 172–73
Ferren, Ed, 172–73, 174, 178, 184
Ficek, Susan, 288
Fiske, Donald, 107, 114, 115–16, 122, 124
Fleming, Reggie, 40
Fletcher, Cliff, 80, 82, 231
Forbes, David, 166, 168, 169, 172, 177, 232, 287, 288, 298–99
Ford, James, 183
Foster, Newton, 1, 2
Foster, Susan: Carl's death foreshadowed, 325–26; as Carl's "gatekeeper," 213, 242–44; as Carl's support system, 33, 44–45, 61–63, 100–101, 241, 332; honoured by Leaf Alumni, 329–30; honoured by Oldtimers for pension battle, 272–73, 276; as landlord, 108–14; life after Carl, 328–33; marriage to David Horton, 91–92, 112; at McGill University, 1, 3–5, 57; meets Carl Brewer, 1–3; meets with Carl in Montreal, 3–5, 59–63; real estate career, 96–97, 108; relationship with Carl, 239–54;

relationship with Carl begins, 60–63, 93–95; role in Carl's arbitration case, 124–25, 127–28, 239–41, 244; role in Eagleson investigation, 144–47, 151, 212, 239–41, 244; role in pension battle, 113, 201, 239–41, 244; teaching career, 91, 108, 112; travels with Carl, 132, 180–81, 204–5, 234–38, 245–46, 255–58, 278–83, 294–96, 301–3, 313–14, 317
Fotiu, Nick, 149
Frank, 220–21, 223
Fraser, Rick, 111–12, 117–18
Freitas, Joe, 174, 302
Fullerton, Dr. Gary, 316–17

G

Gadsby, Bill, 73, 74, 164
Gadsby, Edna, 164
Gallinger, Ralph, 248–49
Gans, Arthur, 120, 132–36
Gardner, Cal, 272
Gartner, Mike, 179
Garvey, Ed, 153–56, 158, 166–67, 170, 175–76, 179, 215, 216, 266, 298–99
Geoffrion, Bernie "Boom Boom," 33
Gibson, Judge Keith, 115–16
Giffin, Don, 77–78
Gillis, Diane, 265, 266, 286, 287
Gillis, Mike, 233, 264–70, 286
Glennie, Brian, 332–33
Goldblatt, Marvin, 148, 215, 266
Goldham, Bob, 74, 161–62, 164
Goodenow, Bob, 170, 211, 219, 257, 292
Goodman, Justice Allan, 188
Gordon, Michael, 125, 126–27
Gorton, Judge Nathaniel, 287–89
Graham, George, 56, 141
Granger, Cam, 1–2
Gray, Malcolm, 152, 216
Greenglass, Mort, 130, 131
Greenspan, Brian, 286
Gregory, Jim, 198, 322
Gretzky, Wayne, 177–78, 188
Griffiths, Allison, 143, 163, 168, 182, 207, 212
Gross, George, 46–47, 63, 68, 129, 291

H

Hagman, Matti, 279
Harkness, Ned, 76–77
Harloff, Glen, 220, 222–23
Harris, Billy, 13, 30, 86–89, 141, 164, 166, 272, 323–24
Harrison, Jim, 146–47, 166, 169, 193, 202, 229, 232, 233

Index

Index